The Fifty-Eighth
North Carolina Troops

ALSO BY MICHAEL C. HARDY
AND FROM MCFARLAND

*The Battle of Hanover Court House: Turning Point
of the Peninsula Campaign, May 27, 1862* (2006)

*The Thirty-seventh North Carolina Troops:
Tar Heels in the Army of Northern Virginia* (2003; softcover 2009)

The Fifty-Eighth North Carolina Troops

Tar Heels in the Army of Tennessee

MICHAEL C. HARDY

McFarland & Company, Inc., Publishers
Jefferson, North Carolina, and London

LIBRARY OF CONGRESS CATALOGUING-IN-PUBLICATION DATA

Hardy, Michael C.
The Fifty-Eighth North Carolina troops : Tar Heels in the Army of Tennessee / Michael C. Hardy.
    p.   cm.
Includes bibliographical references and index.

ISBN 978-0-7864-3438-1
softcover : 50# alkaline paper ∞

1. Confederate States of America. Army. North Carolina Infantry Regiment, 58th. 2. North Carolina — History — Civil War, 1861–1865 — Regimental histories. 3. United States — History — Civil War, 1861–1865 — Regimental histories. 4. United States — History — Civil War,1861–1865 — Campaigns. 5. Confederate States of America. Army. North Carolina Infantry Regiment, 58th — Registers. I. Title. II. Title: 58th North Carolina troops.
E573.558th.H37   2010   973.7'4256 — dc22   2010031956

British Library cataloguing data are available

©2010 Michael C. Hardy. All rights reserved

No part of this book may be reproduced or transmitted in any form or by any means, electronic or mechanical, including photocopying or recording, or by any information storage and retrieval system, without permission in writing from the publisher.

Front cover image: Confederate prisoners at a depot in Chattanooga, 1864 (Library of Congress); background ©2010 Clipart.com

Manufactured in the United States of America

McFarland & Company, Inc., Publishers
Box 611, Jefferson, North Carolina 28640
www.mcfarlandpub.com

Table of Contents

Preface ... 1

1. December 1861: The Mitchell Rangers ... 5
2. 1860–1862 ... 12
3. May 1862 ... 20
4. January–July 1862 ... 24
5. August–October 1862 ... 34
6. November 1862–September 1863 ... 44
7. September 1863 ... 64
8. September–December 1863 ... 80
9. December 1863–May 1864 ... 94
10. May–July 1864 ... 109
11. July–December 1864 ... 128
12. January–May 1865 ... 148
13. 1865–Present ... 168
14. The Fifty-Eighth North Carolina in Perspective ... 185
15. Looking for the Fifty-Eighth North Carolina Today ... 189

Appendix A: Fifty-Eighth North Carolina Troops Roster ... 193
Appendix B: Fifty-Eighth North Carolina Parolees ... 223
Appendix C: Members of the Fifty-Eighth Who Deserted and Joined the Union Army ... 226
Chapter Notes ... 229
Bibliography ... 239
Index ... 247

Preface

The time of year bore no resemblance to the late summer of 1863 when the Fifty-Eighth fought at Chickamauga. It was a cold winter's afternoon in north Georgia, in February 1998. I had been to a Civil War show in Dalton and was on my way back to my home in western North Carolina. I had purposely left early enough to stop at the Chickamauga National Battlefield Park to look for the Fifty-Eighth's battlefield marker. A stop by the information desk at the park headquarters had produced a map and rough directions on finding the marker. Alone and cold, I stumbled around Snodgrass Hill looking for the granite tribute. This was my second trip to Chickamauga. The first had come a decade earlier on a family outing. I had almost given up searching when I finally saw the monument through the barren trees. A small footpath to the monument told me that I was not the only one in search of the Tar Heel marker. Both the walk all over Snodgrass Hill and the discovery of the marker led to a warmth inside. I was already at work on my first book, and in the back of my mind, I am sure that the idea of writing about the Fifty-Eighth was already germinating. Since that cold winter day, I've been back to Snodgrass Hill and the Fifty-Eighth's marker a half dozen times. In August 2009, I even got to camp on Snodgrass Hill, working as an interpreter portraying the Fifty-Eighth.

Since the 1860s, there have been thousands of books written about the American Civil War. Major and minor personalities, battles great and small, weapons, ships, and civilians have all received the attention of the historian. The material on Gettysburg, and especially on Lincoln, is overwhelming. Yet, there are still thousands of stories that have not been told.

North Carolina sent more than seventy regiments into Confederate service. The service of some of these regiments is legendary: the First North Carolina Volunteers at Big Bethel Church in June 1861; Anderson's brigade in the Sunken Road at Sharpsburg in September 1862; the Twenty-Sixth North Carolina at Gettysburg in July 1863; the Thirty-Seventh North Carolina at Spotsylvania Court House in May 1864; and the Fourth and Fourteenth North Carolina at Appomattox in April 1865. These actions led to a motto adopted by the veterans themselves after the war: "First at Bethel, furthest to the front at Gettysburg and Chickamauga, and last at Appomattox." It is one of those statements, "Furthest to the front at ... Chickamauga," that is the focal point of this book.

There were four regiments from North Carolina to serve permanently in the western theater during the war: the Twenty-Ninth, Thirty-Ninth, Fifty-Eighth, and Sixtieth North Carolina Troops. Two other regiments, the Sixty-Second and the Sixty-Fourth, served briefly in Tennessee before being transferred back to North Carolina. The Sixth North Carolina Cavalry also spent some time in the western theater.

Most of the 2,000-plus men who served in the Fifty-Eighth North Carolina troops can be termed "unwilling volunteers." These men enlisted just prior to, or right after, the first Confederate Conscription Act was passed in April 1862. They volunteered because they had to. Some in the regiment, like most of the men in Companies L and M, were conscripts, forced into service at the point of the bayonet. After thirteen months of garrison duty in east Tennessee, and numerous desertions by the unwilling volunteers, the Fifty-Eighth went on to perform well, especially at Chickamauga, Tennessee, in September 1863; Resaca, Georgia, in May 1864; and Bentonville, North Carolina, in March 1865. At each of these battles, the Tar Heels of the Fifty-Eighth pierced the Federal lines.

Through enlistment, garrison duty in east Tennessee, desertion, the heat of battle, and the boredom of camp life, this is the story of the Fifty-Eighth North Carolina Troops. It is told, as much as possible, in their own words, using their diaries, letters, and post-war reminiscences.

A project of this length could not have been possible without the help of countless individuals. The most important are the hundreds of descendants with whom I have had the privilege of talking over the course of a decade-plus of research. They are the ones who have preserved letters, diaries, family stories, and photographs. These wonderful folks have shared their family treasures with me, and I take great pride in being able to help preserve their family history.

Special thanks also go to the librarians and archivists at numerous institutions, including the public libraries in Ashe, Watauga, Caldwell, Avery, Mitchell, Yancey, and McDowell

Historian Michael C. Hardy spent more than a decade researching and writing this history of the Fifty-Eighth North Carolina Troops. He is pictured here with the Fifty-Eighth's monument at Chickamauga in 2008.

counties. The historical societies in Avery (Cindy Peters), Mitchell (Irene Sparks), and Caldwell (John Hawkins) counties were also extremely helpful. Also in this list are the librarians and archivists at the Appalachian Collection at Appalachian State University; the Southern Historical Society Collection at the University of North Carolina, Chapel Hill; the North Carolina State Archives and the North Carolina Museum of History in Raleigh; and the United States Army Military History Institute in Carlisle, Pennsylvania. The historians and rangers at Bentonville Battlefield and the Bennett Place in North Carolina, Chickamauga-Chattanooga National Military Park, and Kennesaw Mountain National Military Park were also very helpful.

Countless others either provided information or worked as sounding boards for ideas and thoughts about the regiment. This list, albeit incomplete, includes Skip Smith, Chad Marley, Tom Belton, Jim Priesmeyer, the late Sanna Gaffney, David Long, Marilyn Crosbie, Barbara Bledsoe, Claudia McGough, Tense Franklin Banks, Lee White, Robert Marshall, Benny Hayes, Chris Watford, and Jeffrey Weaver.

Two individuals bear special appreciation. Leta Cornett, of Watauga County, deserves credit for re-discovering the Delap Family Cemetery in Campbell County, Tennessee. Over sixty members of the Fifty-Eighth North Carolina Troops, along with men from other regiments, are buried here, and we are all grateful for her research and work at finding these graves that had been lost to history.

The other individual is Michael Ledford, the most knowledgeable person about Yancey and Mitchell counties and the war. There were times that we talked two or three times a day, trading names, dates, cemeteries, and stories. More than once we could be found tramping through a cemetery in the snow or in the rain, looking for the graves of men who served in the Fifty-Eighth. Michael also read and commented on the manuscript.

And finally, Daphne Baird of Williamsburg, Kentucky, read the manuscript for me, finding all sorts of problems with consistency. That should be expected, considering it took three years of starting and stopping to finish this.

Lastly, my beloved Elizabeth loves this story, especially John and Fannie Palmer, almost as much as I do. She's tramped battlefields, dug in archives, helped translate letters, read e-mail, and read the manuscript more than once, making me look like a much better writer. What would I do without her?

I do hope you enjoy this history of the Fifty-Eighth North Carolina Troops. These men, like so many others, have waited too long for their story to be told.

CHAPTER 1

December 1861: The Mitchell Rangers

There was a very loud "snap" as the hammer struck the percussion cap. A split second later, this "snap" should have been followed by a "crack" as the flame produced by the cap ignited the black powder in the chamber of a revolver. But there was only a "snap." It was Saturday, April 5, 1862, and neighbors David Oaks and John B. Palmer "were arguing over cattle." Palmer was trying to purchase the cattle from Oaks to feed his soldiers in the Mitchell Rangers. Just what was said to anger the thirty-year-old Oaks enough to pull his pistol to shoot Captain Palmer is unknown. Palmer quickly extracted his own pistol and "shot him on the spot." "Uncle" Jacob Carpenter, who kept local death records on scraps of paper, recorded that "David Oakes ag 30 [died] apr 5 1862. Shote by John Parmer in ware." Much of the history of the Fifty-Eighth North Carolina Troops is just as tragic and just as frustrating to modern historians as this isolated event in the life of one of its commanding officers.[1]

Pre-twentieth century warfare has often been painted with broad brush strokes. Who can forget the image of the plumed captain, leading his infantry or cavalry company while gloriously mounted on a noble steed? After war's end, the captain returns home to the bosom of his waiting family. While the honored dead are memorialized, the battles that won the war are nearly bloodless. War was perceived as a glorious adventure between honorable opponents, fought on pre-arranged fields of contest.

When war came to the United States in 1861, many leaders in the South were the first to depart from the notions of conventional warfare, just as they had done to win the American Revolution. Bands of partisan rangers, state rangers, and legions began to answer the call of their new nation. Virginia created the "state rangers" in 1861, and the Confederate government authorized partisan rangers in 1862. Both organizations sought to give credence to irregular forces. These rangers were organized and ordered to operate behind enemy lines or in areas which frequently changed hands. Partisan bands were raised across the South, especially in Virginia, Tennessee, and the trans–Mississippi theater. By 1864, all partisan ranger organizations, with the exception of the one led by John H. Mosby in Virginia, had been disbanded and the men formed into traditional front-line combat regiments.

Legions were also extremely popular in the early days of the Confederacy. A Confederate legion was composed of a regiment of infantry, a battalion of cavalry, and a battery of artillery. These quasi-military organizations were ideally suited for local defenses, and there were quite a few formed in the first year of the war. They included Cobb's Legion, led by Thomas R. R. Cobb; Hampton's Legion, led by Wade Hampton; Whitfield's Legion, under the command of John W. Whitfield; Hilliard's Legion from Alabama; and the memorable Thomas's Legion of Cherokee Indians and Mountaineers from North Carolina.

Many men sought to raise irregular bands for state or Confederate service. One surprising would-be legion leader was Mitchell County resident John Boynton Palmer. Palmer was born in Plattsburg, Clinton County, New York, on October 13, 1826. His mother was Charlotte Sailly, and his father was John Palmer. The senior Palmer was a lawyer, county judge, member of the state assembly, and in 1817 and 1837, a representative in the United States Congress. He died in 1840, and John B. Palmer moved to Detroit, Michigan, where he lived and worked with a brother, brother-in-law, and sister. Palmer became an involved citizen in the affairs of Detroit. He was a merchant who helped charter the Detroit Savings Bank in 1849, was a director of the Detroit Board of Trade in 1856, and served as president of the Detroit Literary Society in 1857. In October 1852, Palmer married Frances (Fannie) Marvin Kirby, of New York. Her parents were Col. Edmund Kirby and Eliza Brown. The wedding of Kirby and Brown was attended by celebrities: the Marquis de Lafayette and President John Quincy Adams. The Palmers, in turn, traveled in some of the most elite circles of Detroit society. John B. and Fannie Palmer had one son, Edmund Kirby Palmer, born in 1854.[2]

For some unknown reason, possibly because of his health, or because of the influences of his North Carolina friends, the Childs family, or simply because the noise of a growing city became a bother, Palmer chose to move from bustling Detroit to rural western North Carolina in the late 1850s. In 1858, his home, called Grasslands, was constructed in what was then Watauga County. The home was "the finest house in all the area." Palmer was described as "a man of medium build, slightly gray and very handsome. Everyone who knew him liked him." It is possible that Palmer continued to be a merchant. According to the 1860 Watauga County census, he was a farmer, not a slave owner, and was the wealthiest man in the Toe River Valley.[3]

Palmer was very active in local affairs. When Mitchell County was formed from parts of Watauga and Yancey counties in January 1861, he was elected associate justice for the Pleas and Quarters court. He was also elected treasurer of public buildings for Mitchell County. In addition, he was one of the commissioners appointed to select a seat for the new county.[4]

When war came between the southern and northern sections of the United States, Palmer chose not to return to his native state of New York, but instead cast his lot with the South. Both John and Fannie had relatives who fought for the Union. It is still unclear why the Palmers chose to ally themselves against family and friends.

The first months of the war came and went, and families from the Toe River Valley sent their husbands, fathers, brothers, and sweethearts to fight for the South. The Palmers chose to remain out of the conflict for those first few months. The newly founded Confederate States of America was able to establish a government, and its armies succeeded in winning military victories over the Federals at Ft. Sumter, Bethel Church, Bull Run, Ball's Bluff, and Wilson's Creek. But as summer slipped into fall, the Confederacy began losing the advantages it had gained during the first six months of the war. Men were volunteering in fewer numbers, and those in six- or twelve-month regiments were beginning to refuse to re-enlist. The Confederate government was pursuing a less aggressive strategy, and the North, which was actively recruiting more men, began to launch campaigns that would prove successful.

Western North Carolina in 1860 was still largely an untamed wilderness on the edge of the frontier. The area was sparsely settled. Some Cherokees inhabited the southern portion of the mountains, and no railroad had yet breached any of the gaps from the east or south. Commerce continued to flow up and down the mountains in wagons on poor roads. Some of these roads had been in existence for centuries, carved out of the landscape by the no-longer-present bison and elk that once roamed the hills and valleys. While modernization had begun to take place in large cities, the people of western North Carolina still practiced many of the old ways, as had their ancestors who had arrived 100 years before. Their speech patterns remained tied to those ancestors and distant relatives who lived across the Atlantic Ocean in Scotland and Ireland. People lived in tightly knit communities, much as their ancestors had, and most people lived near immediate and distant family members. However, mountain people were never completely cut off from the rest of the world. Though travel was arduous, it was possible. Literacy rates were high for the time period, and news flowed into communities in the mountains as quickly as in other rural places across the country. Education was highly prized by young and old alike.

Even before North Carolina left the Union, hundreds of men from Western North Carolina were volunteering to serve the state and the new Confederacy. North Carolina seceded in May 1861, and by October, an estimated 4,400 men had volunteered, one in fifteen mountaineers, as compared to one in nineteen for the rest of the state. Palmer recruited the men for his new command from the surrounding countryside of the Toe River Valley.[5]

The Toe River derives its name from the Cherokee word Estatoe. All of the creeks and branches in the valley form the Toe River, which, after winding through the Unaka Mountains, becomes the Nolichucky River and passes into Tennessee. It was not until 1778 that the Toe River Valley was officially opened to settlement, even though there is no doubt that white settlers had arrived prior to that date. Samuel Bright obtained a land grant in March 1780 on the North Toe River. He then carved out a road to Tennessee known as Bright's Trace. It is believed that the area where Bright settled had been in the possession of William Davenport as early as June 1774. Other families soon followed, including the Wisemans, Davises, and Pendleys. They settled the area around Linville Falls and the Bright settlement. By the 1790 census, there was a total population of 300 people in the whole valley.[6]

By the turn of the nineteenth century, Bright had sold out and moved on, and the Childs family, from Massachusetts, occupied the old Bright settlement. New families continued to move into the region. The Toe River Valley had been a part of Burke County until 1791, when Buncombe County was created. In 1833, Yancey was created and encompassed the area. Another new county was created in 1849 and named Watauga. This new county took in a portion of the North Toe River. Mitchell County followed in 1861, and the Toe River Valley was split between Yancey and Mitchell counties. The county seat for Mitchell was established at Childsville, the home of the Childs family and the former Bright settlement, and was renamed Calhoun.

Palmer, who had been so influential in the formation of the new county, began recruiting a mixed company of infantry and cavalry in late 1861. The reasons for Palmer's participation are unknown. At the age of forty-five in 1861, he was not liable for conscription. One possible reason for his enthusiasm might have been the recent bridge burnings.

In September 1861, an east Tennessee native, the Rev. William B. Carter, approached Federal officers in Kentucky with the idea of destroying the vital railroad link that ran through east Tennessee. Once the line was out of commission, regular Federal soldiers could move into the area while local loyalists mobilized to strengthen Federal control of the area. The officers and exiled politicians liked the idea, and Carter traveled to Washington,

D.C., to present his idea to Abraham Lincoln, Simeon Cameron, and George B. McClellan. With their approval, Carter was back in Kentucky, and then east Tennessee, organizing men to burn the bridges. The night of November 8 was set for the bridge burners' covert operations. Carter sent word back to Brig. Gen. William T. Sherman, departmental commander, urging the troops to move quickly. Brig. Gen. George Thomas moved six regiments to Crab Orchard, Kentucky, about forty miles from Cumberland Gap, but Sherman's lukewarm support began to wane. Sherman feared that the Confederate forces were getting ready to launch their own attack and would not allow his forces to advance. It is unknown whether or not Carter was aware that Sherman had pulled his support. Regardless, Carter launched his attack, and on the night of November 8, five of the nine bridges were destroyed. Loyalists mobilized in several different towns and counties, including Elizabethton, where 1,000 Unionists gathered, organized companies, elected officers, and began stockpiling supplies. Regular Federal soldiers did not arrive, but Confederate reinforcements did. Several of the bridge burners were captured and hanged. Responding to the suppressed Union threat, North Carolina Governor Henry Clark offered two regiments for service in the area, and the Twenty-Ninth North Carolina Troops was in Cocke County, Tennessee, by December 3, 1861. An article ran in an Asheville newspaper stating that up to 1,000 loyalists had been driven out of east Tennessee into Madison County, just to the north. These numbers were greatly exaggerated. However, local officials were aware of problems in the area.[7]

Most of Palmer's recruits were from his neighbors in the southern sections of present-day Avery County. The "Mitchell Rangers" was mustered into service on December 31, 1861. There were sixty-three enlisted men, all farmers. The oldest was Lewis Vance, born in 1802 or 1803. The fifty-nine-year-old Vance enlisted with two of his sons, Thomas and William. On the other end of the age bracket, several fifteen- and sixteen-year-olds enlisted. They included Samuel Blalock, Erwin Carpenter, Henry Dellinger, David Franklin, and James Riddle. Carpenter and Dellinger were later discharged, presumably for being underage. Twenty-six of the sixty-three enlisted men were twenty years old or younger. Eleven were thirty or older. The average age was twenty-four. All but Frederick Tobey, James Conley, and Lewis Vance were native Tar Heels. Vance was from South Carolina and Tobey and Conley hailed from New York.[8]

Henry T. Dellinger (Company A), pictured here (right) after the war with his brother James, joined the Mitchell Rangers at the age of 16 in December 1861. Because of his youth, he was rejected for service (courtesy Tense Franklin Banks).

Helping Palmer command the group were Martin Wiseman,

John Ollis, and John Wiseman. John Ollis, Jr., was born around 1818. He was 6'11" tall and "had a booming voice to match his height." Although average heights were shorter in the nineteenth century than in the twentieth, tall men like Ollis did exist and were generally quite impressive. Ollis was an overseer for the Avery family, a minister, and a Mexican War veteran. He was elected first lieutenant on December 30. John Wess Wiseman was elected second lieutenant the same day. At the age of twenty, he was the youngest of the company grade officers. Martin Davenport Wiseman was also elected second lieutenant on December 30. He was born on August 13, 1818, in Burke County.[9]

Even as winter settled on the mountains of western North Carolina, men continued to join the Mitchell Rangers. The men who saw the war as a grand adventure were long gone. Palmer's men enlisted out of a sense of patriotism, not to the Confederacy, or even the state, but to their homes scattered around the Linville Falls sections of Burke and Mitchell counties. The high country of western North Carolina had only recently been settled, and was sparsely inhabited. Most the families were interrelated and the natures of the people in the mountain South were markedly different from those of their lowland neighbors. The primary motives for enlistment among these men were home, embodied by the fireside, wife, and children, and the communities from which they hailed. They were in the army to protect their local interests.

Frederick Tobey, a native of New York, was promoted to captain after John B. Palmer was promoted to lieutenant colonel. He served as captain of Company A until the regiment was reorganized in April 1865, when he was transferred to Company D. Tobey moved to Lincoln County after the war (courtesy the North Carolina Department of Archives).

The Mitchell Rangers was a "part-time" organization. The men only served when needed. The rest of the time, they were free to return to their homes and look after their families and farms. Undoubtedly, this agreement was satisfactory to the local men who joined. Hundreds of men had already poured out of the area and into regiments that were no longer even in the state. Palmer's command provided protection to the families whose loved ones were off serving as soldiers. Part of the organization was infantry, and part was cavalry, though the distribution between the two segments is unknown. A cavalryman was expected to provide his own mount. Romulus W. Brown, who enlisted with the large group on December 30 and was from McDowell County, brought his own horse, "The Star of the West." According to a family story, the horse had been purchased by Romulus's father, John, in Texas at the start of the war. The Star of the West was a "swift saddle horse."[10]

On January 7, the first group of new recruits arrived in camp, most likely Camp Martin, established on Palmer's estate beside the Linville River. The flat bottoms to the south of the house provided a good camp and staging ground. Six men enlisted that day, including Phineas and Tillman McCurry, whose brother Walter had enlisted on December 30. Alfred

First Sergeant James M. Green (Company K) transferred from the cavalry to the Fifty-Eighth on July 29, 1862. He was wounded during the battles of Chickamauga and Kolb's Farm but survived the war (courtesy Robert Morgan).

A. Carpenter also signed up. Two of his brothers, Erwin and Jonathan, had already joined on December 30. Three days later, Charles Baily joined the Mitchell Rangers.[11]

Palmer wrote Governor Clark on January 10 regarding a number of issues. It seems that the governor had also issued a commission to Mr. Pearson, who was to raise a company in Mitchell County. Clark had to soothe Palmer. "When Captain Pearson was appointed, I was not aware or had lost sight of the fact that he was a resident of Mitchell County," the governor wrote. Palmer believed that Pearson's appointment had been because Clark had lost faith in him. The governor responded, "I have to state that I have no reason to feel dissatisfaction with your conduct as an officer or to doubt your loyalty to our State and the Southern Confederacy. I was ... convinced, both to your skill and judgment and devotion to our cause, before a commission was given to you, and I have since had no reason to change my opinion." The Mitchell Rangers were to remain in service as long as the governor saw a need, to battle "foes [within] or beyond the borders of the state."[12]

New men continued to trickle in. On January 14, David L. Carpenter, Samuel W. English, and Matthew Sparks joined, followed by Samuel H. Gaddy on the seventeenth. Palmer slightly reorganized his command on January 21. Cpl. Alexander G. Havener was reduced back to the ranks that day, and then given a furlough without pay. According to the records, he never returned to Palmer's command. Thirty-five-year-old John A. Hensley was appointed corporal to take his place. Also promoted was Samuel English, who was assigned the rank of sergeant. A week later, John M. English, a Mexican War veteran and brother to Samuel, enlisted along with three others: James M. Green, James Stewart, and Thomas J. Wiseman.[13]

Palmer and his neighbors in the Mitchell Rangers spent the winter of 1861–1862 ready to protect their homes and families in the wilds of western North Carolina, although there was as yet no imminent threat. For many, it was their last winter on their beloved mountains and in the hollows among the towering trees.

CHAPTER 2

1860–1862

"No troops from North Carolina."—John W. Ellis

The South was in a state of turmoil when John and Fannie Palmer chose to make western North Carolina their home. Ever since the early days of the republic, one state or section of the country often had threatened secession from the Union. The conflict usually arose over differing views of constitutional authority, with economic reasons coming in a close second. The debate had been heated since the introduction of the Wilmot Proviso in the United States Congress in 1846. This proviso, attached to an appropriations bill, declared that any new territory acquired from Mexico as a result of the Mexican-American War would forever be free from the institution of slavery. This would have given free states a permanent majority in the Senate.

The Mexican-American War had been fought largely by Southerners, and many in the South were angered by the proviso. The Wilmot Proviso brought out many Southern extremists, like western North Carolina's Thomas Clingman, who desired a Southern confederacy. The Compromises of 1850, which regulated the expansion of slavery in the new territories, calmed the storm for four years. In 1854, the Kansas-Nebraska Act was passed, allowing two new territories, Kansas and Nebraska, to chose for themselves if they were going to be admitted as free states. Not only did the passage of this act lead to the demise of the Missouri Compromise, but it reopened the slavery debates and led to the foundation of the Republican party in the North.

The new Republican party was opposed to the expansion of slavery into the new territories and endorsed the belief that free labor was superior to slavery. Members of the party wanted to see America modernized, emphasizing higher education, banking, railroads, industry, and cities. John C. Fremont was the party's candidate for president in 1856. His campaign slogan was "Free soil, free labor, free speech, free men." The party had no support in the South, and many Southerners viewed the party as a dissentious organization that threatened civil war.

Kansas and Missouri became a bitter battleground between the free-staters and pro-slavery factions. A mini-civil war raged by 1856, and abolitionist John Brown came to the forefront. John Brown escaped from Kansas and went to New York where, in 1858, he drew up a constitution for a "Negro republic to be founded in the mountains of Virginia." A group of wealthy abolitionists, the Secret Six, funded a revolution led by Brown. On October 16, 1859, Brown, with twenty-one followers, seized the arsenal at Harpers Ferry, Virginia, with plans to arm themselves and other slaves to start a guerrilla war in the Appalachian

Mountains. Brown was apprehended, tried for treason, and executed. All of the state's newspapers carried accounts of Brown's actions, and the raid sent tremors across the nation. When it became known that the raid was sponsored by prominent Northern abolitionists, the public became alarmed, viewing the action not as the work of a lone fanatic, but as the ultimate scheme of the abolitionists. The real problem came when Brown's body was borne through the cities of the North. Church and town bells pealed, prayers were offered, and elegies read. In western North Carolina, public meetings were held in at least five counties: Buncombe, Henderson, Madison, Caldwell, and Yancey. Militia units were created to respond to such threats in their own communities. Calls went out for mountain Southerners to stop buying goods manufactured in the North, and to return to cottage industries.[1]

In April 1860, the Democratic Convention met in Charleston, South Carolina, to nominate a presidential candidate. A Burke County native, William W. Avery, headed the committee that drafted the party's platform of congressional protection of slavery. The platform failed to acquire enough votes for passage, and the delegates from the Deep South states walked out. When the convention met again in Baltimore on June 18, the members refused to re-admit those who had walked out of the convention in Charleston. Virginia then withdrew, along with most of North Carolina's delegates. Stephen Douglas of Illinois emerged as one candidate for the Baltimore group. On June 23, the "Seceders Convention" was held in Baltimore, and Vice President John Breckinridge was nominated. Yet another candidate, John Bell of the Constitutional Union party, entered the fray. The split in the Democratic party allowed the election of the Republican party's nominee in November 1860: Abraham Lincoln. No votes for Lincoln were garnered in North Carolina, as Lincoln did not appear on the ballot. Breckinridge carried the state by a small majority over Bell, with Douglas receiving few votes.

David Carpenter joined the Mitchell Rangers (Company A) at the age of 22 in January 1862. He transferred to the Fifth Battalion Cavalry in June 1862 and was later captured. Carpenter died in the prison camp at Point Lookout, Maryland, in October 1864 (courtesy Mildred Guthrie).

Reaction to Lincoln's election was swift. South Carolina called for a state convention, and on December 20, unanimously voted to secede. It was rapidly followed by Mississippi, Florida, Alabama, Georgia, Louisiana, and Texas. While Clingman, Avery, and North Carolina Governor John Ellis were applauding the actions of South Carolina, another western North Carolina politician, Zebulon Vance, was urging restraint. In a letter written in December 1860 to William Dickson, member of the House of Commons from Caldwell County, Vance wrote, "We have everything to gain and nothing on earth to lose by delay, but by too hasty action we may take a fatal step that we *never* can retrace — may lose a heritage that we can never recover."

Public meetings began breaking out in the mountain counties. In Caldwell County, a "Union Meeting" was held in late December. Lawyer Walter W. Lenoir introduced a motion for the chairman, Joseph Norwood, to appoint a committee to draft resolutions. Lenoir and six others were appointed to the committee and went to work. The resolutions recognized the right of a state to secede in the face of "an intermeddling spirit of many persons in the non-slaveholding South." If attempts of a peaceful and constitutional settlement failed, then "the South must demand, and if necessary, force, a separation of the two sections." And, "if any one or more of the states should attempt to secede from the Union ... it is the wisest policy of the federal government to recognize immediately their separate national existence."[2]

Vance, who represented much of western North Carolina in the House of Representatives, wrote to Lenoir just a few days after the Union meeting in Caldwell County. "The crisis here is rapidly approaching its denouement," Vance wrote. The Union had already been dissolved. "Must N.C. and the other border states go with them is our question? We are not compelled to do so." Vance then advanced an idea of a new confederation "composed of the border slave and free states. In this way we preserve this Capitol, the public lands, the form and prestige of the old government, secure greater homogeneousness, and finally re-organize and reconstruct the whole Union around this grand and over-shadowing nucleus!" This new "Central Confederation" would then entice Georgia back into the fold, and the other Deep South states would be forced to follow. "As for New England," Vance wrote, "we would *kick* it out if it refused to secede, and would never let it back unless as the single state of New England." Lenoir responded a few days later and likewise professed his loyalty to the constitution "the union, the laws, the treaties and the flag of our country." He believed the resolutions that Caldwell County had passed showed

> that I stand out as stoutly as any southern man ought for full justice from the north as an indispensable condition to union with the north, or any part of it. But if we are going to have an entire separation from the north, I am opposed to joining our state with the schemes and politics of the cotton states, and prefer a union with Virginia, Kentucky and Tennessee, with Maryland, Delaware and Missouri if they would join; or even our separate independence. I am utterly opposed to reopening the slave trade, have no faith in the new political dogmas which I believe they will engraft in their constitution, and have no desire to engage in the silly project of trying in vain to carry slavery into Mexico and Central America.... Nor do I wish to take part in a civil war between the North and the South, for the possession of those God forsaken regions, which will be sure to come about unless we have a central government to keep the peace.[3]

In nearby Yancey County, the reactions to secession and North Carolina's "watch and wait" attitude were just the opposite. "The political excitement is very intense," Burnsville merchant John Bailey wrote to his brother. "[Bayles M.] Edney and [David] Colman made speeches in favor of secession. The majority of Yancey ... is in favor of secession." Samuel Deaver of neighboring Madison County wrote to Vance in late January: "Your enemies in the County [Yancey] is trying to make Capital of your Being A union man.... At Burnsville last Weeke ... they hung you in Efigy." Not everyone in old Yancey was in support of secession. A "worthy friend" wrote to the *Weekly Standard*, "A large portion of [Yancey] are for the Union, whatever designing men may say." It is also believed that a Union meeting was held in Yancey in early January 1862.[4]

Ashe County to the north also held rallies. The first was in October 1860. Vance, former congressman Nathaniel Boyden, and James Leach were present, and the crowd was thought to number between 4,000 and 5,000 men and women. The Salisbury Brass Band wooed the crowd. A second pro–Union meeting was held at the courthouse in Jefferson in January 1861. The meeting was attended by both Democrats and Whigs, and pledged that the citizens of the county "are as immovably attached to the institutions of the South, as deeply deplore

The soldiers in the above photographs are pictured wearing a woolen battle-shirt, a very popular style during the early days of the war. At top are brothers William and John Vance (Company A). Below them, on the left, is Israel Team (Company E), and on the right is David Franklin (Company A) (Vance brothers courtesy the Avery County Historical Museum; Team and Franklin courtesy Tense Banks).

the election of Lincoln and Hamlin, and have as much abhorrence of the personal liberty laws of the North as any people on this continent; but ... we can see no safety for our institutions and no remedy for our ills in a dissolution of the Union."[5]

While his exact actions are unknown, John B. Palmer actively campaigned against secession in Watauga and probably Mitchell counties.

Legislators in Raleigh met and, on January 29, adopted a bill imploring the male citizens to vote on February 28. They were to vote on the question of calling a convention and to elect 120 delegates. By a slim majority (50.3 percent, or 651 votes), the call for a convention was rejected. The mountain counties were as torn as the rest of the state. Ashe, Watauga, and Caldwell rejected the measure by more than 60 percent. McDowell rejected it by 50 percent, and Yancey was in favor of the measure by more than 60 percent.

Tensions continued to mount between the northern and southern sections of the country in March and April 1861. A peace conference in Washington, D.C., ended with failure on February 27, and Lincoln's inaugural address on March 4 did nothing to help ease anxiety. For the next few weeks, secessionist newspapers continued to fan the flames of war in the state. By mid–April, the die was cast. Lincoln chose to reinforce the garrison at Fort Sumter in Charleston, South Carolina, and the Confederates in South Carolina, on April 12, attacked the fort, which capitulated the next day. On April 15, Lincoln called for 75,000 volunteers, including two regiments from North Carolina, to go into South Carolina and stop the rebellion. Governor Ellis responded to Lincoln: "Your dispatch is received, and if genuine (which its extraordinary character leads me to doubt), I have to say in reply that I regard your levy of troops for the purpose of subjugating the states of the South, as in violation of the Constitution and a usurpation of power. I can be no party to this wicked violation of the laws of the country, and to this war upon the liberties of a free people. You can get no troops from North Carolina."[6] On April 17, Virginia voted to leave the Union, and Governor Ellis called for 30,000 North Carolina troops and a special session of the legislature to meet in two weeks.

War fever ran rampant across the state. A brass band played in Yancey County on April 18, boosting already soaring military spirits. Yancey produced its first company, led by Capt. John S. McElroy, for service on May 1. It eventually became Company C, Sixteenth North Carolina Troops. Watauga County raised its first company on May 11, 1861, the Watauga Rangers, led by former state representative George N. Folk. This group later became Company D, First North Carolina Cavalry.[7]

Behind these new companies was the old militia system. The militia system in North Carolina dated all the way back to the 1660s. Early settlers were expected to own their own muskets, powder, and shot, and men between the ages of seventeen and sixty were required to serve when the council deemed necessary. Usually, a military crisis, such as the Tuscarora War (1711–1712) or the American Revolution, was needed to bring about a reorganization. During the latter, the age requirements were changed to between sixteen and fifty, and the state was divided up into six militia districts. As the militia system progressed into the nineteenth century, it gradually became ineffectual, and annual musters were likely to be social occasions, often with much drinking and fighting, rather than days to sharpen one's military training. While members not present were often fined for their absenteeism, most of the county turned out for the social event. News and gossip were shared along with food and, later, whiskey. Fights usually broke out, at times turning tragic. An Asheville newspaper recorded in June 1846 that "an affray occurred at the muster ground ... in Yancey County, on Saturday last, in which a young man named Roberts was stabbed ... and died the following

Monday." In Watauga County shortly before the war began, Joseph B. Todd, clerk of court, had to stand in the courthouse door and brandish his sword, trying to keep the sheriff and others from riding their horses through the courthouse. Despite the ineffectualness of the old militia system, it at least gave to future soldiers a rudimentary introduction into military formations and maneuvers.[8]

Virginia passed an ordinance of secession on April 17, followed by Arkansas on May 6 and Tennessee the following day. On May 1, the North Carolina legislature met in a special session. The House of Commons unanimously passed a bill to a call a convention to consider withdrawing North Carolina from the Union. The bill to call the convention appeared before the state house, and with three dissenting votes, passed that body. The date set for the convention was the twentieth. The convention removed North Carolina from the Union, and, over the next thirteen days, other measures were passed. Governor Ellis was authorized to tender military aid to Virginia; a commissioner was appointed to the Confederate government; five million dollars were set aside for public defense; and the governor was authorized to enroll 10,000 troops, with another 20,000 to serve for twelve months and to be paid a ten-dollar bounty.[9]

What has been termed "the ablest political body ever assembled in North Carolina" met in Raleigh on May 20. Unanimously, the delegates passed the ordinance of secession. Bells pealed and cannons boomed, announcing the moment. Within an hour, the delegates had also passed an ordinance ratifying the Provisional Constitution of the Confederate States of America. On May 21, President Jefferson Davis issued a proclamation welcoming North Carolina into the Confederacy. That same day, the delegates signed the ordinance.[10]

Thousands of men began to pour out of coastal villages, urban centers, and mountain hollows and ridges to join local companies. These new companies gave themselves fanciful names, like the "Hornet Nest Rifles" from Mecklenburg County; the "Confederate Guards" from Beaufort County; the "Gilford Dixie Boys" from Guilford County; the "Dixie Invincibles" from Hyde County; and the "Shady Grove Rangers" from Lincoln County. On May 13, 1861, the First North Carolina Volunteers was organized, and on June 10, 1861, fought in the first land battle of the war, at Bethel Church, Virginia. Other regiments from the Old North State were soon mustered into service and quickly made their way into Virginia. Three North Carolina regiments were present when the first major battle of the war, fought at Manassas, took place on July 21, 1861.[11]

Fort Sumter, Bethel Church, and Manassas were all Confederate victories that sent the Federals reeling back into their defenses. However, these losses also stiffened the Federal resolve. There were many, North and South, who had thought the war would be over with one big battle and in six months or less. Many now realized that the affair would last considerably longer. The South faced numerous logistical problems. While men were joining regiments by the score, these men were green recruits who had to be trained. An even worse problem was the lack of supplies, like rifled muskets, tents, and saddles for the cavalry. The South did not have these munitions of war, and the industry base necessary to manufacture the needed items was almost non-existent in the region. To further complicate the situation, the North's navy was able to blockade Southern ports, preventing needed goods from flowing in. And the North's superior navy was able to deliver troops to any point along the South's coastline for an attack, a fact that soon became apparent to North Carolinians.

Not long after leaving the Union, North Carolina began work on a series of defensive works along the Outer Banks and farther south along the Cape Fear River. The actions of the state were not entirely defensive. The state also commissioned several small steamers to

Eli Church (Company I), pictured here after the war with his wife, Louisa, son Abner, and granddaughter Mary Louisa Baxter Hodges, served only a brief time in the Fifty-Eighth. He volunteered on July 24, 1862, and transferred to the Fifth Battalion North Carolina Cavalry on July 27, 1862 (courtesy Gary Hodges).

ply the waters off the Outer Banks. In one six-week period, the *Winslow* was able to capture sixteen Federal ships. Wishing to put an end to the harassment, the Federal forces focused their attention on the area. On August 28, 1861, Fort Clark fell to a combined Federal naval and army assault. Fort Hatteras surrendered the following day. Roanoke Island was lost in February 1862, and was then used as a base for Federal attacks on the interior of eastern North Carolina.

Other victories were won by the Confederates in 1861, including Ball's Bluff in Virginia and Wilson's Creek in Missouri. Success had also been achieved in Kentucky and Arizona. Had the Confederates been able to mount a successful offensive campaign into Maryland or Pennsylvania, then the effort to establish independence might have become a reality. However, as 1861 slipped into history, the Confederacy's momentum slipped as well.

Chapter 3

May 1862

"I will make an honest effort of it."— Zebulon B. Vance

On the other side of North Carolina, far away from Palmer and the Mitchell Rangers, a native mountaineer was attempting to organize a new command. Zebulon Baird Vance was a lawyer and politician from western North Carolina. At the start of the war, he was serving in the United States House of Representatives. Vance openly campaigned for North Carolina to stay in the Union, but only until Lincoln called for troops from North Carolina to go into the deep South states in order to force them back into the Union. Lincoln's actions propelled North Carolina into secession. Once his state's direction was clear, Vance helped raise a company of volunteers from his native Buncombe County, the Rough and Ready Guards, mustered into service on May 3, 1861. Vance was chosen as the captain. The Guards became Company F of the Fourteenth North Carolina State Troops on June 6, 1861. He served until August 27, 1861, when he was elected colonel of the Twenty-Sixth North Carolina Troops. Vance was only 30 years old.

The Twenty-Sixth North Carolina was in Raleigh until September 2, when the regiment moved to Morehead City and Bogue Banks. In January 1862, the Twenty-Sixth was transferred to the New Bern area to help construct defensive works. During March 12 through 14, Vance and the Twenty-Sixth fought their first battle just south of New Bern. The engagement was a Confederate loss.

Prior to the battle of New Bern, Vance was contemplating raising a legion. On March 4, he wrote Allen Turner Davidson, a Confederate Congressman and cousin of Vance:

> I have the offer of some new companies from the mountains. In thirty days, I could raise another regiment for the war, two companies of cavalry & one of artillery. This would make a handsome brigade with which I would like to take the field on active service. Do you suppose the president would give me authority to raise it? If so, I would pledge myself to raise it in 30 days. Can't you feel the authorities for me? ... If you think it probable I would run up to Richmond for a "few days"— I am exceedingly tired of watching and waiting behind ditches; and really believe I could better serve my country now by using my influence in the mountains to raise troops than in any other way.

On the reverse of the envelope was written: "Authority to raise troops [,] but can't promise he shall be General." So, Vance had his permission to raise a legion, but no promise of higher rank.[1]

Vance and the Twenty-Sixth fought well at New Bern, and both the colonel and his regiment received praise throughout the press. The surge in popularity, combined with the recent approval of the Conscription Act, prompted Vance to pursue the idea of a legion. He wrote to George Wythe Randolph, secretary of war, asking authority to raise two regiments of infantry, two companies of cavalry, and an artillery battery. He believed that he could accomplish this in just thirty days. Two weeks later, Vance had his approval and wrote a dispatch to be published in newspapers across the state. The article stated that Vance had been authorized to "raise a LEGION for the war." Vance wanted "an additional regiment of Infantry, two companies of cavalry, and one company of artillery." It could be that the Twenty-Sixth North Carolina would be the core infantry regiment that Vance had in mind. A bounty of $100 was to be paid to each new recruit. The government was to furnish the best arms in the Confederacy. Vance encouraged new recruits, either singles or by companies, to "turn out, and let's make short work with Abe."[2]

However, Vance had no sooner announced his plans for the legion when problems arose. Vance undoubtedly wrote to Governor Henry Clark, trying to gather some of the new companies from the state's camps of instruction for his new legion. Clark was politically opposed to Vance and wrote, through the state adjutant-general's office, that the number of troops requested by the president from North Carolina were already in the field and the troops in camp were being raised as a reserve as required by law. "For these reasons," the governor wrote, we are "not inclined to encourage further the formation of new companies, considering it better policy to fill up those already in service, if an increase of force be necessary." Clark had already denied Vance's request for recruiting instructions in an earlier letter.[3]

Unable to use any of the new companies that had already tendered their services to the state, Vance started to recruit men on his own. He turned toward the mountain counties. One new company for his legion was recruited in Caldwell County. Vance was already known in the county, having practiced law there while on the circuit. Two of the companies in the Twenty-Sixth were also from Caldwell. Vance turned to a fellow lawyer, Walter W. Lenoir, to help raise the legion. Lenoir was a grandson of Gen. William Lenoir of Revolutionary War fame and was attached to his brother's company of the Twenty-Fifth North Carolina Troops. He had just been offered a lieutenancy. Lenoir was back in Caldwell County on April 30 "for the purpose of joining and assisting in raising a company ... for Vance's Legion." Lenoir did not express much hope. "The prospect of forming the new company here does not seem very bright," he wrote in his diary. "I will make an honest effort to encourage it."[4]

War-time image of Zebulon Baird Vance, who tried to raise "Vance's Legion" in early 1862. Vance's Legion failed, and one of the companies transferred to the Fifty-Eighth. Vance went on to become governor (courtesy the North Carolina Museum of History).

Other misfortunes befell Vance. He applied to his superiors for a furlough so he could go back to western North Carolina and recruit men for the legion. The request was denied. On April 21, Vance's former fellow law student, Burgess S. Gaither, wrote to the secretary of war, asking that Vance be granted a furlough to go and organize his new legion. Vance, in a letter to the secretary dated May 2, denied having asked Gaither to intervene on his behalf. However, Vance used the opportunity to address the secretary regarding his furlough. "The late Secretary Mr. Benjamin, authorized me to raise a certain number of troops for the Confederate Service," Vance wrote. "Gen. Holmes refuse to permit me to leave camp for that purpose, though the troops are ready to be mustered ... twice as many more as I called for. I know not what to do with them, and asked Mr. Gaither to consult you in regard to the matter. But it makes no difference. I suppose it to be an indirect method of repealing the authority granted to me."[5]

A company, or possibly two, was organized in Caldwell County for the legion. These men left Caldwell County on May 15 and started for Kinston, North Carolina, where Vance and the Twenty-Sixth North Carolina were located. Lenoir wrote that the Twenty-Sixth's band left on May 15. Another Caldwell County man, George Washington Finley Harper, kept a diary of his travels. The Caldwell County men were in Salisbury by the evening of May 19 and in Goldsboro the following evening. On May 21, they were in the camp of the Twenty-Sixth North Carolina, where old acquaintances were undoubtedly renewed and elections for officers were held. Thomas Dula, who had run as a secessionist candidate during the February 1861 call for a convention, was elected captain, Lenoir was made first lieutenant, and Emanuel Hendrick was second lieutenant.[6]

On May 24, the company left Kinston and spent the night in Raleigh. Harper wrote that the troops spent the nights of May 24 and 25 quartered in the Baptist church. The next day, the company was moved to Kittrell Springs, in Granville County, to engage in "clearing off and triming up a grove of old field pines for camp and building tents." Another commander offered his company to Vance. Lewis A. Johnson was organizing a cavalry company in Anson County and apparently offered his company for service in the legion. Walter Lenoir wrote of two other groups of men in camp for the legion. The first was "an infantry company, or rather part of one from Rockingham county," and another an "infantry company from Alleghany county."[7]

For Vance, his time had expired. He had been allowed only until May 17 to forward the muster rolls of his command to Richmond. On that day, he wrote to George Randolph that his companies "were scattered over different portions of the State, in counties remote from the Telegraph & daily mails." Vance had been unable to get those promised companies into camp. "The scheme is therefore a failure unless you will have the kindness to allow me a week or two to get my rolls & return them to you office." This request for an extension of time was taken to Gen. Robert E. Lee by D. W. Barringer, who forwarded it to the secretary. Randolph claimed that he had no power to extend the time period given to Vance. Two telegrams went out to Vance on May 19 and on May 21. The first stated that if Vance "had the whole number requisite for organization actually enrolled on the 17th inst. they will be received." The second note asked Vance to send in those muster rolls.[8]

"My Legion is thriving and will yet be a success I think," Vance wrote to his wife on May 25 from Kinston. Alpheus M. Erwin was appointed by Vance to act as the commissary agent for the legion. He arrived at Kittrell Springs on June 4. Apparently, Captain Dula's company was the only company in camp. Erwin reported to Vance that just four or five men from the Anson County cavalry company were in camp. The others were expected at any time. Erwin also informed Vance that one of his new men had died: Sydney Settlemire, a Caldwell County resident, stricken with typhoid fever.[9]

Time had really run out for Vance and his legion. On June 15, he wrote to Randolph, stating that he found "it impossible to raise and organize troops with both state and Confederate authorities against me, and have therefore quit trying to get my companies together." Vance asked the secretary of war to issue orders regarding the disposition of the companies he had in camp. Companies made up of men who were not liable for conscription were to be disbanded, with men of conscription age assigned to old regiments. Full companies of volunteers were to be transferred "to regiments needing companies to complete them." Walter Lenoir recorded in his diary that Dula "has gone to the Western part of the State, with Col Vance's permission, for the purpose of attaching the company to some of the unfinished regiments or battalions, still in process of formation there." The men in the company from Caldwell County did not have long to wait.[10]

Chapter 4

January–July 1862

"On our way to the Civil War."— Pvt. Wesley Presnell, Company D

The war was not going well for the Confederacy at the beginning of 1862. Early victories in 1861, like Fort Sumter and Bull Run, had given way to defeats at Forts Henry and Donelson, Bowling Green, and Pea Ridge. Port Royal, South Carolina, was taken in November 1861; New Bern, North Carolina, fell in March; and the port of Savannah was closed on April 11. New Orleans and the Mississippi River were lost by April 25. Northern Virginia was lost that same month, and by the first of May, a Federal army sat on the outskirts of the Confederate capital in Richmond. Supplies, such as uniforms, rifled-muskets, and lead were in short supply across the South, and the blockade that would eventually strangle the South was already taking its toll.

Little information exists on the activities of Palmer and his Mitchell Rangers during the early months of 1862. On January 14, Palmer was ordered by Adjutant General James B. Martin to release the prisoners he had collected, provided that they had taken the oath of allegiance. The arms that these unnamed prisoners had were to be retained for "public service." Palmer was also "to protect citizens from mobs or any illegal proceedings." In mid–February, he was ordered to Raleigh, possibly to pick up pay and articles that he had requisitioned. On March 13, Palmer either asked for, or received, a large amount of supplies, including 115 cartridge boxes, waist belts, and cap pouches; 95 bayonet scabbards; 20 pounds of rifle powder; 100 pounds each of buckshot and lead; 1,000 musket caps; 6,000 shotgun caps, 20 saddle bags and holsters, and 20 flint and steel pistols.[1]

Though there were few actual duties to engage them, not all of the Mitchell Rangers' time was spent on their farms. On the first of May, the *Asheville News* reported that "Capt. Palmer's company from Mitchell, a splendid body of mounted men, and one company from Tennessee, are co-operating with the Madison and Buncombe troops." The article stated that the troops were trying to blockade the passes in Madison County, and that up to forty men had been captured, along with 100 guns.[2]

As early as December 1861, there had been serious talk of enacting a conscription bill, an attempt to swell the ranks of the Confederate army. The government realized that by the spring of 1862 the Confederate army and any chances of a Southern nation would be crippled when the men in more than 150 regiments, who had enlisted to serve one year, could go home. To combat these losses, the Confederate Congress passed the Furlough and Bounty Act in December 1861. This new law granted all men who had enlisted for one year a $50 bounty and a sixty-day furlough if they re-enlisted. However, these measures fell woefully short. On March 28, Jefferson Davis submitted a bill to the Congress requiring all white, able-bodied men, between the ages of eighteen and thirty-five, to serve for three years or the war. The bill passed the Confederate Congress on April 16. Five days later, a supplementary act was passed exempting teachers, ministers, state employees, industrial workers, and slave owners.

Conscription fell hardest on the yeomen farmer class. Throughout much of the state, it was time for spring planting, and the small- to middle-size farms, which had already sent a son or two, or possibly a father, were devastated. The Conscription Act was the most despised statute ever issued by the Confederate government. The law removed the power of recruiting and raising regiments from state hands and placed that power within the central government. Ironically, if a Southerner were asked what he was fighting against in the Civil War, he might have said he was against the intrusion of the government into his affairs. Many Southerners voiced their displeasure with their feet: they simply walked off their farms to hide in the swamps and woods, creating an additional burden on their families and on the government.

The conscription law stipulated that regiments in the process of forming had until May 17 to organize. That date was later pushed back until July 8, and then August 1. The act of conscription was an attempt to encourage enlistment by men who had otherwise been lukewarm in their sentiments toward the army. These unwilling volunteers could elect their officers just as the men who had enlisted in 1861 had done. They could also collect a bounty. Men who waited until they were conscripted could do neither, and were often assigned to any regiment that needed more men rather than having the opportunity to serve with friends and neighbors.[3]

By May 1862, Palmer had recruited one infantry company, the Mitchell Rangers, and two cavalry companies, known collectively as "Palmer's Legion." The "Mitchell Cavalry" was one of the two cavalry companies. Authority to raise the company

Like several other members of the Mitchell Rangers (Company A), James H. Wiseman transferred to the Fifth Battalion, North Carolina Cavalry (courtesy Tense Banks).

Born in New York, John B. Palmer was the only colonel of the Fifty-Eighth North Carolina Troops. In November 1863, he became commander of the Department of Western North Carolina (courtesy the North Carolina Department of Archives and History).

was granted to Sgt. Samuel W. English on May 13. The other cavalry company was the "Burke Rangers." Junius C. Tate was given permission to recruit this company on May 15.[4]

Just what occurred during the next six weeks remains clouded in confusion. One line of thinking is that Palmer began to recruit the Fifth Battalion Partisan Rangers during this time. On a company muster roll card located in the Compiled Service Records for the Fifty-Eighth North Carolina, one entry reads: "The 5th (Palmer's) Battalion North Carolina Partisan Rangers, consisting of seven companies, was organized under the authority of the Secretary of War dated May 13, 1862." However, Palmer wrote to Confederate Adjutant and Inspector General Samuel Cooper that once the legion was disbanded, "I organized the Infantry into a Regt and the cavalry into a Battn, both continuing to form parts of my command." Palmer ran an advertisement in the *Asheville News*, appearing on July 31, stating that he been authorized by General Edmund Kirby Smith to "increase his FIVE COMPANIES of Infantry to a FULL REGIMENT, And his TWO COMPANIES of CAVALRY to a BATTALION." Interested company commanders were to report to Palmer at Camp Martin in Mitchell County. It is clear that both Palmer's Legion and the Fifth Battalion Partisan Rangers were unsuccessful. Their failure to materialize has less to do with Palmer personally and more to do with the Confederate government, which had started to dislike the idea of legions.[5]

With the threat of conscription and the family and community dishonor entailed with avoiding enlistment, new companies started to form in the mountains of western North Carolina. Jacob Bowman began to recruit the first. Bowman, a farmer and state representative, raised the second company from Mitchell County. Bowman had been the person to introduce the resolution into the state house creating Mitchell County in 1860. He gained authorization from the secretary of war on May 13, and began to raise his company. On May 17, Bowman, at the age of thirty, was elected captain. John C. Green, thirty-two, was elected first lieutenant. William Garland was chosen second lieutenant. He was thirty-eight years old. His cousin, twenty-one-year-old John C. Garland, was elected third lieutenant.[6]

Since there were no newspapers in Mitchell or the surrounding counties, recruitment for companies was largely accomplished by word of month. Bowman might have spread word that he was raising a company by speaking to family members or friends whom he met on the street, or possibly at church. At times, men who wished to raise companies gave stirring speeches. Early war speeches had been designed to entice men into joining, speaking of a single battle in which the Yankees would be whipped with the entire war over in just three months. Those first recruits were the young men who rushed off to war in early 1861 and saw the conflict as a grand adventure. Starting in the fall of 1861, everyone could see that this was to be a protracted conflict, and men enlisted out of a sense of responsibility to their families and their state. If Bowman gave a speech, he might have mentioned those that had gone on before. But his speech also contained the fact that the men listening to his voice were required to serve. That was the law. It is also doubtful that the new soldiers received a farewell dinner or presentation of a company flag made by the local ladies. The time for such morale-boosting gestures had passed.

On May 17, ninety-two men joined Bowman's company. Their ages ranged from two sixteen-year-olds, Greenbury Young and Henry C. Herrill, to five men over the age of fifty. The oldest was Jackson Stewart, who was fifty-eight. Overall, they averaged just over twenty-seven years of age. Almost all of them were farmers. Thomas Young and Gibbs Garland each listed his occupation as clerk. Sydney Prestwood was a saddler, and Leonard Buchanan was a Baptist minister. Another soldier joined on June 1, two on June 27, four on July 12, three on July 16, and four on July 19. Azor Pritchard and Robert F. Baker both transferred from Company I, Twenty-Ninth North Carolina Troops, also during July. Forty-one-year-old Thomas Gardner was rejected for service, even though he later rejoined the regiment.[7]

Thomas Buchanan joined the regiment as a substitute for Thomas B. Young. On May 17, Young joined the regiment, then, after Buchanan's arrival, was discharged. The new conscription law allowed a man who had been conscripted to hire a substitute to take his place within the ranks. Thomas Buchanan was forty-two years of age at the time he was employed by Young and beyond the age of the new law.[8]

The "Yancey Boys" were the next company formed. William W. Proffitt, the sheriff of Yancey County, began recruiting this company in late May after gaining approval from the secretary of war on May13. Proffitt was thirty-four years old and was elected captain. Also on May 29, twenty-two-year-old Jonathan Horton was elected first lieutenant; twenty-five-year-old Suel Briggs was elected second lieutenant; and forty-seven-year-old Benjamin Moss was elected third lieutenant. Horton and Briggs were farmers, and Moss was a carpenter. There were sixty-seven men who joined the "Yancey Boys," plus the four officers, on May 29. Their average age was twenty-five years old. As with the other two companies, the members were almost all farmers. Besides Lieutenant Moss, Skelton Fox, Robert Holcombe, Swinfield Howell, and John Hunley all listed their occupation as carpenters. Larkin Jones was a blacksmith; William Austin was a teacher.

Yancey County, formed in 1833, was one county west of Mitchell County. Burnsville was the county seat, and Mt. Mitchell, the highest mountain east of the Mississippi River, lies in the southern part of the county. On June 16, twenty-three other men joined the company, which was officially mustered into service that same day. There were two sixteen-year-olds in the ranks: William Anglin and Thomas Sheppard. Sheppard had already attempted to join Company B, Twenty-Ninth North Carolina, but had been rejected due to his age.[9]

James Fox, a member of the Yancey Boys, was soon elected to the position of musician, as he played a fife. After the war, Fox recalled the unusual election process that sounds like something from a children's story. "It seem that another soldier in the company also played the fife and was interested in becoming company fifer," Fox told his family. "The same then as now, the company commander passed the buck. [Fox] was told to start playing the fife and to start walking in one direction, and the other man was told to do the same, except to walk in the opposite direction. The fifer who had the most soldiers following him was elected as the official fifer."[10]

In Watauga County, two counties to the northeast, the Rev. Drury Harman was attempting to raise another company. Harman

Larkin Jones was born in Wilkes County and worked as a blacksmith in Yancey County prior to enlisting in Company C in 1862. He was promoted to musician and carried his drum for much of the remainder of the war (courtesy Michael Ledford).

was thirty-six years old, the former pastor of the Cove Creek Baptist Church, and the Watauga County register of deeds. Like Bowman and Proffitt, he gained approval from the secretary of war on May 13 to raise a company, and was elected captain of that company on June 27, 1862. Helping him with command were Benjamin Baird, thirty years old and a farmer; twenty-eight-year-old William Mast, who had just returned with his family from a failed attempt to relocate to Texas; and William M. Howington, who was twenty-five years old. Baird was elected first lieutenant, Mast, second lieutenant, and Howington, third lieutenant. Howington had previously served in Company D, First North Carolina Cavalry. Sixty-five men enlisted on June 27, and an additional fifty-five enlisted on July 7. Ten other men enlisted in June and July. The men averaged twenty-seven years in age, and save for the Reverend Harman, shoemaker John Danner, and blacksmith Michael Mitchell, all of them were farmers. The youngest was William R. Cox, a mere lad of fifteen. Hezekiah Thomas and William Calaway were only sixteen. William S. Gragg came from Company B, Thirty-Seventh North Carolina Troops. Ten additional men transferred out of the "Yancey Boys" to join Harman's regiment. Boone was the county seat of Watauga County, formed in 1849.[11]

Mexican War veteran John C. Keener next attempted to recruit a company. Keener was born in 1818 in Carter County, Tennessee. He served in Company D, First North Carolina Volunteers, in 1847, then returned to the Toe River Valley to raise a family. Keener likewise gained permission on May 13 from the secretary of war to recruit a company. On June 25, forty-one men from Mitchell County enlisted in Keener's company. Keener appears to have had trouble recruiting the rest of his men. A standard infantry company of the time period consisted of one hundred men. Palmer's company had come from the southern end of Mitchell County, and many members of Captain Bowman's company had come from the northern end of the county. While several men transferred from Captain Bowman's company to Keener's, it appears that Keener had to travel to Caldwell County to finish his recruiting. On June 27, thirty-one men, mostly from Caldwell County, joined his company. Another seventy-six Caldwell County men joined on July 5, with an additional twenty-five men joining over the next month. By the end of July, Keener had 174 recruits in his company. Their average age was twenty-five years old. The youngest members were three sixteen-year-olds: Israel Coffey, Samuel Denney, and Jasper Ledford. Coffey was from Caldwell County, and Denney and Ledford hailed from Mitchell County. Helping Keener with command was Alfred T. Stewart, a twenty-eight-year-old farmer from Caldwell County. Stewart had joined Company F, Twenty-Sixth North Carolina, in July 1861, and served as third lieutenant until April 1862, when he was defeated for re-election. He was elected first lieutenant of Keener's company on June 25. Keener was also assisted by seventeen-year-old Doctor Estes, who had joined Company F, Twenty-Sixth North Carolina, in July 1861, and served as a private until being elected second lieutenant on June 25. James B. Marler, who enlisted in Caldwell County at the age of thirty-one, was also a farmer and was elected third lieutenant. The only man who did not list his occupation as a farmer was thirty-three-year-old Thomas J. Coffey, who gave his occupation as merchant.[12]

Established in 1842 and named for Col. Joseph McDowell of King's Mountain fame, McDowell County supplied the next company. Thirty-year-old Jason Conley, a farmer, enlisted 114 men on July 14. On the next day, Conley gained official sanction from the secretary of war to recruit his company. Conley was elected captain. Caleb O. Conley, Jason's cousin, was elected first lieutenant. John H. Morris was elected second lieutenant, and James D. Morrison was elected third lieutenant. Caleb Conley was twenty-nine, Morris was thirty-four, and Morrison the oldest at thirty-five. All of the men were farmers or farm laborers, except Benjamin Woodside, who was a printer. They averaged twenty-seven years of age. Daniel Mosteller, one of the new privates, had just returned from a four-year stint trying to make a new life in Arkansas and Missouri.[13]

Yet another company was raised in Yancey County. John W. Peek, a fifty-one-year-old clerk, recruited a company in Burnsville. Peek first saw military service in the 1830s, serving in a Yancey County company helping with the Cherokee Removal. Peek's new company was raised between July 8 and July 15. Seventy-six men joined on July 11, and another eight the next day. Ninety-eight men total joined the company before July 15. One of the new recruits, John W. Edwards, provided this glimpse of the recruitment process: "Word was sent out through the settlement for all of conscript age to come in. Capt. Peak [sic] came around and said as I had to go in I had better go in his company. We were acquainted and a little [connected.]" Peek was elected captain. Forty-year-old John Tipton was elected first lieutenant. The other two officers were youngsters. James Gardner was a nineteen-year-old farmer when he was elected second lieutenant, and Cornelius Byrd was a twenty-year-old farmer when elected third lieutenant. The average age of the men was almost twenty-six years old. Lynville Edwards and James Hughs were both sixteen years old. Moses Byrd, Thomas Howell, and Levi Wilson all transferred from Company G, Twenty-Ninth North Carolina Troops, to the new company. After the company was mustered into service on July 15, John C. Hogler and Joseph H. Hollifield's enlistments were cancelled for unknown reasons. All the men save Peek were farmers.[14]

Capt. James B. Marler enlisted in Caldwell County in June 1862. The next month, he became third lieutenant of Company E of the Fifty-Eighth. He rose through the ranks to become captain in August 1864. However, he was dropped from the rolls of the regiment in April 1865 for being absent for six months (courtesy Ralph Marler).

Palmer's next company was one that had volunteered to serve with Vance's Legion. Once the legion had failed, Captain Dula, according to Lt. Walter W. Lenoir, traveled "to the Western part of the State, with Col. Vance's permission, for the purpose of attaching the company to some of the unfinished regiments or battalions, still in the process of formation." Dula's company was originally mustered into service by Colonel Vance on May 23, 1862, even though it appears to have never formally belonged to Vance's regiment. Seventy-five men were on the rolls on May 23. It appears that the company was back in Caldwell County from July 11 until August 11. On July 16, an additional sixteen men joined the company. Their average age was almost twenty-seven years old. Robert Bryant and Robert Gilliland were both just sixteen. The oldest was Abner Triplett, who was fifty-six. Forty-eight of the men are listed as coming from Company I, Twenty-Sixth North Carolina, while another four men had previously served in Company F of the Twenty-Sixth. As with the

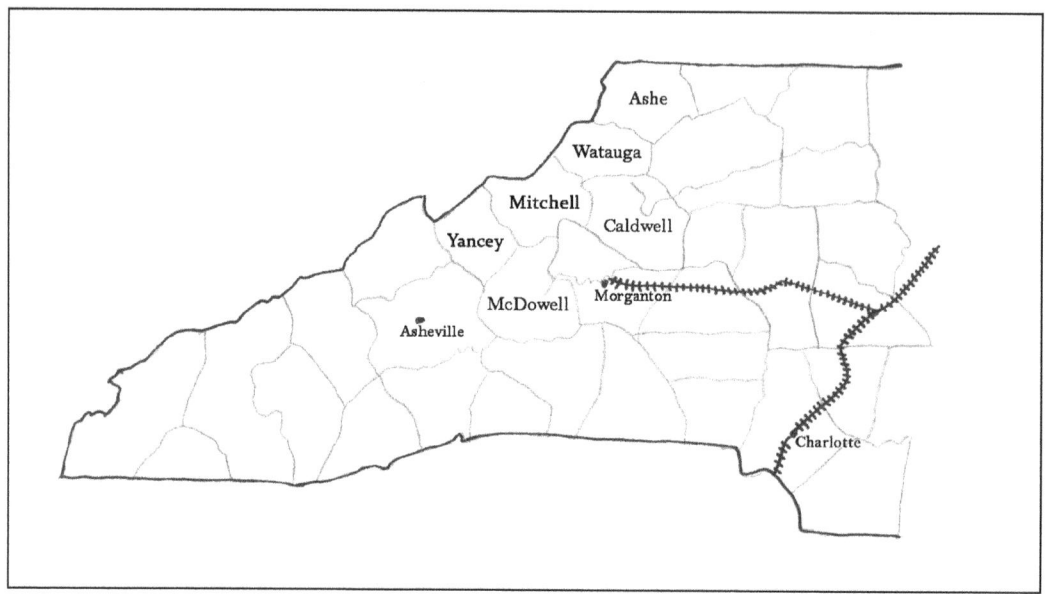

The Fifty-Eighth North Carolina came from Ashe, Watauga, Mitchell, Yancey, Caldwell, and McDowell counties, all located in western North Carolina.

other companies, all of the men were farmers save merchant George Harper, lawyer Walter Lenoir, blacksmith's apprentice James Fletcher, and clerk Robert Smith. Lenoir left the company in July 1862, taking command of Company A, Thirty-Seventh North Carolina Troops.[15]

Following the former company of Vance's Legion came another company from Watauga County. This company, known as the "Watauga Troopers," began recruiting members on July 15, when forty-four men joined. William Miller, a forty-eight-year-old farmer, was elected captain. Miller served in the United States Army when the Cherokee were removed to Oklahoma, and then in Company D, First North Carolina Volunteers, during the Mexican War. When the war came, he enlisted in Company D, First North Carolina Cavalry, on May 11, 1861. Miller served until February 15, 1862, when he was discharged by reason of a "broken down constitution." Thirty-two-year-old William M. Hodges was elected first lieutenant. A brickmason, twenty-eight-year-old Jordan C. McGee, was elected second lieutenant. James H. Horton, twenty-one years old, was elected third lieutenant. Thirty more men joined the regiment on July 24, and all seventy-four men were mustered into service on July 25. Thirteen of those men came from other companies in the future Fifty-Eighth. Bartlett Hilliard had attempted to join the Thirty-Seventh North Carolina, but had been rejected. He was able to join the Watauga Troopers. George Grubb transferred from the Fifth Battalion North Carolina Cavalry. Ephraim Miller was fifteen years old, and Solomon Smith was sixteen years old. The average age of the Watauga Troopers was twenty-five and a half years. All were local men, save Moretz Weisenfeld, who was from Prussia. All the men were also farmers, save McGee, blacksmith Gilson Davenport, and teacher Alfred Davis.[16]

Still another company came from Mitchell County. Samuel Silver, already serving as second lieutenant in Keener's company, started working to form a new command. Most of the men for this new regiment were already members of other companies, and they simply transferred to this new command. Occupying the position of third lieutenant was another private from the Mitchell Rangers, David Chandler. He was a twenty-eight-year-old farmer. Leonard M. Buchanan, a Baptist pastor who had served in both Palmer's and Keener's companies, was elected second lieutenant. Buchanan was fifty-two years old. Joining Silver, Chandler, and Buchanan as company officers was Jonathan Duncan, also a former member of Keener's company. Duncan was thirty-one years old and a farmer. By July 29, when the company was mustered into service, a total of eighty-four men had joined the regiment. Most were Mitchell County men, joined by ten from Caldwell County. The average age of the new recruits was twenty-five years. Henry Fox was fourteen years old, and Alexander Fox was fifteen years old. Both hailed from Caldwell County. All were farmers, save Nathan Morgan, a miller, also from Caldwell County.[17]

In the northwestern corner of the state, in Ashe County, which was formed in 1799, work was underway to recruit a company of men from the conscript population. According to one of the conscripts, "all conscripts who would voluntarily surrender themselves [would have] the privilege of volunteering in Captain Gentry's company. About fifty, though intimidation and fear, had reported and volunteered." This company was mustered into service on July 20, 1862. Elected captain was a thirty-four-year-old farmer, William Gentry. Serving as first lieutenant was thirty-two-year-old Calvin Eller. Twenty-five-year-old Poindexter Blevins was elected second lieutenant, and forty-three-year-old Edward Blevins was elected third lieutenant. Ninety-nine men were mustered into service. They averaged twenty-six years of age. Henry A. Houck was the oldest at sixty-one years of age. All were farmers except Leander Hurley, who was a weaver. Abraham May was from Alabama, and Jacob King was born in Illinois.[18]

Each company normally had four commissioned officers, elected by the men in the company. The captain was in charge of each company, and his three lieutenants helped him command the enlisted men. The process of electing company officers was a traditional rite, and often did not allow the best qualified man to be elected to the position, only the most popular or the one with the most relatives in the new company. The captain was responsible for the administrative supervision of the company and responsible for the tactics of the company. He made sure that the company clerk, quartermaster, and commissary were doing their jobs properly and on time. He supervised the bi-monthly returns, on which the payment of the men was based. The captain also instructed the lieutenants and the non-commissioned officers in their duties. He drilled the men in company-level tactics, including maneuvers and firing, and often dispensed judgment for lesser breaches of military discipline. If the captain was away on duty or leave, then the first lieutenant stepped into his position for the duration of the captain's absence.

A typical company had eighty enlisted men. A set of non-commissioned officers, five sergeants and eight corporals, was appointed by the captain. The hardest working man in the company was the first, or orderly, sergeant. This sergeant received his orders from the captain and was responsible for seeing that they were carried out. He kept the company roster and was responsible for calling the roll at least twice a day. The first sergeant filled out the morning report and the sick report, and was to be watchful of all company property. He also supervised the company clerk, company quartermaster, and company commissary. He formed the company at prescribed times on the color line, supervised the other non-commissioned officers, assigned members of his company to details, inspected his men, and was usually the person who made arrests and confined enlisted men, under orders from the company commander. Sergeants in general were to be "quiet" with an "imperturbable temper, combined with firmness and resolution." They were not to show "partiality and favor to individuals" and to avoid "harsh and violent treatment" of the men under their command. Sergeants were permitted to "shoot men down when they attempted to run away" and to "see that the men fill their canteens with water, not with whiskey."[19]

It is unclear where the new regiment was mustered into service. One post-war source, by Jonathan B. Miller, a member of the Watauga Troopers, states that the first eleven companies "were mustered into service ... at Johnson's Depot, Tenn[essee] in the summer of 1862." Another post-war source, a history of the regiment written by Caldwell County's George W. F. Harper, states that the regiment was "organized in Mitchell county, North Carolina, 24 July 1862." Either location could be correct. The new organization was labeled the Fifty-Eighth Regiment, North Carolina Troops, and officially mustered into service on July 29, 1862. Palmer was promoted to colonel and given command. His original command, the Mitchell Rangers, became Company A, and Martin D. Wiseman became captain. Captain Bowman's Mitchell County company became Company B. The Yancey Boys followed as Company C. Their captain, William W. Proffitt, was elected lieutenant colonel, and Lt. Jonathan Horton became captain. Drury Harman's command from Watauga County became Company D. Captain Keener's mixed company of men from Mitchell and Caldwell Counties became Company E. Keener was elected major and Alfred Stewart advanced to the rank of captain of Company E. The McDowell Rangers became Company F, and Captain Peek's Company from Yancey was selected as Company G. Captain Dula's Caldwell County company became Company H, and the Watauga Troopers was selected as Company I. There was no letter J in the company designation, because of its similarity to the letter I. So, the other Mitchell County company, under Captain Silver, became Company K. Most infantry regiments only had ten companies. The Fifty-Eighth was mustered in with eleven. Captain Gentry's company, from Ashe and Watauga counties, became Company L.[20]

Lt. Col. John C. Keener was not only a member of the Fifty-Eighth, but also a veteran of the Mexican War (courtesy Marie Bost).

Regardless of where the regiment was mustered into service, it soon left the Toe River Valley. Caldwell County's John Coffey penned some verses to remember the events, writing that "twas a hard thing to part with the little ones so gay/That was playing in the yard around the door/My wife sob[b]ed aloud when I started away —/Saying farewell I shall [see?] you no more." William H. Younce, one of the conscripts in Ashe County, recounted his experience in a post-war reminiscence entitled *Adventures of a Conscript*. Younce was forced into the Confederate Army after being caught while trying to slip off to Tennessee. On the day his company left Ashe County, a crowd had gathered "to say goodbye to the boys. I was the hero of the occasion, and the crowd became so enthusiastic that I was carried on the shoulders of some of the younger men to a platform and forced to make a short talk.... It was now time to start and after the goodbyes had all been said by weeping mothers, wives, sisters and children, I lined the men up in double file and gave the order to march. It was forty miles to the railroad [at Johnson's Depot], but nothing unusual happened on our journey."[21]

Another soon-to-be soldier, Wesley Presnell, recalled the "barn loft" in the "old log barn of James Blair (at the Eggers place) ... where the boys of Co. D, 58 Regt. spent their first night of camp left." Presnell and his comrades "passed down Elk Valley on our way to the Civil War."[22]

CHAPTER 5

August–October 1862

"I never knew what it was to leave you before."— William Bailey, Company C

Many of the regiments from North Carolina had already seen hard service before the Fifty-Eighth was formed. Major battles in the east, such as the Seven Days' campaign in Virginia in June and July, had inspired heroic deeds from the men of the Tar Heel state. However, the Fifty-Eighth was not destined for the bloody ground of Virginia. The regiment's first months of service were to be spent in an area where the foe could not always be easily distinguished from friends.

The Fifty-Eighth was sent to east Tennessee for several reasons. Unionists had been slipping out of western North Carolina and heading through east Tennessee to one of the recruitment camps the Federals had established in Kentucky. Men were needed to guard the railroad bridges, which had already proven vulnerable to attack. Cumberland Gap, and other gaps in southwest Virginia, were in the possession of the Federal army. And, a few months earlier, Union General Henry Halleck had assembled a force of 125,000 men, the largest force mustered to date. While this force had been disbanded by June, the ability of the Federals to organize such a large force so quickly weighed heavily upon the Confederate command.[1]

Everyone in Palmer's command was new to his job. Palmer commanded the entire regiment. He was responsible for seeing to the men's well-being and health; their clothing, equipment, and arms; the tentage and sanitation of their camp; and the instruction of his officers. Palmer had a staff to assist him in his responsibilities. Lt. Col. William W. Proffitt and Maj. John C. Keener helped command the regiment. Added to this was an adjutant, Edmund Kirby.

Edmund was Fannie Palmer's first cousin. He was born in 1830 in Aroostook, Maine. His father was a member of the First United States Artillery who was killed in Florida during the Seminole Wars. Edmund attended schools in Richmond, Virginia, before graduating from the Virginia Military Institute in 1861. While at VMI he witnessed the execution of John Brown. After graduating, Kirby was drill master at Camp Lee in Richmond, served in a Tennessee Regiment, and was in an artillery company before being requested by Palmer to transfer to the Fifty-Eighth. Kirby most likely served as drill master while performing the task of adjutant. The adjutant worked almost like a clerk, keeping the regiment's supplies coming in and lining up the regiment for inspections and drill. He was assisted by a sergeant major, the highest ranking enlisted man in the regiment. This post was filled by thirty-six-year-old Harrison Herndron. He was from Habersham County, Georgia, and had possibly served in Company H, First Georgia Infantry, prior to joining the Fifty-Eighth. Marcus

Bearden, from Buncombe County, was appointed assistant quartermaster. A native of Ireland, twenty-six-year-old Joseph J. Mason, was appointed assistant commissary of subsistence. Mason had been a merchant in Burnsville prior to joining Company C. James Conley transferred out of Company B, Fifth Battalion North Carolina Cavalry, to serve as quartermaster. Serving as ordnance sergeant was John Hensley, who transferred from Company A. Occupying the position of regimental surgeon was Waighstill Avery Collett. In 1856, Collett graduated from the Jefferson Medical College in Philadelphia. He then took up his practice in Morganton, in Burke County. Collett also served as a permanent member of the North Carolina State Medical Society. These men constituted the field and staff of the Fifty-Eighth.[2]

Portions of Palmer's command were in Washington County, Tennessee, by the first of July, and went into quarters at Camp Stokes, near Johnson's Depot. It appears that ten of the companies were present by the end of the month. In 1862, Johnson's Depot, now Johnson City, was little more than a stop on the East Tennessee and Virginia Railroad. There were two stores and a few homes in the hamlet.[3]

Just as the families and communities—now deprived of their husbands, fathers, and sons—had to adjust, so did the men themselves. At home, the men had been the masters of their own lives. While many of them worked incredibly hard on their small farms, they were able to choose what they did each day. Now, their lives were controlled by the beat of the drum, calling them out to drill, to dinner, to post guards around the camp, or, when they were sick, to visit the regimental surgeon. "We have roll call at 5 A.M.," wrote Company E's Langston Estes about the new recruit's day. His first drill began not long afterwards and lasted until 6 A.M. "Breakfast at 7:00. Drill at 8:30 till 11:00. Dinner and roll call at 12:00. Drill from 2 [till] four P.M. Dress parade from 5–6. Roll call at 7 P.M. Drum beat at 8:00 to put out all light and go to bed."[4]

Edmund Kirby was promoted to lieutenant colonel just prior to the battle of Chickamauga, in which he was killed (courtesy the North Carolina Department of Archives and History).

This intense amount of drill was necessary, turning rural mountain men into soldiers equipped to fight in a not-so-modern war. The men learned to march, both in ranks and in a column. Every formation, from roll call in the mornings to the line of battle in which the men fought, was done in ranks. According to a tactics manual of the period, "each company will be formed into two ranks, in the following manner: the corporals will be posted in the front rank, and on the right and left of platoons, according to height; the tallest corporal and the tallest man will form the first file, the next two tallest men will form the second file, and so on to the last, which will be composed of the shortest corporal and the shortest man." The back rank of men was to be 13 inches from the front rank of men. In a traditional regiment of ten companies, the fifth company in line was designated the color company, with the regiment's flag and color guard, composed of six men, posted on the company's left end. William Gouge (Company E) estimated in a letter home that the regiment drilled for seven hours a day. During this time, they learned to form ranks, how to march in a straight line, by the right and left flank, at an oblique, and in a column, and by the rear rank.[5]

Langston Estes wrote home on July 23 that on the previous day, he was issued "a gun, napsack, a cartridge box, a cap box, a canteen and a Heiversack [haversack]." It is unclear just what type of firearm that Estes and his comrades were issued. Chances are, it was one of the .69 caliber, smoothbore muskets that were so common early in the war. The musket, weighing ten pounds, fired a buck-and-ball load, consisting of a .64 round ball, with three .30 caliber buckshot on top. These four pieces of lead were wrapped together in paper with 100 grains of black powder and tied with a string. Forty rounds were carried inside the soldier's cartridge box, a leather box, usually with a leather sling, slung over the left shoulder and worn on the right hip. The cap box held a like number of percussion caps, small copper cups with a chemical called fulminate of mercury inside. One of the things that a soldier learned was how to fire his musket. At the command of "load," the soldier placed the butt of the musket on the ground, barrel out, and tilted across the body, but away from his face. While holding the musket with his left hand, he retrieved a cartridge from his box with his right hand. The soldier then bit the end of the cartridge, exposing the powder. Next, the whole package was dumped down the barrel, and the ramrod, located beneath the barrel, was removed and used to push the entire load all the way down the barrel. Failure to seat the load properly could cause the barrel to rupture when fired. After returning the ramrod, the soldier raised the musket, and after balancing it with his left hand, retrieved a percussion cap from his cap pouch and placed it on the cone, or nipple, of his musket. He was then ready to fire his musket. When the order of "Aim" was given, the soldier cocked his musket and raised it to his shoulder. When the order "Fire" was given, he pulled the trigger. The hammer struck the cap, and the ensuing sparks lit the powder, causing it to explode and send the balls down range. A good soldier of the time period could fire three rounds a minute. The loading of the musket, and the firing, in groups, by files, or at will, was gone over countless times in drill.[6]

Estes also mentioned receiving a knapsack and a haversack. The knapsack was worn on the back and contained extra clothing, with a blanket affixed to the top. When loaded improperly, the straps of the knapsack dug into the shoulders, and many soldiers preferred a blanket roll instead. The piece or two of extra clothing could be rolled up, possibly with a small tent or poncho, or gum blanket, tied at the ends, and worn over one shoulder. The haversack was usually a cotton bag with a shoulder strap and was worn over the right shoulder and left hip. While on the march, a soldier kept his rations in this bag. He also carried his plate and fork, and at times fastened a tin cup or "mucket" to the bag. While they were white when issued, the haversacks quickly took on a greasy appearance. The canteen was likewise worn on this side.

This cartridge box is thought to have been used by a member of the Fifty-Eighth (courtesy the North Carolina Museum of History).

"[W]e get a pound of meat a day,"

recorded Jonathan Green (Company D) in his letter home, and "18 ounces of flour." He made no mention of vegetables. Prior to the war, pork was the mainstay of most meals for rural people. A hog could be put out to forage liberally in the surrounding woods. In late fall, hogs were slaughtered, salted, and placed in the smokehouse to cure, providing meat for the next year. The meat supply was supplemented by venison, and occasionally poultry, fish, and steak, even though beef did not keep well. Potatoes were a staple, along with beans, corn, apples, and berries. The climate of the mountains produced short growing seasons.

Most soldiers organized themselves into groups that cooked and, at times, slept together. The groups were called messes and consisted of three or four men or more. They usually took turns preparing food for the mess, gathering firewood, or other camp chores. The mess to which Langston Estes belonged consisted of Henry, Henderson, and Doctor Estes; Joseph Dickson; John Medaris; Alfred Holyfield; and Jasper, Hight, Newton, and "P" Moore. "I think they are all very good fellows," Arthur McFalls (Company A) wrote home, telling his wife that his mess contained eight men.[7]

Sickness soon invaded the regiment. It could have resulted from the lack of sanitation or from improper food preparation. William Bailey (Company C) wrote home to his wife on August 16: "I am not well at this time, my old complaint is bothering me again." William Gouge (Company K) informed his family that he was "well ... ever since I left home. But there are a great many sick here. The cases of sickness are mostly measles. I expect I shall have them myself for there is no chance to keep from them in camps." Even though many of the cases were not serious, some were. Nathan Morrow (Company H) died in Caldwell County on August 3. This was followed by the first camp death, Lorenzo Horton, who died of "typhoid fever" on August 25.[8]

Even though they had only been gone a couple of weeks, many of the men were terribly homesick. Jonathan Green (Company D), wrote home in July: "I would like to see you all once more but i dont know whether i ever will or not without you can come down for we cant come when we want to [.]" William Gouge (Company K) told his family that they did not "know how bad I want to be at home to help take care of my little children and enjoy their delightful presence." A Yancey County private wrote to his family: "You know I want to see you all, But I cant tell when I shall see you. I never knew what it was to leave you before." Green B. Woody (Company C) wrote home a couple of weeks later, after being denied a furlough home, "You can't guess how it hurt me to have to give out and lay down in my tent and don't know if I shall ever see you again." These same sentiments were widespread over the entire regiment.[9]

Camp life was not always safe. The records for the regiment state that Albert

Albert J. Franklin (Company A), shown here wearing a battle shirt, was struck by lightning not long after the Fifty-Eighth transferred to Tennessee. He survived the lightning strike and the war (courtesy Tense Banks).

Franklin (Company A) was struck by a bolt of lightning on or about August 15. While Franklin was not killed by the jolt, his family claims that "he never fully recovered" from the ordeal. Another private, John Oxford (Company E) of Alexander County, was bitten by a rattlesnake while he was in camp at Johnson's Depot in October 1862. According to the family, John was unconscious for several days, and his brother James remained behind to care for him. John was discharged from the army on an unknown date.[10]

Palmer's command was not all together in one place. Company H, under Captain Dula, did not leave Caldwell County until Tuesday, August 12. By Saturday, August 16, the company was at Crumley's near Johnson's Depot. The next day, Company H moved to Camp Stokes. Some of the regiment was at Carter's Depot, some at Zollicoffer, and the balance at Johnson's Depot.[11]

The regiment's preliminary training and equipping soon came to an end. On August 25, the regiment was assigned to the division of Brig. Gen. Carter Stevenson. Just a few days prior, on August 14, Stevenson had been given the task of capturing the Federal garrison at Cumberland Gap. Born in Virginia in 1817, Stevenson was an 1838 graduate of West Point and had seen service in both Florida and Mexico. He was dismissed from the United States Army in June 1861, becoming colonel of the Fifty-Third Virginia Infantry. He was promoted to brigadier general on February 27, 1862.[12]

Stevenson's superior and District of East Tennessee commander, Maj. Gen. Edmund Kirby Smith, had launched an attack into Kentucky, bypassing the Federal garrison at Cumberland Gap. Smith, a cousin of Colonel Palmer's wife, Fannie, was born in St. Augustine in 1824. Like Stevenson, he was a graduate of West Point and had seen combat service during the Mexican War. He resigned from the United States Army in April 1861 and was commissioned a lieutenant colonel in the regular Confederate army. Later, he served on the staff of Joseph E. Johnston. Smith was promoted to brigadier general in June and wounded in the neck and shoulder a month later at the battle of Manassas. Promoted to major general in October 1861, Smith was placed in command of the District of East Tennessee on February 25, 1862.[13]

Following the battle of Shiloh, the Federal army had been split. Ulysses Grant took his command toward Vicksburg, and Don Carlos Buell moved toward Chattanooga. The overall Confederate commander of the area, Braxton Bragg, was able to move his force from Tupelo, Mississippi, to Chattanooga before Buell could arrive. Nashville, Tennessee, had been in Federal control since February 25, and Buell used the area as his base. Bragg and Smith, meeting in Chattanooga, devised a plan in which Smith would capture Cumberland Gap, then reinforce Bragg, destroying Buell and re-capturing Nashville. However, Smith was lured by the promise of 25,000 to 30,000 Kentuckians who were waiting for the Confederate forces to appear before enlisting. On August 16, Smith left Stevenson with 9,000 men on one side of Cumberland Gap and took 10,000 men through another gap into Kentucky, stopping at Barboursville, 29 miles north of Cumberland Gap. The Federals at the gap were effectively cut off from their supplies. While at Barbourville, Smith wrote Bragg, informing him that the there were no supplies to be foraged and that the roads back to Tennessee were bad. "I find that I have but two courses left me — either to fall back for supplies to East Tennessee or to advance towards Lexington for them." Smith chose the latter, believing that a retreat back to Tennessee was "disastrous to our cause." Smith called for a brigade from Stevenson and set off for Lexington.[14]

Stevenson set out looking for his own reinforcements. The Federals had yet to evacuate Cumberland Gap, and he felt that he needed more men. In his orders, Stevenson was allowed "to call on the North Carolina Regiments at Jonesborough, Greeneville, and Johnson's Depot, and also on the regiments at Knoxville and Loudon." On August 25, orders went out to Colonel Palmer to move his regiment towards Cumberland Gap. Palmer was ordered to issue his men rations for three days and 40 rounds of cartridges. An additional 20 rounds per man were to be carried in the wagons. J. Francis Belton, Smith's assistant adjutant-general, cautioned Palmer to make sure the Fifty-Eighth was "not encumbered with any superfluous or unnecessary baggage." Only five "wagons will be allowed to a regiment and not more than one tent to each company. All other property, including the trunks of the officers, must be left at the railroad or turned over to the proper department for storage."[15]

Lt. Gen. Edmund Kirby Smith was the Fifty-Eighth's first departmental commander in east Tennessee (courtesy the Library of Congress).

One officer in the Fifty-Eighth reported the weather as "hot and dry" as the regiment boarded the train at 7:00 A.M. on August 27 for the first portion of the trip. Once the men reached Morristown, they disembarked and slept without tents. The next day, the 40 rounds of ammunition prescribed to the men was issued, and the regiment struck out at 10 o'clock in the morning, camping that night near Bean's Station. On August 29, again a hot and dry day, the regiment crossed both the Clinch Mountain and the Clinch River, and camped within three miles of Tazewell, Tennessee, covering thirteen miles. The regiment's wagons did not arrive, and Lieutenant Harper recorded that he and three of his companions "slept ... on and under one shawl in the open air. [The] Regiment fed on green corn and bacon." The following day, the regiment moved one mile and went into bivouac at Camp Reynolds, near Tazewell. For the next two weeks, the regiment followed the routine of camp life: drills, inspections, and guard-mounting rotations. The Federal force at Cumberland Gap was only twelve miles away. Harper recorded in his diary a regimental review and inspection on Sunday, September 14. Regulation prescribed reviews and inspections on every Sunday.[16]

The Federal garrison at Cumberland Gap was on quarter-rations, and those rations were about to run out. By September 12, the men had been without bread for six days and no food was available for the remaining mules and horses. Some of the mules had already been slaughtered to feed the soldiers. On the night of September 16, as many supplies as could be transported out of Cumberland Gap were sent to Manchester, Kentucky. Supplies that could not be carried off were buried or destroyed. The roads throughout the area were mined and cannons were spiked. On the evening of the seventeenth, the Federals left Cumberland Gap and headed north toward Ohio. The remaining buildings were burned, and the magazine exploded.[17]

Confederates were quick to follow the retreating Federals into the gap. The Fifty-Eighth broke camp on Friday, September 19, and headed through Tazewell. The regiment

A war-time wood-cut illustration of Cumberland Gap.

crossed Powell's River at 9:00 P.M. before stopping for the evening. The next day, the Fifty-Eighth arrived and "moved to [the] top of [the] Gap and camped on West and Va. side." Many were amazed at the level of destruction. A letter, possibly written by Tilman Silver (Company K), recalled that when the regiment reached the gap, the men found that the Federals "had buried meat, flour, salt, rice, and guns and had heaped the dirt upon them like graves. The prisoners told our men what it was. They went to digging, and they got a lot. They had put rocks at the head and foot of the dirt so that our men would think it was graves and would not dig." Arthur McFalls (Company K) went into even more detail, writing that he believed that

> there are five hundred thousand pounds of lead left in their commissary house and melted by the burning of the house. This lead we are taking up for the government with many other things such as pot racks, picks, cross bars and broken guns. The ground is literally covered with pants, coats, tents, shirts and almost all manner of clothing and almost all kinds of Yankee ingenuity they have destroyed about twenty thousand stands of small arms, spiked the cannon and pushed them off of high bluffs and drove some of them perfectly full of balls.... Kettles in rolls, broke their bottles and plates, mashed their tin cups....

Lieutenant Harper also commented on the "great destruction of Yankee property." However, he seemed glad to be "camped in Yankee tents."[18]

Palmer had to cope with hundreds of Federal prisoners. On September 23, he wrote to department headquarters in Knoxville asking what he was to do with all these men. Some of the captured soldiers were from Northern states, and some were from east Tennessee. Charles Stringfellow, the assistant adjutant-general, told Palmer that he was to "make no distinction between those from East Tennessee and the Northern States" when the soldiers had been taken under arms. "Union men who are willing to renounce their opinions and join the Army will of course be permitted to do so." However, these former soldiers could not simply be paroled and left in east Tennessee. "Those not for us are against us and must so be treated."[19]

On September 24, three members of the Fifty-Eighth — Joseph H. Green (Company C), Carroll Hicks (Company D), and Eli James (Company E) — were killed by the explosion of a "keg of powder." Family history relates that John Wesley Hicks, possibly the John Hicks in Company E, lost an arm when a "powder house blew up." It could be that the barrel had been mined by the Federals, or simply that it was mishandled by the Confederates. These three were the first battlefield-related deaths of the regiment.[20]

Stevenson continued north with his division, taking his men to Danville, Kentucky. The Federals continued their retreat, traveling through the mountains to the northeast, with Confederate cavalry harassing them the entire time. Colonel Palmer, with his regiment, the Fifth Battalion North Carolina Partisan Rangers, and Hilliard's Alabama Legion, was left in charge of the captured Federal stores at Cumberland Gap, and with an untold number of Federal prisoners. Palmer was also ordered to remove all of the obstructions from the surrounding roads.[21]

Palmer established his headquarters and set about to work. Lieutenant Harper (Company H) and adjutant Edmund Kirby split the duties of assistant adjutant general for Palmer. Most of their time was invested in chasing bushwhackers and paroling prisoners. However, there was always time for fun, as related in this postwar account. James Anglin was a private in Company C. Anglin's company was camped on the side of the mountain, and

> Palmer, who was stationed near the foot of the mountain, was quartered in a shack which stood in the center of a large field. Mr. Anglin, with a number of his comrades, rolled a cannon wheel down the side of the mountain towards [Colonel] Palmer's shack. The wheel went down the mountain, gaining more and more speed, and ran across the field in the direction of the shack, but a short distance before reaching it, it hit a rock which caused it to bounce completely over the shack, hitting and killing Palmer's horse.
>
> Hearing the commotion, Palmer ran out of his shack and when he learned what had happened he mounted [another] horse and rushed up the mountain to Captain Briggs' camp and commanded him to have the roll called, expecting to find those absent who played this prank, but when the roll was called every man was present and Palmer never learned the identity of the guilty ones.[22]

Evidently, the pranksters decided to stay anonymous.

Events were going well for the Confederates in Kentucky. While tens of thousands of men were not flocking to the Confederate armies as Morgan had predicted, the Confederate forces were able to win victories. Kirby Smith won one of the most decisive Confederate victories of the war at Richmond, Kentucky, on August 30. He captured Lexington, Kentucky, on September 2 and the capitol at Frankfort the next day. Gen. Braxton Bragg started out on August 28, first feinting towards Nashville, then, on September 7, moved toward Glasgow, Kentucky. On September 17, Bragg captured the Federal garrison at Munfordville. Bragg then proceeded to Frankfort and helped facilitate a new Confederate government in the capital. Nevertheless, the Federals from Louisville were on the move, and Bragg started to fall back. On October 8, a portion of Bragg's army met a portion of the Federal army at Perryville. Although Perryville was a tactical victory for Bragg, he chose to fall back into Tennessee with his bounty of foraged supplies.

Orders came to Palmer's command at Cumberland Gap on September 29. Palmer, who was attempting to get a telegraph line run into Cumberland Gap, was to take two-thirds of his infantry and three companies of cavalry to London, Kentucky. The balance of his command was to stay behind in Barbourville, about equal distance between the Gap and London. Palmer was ordered to keep "Regular scouts ... on the route from Cumberland Gap to Mount Vernon, and to supply escorts for "all trains and couriers." Bragg also ordered 200,000 rations to London, and 100,000 to Cumberland Gap "as soon as practicable." The expedition stepped off about the first of October and was composed of sixty members of the Fifty-Eighth, including Company E, "40 Indians and 90 Cav with 3 days rations." According to John Blair (Company E),

> We marched up the River for 30 miles and encamped at an old torys house so as to scare the country road about there we got there the next day and 40 of us and some of the Indians started out on a scout went to one house and the first thing I saw was a man putting flat try to git across a field and a little boy running in the other direction hollering runn Daddy runn and some of the boys shot at him but it was so far that they could not hit him we shot at 3 others the same evening but did not kill none of them it beaing to far the balls could not reach them we made a search for arms but found nothing but a little brandy some of the boys drunk and we returned to camp next morning we started out a gain and did not go more than 2 miles till we were fired on by some scoundrels but did not hit us they was on a hill and our pickets past just [between] them and did not see them when they fired on us we returned the fire and charged up the mountain but it was to steep and rough that we could not ketch them they had level ground to runn on and I tell you they made use of there legs We got there coats we followed them for 3 or 4 miles we caught 5 Yanks and 15 stand of arms and returned to the Gap Sunday nearly worn out running over the mountains.

A short rest was in order before orders came again on October 13 for the men to prepare three days' worth of rations. They, save Company H, moved into Kentucky on the sixteenth, but returned the same day.[23]

Bivouacked back in their old camp, the Fifty-Eighth soon bore witness to the retreat of Braxton Bragg's and Kirby Smith's armies. Their entire forces, instead of moving back through the routes that they had used to advance north, used Cumberland Gap for the journey back to Tennessee. Starting on October 17, and continuing through October 23, Lieutenant Harper (Company H) confided in his diary the movement of troops was "a constant stream of men, horses, mules, wagons, etc." On the eighteenth, Harper noted the passing of Bragg himself. William Horton of Company I wrote on October 23: "I have seen more men and more stock in the last week than I thought was in the war."[24]

For a brief time, the Fifty-Eighth was assigned to the brigade of Archibald Gracie, Jr. Gracie was born in New York City and educated in Heidelberg, Germany, and at West Point. The beginning of the war found Gracie a captain in the famed Washington Light Infantry. He served in the Third Alabama Infantry and the Eleventh Alabama Infantry before being elected colonel of the Forty-Third Alabama Infantry. While his promotion was not voted upon

Maj. Gen. Henry Heth was just one of many the departmental commanders under whom the Fifty-Eighth served in east Tennessee (courtesy the Library of Congress).

by Congress until April 1863, he is listed as a brigadier general commanding the second brigade under division commander Henry Heth on October 31, 1862. Along with the Fifty-Eighth, the Forty-Third Alabama, Fifty-Fifth Georgia, Sixty-Second and Sixty-Fourth North Carolina Regiments, and the Newman Artillery were in Gracie's brigade.[25]

"Clear, cold," was Lieutenant Harper's diary entry for Friday, October 24. The regiment had received orders to move about 35 miles south to Big Creek Gap. But not all the regiment was going. Sickness still plagued the men. At least eleven members of the Fifty-Eighth had perished since coming to Cumberland Gap in mid–September. Three had died as a result of wounds on September 24. The others had died of unknown causes or of disease. They included Alfred Conley, who died of a "fever"; Merit Curtis, who died of "typhoid fever"; and Elias Whisenhunt, who died of the "measles." All three were from McDowell County and served in Company F. While the loss of eleven men was tragic, it would pale in comparison to the ordeal the Fifty-Eighth was about to undergo.[26]

CHAPTER 6

November 1862–September 1863

"At times I grew melancholy and despondent."—William Younce, Company L

As the Fifty-Eighth left the expanse of Cumberland Gap, the Confederacy as a whole was quiet. Bragg and his army were at Murfreesboro, watching the Federals at Nashville. Kirby Smith's forces were positioned across east Tennessee. In Virginia, Robert E. Lee's storied army had pushed the Federal Army under George M. McClellan off the Peninsula, had soundly defeated Maj. Gen. John Pope's Army of Virginia at Second Manassas, and had captured the garrison at Harper's Ferry. However, the Army of Northern Virginia had fought to a standstill along Antietam Creek in Maryland, and had retreated back into Virginia. It was now positioned across Virginia from Winchester to Fredericksburg. In the west, John Pemberton commanded the Department of Mississippi and Eastern Louisiana, and was in charge of keeping the Mississippi River under Confederate control, a hard task considering New Orleans had fallen in the spring of 1862, with the northern portion of the river also falling into Federal hands.

Bragg was in need of reinforcements, and the only available men were in east Tennessee. Smith had no desire to release any men to Bragg, whom he disliked. On October 24, Bragg was given the authority to use the men in east Tennessee "for such time as the exigency of the operation may demand." Smith could decide which troops to send, and if he wanted to go with them. Two divisions, one under John McCowan and the other under Cater Stevenson, were sent to Bragg. The first group left on November 9. Smith joined his troops in mid–December, leaving General Henry Heth in charge.[1]

An effort to reorganize the troops in the Department of East Tennessee began at the end of October. The remaining division left in east Tennessee was structured into three brigades. The first brigade was placed under the command of Col. R. W. Hanson, and was composed of the Second, Fourth, Sixth, and Ninth Kentucky Infantry Regiments, with Graves's and Cobb's artillery batteries. This brigade constituted the department's reserve and was stationed at Shelbyville. The third brigade—consisting of the Twentieth, Twenty-Eighth, and Forty-Fifth Tennessee Regiments, along with the Sixtieth North Carolina Troops, with two batteries of artillery—was under the command of Col. F. M. Walker. This brigade was stationed as the army's left. The second brigade, constituting the army's right, was commanded by Col. John B. Palmer. His command, according to the official orders, was comprised of the Eighteenth and Thirty-Second Tennessee, Thirty-Second Alabama, Fourth Florida, and two batteries of artillery. No mention of the Fifty-Eighth was made in the order. Palmer's brigade was stationed at Big Creek Gap.[2]

East Tennessee was still openly hostile to Confederate authority. Mass arrests of suspected Unionists, deportations, and hangings had done nothing to bring the section of the state into the fold of the Confederacy. To Kirby Smith, east Tennessee was a land "more dangerous and difficult to operate in than the country of an acknowledged enemy." On April 8, 1862, President Jefferson Davis had declared east Tennessee an enemy territory, suspended the writ of habeas corpus, placed the area under military police, and prohibited the distillation and sale of alcohol. Controlling east Tennessee, and guarding the railroad that ran through the area, the only direct line between Virginia and Georgia, soon occupied much of the Confederacy's time and resources.[3]

The trip from Cumberland Gap to Big Creek Gap was difficult for the Fifty-Eighth. The regiment left Cumberland Gap at 2 P.M. on October 25 and made ten miles before dark. The next morning, the Tar Heels awoke and found the ground covered with snow. The men covered between sixteen and eighteen miles October 26, all the while wearing "bad shoes." According to one soldier, the men "camped in a nice grove" that evening. "Night snowing fast," recorded another member of the regiment; "made large campfires, raised tents and slept comfortably." Green B. Woody penned a letter home on October 29, describing his chilly travels:

> I can inform you that we left the Gap Saturday the 25th at 1 o'clock and march 10 miles west and camp in Powell Valley and just before day it commenced snowing. The ground was gray at daylight. We marched at 8 o'clock and by 10 there was a good tracking of snow. At 12 the large snow commenced flying fast and the wind blew in every direction. It was bad traveling meeting the wind. I gave 50 cents to git my gun and napsachall (carried) and it saved me for I should of gave out. Some of the boys did not reach camp that nite. Wyatt and Jim Slagle like to of gave out. We camped at 4 o'clock and bilt fires. I had a good fire when the boys got there and by dark the snow was ankle deep but I can inform you I slept good and warm. I have got that pillow yet and was a great beautiful morning on Sunday.

The following day, the regiment marched five miles and went into camp near a church at Big Creek Gap.[4]

Palmer's command, as reported in December 1862, now reflected the men who actually made up his brigade. Just when the brigades were reorganized is unknown. Both the First and Fourth Battalions of Hilliard's Alabama Legion were members, along with the cavalry battalion of Smith's Georgia Legion, under the command of Lt. Col. John R. Hart. The three companies of the Fifth Battalion, North Carolina Cavalry, were also present, along with the Fifty-Eighth and Sixty-Fourth North Carolina Troops. The Barbour Artillery, from Alabama, rounded out the men at Big Creek Gap. Lieutenant Harper was assigned to headquarters as acting assistant adjutant general, or Palmer's chief of staff. Adjutant Kirby reported that on December 12, the Fifty-Eighth contained 1,082 men.[5]

Tracing the movements of the Fifty-Eighth over the next ten months is next to impossible. The regiment seemed to be seldom stationed together as a whole, with some companies at Big Creek Gap and others at Jacksboro. The regiment officially called Big Creek Gap home until December 23, when headquarters was removed to Jacksboro. The town of Jacksboro had abundant springs to supply the regiment with water. The first Confederate commander in the area, Brig. Gen. Felix Zollicoffer, established his headquarters in Jacksboro, using the courthouse. Troops were quartered in the Franklin Academy, and the Methodist Church became a hospital.[6]

One of the chief responsibilities of Palmer's command was to round up bushwhackers and keep the local pro–Union populace in check. Campbell County Unionists outnumbered local pro–Confederates more than two to one. Many members of the Fifty-Eighth undoubtedly encountered Reubin and Obedience Delap Rogers. They lived at the foot of the mountain between Jacksboro and Big Creek Gap. They were active in recruiting and piloting across the mountain local men who wanted to join the Union army. Members of the Fifty-Eighth were constantly being sent out on "scout," looking for these groups of men trying to make their way through one of the gaps. "I am to go out on scout with 9 others. We don't know where to. And 8 other men are to go after some bushwhackers," Langston Estes reported in late November.[7]

Bushwhackers were the biggest threat. Jonathan Miller of Company I later recorded these observations:

> The winter was spent in out post duty guarding this and other passes in the Cumberland mountains, and making several expeditions into Kentucky, most of which were commanded by Capt. Miller. The writer well remembers being along on one of these expeditions and the strict discipline under which we were subjected. Every man was required to keep his place. No stragling nor "foraging" was allowed when Capt. Miller was in command. It was wise and prudent of the captain, for there were numerous "Buchwhackers" on the ridges watching our every movement, men who neither favored the cause of the North nor the South. They preferred to be allowed to do as they pleased — did not want either army to invade their soil.[8]

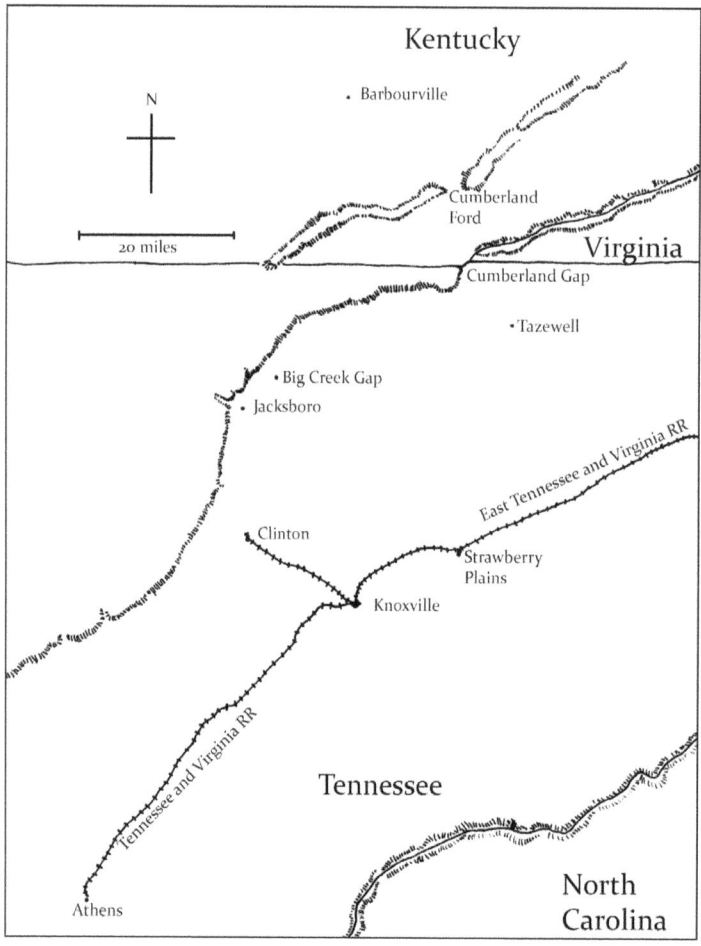

From August 1862 until September 1863, the Fifty-Eighth was stationed in east Tennessee.

Fighting bushwhackers was a much harder task than fighting soldiers on a battlefield. On a battlefield, the foe wore a uniform and rallied to a flag. Bushwhackers seldom wore uniforms. They were citizens and dressed accordingly. A local that one might pass on the road could easily be headed to inform a band lying in ambush farther up the path. Bushwhackers, also referred to as guerrillas, did not heed the accepted codes of military conduct. They did not stand and fight as regular troops did. Coming back from one scouting trip, Estes reported that he had "started out to take up some bushwhackers, But they shot at us every chance. So we returned. One ball came close to me but didn't hit anybody." Fighting guerrillas was difficult and dangerous. "While we were out from Friday till the next Thursday we took between 10–20 prisoners, and wounded 2 and then hung them. It was awful to see them hanging up to an appletree," Estes continued in his letter. The bushwhackers "wounded 2 of our regiment. One was Rufis Robbins had his thumb cut off [and] was wounded in the right shoulder. The other one was in Capt. Wiseman's company. He was shot across the breast. We burnt 7–8 houses for them and destroyed close to 200 bee stands and other things accordingly." Garrett Gouge, in a letter home to his wife in the spring of 1863, backed up Estes's recounting of the brutality of bushwhackers: "I saw a man shot the 16th day of this instant for bushwhacking and stealing horses.... Tennessee cavalry shot him. He had six balls shot in him."[9]

Just how many scouting missions the members of the Fifty-Eighth launched is impossible to tell. An undisclosed number of the regiment's men raided into Scott County, Virginia, on November 11 and 12, 1862. On April 2, 1863, Company E of the Fifty-Eighth was sent to Bear Creek Gap with portions of the Fifty-Fifth Georgia and the Sixty-Fourth North Carolina, on a scouting mission. The next month, possibly the whole regiment moved into Kentucky. By May 9, it was bivouacked on the Wolf River at Camp McGinnis. The men stayed at camp until May 17, when they moved toward Monticello, Kentucky, arriving four miles from town the next day. The regiment bivouacked at Bethuda Church until May 25, when it moved back to the Wolf River, arriving at Camp McGinnis at sunset. The men returned to Tennessee on May 27. These movements were an effort to counter a rumored advance by the Federals and to lead the Federals into believing that the Confederates were going to attack.[10]

James Fox (Company C) told his family, after the war, that during one of these raids, he and "one of his brothers were told to steal in at night and set fire to a certain house. Under possible penalty of death, he told the officer who gave him the command 'We won't do it.' Two other soldiers hearing the command immediately volunteered for the arson job ... in explaining his refusal to obey the command.... I can remember that he said shooting at men who were shooting at you is one thing, but burning a house where probably only women and children lived was another."[11]

Very little time was actually spent chasing bushwhackers, and the members of the Fifty-Eighth found themselves passing an abundance of time in camp. One officer of the regiment wrote: "Camp — nothing to do, getting board." It was a common complaint. While most regiments were quartered in tents or improvised structures made of logs with canvas roofs, it appears that the Fifty-Eighth spent most of the winter of 1862–63 in houses. William Gouge (Company K) made mention of a house where he was quartered in Jacksboro. "I have a good tight room to stay in," he wrote on February 15. Tilman Silver (Company K) wrote to his family on March 15: "We are staying in the courthouse in Jacksboro. I am sitting in the window with my back against the glass and brother Levi is sitting in the next window writing a letter." Lieutenant Harper (Company H), who was serving on brigade staff, moved into headquarters. "High living," he confided in his diary.[12]

Palmer's command continued to grow. Toward the end of October, or possibly the first of November, his twelfth and last company arrived in camp. On September 26, ninety-one men were mustered into service in Boone in what became Company M. The company was commanded by twenty-seven-year-old Jonathan L. Phillips, a schoolteacher from Ashe County. Phillips was a former officer in the Ninety-Eighth North Carolina Militia. Helping command the regiment was thirty-two-year-old George W. Hopkins. Twenty-nine-year-old Thomas Ray, a farmer, was elected second lieutenant. Lastly, John R. Norris, who was serving as a private in Company B, Thirty-Seventh North Carolina Troops, was elected to the position of third lieutenant. The thirty-four-year-old Norris had enlisted on September 14, 1861. He was mustered in as a sergeant, but later reduced back to the ranks. Norris was wounded in the leg during the fighting at Mechanicsville, Virginia, on June 26, 1862. He was listed as a deserter from the Thirty-Seventh when elected to the position of a lieutenant in Company M. While Norris might not have been the best soldier, he had experience that the others did not. Norris was from Watauga County, while Phillips, Hopkins, and Ray were from Ashe County. The company did not report for duty until the end of October or the beginning of November. On November 2, Captain Phillips submitted a receipt for the money he had paid out-of-pocket for rations for fifty men while they moved from Watauga County to Knoxville, a trip that lasted nine days. Francis Wilcox, an unwilling volunteer who had moved to Kentucky prior to the war, but was back in Ashe County visiting family, recalled that he was recruited by Lieutenant Ray. On "the 6th day of November" Ray and Wilcox left North Carolina, "arriving at Big Creek Gap on or about the 11th or 12th of November."[13]

While Lt. George Harper was attached to the brigade headquarters and had freedoms that enlisted men did not have, his diary relates what many of the men did during their free time. He was constantly reading, and documented his reading through *Bride of Lammermoor*, *Bible on Atheiam*, *Monastery Draughts*, and *The Abbott*. Once the weather turned warm, Harper recorded being able to go "boatriding and fishing" and later, "bathing." He even made mention on January 21 of playing chess.[14]

Soldiers seemed to spend most of their time looking for letters from home or writing letters to their loved ones. "Dear brother and sister," started a letter from George McGuire (Company L) on December 18, "It is with pleasure that I seat my self this morning to write a few lines to you." Jesse Hawkins (Company E) started his letters similarly, writing to his wife and mother: "I Seat my self with pen in my hand to let you know that I am well at this tim hopin these few lines may come safe to hand." Most missives from the time period start in like fashion. Soldiers wrote about everything in their letters home: food, men who had died or were ill, funny instances from camp life, where they were or where they had been, and where they thought they were going. When letters were late, or did not arrive in an acceptable time, the soldiers became worried. Often, the soldiers preferred to give their correspondence to soldiers on their way home instead of trusting the "rapid and unfailing mail," as one member of the Fifty-Eighth described it.[15]

James T. Fox, pictured here after the war with his wife, Mary Ann Bennett Fox, served as a fifer in Company C. He is listed as having deserted on August 15, 1864 (courtesy Connie Seibert).

All soldiers expressed the desire to be at home with their loved ones. William Gouge (Company K) wrote his parents on February 15: "I would like to see you all. I hope to live till this war ends and get home to see you all and to enjoy home one time more." Jesse Hawkins's wife wanted him to get a furlough and come home. He told her in a letter in March that "there is [no] chance of getting a furlough[.] I cant tell when I will get home[.] I wood bee glad to get to come home to make [a] crop." Langston Estes (Company E) hoped that the regiment would be transferred to Johnson's Depot. "If we cant go there we want to go to old NC We will go any where rather than stay here in this valley along the Cumberland Mountain." John B. Hughes (Company K) also expressed the desire to go home when he wrote, "I can say to you that I should bee glad to git to come home and see you all one time more but at this time I cannot though don't let this put you out of hart."[16]

In the letters of soldiers, only the topic of food came close to surpassing the coverage given the desire to return home. The winter of 1862–1863 was hard on the men. Langston Estes informed his family on February 1 that he and his comrades had "beef to eat and some pork we get at night — vegitables are hard to get But we get tolerable enough." By spring, things began to improve. Garrett Gouge informed his wife: "We draw a half-pound of meat to the man a week and we draw all the sugar, rice, peas, salt and vinegar ... enough bread and a little flour." A month later, Jesse Hawkins wrote to his wife and mother that he got "1 Pound [of bacon] for 7 days But I fair very well what I lack in drawing ... I can get what Milk and Butter I want." When they were not telling the folks back at home what they had, they were asking for items from home, or were wishing to be at home. "I would like to ... set down with you to breakfast and drink some milk and coffee and eat Some buter and porck and many other things," wrote George McGuire. Enlisted men were issued their rations by the army, through the regimental commissary. Officers were not so lucky. They were required to purchase their food, often from civilians in the area. At times, the officers had a camp servant prepare their food, even though no camp servants are mentioned in the records of the regiment. There was a cook named Bill Jackson listed in the roster, but Jackson's race and origins are unclear. He died of unknown causes on October 25, 1862, at Big Creek Gap. At other times, officers dined with local pro–Confederate families, paying for their meals.[17]

Occasionally, the men had visitors from home. Ella, wife of Lieutenant Harper, arrived on November 30 and probably stayed until December 9. On May 1, Harper recorded the arrival of Fannie Palmer, Colonel Palmer's wife. Harper had dinner with her and the colonel on Sunday the third. While his diary does not say when she left, active campaigning started soon thereafter, and she was probably back home at Grasslands, along the Linville River.[18]

According to army regulations, the men were mustered every two months to be paid. Company officers labored over two copies of printed forms provided by the adjutant and inspector general's office for days, recording who was present, who was absent with or without permission, and who owed the regiment for missing items, like musket cartridges. The men were inspected, and once the paymaster arrived, the men were paid. Records indicate that Pvt. James Anglin (Company C) was mustered, and presumably paid, on February 28, April 30, August 31, October 31, and December 31, 1863. The pay scale, according to Confederate regulations in 1863, was:

Private	$11.00 per month
Corporal	$13.00 per month
Sergeant	$17.00 per month
First Sergeant	$20.00 per month
Sergeant Major	$21.00 per month

Second Lieutenant	$80.00 per month
First Lieutenant	$90.00 per month
Major	$130.00 per month
Lieutenant Colonel	$170.00 per month
Colonel	$195.00 per month

Officers were paid privately rather than in front of the regiment.[19]

There were forms for everything in the Confederate army: clothing, stationery, food, special requests, and furloughs home. On March 3, 1863, Captain Phillips (Company M) requested three jackets, two pairs of pants, and sixteen pairs of shoes for his company. A few days later, on March 16, Captain Bowman (Company B) filled out a requisition for his company, asking for one coat, twenty-nine pairs of pants, thirty blankets, and forty-four pairs of drawers.[20]

Every morning the men fell into ranks for roll call. Every man was expected to be in line once the drums and fifes ended. Those late were to be punished. The first sergeant, under the watchful eye of the company commander or one of his lieutenants, called the names of the men. He then made out a morning report of the men present, absent, in the guard house, or sick. Once the captain signed the morning report, it was taken to the adjutant, who compiled all of the reports from the companies and presented them to the commanding officer. The daily guard details were created, usually drawing a number of men from each company, which the first sergeant presented to the daily officer of the guard. The men who were reported to be sick and still in camp were taken to the regimental surgeon by the first sergeant. The surgeon examined the men and determined who was sick enough to be sent to the hospital, or who should return to their camps to be either confined to those quarters or put on restricted duty.[21]

All regiments were prone to camp sickness. Confederate Surgeon General Samuel Moore wrote in the fall of 1861 "that while there has perhaps been much sickness which could have been avoided, yet the experience of all military life shows that new troops, whether regulars or volunteers, are sick in vast numbers during the early period of their service." During the winter of 1862–1863, sickness, disease, and death ran unabated through the Fifty-Eighth. Most men from rural backgrounds had never been exposed to many of the childhood diseases so common in camp. Measles was one of the worst, transmitted by the close contact of the men with each other. While the infected men were often quarantined, the contagion still spread rapidly. Edward Towery (Company F) on November 15, Grandison Shepherd (Company C) on November 20, and William McVay (Company B) on March 24, 1863, all reportedly died of measles.[22]

Measles often led to a breakdown of the immune system that could lead to pneumonia. One in four men who contracted the respiratory disease later died. In many cases, the records simply state the soldier died of the "fever," and it is impossible to differentiate between pneumonia and typhoid. Frequently contracted through water contaminated by the improper disposal of excremental matter, typhoid killed thousands throughout the army. William L. Brown (Company H), Adam Eggers (Company D), John W. Hunter (Company C), Thomas McKinney (Company A), Joseph Stewart (Company A), and Alfred Watson (Company M) are all listed as having died of the "fever" or "brain fever" while the regiment was stationed in Campbell County. In all, at least sixty men of the Fifty-Eighth perished that winter. Most of their records do not list a cause of death. These men were buried in a local cemetery.[23]

The amount of sickness within the companies was also something the soldiers wrote about in their letters home. "The boys are almost all on the [mend]," wrote William Gouge (Company K) "except Bartley Wilson. He is very low. I don't think he will ever get well. He has been worse yesterday and today than he has ever been." Garrett Gouge (Company K) wrote of William in April: "Brother William is not well and at this time I cannot tell what is the matter with him. He is in his tent yet." From his Camp at Big Creek Gap, Langston Estes (Company E) informed his family in March, "There's a lot of sickness in camp seven died at Jacksboro this week. None has died in this Co. since Finley Coffee died." Even officers were not immune to the sickness in camp. Captain Jason Conley of Company F died on October 31, 1862, First Lt. John C. Green of Company B died on January 28, 1863, and First Lt. David Chandler of Company K died of the "sickness" on March 31, 1863. The regimental surgeon, Waighstill Collett, was absent sick in March and April 1863.[24]

With the death of so many, there was a constant stream of letters back to North Carolina, offering those loved ones at home the sad news of the passing of members of the family. John W. Bailey (Company C) had to write this letter to his brother and sister back home in July 1863 about the death of Thomas Bailey (Company B):

> A sense of duty impels me to communicate to you the sad [news] the death of our Brother He is before me cold and silent in the chill embrace of death he died a little before nine o'clock to nite. About the last words he uttered before in an audable voice was that he was not afraid to die said he wanted to go to Jesus.... He has been growing weaker every [day] he left your house everything about him appeared to be dormant and inactive, consequently he was very sleepy and stupid. was somewhat resless of nights but would general sleep during the day he did not appear to think that was geting worse but I could see that he was and told him of his fast approaching death. Communicate the news to Isaac.[25]

Considering the amount of sickness and death, the morale of the regiment was understandably low. Within the officer corps, twenty-five men were lost. Officers, unlike the enlisted men, were allowed the opportunity to resign. The reasons for these losses were as varied as the men themselves. Three men, First Lt. John C. Green (Company B), Capt. Jason Conley (Company F) and First Lt. David Chandler (Company K), died of disease within the first year of service. The most common reason for resignation was old age. Lt. Col. John C. Keener, who had taken William Proffitt's place after he resigned of "phthisis pulmonalis" on April 25, himself resigned on June 16. Keener gave this reason: "I am near fifty years of age [and] now consider it my duty to retire from the [service] for the purpose of going home to attend to the wants &c. of my family." Palmer added this "endorsement" to the back of Keener's resignation letter: Keener "is not competent to perform the duties of the office he holds and the interests of the public service demand, in my opinion, that his resignation be promptly accepted." The family story has it that Keener's son, John A. N. Keener, was ill and that Lt. Col. Keener had asked for a furlough home. The Confederate government was denying furloughs at the time, in an effort to curtail desertion, and Keener's was rejected. His son died, and Keener resigned from the army.[26]

Others resigned for the same reasons. Capt. Martin Wiseman (Company A) resigned on July 4, stating, "I am over 45 years of age and my fam[i]ly is in a condition that requir[e]s my attention at home being all of the female sect and no man person on the primises; also feeling a[n] incompaceny of filling the officer which I now hold." Wiseman's first lieutenant and neighbor, John Ollis, gave about the same reason: "I am over fifty years of age and I am too weakly constituted to perform the duties of my office. Second[,] that I do not feel myself competent and do not believe that I can acquire sufficent knowledge of military affares to perform the duties of a lieutenant." His resignation was accepted on June 17. Others resigning for the same reason include Capt. John Peek (Company G), Second Lt. Jackson Stewart (Company B), and Capt. William Miller (Company I). Miller added that not only was he old, but "my hearing [is] such that I cannot understand the commands when g[i]ven at a distance." Stewart's resignation was accepted on April 25, Peek's resignation was accepted around May 5, and Miller's on August 14.[27]

Some of the older officers were also considered incompetent. Palmer wrote that Keener was incompetent, and Captain Wiseman and Lieutenant Ollis both stated that they were likewise ill-equipped on military grounds. Also, First Lt. John C. Garland (Company B), submitted his resignation on December 18, 1862. His reasoning was that "I feel myself incompetent of discharging the duties of a commissioned officer." His resignation was accepted on January 20, 1863. Lt. John Tipton (Company G) resigned on March 26, stating that he was "wholly incompetent for the duties and responsibilities of the office [of 1st Lieutenant] through a want of education, [and] military skill." His resignation was accepted on May 15, 1863. Some of the officers who resigned probably feared the upcoming Boards of Examination. Created by the adjutant and inspector's office in May 1863, these brigade-level boards examined current and prospective officers, making sure that they were competent enough to perform under the rigors of military life.[28]

Sickness also led to resignations. Jackson Stewart claimed to have been in "ill health" for three months prior to submitting his resignation. Company C's Second Lt. Benjamin Moss was out sick from December 25, 1862, until June 30, 1863. Moss suffered from a "enlargement of knee joint [and] arthritis." He resigned on August 1. John Morris, second lieutenant of Company F, resigned in January due to "pulmonary consumption." Captain William Gentry (Company L) resigned on June 1, due to his "pulmonary disease."[29]

Several of the officers were even absent from their commands and dropped. Sergeant Major Harrison Herndon deserted sometime in May of June 1863 and was replaced by James Inglis (Company H). Three of Company G's officers were absent. Lt. James W. Gardner disappeared from the records after being declared absent without leave in March and April 1863. George Hopkins and Thomas Ray were both transferred from Company M to Company G, but neither ever appeared as active within the company. Hopkins was on detached service in North Carolina when he was transferred on June 15, and when he failed to rejoin the regiment, he was dropped on November 16. Ray was transferred in May but resigned on June 5, "apparently without having reported for duty." Capt. Drury Harman, while not a deserter, fell back upon his pre-war occupation when he resigned. "I consider, having been for years a minister of the Gospel," Harman wrote in March 1863, "that I am unfitted by the want of military talent and acquirements for the position which I now hold in the army." His resignation was accepted at the end of the month.[30]

All of these losses were exacerbated by those officers who resigned, or were demoted back to the ranks, over some personal grievance. Feeling ill will towards the commanding officer was common during the first year of the war. The commanding officer was attempting to take raw, undisciplined men and turn them into competent officers and soldiers. Isaac Bailey, who later served as captain of Company B, wrote to his sister in October 1862, "That old Palmer has not had me under arrest any more. But he has had all of the commissioned officers under arrest since that time." It is unclear just why Palmer had all of the officers under arrest, but his actions had serious repercussions. Many of the officers of the Fifty-Eighth who resigned for other reasons might have been able to tack on some grievance. Capt. Jacob Bowman (Company B) resigned on March 5, stating in his resignation letter that the "charges having been made against me as so serious a nature as to impair my influence with the company under my command[.] I feel that the interest of the service and a proper self respect demand that I should tender my resignation." Bowman's resignation was accepted on April 16. The charges preferred against Bowman are apparently lost to history. Lt. Edward Blevins (Company L) found himself under arrest at the beginning of 1863 and charged with "conduct unbecoming an officer and a gentleman." Instead of facing a court-martial, Blevins resigned on January 5, and, when his resignation was accepted, he enlisted as a private in his company. Lt. Milton Hampton (Company C) found himself under arrest for unknown reasons on June 30, but was back to duty and promoted to first lieutenant on August 14.[31]

Individuals were not the only ones who appeared dissatisfied with where the regiment was stationed or who its commander was. In mid–January, Capt. Thomas Dula (Company H) wrote to Governor Vance, asking that his entire company be transferred to "Col. Radcliffe." James Radcliffe was the colonel of the recently created Sixty-First North Carolina Troops. Radcliffe "has only eight Companies and is wanting two more[. We] would like very much to be attached to his command." Dula continued, "Col. Palmer has twelve Companies of infantry troops, two more than he has a right to." Company H remained in the Fifty-Eighth for the duration of the war.[32]

The low morale and problems within the officers' corps extended to the common soldier in the ranks as well. Back in September, Langston Estes had written home about the lack of furloughs, blaming Colonel Palmer. "If he don't do better he will git his men hating him," Estes wrote. "The most of the men is giting against him anyhow." Instead of revolting against their commanding officers, often family members that they, the enlisted men, had themselves elected to these positions, the soldiers in the ranks chose to desert instead.[33]

Every regiment, North or South, had deserters, men who left their regiments without a furlough. A soldier often went to his company commander and asked for a furlough home. The paperwork was filled out and taken to the regimental commander, who approved or declined the soldier's request. If approved, the soldier was given a piece of paper saying that he

John L. Ollis was already forty-three years old when he volunteered in December 1861. He was elected to the post of first lieutenant of Company A, but resigned in June 1863, stating that he was too old to serve (courtesy Doyle Ollis).

had permission to be away from his regiment for a certain length of time. Men caught without this slip of paper could be arrested, jailed, and returned to their commands for punishment. Coming up with precise desertion numbers for the Fifty-Eighth is next to impossible. Too many gaps exist within the available records. But some glimpses within the regiment provide a good idea of just how much a problem desertion was.

Even as the regiment was being mustered into service in late July 1862, there were numerous men absent from their commands. In Company G, twenty-five men were not present. Of that twenty-five, sixteen never reported for duty with the Fifty-Eighth. Those who did come back arrived in the spring, but were likely to desert again. By November 30, fifty-three men had been declared absent without leave. On November 5, an additional twenty-five men were declared absent. All of these men were from Company M. It appears that most of the conscripts in Company M were granted furloughs for ten days on October 25, while a smaller group was granted furloughs for fifteen days. All but three, William Hampton, Nicholas Keller, and William Keller, failed to return. By the end of the year, at least an additional forty-five men had left the regiment.[34]

Men left for a variety of reasons. Some wanted to escape the hardships of being a soldier. The constant drill, bad weather, poor food, and discipline wore on some soldiers. "The guard duty while at Big Creek Gap," wrote Jonathan Miller (Company I), "were excessive, and the command suffered severely from privation and exposure." For others, leaving their wives and small children with no one to fend for them prompted them to head back home during planting and harvesting season to provide for their families. A few were cowards, and the thought of being in a battle scared them from their place among the ranks. However, most deserted from a lack of support for the Confederacy. They were not necessarily Unionists, but many men simply wished to be left alone and not involved in the conflict at all, on either side. Finally, some were Union supporters. Ashe County's William Younce (Company L) was one such man. Conscription forced him into the Confederate army. Prior to joining the Fifty-Eighth in east Tennessee, Younce had already tried to slip off once and had been caught. He reluctantly joined the Confederate army. Younce only spent about two weeks in camp. "At times I grew melancholy and despondent," he wrote after the war. Younce had "registered an oath in heaven that I would never fight for the Southern cause, and bear arms against my country, and in the bitterness of my remorse I cried out: 'Why did not my tongue cleave to the roof of my mouth before taking the oath of allegiance to the Jeff Davis Government? Why did I not let them take my life?'" Younce found three like-minded associates: "Robinson, Roark, and Reedy." The "Robinson" was Wilborn Robison. There were three Roarks in Company L: Joshua, Solomon, and William. The one Reedy in Company L was George W. Reedy.[35]

Starling Patterson Green served just a short time in Company A of the Fifty-Eighth. He enlisted in March 1863 and deserted in June 1863. He later served in the 13th Tennessee Cavalry (U.S.) (courtesy Robert Morgan).

Younce and his colleagues planned for several days, pondering the best way and time to quit the

Confederate army. It was Younce's intention to head back to the mountains and "wait for the nearer approach of the Union army, and then make a last desperate attempt to get inside the Union lines." So "about the first of November," during the afternoon, the group "flanked the guards and soon found ourselves in the country among the hills." That night, they traveled along the road, and when daylight came, took to the woods. The next night, they stopped. "We were so worn out for want of rest and sleep that we lay down on the cold ground ... with no covering ... and slept soundly until morning." After a "scanty breakfast" from the rations they had brought, Younce and his companions continued to travel through the woods and minor roads.

Finding themselves famished, they spotted a small house and took the chance to approach the house looking for food. "We were cordially received," Younce wrote, "and told that supper would be prepared for us, and that we were welcome to remain over night." After a good meal, the men were shown to a room, where they spent the night. Early the next morning, a call for breakfast came. Younce and the others dressed themselves, but found the door locked. When the door was opened, they found to their horror a "half dozen muskets in the hands of as many Confederate soldiers." Their "genial host" for the evening just happened to be the Confederate enrolling officer for the area. He had suspected that his guests had been deserters, and once they had been fed and locked into their room, had sent for Confederate soldiers to take charge of his unsuspecting prisoners. Their host still expected to feed his prisoners breakfast and ordered the four out onto the porch to wash. "We followed as he directed," Younce chronicled, "the soldiers holding their guns in readiness for any emergency.... When we reached the porch near the corner of the house Roark and Reedy made a dash for liberty."

> Quick as thought they dashed around the corner of the house, leaped over a low fence, and started across an open field toward a wood about two hundred yards away, the guards were on the alert, and four of them dashed around the corner after them, getting in plain view of them just as they were leaping the fence. I stepped to the corner just in time to see each guard place his gun to his shoulder, take deliberate aim, and fire. For a moment I held my breath, for I fully expected to see both boys fall, as they were not more than twenty-five yards from the house, but strange to say, neither one of them was touched, and had they continued it is possible that they might have reached the wood and escaped. While the guards were re-loading they might have gotten beyond their reach; but they both stopped, turned around and came back. We then went into breakfast, while the guards stood in the room and at the door. We ate but little, in fact Roark and Reedy, after their excitement, ate nothing.

The four were taken to Rogersville and placed in the jail. A day and a half later, they were escorted to Knoxville via the train. Younce and his associates were lectured on the duty of young Southern men. Younce told the provost marshall that they were not deserters and had "simply started to our homes, expecting to remain a few days, and then return to our regiment." Younce was pleading the "absent without leave" clause, even though his intent was to escape and join the Union army. A soldier was declared absent without leave when gone for fewer than sixty days and expected to return. Even though Younce had been in the army for just a couple of weeks, he was attempting to manipulate the system and save his own neck.

The foursome was secured in the overcrowded jail in Knoxville, awaiting the next day and their fate. Fortune was kind to Younce and his comrades. They were sent to a camp on the eastern edge of town and placed under guard for about two weeks. After being released, they worked as teamsters, taking supplies to Kingston, and returning on the train sometime around December 22. When they returned, a sergeant and four men from the Fifty-Eighth were waiting for them. Younce and the others were escorted back to camp. Younce went straight to Colonel Palmer. He walked into Palmer's headquarters, saluted the colonel, and said:

> Colonel, we have been absent without leave, and we now report for duty, and beg that you will pardon us for this offense." He then proceeded to give us a lecture as to our duty, and said he hoped this would be a lesson for us, and that we would never commit an error like this again, and assured us that if we ever should that we would be punished to the full extent of the law. "And now" said he, addressing the guard, "you are discharged"; and turning and addressing us, said: "Now boys, go to your quarters, and be better men in the future."[36]

Not everyone who deserted got off as easily as Younce and his associates. The Articles of War, the rules that governed the armies, stated in Article 20 that any soldier (or officer), that has received pay and hence been mustered "and shall be convicted of deserting ... shall suffer death, or such other punishment as, by the sentence of a court-martial, shall be inflicted." A soldier who deserted could be convicted of a crime and executed for that crime.

Officers often tried other means of deterring men from leaving their companies. George Harper recorded in his diary in March 1863 that one soldier of his company had been tried for desertion and "received the penalty of [the] Court Martial ... 50 lashes, ball and chain, etc." Solomon Greene, Jr. (Company D), was court-martialed for desertion and ordered to "'mark time' for two hours each day for ten days." Marking time was marching in place. Albert Shehan (Company F) was sentenced to wear a ball and chain for forty days. Arthur McFalls, who served in both Companies A and K, related in a letter home in August 1863 that he was "out of the guard house at last. I was confined 6 months, 11 days." A family story relates how Wesley Cannon (Company H) was ordered to burn a woman's barn or corn crib. He refused, and was court-martialed for disobeying orders. While on his way to serve his sentence in Richmond, Virginia, Cannon and another soldier, after the guard fell asleep, jumped off the train and made their way to Federal lines. It appears that most of the deserters who returned were granted leniency.[37]

Sgt. A. Colman Craig (Company H) was present through August 31, 1864. He survived the war, but does not have a parole in his Compiled Service Record (courtesy the North Carolina Department of Archives and History).

Military justice was not the only concern. Soldiers also faced pressure when they returned home. Empsey Gragg deserted in May 1863 and headed back home to Watauga County. Gragg's wife had written him a letter, stating that his family was "suffering for the want of something to live on," and Gragg had come home to check on things. During the July meeting of Gragg's church, they moved that "Brother Emsey Gragg had left his Regiment in the Army without leave, agreed to send a committee to see Brother Gragg and report the facts." Gragg came to the October meeting of the Cove Creek Baptist Church and "made acknowledgement for his act of desertion and promised to return to his Regiment as soon as he could." Gragg did return, and was reported under arrest in January and February 1864. He would later desert again.[38]

Another section of the Articles of War stated that any soldier "who shall be convicted of having advised or persuaded any other officer or soldier to desert the service of the Confederate States" could be put to death or subjected to some other punishment. Many soldiers were indeed persuading others. Francis Wilcox (Company M) confessed that he was "getting homesick to see Kentucky and I told some of Company M I was going home soon. They asked if I would like company they would go with me. I told them yes. I'd be please to have them." Those going with Wilcox that cold night in December 1862 included fellow Company M members Daniel Graham; brothers Jefferson and Thomas Greer, a cousin, Isaiah Greer; Isaiah's nephew Phillip Greer; George W. Lorance, a brother-in-law to Isaiah Greer; and Robert Jones. The party found a man loyal to the Union and paid him $16.00 to serve as a guide. They were soon within Union lines. None of these men ever returned to the Fifty-Eighth.[39]

William Younce (Company L) was another soldier trying to induce others to leave with him despite his previous unsuccessful desertion experiences. Once he rejoined the regiment, the winter doldrums set in, and Younce once again began to talk, "constantly sowing seeds of discontent among the boys, always talking for the Union, and against the South, to those whom I could trust." Younce estimated that "at least half of the regiment or perhaps more were just as loyal to the Union as those who wore the blue."[40]

Many of the soldiers with whom Younce talked were concerned about their families at home. They told Younce: "If I were like you [young and single] I would go but I have a family — a wife and little children, who will cry for bread. How can I leave them to suffer? It may be the war will end before long, and I can then go home." When a soldier deserted, he was not able to simply return home to care for his family. While the deserter might stop by his home from time to time, if he lingered, he might be caught. Some deserters were executed on the spot when they were apprehended. Others were taken to a military prison or, if they were lucky, sent back to their regiments. Their families were labeled as Unionists, and any help sent to the counties by the Confederate government for the relief of the families of loyal Confederate soldiers was denied to them.

At first, the county governments tried to help all the destitute residents of their areas. Yancey County, in September 1861, had levied a tax in an attempt to provide equipment for the militia, uniforms for the volunteers, and care for the families of those in Confederate service. However, the property owned by soldiers was exempt from this special tax. In the fall of 1862, Caldwell County appropriated $1,000 to buy corn

Arthur McFalls was thirty-four years old when he volunteered in June 1862. On July 29, 1862, the day the Fifty-Eighth was formally organized, McFalls transferred to Company K. He was killed on September 20, 1863, at Chickamauga (courtesy Beth Stoney).

for the families of soldiers. Joseph C. Norwood of Caldwell County allowed the families of soldiers to cultivate gardens on his land in 1863.[41]

Younce chose the evening of February 10, 1863, for his second attempt to leave the Confederate army. He had recruited eight accomplices from Company L: James Callaway, Nathan Cox, Jason Jones, Jesse Jones, Memoch Jones, Andrew Lovelace, Wilborn Robison, and William Wallis. The group waited until dark, after tattoo had sounded, and everyone was asleep. They gathered the supplies that they had been collecting and set out toward North Carolina. After ten days of traveling through the mountains, keeping to the summits so they might see for miles on each side, one of the members of the group grew ill. Younce did not mention his name in his record of the excursion, but he appears to have been one of the Joneses. After a few days, the man became too sick to continue. "In spite of all we could [do he] could go no further, and begged that we go on, and let him die alone," Younce chronicled after the war.

> He said if we undertook to take care of him, we would all be captured, and for us to leave him and save ourselves. We could not think of leaving him alone. Of course his brother would not go and leave him to die alone. We gathered a lot of dry leaves and made a bed for him under the trunk of a fallen tree, and gathered bark from trees and covered him to protect him from the rain, and placed him there as gently as we could, and as the tears coursed down their faces we bade the boys good-bye and started on our journey. The young man sat on the log, beside his sick brother's bed, and waved his hand to us as we disappeared around the side of the mountain.... I have never known what became of these brothers.[42]

Both brothers did survive. Jason Jones returned to the army on April 23 and Jesse Jones was back with the regiment on March 3. Three others also later returned to the Fifty-Eighth, for a total of five out of the original nine members of the group. Younce himself seemed incapable of staying out of the Confederate army. He later served in both the Virginia State Line and the Twenty-First Virginia Cavalry.[43]

For those who decided to stay out of the service more permanently, the mountains were logical places to hide, providing many almost inaccessible caves and hollows that the deserter had likely known all of his life. Every few days, the soldier would need to come out from his hiding spot to secure food. Or, a family member out to feed the hogs might drop off some provisions at a prearranged location. Thaddeus Braswell (Company E) supposedly took to hiding out in a cave on the southern slopes of Beech Mountain right after enlisting in 1862.[44]

In 1863, several officers from the Fifty-Eighth, along with a few men, were sent back to their respective counties to round up those who had overstayed their furloughs. In January and February 1863, Lt. Calvin Eller (Company L) was sent to Ashe County; Lt. Jordan McGhee (Company I) was sent to Watauga County, Lt. Adam Lingle (Company H) was in Caldwell County; and Lt. William Coffey (Company E) was also in Caldwell County. Capt. Samuel Silver was in Mitchell County for this reason in March and April 1863. First Sergeant Elisha Hurley (Company L) was also sent back to Ashe County in May and June of that year. Lt. George Hopkins (Company G) was in Yancey County in June 1863.

Confederate regulation specified a reward of $30.00 per deserter who was apprehended and delivered to the proper Confederate authorities. Company F's commander, Capt. Caleb Conley, ran an advertisement in the January 7, 1863, edition of Marion's *Mountain Mercury* publically announcing a reward of $180 for the "apprehension and delivery to me, of the following deserters ... $30 for each one. I will give $15 for each one's confinement in jail: Erwin Shepherd, Anderson Robbins, Anderson Shepherd, Pinkey Shehan, Albert Shehan, and Anderson Loven." In June 1863, Watauga County's Ransom Hayes was paid for keeping eight deserters from the Fifty-Eighth in the local jail. Hayes received seventy-five cents per day for keeping Eli Harmon, Ranson Teaster, Elisha Trivett, and Duke and Michael Ward, all members of Company D.[45]

Desertion was a problem all across the Confederacy, and, in 1863, the Confederate government tried to take steps to curtail the problem. In February, Adjutant and Inspector General Samuel Cooper issued an order dropping from the rolls officers who were absent without leave longer than thirty days. In April, he forbade the whipping of soldiers as a punishment for desertion. Whipping, also known as flogging, had been practiced in the United States from 1776 to 1861, except for a few years after the War of 1812. Another act passed that day reaffirmed the death penalty for desertion. A final act that month prevented officers and soldiers from being paid while absent without leave.[46]

Both state and national governments were doing all they could to get the men absent from their commands back into their respective regiments. On January 26, 1863, North Carolina Governor Zebulon B. Vance issued a proclamation asking these men to return by February 10. Those that did so were to receive "no other punishment than a forfeiture of their pay for the time they have been absent without leave." Those who had not returned to their respective regiments, once apprehended, were to be tried for their act of desertions and "upon conviction be made to suffer death." Vance appealed to the soldier's sense of honor:

> Many, after carrying their country's flag in triumph through various bloody conflicts and making for themselves a name of which their children's children might have been justly proud, have forfeited it all by absenting themselves at a moment when their own State is invaded and about to be desolated by a brutal, half-savage foe.... I appeal to them to stand by their country yet a little longer, and not to sully by desertion the bright and glorious reputation of the State which they have helped to win on a hundred hard-fought fields.... Let no one, unmoved by this appeal to his patriotism and honor, suppose that he can remain at home with impunity.

It would appear that scores of men who had either deserted, or were at home on expired furloughs, had returned to the Fifty-Eighth by the end of April.[47]

Confederate President Jefferson Davis also tried his own amnesty proclamation to entice those who were absent from their regiments to return. His declaration, dated July 31, granted a "general pardon and amnesty to all officers and men within the Confederacy now absent without leave who shall with the least possible delay return to their proper post of duty." Absentees had twenty days to return to their commands. Davis then appealed to his "countrywomen, the wives, mothers, sisters, and daughters ... to use their all-powerful influence in aid of this call ... to take care that none who owe services in the field shall be sheltered at home from the disgrace of having deserted their duty to their families, to their country, and to their God." Few members of the Fifty-Eighth answered Davis's call to return to their regiment.[48]

An additional possible reason for the high desertion rates among the members of the Fifty-Eighth could be that they were a part of an overall weak organization. Department commanders were constantly changing. Maj. Gen. Edmund Kirby Smith was in charge of the Department of East Tennessee when the Fifty-Eighth arrived at Johnson's Depot. Three weeks later, Smith began his campaign to liberate Kentucky, and departmental command fell upon Maj. Gen. John McCowan. He commanded from August 24 until September 19, when he was replaced by Maj. Gen. Samuel Jones. Jones commanded the department until September 27, when he was replaced by McCowan, who in turn was replaced by Smith on

October 20. Kirby Smith commanded the department until November 11, when he, in turn, was replaced by Brig. Gen. Henry Heth. Brig. Gen. William G. M. Davis replaced Heth on January 17, 1863, only to be replaced by Brig. Gen. Daniel Donelson. Donelson was the Fifty-Eighth's longest serving departmental commander, remaining in the post until April 15, when he died. Donelson was replaced by Maj. Gen. Dabney "Puss-in-Boots" Maury, who only commanded the department until April 27, less than two weeks. Maury was replaced by Maj. Gen. Simon Buckner, who commanded the department until June 26, when he was replaced by Brig. Gen. William Preston III. Preston retained command for a month.

The Department of East Tennessee became the District of East Tennessee around the end of July, and on July 25, Buckner replaced Preston as commander of the area. Buckner was highly critical of the troops under his command. He complained to General Cooper in Richmond at the end of July that he had 2,400 men under his command from the mountains of east Tennessee and western North Carolina whom he would like to replace with 1,000 men from other states. "Fully half of the East Tennessee and North Carolina troops, from the mountain districts, are not to be relied upon." Buckner wrote a few days later, "I repeat my request for their exchange of other troops, for when removed from the temptation of desertion, they will make good soldiers." On September 3, Buckner was replaced by Jones, who continued as district commander after the Fifty-Eighth was transferred out of the area. The Fifty-Eighth had no Robert E. Lee nor Thomas "Stonewall" Jackson to inspire the men to greatness.[49]

Some soldiers were lucky enough to be detailed away from the Fifty-Eighth, away from the drudgery and dangers of being constantly on "scout," and into one of the government shops in Knoxville. The town boasted Confederate meat packing facilities, shoe shops, an armory that manufactured cartridges and percussion caps, along with laborers, wood choppers, railroad hands, blacksmiths, and carpenters. John Scoggins (Company B), Elijah Hall and Daniel Mosteller (Company F), John Kirby (Company H) and William Keller (Company M), were nurses; Charles Higgins and Andrew Younce (Company G), Finley Baird (Company H), and Wilborn Swift (Company I) made shoes; Michael Mitchell (Company I) and George W. Bumgarner (Company L) were simply listed as "detailed." Bartlett Coffey (Company E) was detailed as a cooper at Loudon; J. E. Rankin (Company F) was a druggist; David Walker (Company F) was a blacksmith; James Ramey (Company H) served as a "wood Workman" and a mechanic; Adolphus Benfield (Company K) was detailed a blacksmith; and Jacob Eller and Jesse Jones (Company L) were wood workmen.[50]

At the end of March, the different portions of the regiments were moved to Clinton, about twelve miles from Knoxville. It snowed on the men as they marched south from Jacksboro toward their new position on the Clinch River. It is unclear how of much of the regiment was at Clinton. Lieutenant Harper and John Dugger (Company D) reported being at Clinton, while Elijah Coffey (Company E) stated that he was at Loudon. Langston Estes reported on April 5 that he was suffering a cold while stationed at Big Creek Gap (Company E). William Gouge, also of Company E, wrote on the same day, stating that he was at Clinton. The men expressed regret at having to give up "tight" sleeping quarters for tents. Estes reported that he, "Hite and Jasper [Hight Moore and Jasper Moore] are staying in one tent. Just living in hog heaven." Harper recorded in his diary that on April 7, he "had [a] chimney put up to tent — making it comfortable."[51]

Word arrived at camp that the Federals had crossed the Cumberland River at Williamsburg, Kentucky, and were headed into East Tennessee. On April 15, the Fifty-Eighth moved to meet them, camping in the woods near Jacksboro that evening. The Federals were slowly pushing the Confederates out of Kentucky, and the Federal commander, Ambrose Burnside, reported on April 21 that "a small advance guard [of Federals] crossed [the Cumberland] at Williamsburg and drove a rebel regiment within 6 miles of the Tennessee line." The Federals came no closer, and the Fifty-Eighth remained at Jacksboro on short rations until Sunday the nineteenth, when the regiment returned to Clinton.[52]

A return presented to the Confederate War Department on April 25 gave this glimpse of the department of East Tennessee. The command, with headquarters in Knoxville, was composed of five brigades. The first, under the command of Brig. Gen. Humphrey Marshall, was stationed in Harlan, Kentucky. The second, under the command of Col. G. T. Maxwell, was stationed at Loudon, Tennessee. Brig. Gen. Archibald Gracie, Jr., commanded the third brigade, with headquarters at Bean's Station, Tennessee. The fourth brigade was stationed at Jonesborough, Tennessee, and was commanded by Brig. Gen. A. E. Jackson. Colonel Palmer commanded the fifth brigade, with headquarters at Clinton, Tennessee. Palmer's brigade was composed of the Fifty-Fifth Georgia, Fifty-Eighth North Carolina, the Sixty-Fourth North Carolina, and Barbour's Artillery. Major Keener was reported as being in command of the Fifty-Eighth while Palmer was in command of the brigade. Palmer reported on April 30 that his brigade had 108 officers and 1,551 men present and able for duty in the fifth brigade.[53]

The Fifty-Eighth remained in camp for about a month, rotating on and off guard, drilling, and attending almost numberless dress parades. One officer in the regiment recorded parades on Tuesday, April 28, Sunday, May 3 (possibly in honor of a visit by Mrs. Palmer), and Monday, May 4, possibly for a visit by Brig. Gen. John Pegram. A dress parade usually entailed the men of a regiment turning out in their best, with clothes clean and muskets and leather gear polished. At times, the regiment paraded across a field in front of the commanding officer or his guest. On May 7, the Fifty-Eighth left Clinton for an excursion into Kentucky, returning on May 30. The regiment had no sooner returned than the reviews and inspections commenced again. On June second and third, Col. George Hodge, aide to President Davis, reviewed and inspected the regiment.[54]

As spring burst forth upon east Tennessee, so did military activity. On June 5, Palmer was informed that the Federals were massing at Somerset, Kentucky. Palmer was ordered to have four days' worth of rations cooked and ready to distribute to his men, and to have those men ready to march at a moment's notice. Garrett Gouge (Company K) wrote home on June 6: "We are under marching orders and ordered to cook three days' rations." Palmer was instructed that his movement could be back to Wartburg, Kingston, Loudon, or back to Big Creek Gap.[55]

For reasons that are not quite clear, on Tuesday, June 9, Palmer was replaced as commander of the fifth brigade by Brig. Gen. John W. Frazier. A Tennessee native, Frazier was born in Hardin County in 1827. He graduated from West Point in 1849, then served in both the Second and the Ninth United States Infantry, attaining the rank of captain in 1857. Resigning in 1861, Frazier became lieutenant colonel of the Eighth Alabama Infantry, and then colonel of the Twenty-Eighth Alabama Infantry. On May 19, Frazier was appointed brigadier general. On July 31, Frazer's brigade was composed of the Fifty-Fifth Georgia Infantry, the Fifty-Eighth and Sixty-Fourth North Carolina Troops, and Kolb's Battery. Lieutenant Harper was retained as assistant adjutant general by Frazier.[56]

Regarding Frazier's replacement as commander, Harper wrote that the demotion was "not for any want of confidence in [Palmer's] ability or patriotism" but was due to Buckner's desire for brigadier generals to command his brigades. Palmer apparently had the support of his regimental commanders. "The officers of the 55th Ga Regt.," wrote Harper, "took the initiative [and wrote] a handsome note to the Col. ... expressing their regret that he has been removed from the command, their high appreciation of his abilities as a commander and their regard for him personally. The other Regts have done the same." Harper thought that Frazier was "a good officer [but] this brigade ... to a man would prefer Col. P."[57]

District of East Tennessee Commander Simon Buckner arrived on June 11 to inspect the brigade. Buckner was inspecting not just the Fifty-Eighth, but his entire command. On June 18, he wrote to Samuel Cooper in Richmond, stating that all of his troops, save Gracie's brigade, were in bad condition. "The defenses of the gaps are very imperfect; scarcely any work has been bestowed upon them during the past twelve months." Part of the bad condition to which Buckner alluded might have extended to morale. Cpl. John C. Blair (Company E) wrote to his father on July 15, "From the best information I can gather, the Confederacy is in a gloomey position though I am not like some people whipped before I ever saw a yankee or heard a cannon if evry boddy was like some people we would allready be whipped such men as these I have no use for Old Bragg has fallen back to Chatanuga leaving the enemy in full possession of middle Tennesee."[58]

As Blair and Buckner were complaining, Buckner's "imperfect" defensives were being tested. On June 14, Col. William P. Sanders of the Fifth Kentucky Cavalry (U.S.) set out from Mt. Vernon, Kentucky, and proceeded south. The orders were to tear up railroad tracks and cut telegraph lines. By daylight on the twentieth, they were threatening Knoxville. The Fifty-Eighth, along with the Sixty-Fourth, was ordered from Clinton to Big Creek Gap. The Fifty-Eighth was back in Clinton by the seventeenth. Saturday, June 20, brought another move. At 3:00 P.M., Frazer's brigade headed south on the Knoxville Road, camping for the night at Bell's Bridge. The following day, the brigade moved to "Harbusons cross" and "prepared for [the] raid which was reported to be moving toward us." Another soldier wrote that the Fifty-Eighth "lay in line of battle all night." Garrett Gouge told his father that the regiment went "into a corn field and formed a line of battle and run a string of fence across the field. [We were] in line of battle till day ... they never came." However, Sanders's raiders bypassed Knoxville, continued up the railroad, burning bridges at Strawberry Plains and New Market, and then escaped back into Kentucky, taking ten pieces of artillery and approximately 300 Confederate prisoners.[59]

On Wednesday, June 24, the Fifty-Eighth moved back to Bell's Bridge and went into camp. Garrett Gouge made these observations from camp on June 25:

> We have had some hard marching of late. We have been after the Yankees for eight or ten days but we have not got to see them yet. They have burned a bridge or two on the railroad but they have not done much damage. They were all cavalry. Our men whipped them at Loudoun bridge and kept it from being burned. Then they started to Knoxville and tore up the road. It is reported that they burned the Strawberry Plain bridge. Then our men reinforced so strong they begin to make their escape. Our men got them surrounded and they left their cannons and a great many of their horse and took to the mountains—one here and one yonder to try to get back.[60]

With a heavy rain falling on them, the Fifty-Eighth started to move toward Loudon on the twenty-seventh, arriving on the thirtieth. The regiment remained at Loudon until July 11, when it was replaced by the brigade of Bushrod Johnson.[61]

The regiment, apparently united, continued to move around east Tennessee. The first of August, Colonel Palmer submitted a requisition for forage for his regiment's transportation of baggage. Palmer needed forage for twelve horses, forty-six mules, and four oxen, a total of sixty-two animals. After leaving Loudon, the Fifty-Eighth made camp at Bell's Bridge until August 4. Orders had come the day before for General Frazier to make his headquarters at Cumberland Gap, while the Fifty-Eighth was ordered to relieve three companies of the Fifty-Fifth Georgia at Big Creek Gap. While at Big Creek Gap, Jesse Hawkins (Company E) penned a letter home, writing on August 12 that he was "this evening on the top of the Cumberland mountain on picket." The regiment evacuated Big Creek Gap on July 22, arriving at Jacksboro the same evening. The stay at Jacksboro was short, and the regiment arrived back at Clinton on the evening of the twenty-third about 10:00 P.M. Lieutenant Harper, with three companies, was detailed to command the rear guard as the regiment left Clinton. After a short rest, the regiment was on the road again at 4:00 A.M., stopping at 10:00 that evening at Campbell Station. Once again at 4:00 A.M., the Fifty-Eighth was on the road, this time covering but two miles before going into camp and cooking "rations all night."

The following day, the regiment arrived at Lenoir's Station, to the southeast of Knoxville, staying a couple of days, mostly "in line of battle." While at Lenoir's Station, Pvt. Noah Isaac (Company I) found it a good time to desert. According to the family, Noah found a hollow log to hide in until his regiment passed on. He then returned to Watauga County. From Lenoir's Station, the regiment moved on August 28 to Loudon. Marching was the regiment's lot for the next few days. The regiment usually started before dawn and was often not finished marching until after dark. Through Sweetwater, Riceville, Charlestown, and Georgetown, Tennessee, the Fifty-Eighth marched. Pvt. Levi Winebarger (Company I) used all the movement to slip off on September 1 while at Sweetwater. According to the family, Winebarger "ducked into a wooded area, threw his gun in a hollow log and walked to Kentucky," where he spent the rest of the war working as a carpenter. At daylight on September 8, the men of the regiment, minus a few more men like Winebarger, found themselves in Chickamauga, Georgia, along with the rest of the Confederate Army of Tennessee.[62]

Chapter 7

September 1863

"A braver man or boy never died."—Capt. Isaac Bailey

Things looked bleak for the Confederacy in September 1863. In the east, Robert E. Lee's Army of Northern Virginia had fought to a draw and was forced to retreat from a campaign into Gettysburg. Along the Mississippi River, the last stronghold in the area, Vicksburg, had succumbed to a siege the day after the grand charge in Pennsylvania. And in the central portion of the Confederacy, Braxton Bragg's Confederate army was forced out of its Tennessee position and into the Chattanooga area with barely a shot fired. The latter situation was the source of the Fifty-Eighth's constant movement.

On August 17, the Federal Army of the Ohio started to move south from its Kentucky base toward East Tennessee. Bragg feared that the 62,000-man force that he faced would join with the 20,000- strong Army of the Ohio and attack Buckner in the rear, cutting Buckner's command off from the Confederates at Chattanooga. Bragg, who had been appointed as Buckner's commander on August 6, 1863, ordered Buckner to abandon east Tennessee, save Cumberland Gap, and move closer to the main Confederate army to the west. Buckner's destination was along the Hiwassee River, about thirty-five miles from Chattanooga. Somewhere along the way, possibly when General Frazier received orders to go to Cumberland Gap, the Fifty-Eighth received a new brigade commander: John Herbert Kelly.[1]

Kelly was born in Pickens County, Alabama, on March 31, 1840. Orphaned at the age of six, he was raised by a grandmother in Pineapple, Alabama, until he entered West Point in 1857. Young Kelly was faced with a decision in 1861: to stay loyal to his country or join the state of his birth in secession.

Molton Buchanan, seen here after the war, served in three different companies of the Fifty-Eighth. He enlisted in Company B in May 1862 and transferred to Company E that June. He served in that company until July and transferred to Company K. He served as a drummer for part of that time (courtesy Robert Morgan).

He chose the latter and resigned from the academy. Kelly traveled to Montgomery and was commissioned a second lieutenant in the Confederate artillery. Stationed at Fort Morgan for a brief time, Kelly soon joined the staff of "Old Reliable"—William Hardee. Kelly was promoted to captain and served as Hardee's assistant adjutant general. On September 23, 1861, Kelly was commissioned major of the Fourteenth Arkansas, and during the battle of Shiloh in April 1862, he was commanding the Ninth Arkansas battalion. A month later, Kelly was promoted again, now serving as colonel of the Eighth Arkansas. At the battle of Perryville, Kelly is said to have personally captured the colonel of the Twenty-Second Indiana, and at Murfreesboro, he was wounded in the arm. In September 1863, the twenty-three-year-old Kelly was assigned a newly formed brigade composed of the Sixty-Fifth Georgia, Fifth Kentucky, Sixty-Third Virginia, and the Fifty-Eighth North Carolina. Kelly's unit was known as the Third Brigade, and was assigned to Preston's division, Buckner's corps.[2]

The commander of the Federal Army of the Cumberland was William S. Rosecrans. In late August, he implemented a plan to force Bragg out of Chattanooga by cutting the Confederate supply lines at Atlanta. Rosecrans successfully bluffed Bragg into thinking he was going to cross to the north and east of Chattanooga, while his real intentions were to cross to the south. On August 29, Rosecrans began to move, slowly encircling Bragg from the west. Bragg sought opportunities for offensive operations. To that end, he ordered the corps under the command of D. H. Hill and Buckner to prepare themselves. Buckner's command, including the Fifty-Eighth, was ordered from the Hiwassee to the vicinity of Ooltewah, Tennessee.

The September 4 order found the Fifty-Eighth near a large spring about two miles from Georgetown, Tennessee. On September 5, the day Buckner received his orders, the Fifty-Eighth moved back through Georgetown, covering fifteen miles before camping near another large spring. The following day, the regiment moved to Tanner's Station, starting about sundown and stopping near midnight. On the seventh, according to Private Dugger (Company D), they "cooked four days rations and marched two miles and camped." Instead of a making an advance, however, Bragg changed his mind, based upon reports from Buckner's scouts to the north and Federal demonstrations to the west.[3]

Bragg's continued vacillation was due to a lack of credible information, as well as corps level officers who simply refused to obey his orders. The latter problem followed Bragg throughout his tenure as an army commander. Many of his senior lieutenants disliked him, believing that he was incompetent. In battlefield situations, men like Corps Commander Leonidas Polk refused to carry out Bragg's orders, thus on more than one occasion costing the Confederate army potential victories. Polk was a personal friend of Confederate President Jefferson Davis, who refused to see Polk's inabilities to work with other Commanders.[4]

Finally, on the evening of September 7, Bragg ordered the abandonment of Chattanooga; he was planning to join with Buckner and concentrate near Rome, Georgia. Buckner's corps was to follow Walker's corps and the army's supply train on an easterly track via Graysville. Private Dugger wrote in his diary that the Fifty-Eighth broke camp around ten in the evening and marched all night. They arrived at Chickamauga, Georgia, about daylight and rested until 10:00 A.M., when they again took up the line of march, moving six miles before halting. On September 9, they moved through Ringgold, Georgia, traveling another ten miles before stopping and cooking rations.[5]

With the mountains of north Georgia shielding many of the army's movements, neither Bragg nor Rosecrans knew much about the deployment of the other. Rosecrans firmly believed that the Confederate army was demoralized and in full retreat, possibly as far back

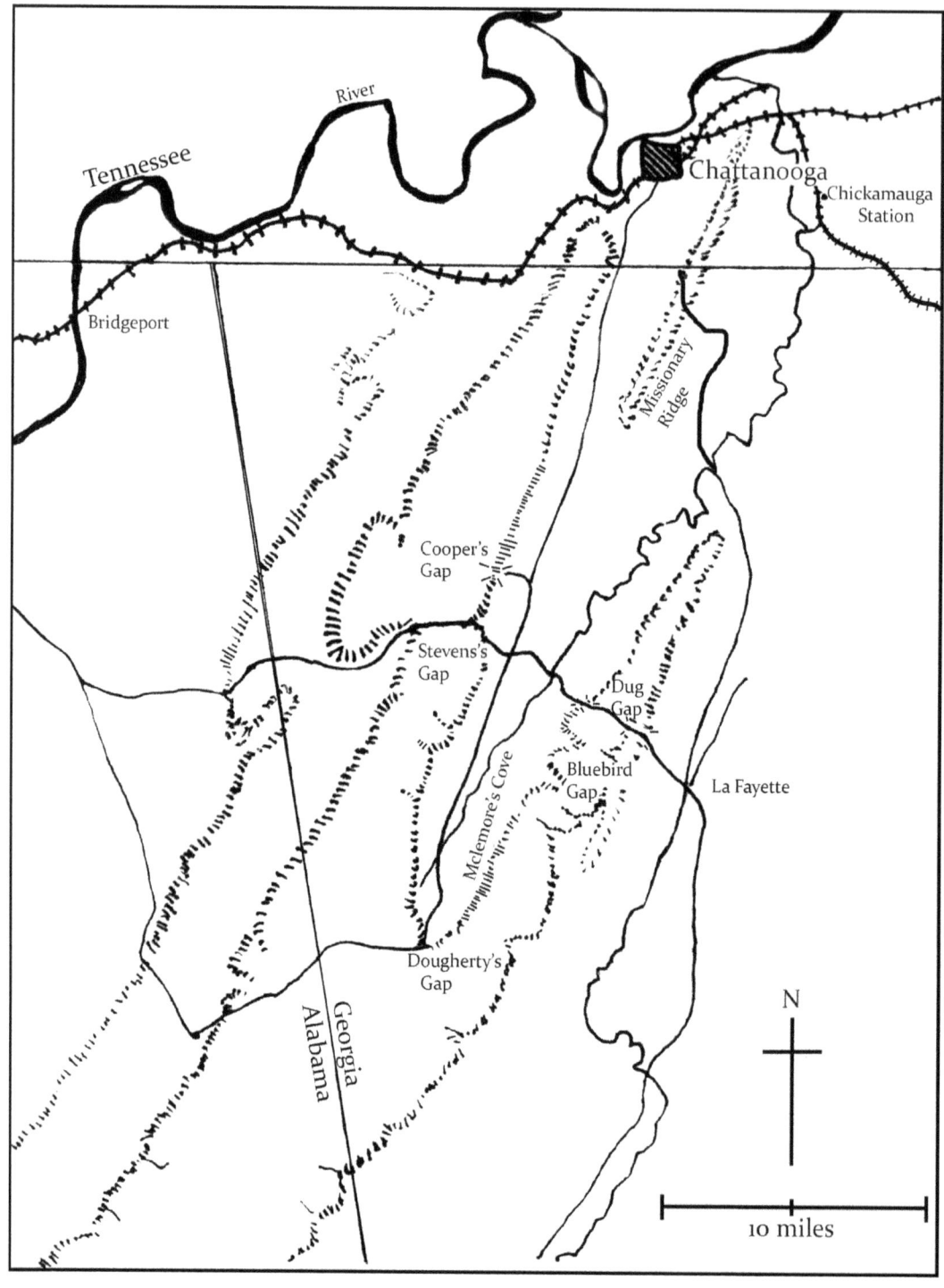

The Fifty-Eighth was all over north Georgia in the fall of 1863.

as Atlanta. Bragg was looking for an opportunity to strike at Rosecrans, and he soon found one. On the evening of September 9, Bragg learned that a portion of the Federal XIV Corps was in McLemore's Cove and was isolated from support. McLemore's Cove was a cul-de-sac, formed by Lookout Mountain to the to the west and Pigeon Mountain to the east. The valley was seven miles long. There were two gaps on the west (Federal) side of the valley, and three gaps on the east side. A division of the XIV Corps, some 5,000 men, had advanced through one of the gaps and was camped near Davis' Crossroads in the Cove. Bragg's plan was to attack the isolated division on multiple fronts, driving them into the narrow end of McLemore's Cove, where they could be captured. He chose a division under Maj. Gen. Thomas C. Hindman to move some thirteen miles and strike the Federals in the flank, while a division under Patrick Cleburne advanced through another gap, striking the Federals in the front. Hindman began moving his division about 1:30 A.M. on September 10.[6]

The Fifty-Eighth fought under General Braxton Bragg's direction at Chickamauga and Chattanooga (courtesy the Library of Congress).

Bragg's plan of action began to fall apart three hours later. General Hill, Cleburne's corps commander, informed Bragg that he could not participate in the attack. Hindman also bogged down four miles from his objective, waiting for Hill and worried about Federals on his right flank. Once Bragg learned of Hill's disposition, instead of cancelling the movement, he substituted Buckner's Corps in Hill's place. Buckner could follow Hindman up Worthen's Gap Road and into the cove.

The Fifty-Eighth had only covered one mile on September 10 before orders came to halt and prepare rations. The men were able to rest for most of the day, until orders arrived that evening and the regiment moved six miles and then went into camp. Buckner arrived at Hindman's headquarters about five P.M. The reinforcements that Buckner brought did nothing to motivate Hindman to attack. Bragg did his best to motivate Hindman, writing at 6:00 P.M., "It is highly important that you should finish the movement now going on as rapidly as possible." and again at 7:30 P.M.: "The enemy is now divided.... It is important now to move vigorously and crush him." Instead of acting swiftly, Hindman, Buckner, and other brigade commanders held a council of war and voted to disregard Bragg's orders.[7]

Bragg's opportunity to destroy a portion of Rosecrans's army was still present on the morning of September 11. During the night, Bragg informed Hindman that his orders could not be changed and that Hindman would attack. That same night, Cleburne's men had removed the obstacles at Dug Gap, one of Hill's problems, and were waiting for the sound of Hindman's attack to launch their own. Hindman still hesitated. In a strange move, he ordered Buckner's two-division corps, camped a mile behind his own men, to lead the attack. There was a single road for all of these men to use, and it took time to get Buckner's

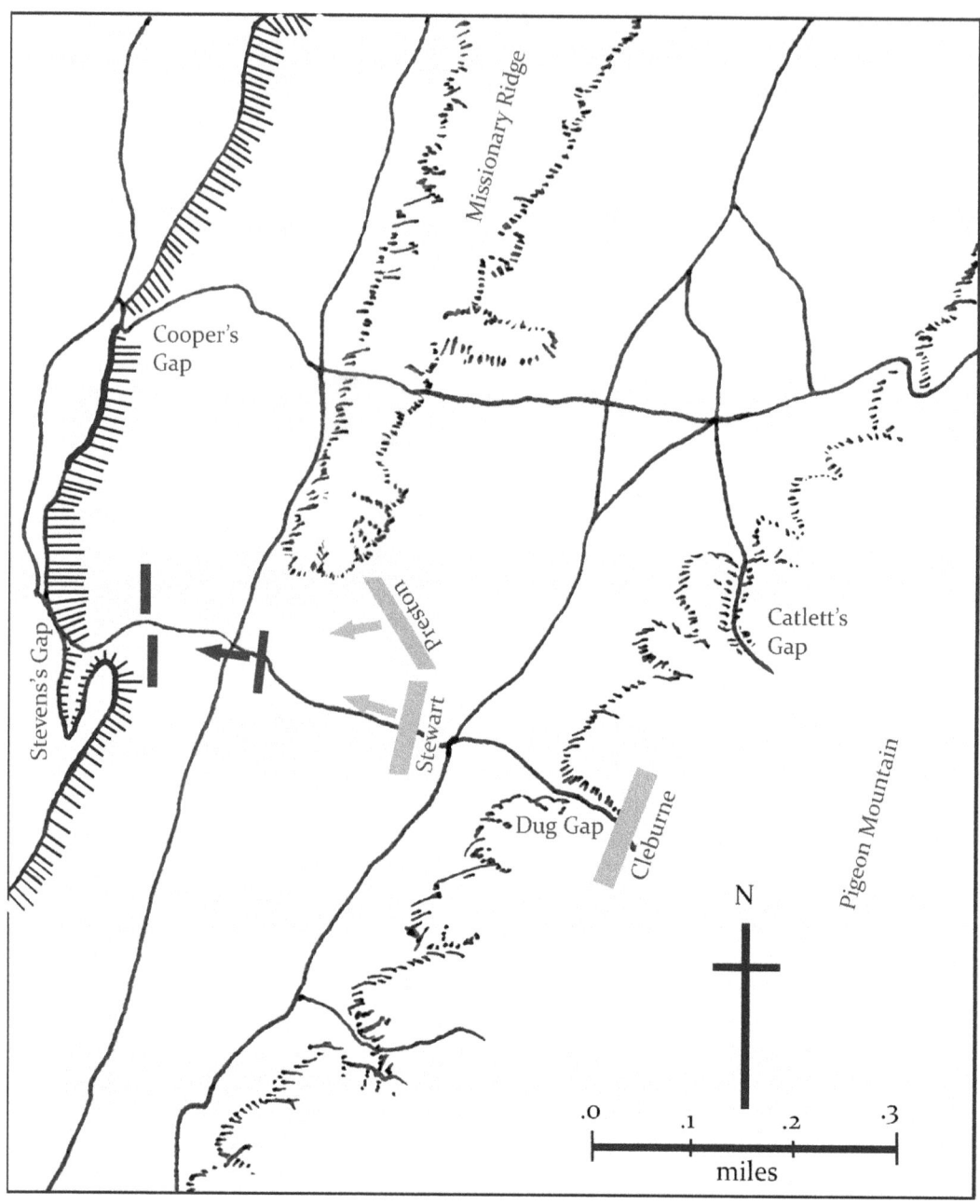

It was due to the disobedience of his lieutenants that Braxton Bragg was unable to destroy a portion of the Federal army at McLemore's Cove.

men into position. Alexander Stewart's division led the way, followed by Preston's division and the Fifty-Eighth. Hindman, who had 15,000 men under his command, was now facing 8,000 Federals. Hindman then decided to retreat and started issuing orders. He then learned that the Federals in his front were withdrawing, and Hindman finally decided to attack. It was close to 4:00 P.M.[8]

Buckner's command was positioned with his left on the spurs of Pigeon Mountain, and his right across Cove Road. He had placed Stewart's division in front, followed by Preston's division, but the order of the brigades is unknown. "The deployment of my column in the midst of a very dense undergrowth," wrote Buckner, "through which the eye could penetrate but a few yards, was necessarily attended with considerable delay and difficulty." Skirmishing had taken place all morning. Once the order arrived from Hindman to attack, Stewart's division advanced. Preston's division, including the Fifty-Eighth, was ordered to move by the flank to the right, and "to form *en echelon* on his right." Anderson's division of Hindman's corps was moved toward Lee's Mill in an attempt to cut off the retreat of the Federals. Cleburne then joined in on the attack, but saw few Federal soldiers. Dugger recalled that after the regiment marched four miles, the Fifty-Eighth engaged the enemy. However, almost all the Federals escaped through Stevens's Gap.[9]

Even though the Fifty-Eighth had been in Confederate service for thirteen months and had seen action while chasing bushwhackers in eastern Tennessee and Kentucky, this appears to be the first time the regiment as a whole was actually drawn up into a line of battle and engaged the enemy. Any causalities sustained by the Fifty-Eighth went unrecorded. The Fifty-Eighth remained in a line of battle on the battlefield until 10 o'clock that evening, when the men "took up a line of march for Lafayette, Ga."[10]

The Fifty-Eighth was a part of William Preston's division. Preston had been the Fifty-Eighth's departmental commander for a time while the regiment was in east Tennessee. Born in 1816 in Louisville, Kentucky, Preston was a graduate of Harvard and a practicing lawyer. During the Mexican War, he served as colonel of the Fourth Kentucky Volunteers. Preston represented Kentucky in the United States Congress from December 1852 until March 1855, and was a minister to Spain from 1858 until 1861. He then served as an aide-de-camp to his brother-in-law, Albert S. Johnston, and on April 14, 1862, was promoted to brigadier general. Preston's division contained three brigades. Brig. Gen. Archibald Gracie, Jr.'s, brigade was from Alabama; Col. Robert C. Trigg's brigade was composed of three Florida regiments and one Virginia regiment. The last brigade belonged to Kelly.[11]

Following the affair at McLemore's Cove, the Fifty-Eighth marched until 2:00 A.M. on the twelfth. After a short rest, the regiment moved on towards LaFayette, "pushing wagons up the Pigeon Mountain." They went into camp about 11:00 P.M. and prepared rations.[12]

Bragg tried to attack a portion of Rosecrans's command at Lee and Gordon's Mill on the morning of September 13. And, once again, General Polk refused to carry out the commander's orders. Polk went into a defensive position and asked for reinforcements. Bragg ordered Polk to once again attack, sending Buckner's corps to support the movement. Again Polk refused, and the opportunity was lost. For the next five days, Rosecrans concentrated his attention on the Army of the Cumberland. While Rosecrans was drawing closer, Bragg was receiving reinforcements, both from Mississippi and from Virginia. From the Army of Northern Virginia, Bragg received two divisions of Longstreet's corps, portions of which arrived on September 18. Chickamauga Creek separated the two armies. Bragg's battle plan was to take the crossings over the creek and turn Rosecrans's right flank, cutting him off from his base in Chattanooga and forcing Rosecrans back into McLemore's Cove. The upcoming fight provided the Confederates a rare advantage. Rosecrans's army numbered 62,000, while Bragg could muster 65,000.

September 14, 15, and 16 brought a reprieve from the marching for the Fifty-Eighth. The men of the regiment remained camped in a grove near LaFayette, resting for the battle they and everyone else knew was coming. On the morning of the seventeenth, the regiment

Both Sgt. Elijah Crump (Company H), on the left, and Capt. Isaac Bailey (Company B), on the right, were seriously wounded during the battle of Chickamauga. Neither returned to the Fifty-Eighth North Carolina Troops (courtesy the North Carolina Department of Archives and History).

set out, marching about twelve miles and going into camp in Peavine Valley. That evening, or possibly the next, Palmer sought to strengthen the field and staff of the Fifty-Eighth. The regiment had been without a lieutenant colonel since the resignation of Keener in June. To fill the void, Palmer temporarily promoted his adjutant, Edmund Kirby, to the post. Kirby spent the evening cutting "four stars out of tin, and affixed them to his collar to designate his rank." The four stars, two on each collar, symbolized the rank of lieutenant colonel.[13]

Fighting erupted on the afternoon of September 18 as Bragg sought to capture two crossings on the Chickamauga River. The fighting took place to the north of Buckner's command and succeeded in pushing the Federals back. Orders came for Buckner's corps to cross over the Chickamauga, and Preston's division used Dalton's Ford as its crossing. Kelly's brigade remained on the south side of the creek. Private Dugger (Company D) recalled that the Fifty-Eighth "lay in a cornfield under the sound of Yankee shells all night." The Fifty-Eighth was witness to thousands of Confederate troops as they spent their night in the cornfield. According to Capt. Isaac Bailey, the men were even denied fires that evening, in fear of giving away their position. Cheatham's division, the largest in the Army of Tennessee, was ordered to the front and chose Dalton's Ford as the place to pass.[14]

About daylight, Kelly's brigade received orders to ford the creek. Some of the men took off their shoes and socks and rolled up their trouser legs. Others might have even removed their trousers. A few probably thought it too much work and plunged into the brown creek water fully clothed. At 8:00 A.M., Preston's division formed a line of battle near the home of the Hunt family. Kelly's brigade, posted in a cornfield, went in to the left of Stewart's division. Kelly posted his regiment: the Fifty-Eighth on the right, Sixty-Fifth Georgia in the center, and the Fifth Kentucky on the left. The Sixty-Third Virginia was guarding the division's ordnance trains. Gracie's brigade was in front of Kelly's, and Trigg's brigade behind. "Here the brigade," reported Kelly, "was subjected to a brisk cannonade from the enemy's batteries." Captain Bailey of Company B wrote after the war: "After remaining in line about forty-five minutes the command was given 'Unfurl your banners.' At this moment the sun broke forth, dispelling the fog, and as our banners floated out on the breeze the Federals, our enemy, General Boynton's command ... commenced playing 'Yankee Doodle' and to move eastward on an almost parallel line with ours."

No losses were reported by the Fifty-Eighth. Stewart's division was ordered elsewhere, and Preston was ordered to move his division to the north-northwest. Trigg's brigade was sent in support of Hood, and Kelly was posted in support of some Confederate artillery. The brigade was subjected to an occasional shelling for the rest of the evening. The only recorded loss of the day was Pvt. Andrew Shehan of Company F, who was "shocked by a bum shell in the left side and shoulder." To protect the left of Longstreet's line, Kelly's and Gracie's brigades constructed breastworks in front of their positions.[15]

William Deyton (Company C) was a carpenter prior to enlisting in May 1862. He deserted twice, once before the battle of Chickamauga and the second time on June 22, 1864, the day of the battle of Kolb's Farm (courtesy Michael Ledford).

Earlier that day, Federal troops set out to destroy what they believed to be an isolated Confederate brigade. This small action quickly escalated into one of the bloodiest battles in the Western Theater of the war. At one point during the day, the Confederates penetrated the Federal lines, cutting Rosecrans off from Chattanooga. Federal reinforcements soon plugged the gap and pushed the Confederates back. Most of the area where the battle took place was extremely wooded, making it difficult for a commander to see a whole regiment, much less brigade and divisional formations. Thus the battle was often waged between regiments, and even at times, companies of men. At the end of September 19, the enemy had held against repeated Confederate assaults. That evening, the Federals pulled back towards the LaFayette Road and entrenched, building breastworks of logs and earth. Meanwhile, General Longstreet arrived from Virginia. Bragg reorganized his army into two grand wings during the night. Longstreet had command over the left wing, while Polk commanded the right. The Fifty-Eighth and Kelly's brigade were now under Longstreet. It was an odd move, reorganizing the Army of Tennessee while a vicious battle raged. In the darkness, with the smoke hanging over the battlefield, Longstreet could not even find some of his commanders.

Frost covered the ground as the soldiers awoke to another day of carnage. It was Sunday, and not only frost but fog and smoke covered the battlefield. The area had been exceptionally dry, and the fire belched forth by the artillery and small arms had caught the thick underbrush on fire at certain points. Some members of the Fifty-Eighth, with combat suddenly imminent, slipped off into the north Georgia countryside. Nine men left on September 17.

One, Pvt. Bartlett Johnson (Company D), left the following day. On September 19, nine more left, including Second Lieutenant William Howington (Company D). Seven more were gone on September 20: twenty-six men in four days. Only thirteen returned. Five of the men, privates Hugh Williams (Company L), Bartlett Johnson (Company D), William Ledford (Company C), and Andrew Harmon (Company D), deserted for the second time. None of these men came back.[16]

Bragg's plan of battle for September 20 was simple: the attack was to start on the Confederate right and move all down the line. The Federals would be cut off from Chattanooga. Once again, Polk failed Bragg, and the attack was several hours late in getting started. The Confederates again penetrated the Federal left, but were driven back. A little after 11:00 A.M., Rosecrans, believing that the shifting of one Federal division had created a gap on his left, ordered another Federal division to shift toward the left. This created a real gap in the Federal lines, just opposite from where Longstreet had massed his wing for an attack. Longstreet had taken all morning to form his men. While Stewart's division moved off to the right trying to find the left of Polk's corps, Longstreet placed Bushrod Johnson's division in the lead, followed by Hood's division. Kershaw's and Humphrey's brigades were ordered to fall in behind Hood. Hindman's division was on the left, with Preston's division in the rear, serving as a pivot for the move to the left as the entire left wing advanced.[17]

Longstreet launched his attack a few minutes after 11:00 A.M. Davis's Federal division was attempting to close the gap in the line when the Confederates struck. Davis's men were swept away. A second Federal division under Phil Sheridan was also swept away. Turning his attention to his right, Longstreet ordered his men to take out massed Federal artillery, which they did, capturing seventeen prized cannons. A portion of Wood's division was soon thereafter forced off the field. Many of the Federals retreated farther north, and prepared a defensive line along Horseshoe Ridge and Snodgrass Hill. The victorious Confederates expected to easily push the Federals out of their hilltop position as they had earlier. However, repeated but disjointed Confederate assaults failed to drive the Federals off the hill.

Earlier that morning, Kelly moved his brigade about 300 yards to the left, supporting three batteries of Confederate artillery. Kelly ordered skirmishers to the front, and four companies marched out under the command of Lieutenant Colonel Kirby. Two of those companies were from the Fifty-Eighth, Companies A and B. The skirmishers advanced towards Alexander's brigade, creating a barrier between the Federals to their front and the main Confederate line. Any attempt to charge the Confederates would be discovered first by the skirmishers, allowing them to fire warning shots as they retreated back

Lt. Gen. James Longstreet arrived in the middle of the battle of Chancellorsville and became the Fifty-Eighth's commander (courtesy the Library of Congress).

The Fifty-Eighth North Carolina spent the night of September 19–20 in this position, at times exposed to artillery fire.

toward their lines. Skirmishers were often deployed with about five yards between each man, allowing a few men to cover a wide front. The skirmishers advanced toward the Creek. "When we had gone nearly half way down through the field, we could see fortifications all up and down the river the full length of the field and about twenty-five yards from the river bank," recalled Captain Bailey.

> Notwithstanding we knew that the enemy was behind the breastworks, we had to advance to feel his strength. So we slowly advanced until we came to the fortifications of fence rails leaning from our advance in the directions of the river to where the enemy had fallen back to and under the bank of the river to draw us over, then to fire on us as we would have to retreat over the fortifications just passed. As soon as the line of skirmishers had passed over the fortifications, the enemy fired from their ranks, three or four men deep, a most galling and enfilading fire into our ranks. We had now ascertained by sad and painful experience what we had been sent out to do.... We were then obliged to retreat through the rail fortifications upon the woods and across the old fields of broom straw waving in melancholy wind, and over a number of our most loved comrades left dead on the field. One of them, Thos. G. Tipton, had just saved the writer's life.[18]

Near the middle of the day, Buckner sent orders to Preston to advance his division. The skirmishers were recalled and Preston placed Gracie's brigade on the left, Kelly on the right, and Trigg in reserve. The men were positioned in a line of battle across the Chattanooga road in front of a house belonging to the Brotherton family. "The enemy in some fields on the north," wrote Preston, "maintained an active fire of shot and shell on my troops" throughout the afternoon. A number of artillery-related injuries were reported, likely occurring at this time. William C. Coffey, quartermaster sergeant, was injured "in the right side by a piece of a bomb shell." Pvt. Joseph Green (Company B) was struck by a shell or piece of a shell "knocking him down and breaking the breast bone." Pvt. James Stewart of the same company lost his hearing by the "bursting of a shell." Sgt. Julius Smith (Company H) was also struck and wounded by a piece of an artillery shell. Around 4:00 P.M., Longstreet came to the conclusion that driving the Federals off Snodgrass Hill would make him "complete master of the field." Longstreet called for his last reserve, Preston's division.[19]

Preston brought two of his three brigades forward. Trigg's brigade was held back to investigate a rumored advance by Federal cavalry. An aide guided Preston's men through the woods and into a field near Snodgrass Hill. Kelly was absent and Colonel Palmer had command of the brigade. "From the edge of Dyer's field," wrote Preston, "the ground descends to a wooded ravine, and after two or three intervening depressions, each succeeding height being more elevated, you reach the summit of the ridge, which is some 200 feet above the level of the plain." It was through these woods and ravines and up this hill that Preston's men needed to charge. Preston positioned Gracie's brigade on the right and Kelly's brigade on the left. Later, when Trigg arrived, his brigade was positioned on Kelly's left. Palmer posted Kelly's brigade with the Fifty-Eighth on the right, the Sixty-Third to their left, and the Fifth Kentucky to the Sixty-Third's left. The brigade was soon ordered to go support Anderson's brigade, which it promptly did.[20]

Colonel Kelly soon returned to command his brigade, and Palmer returned to the command of the Fifty-Eighth. The order to hold fire until close to the enemy was given, and the brigade surged through the woods. The advance sounded, and the division stepped off into the woods. The idea was for Kelly to advance in support of Gracie's brigade. Gracie, however, started off before Kelly could get his men formed. Furthermore, the ravine to the front of Kelly pushed his brigade away from Gracie. Kelly's brigade advanced 300 to 400 yards at the double quick, and under fire almost the whole time. "My men moved with calmness and deliberation," Palmer wrote after the battle. As they neared the top, Palmer discovered that instead of attacking the fortified Federals all along his front, he was actually hitting their line at an angle. The right of Palmer's line stopped just "10 or 12 feet" from the enemy's works.

Once the Fifty-Eighth stopped, the men let loose a volley into the Federal lines. Over the din of battle, someone started yelling that they were firing at friends. The center and the left of the Fifty-Eighth stopped firing for a short time to ascertain the truth, but the right of the regiment continued trading volleys with the Federals, namely the Eighty-Seventh Indiana and the Ninth Ohio. Palmer's old command, Company A, under Capt. Frederick Tobey, appears to have been on the far right of the regiment. Tobey took thirty-four men into the fight. Twenty-two of those were killed or wounded. John Huffman was struck in the thigh; Francis Biddix's right forearm was broken, and he was struck in the hand; Jasper Wise was wounded in the left arm; and William H. Wiseman in the right arm. Joshua Keller, Jeremiah Martin, William McBee, Arthur McFalls, William Phifer, Samuel Poteet, and Theron Sherwood were all killed.[21]

The fire poured into the ranks of the Fifty-Eighth was almost beyond endurance. "Push them men ... push them," yelled Lieutenant Colonel Kirby over the noise of the battle. Just at that instant, Kirby was struck, pierced by four bullets. Palmer, writing to Kirby's brother after the war, stated that two of the balls penetrated two of the newly sewn stars on Kirby's jacket collar. As Kirby fell, three messmates of his, John Eben Childs, Theron Sherwood, and William L. Phifer, all rushed to his side. All three were struck. Childs was pierced by

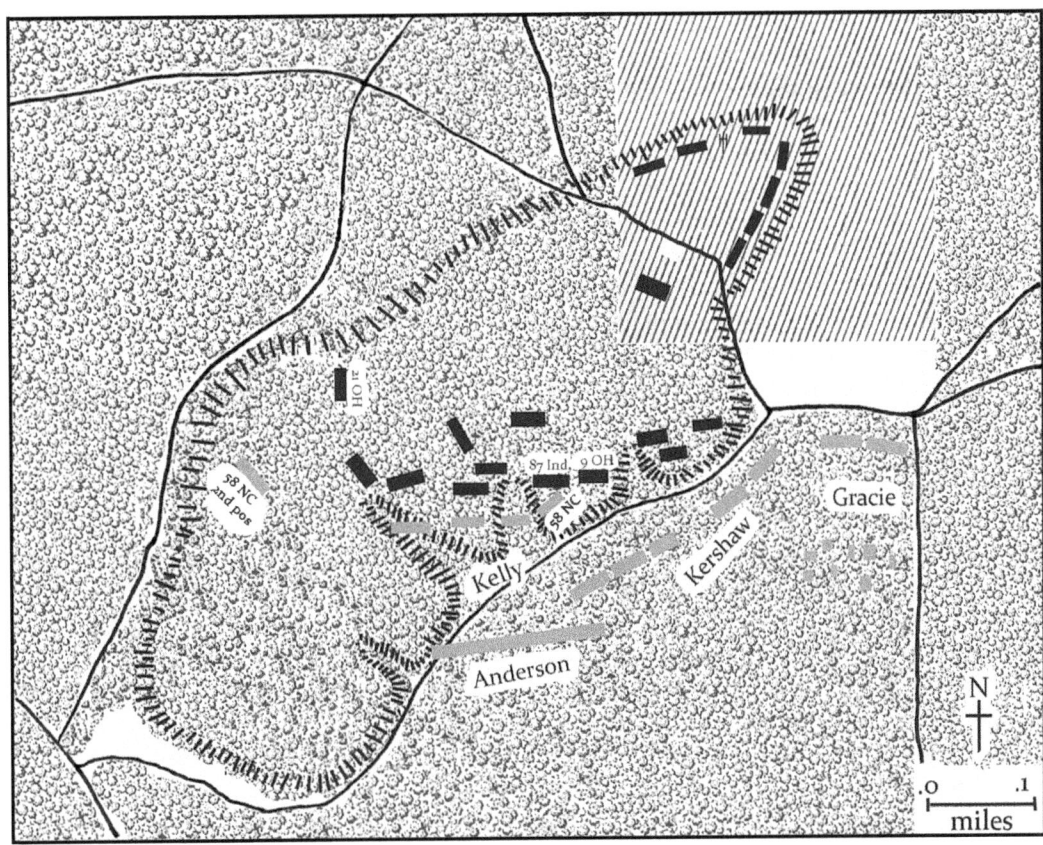

Kelly's brigade, including the Fifty-Eighth, went into action late on September 20 and helped drive the Federals off Snodgrass Hill. The regiment's first position is in the center of the map, and its final position is on the left.

three bullets, two in the head and one in the chest. Isaac Bailey wrote after the war of Childs, "whose smooth girlish face I see before me know, and whose bright sword flashed for the last time in the in the rays of the setting sun as he fell within twenty steps of the enemy's line. His beardless face ablaze with the animation of battle, and his youthful figure transformed into a hero's statue. The dry, parched earth of Snodgrass Hill was never reddened with nobler blood, and a braver man or boy never died."[22]

On the Fifty-Eighth's right, the fire of the enemy was so great and the losses so severe that portions of the regiment started to give way. Palmer rode to the right and rallied his men. Captain Tobey (Company A) soon found himself between the two lines, "with sword raised overhead appealing to his men to rally and come back to the charge," driving them back up the hill. Palmer then noticed that the attack had stalled, and ordered his regiment to lie down and continue firing at the Federals. Had "not the advance been checked by the report that we were firing upon our friends," Palmer wrote after the battle, "we would have swept the enemy from his position at our first charge." Jasper Moore (Company E) had "a passing bullet graze his scalp. He had just rescued his captain whose horse was shot twice from under him." Another soldier, Alfred H. Craige (Company H), was struck in the cheek. According to the family, he swallowed the bullet. Sgt. Theodore McGimsey (Company F) felt a blow to his abdomen and then his arm. It seems that a minié ball was deflected by McGimsey's pocket watch in his vest before striking him in the arm. McGimsey also had two muskets shot from his hands during the battle. Payton Phillips (Company G), according to his family, was "struck in the forehead with a lead pellet and lay unconscious for several hours behind a log where he was hiding. When he awoke, there were many dead bodies, but the battle had moved on. He picked a handful of bones from his forehead" and stumbled off, looking for a field hospital. First Sergeant Elijah Crump (Company H) was struck four times: right leg, right knee, right shoulder, and left foot. He was left between the lines as the Confederates fell back, and all believed that his wounds were mortal. Crump survived the war but never rejoined the regiment.[23]

The Fifty-Eighth stayed in position for about an hour, until 6:00 P.M., when Kelly chose to revive his attack. The Fifty-Eighth was pulled back and marched by the left flank beyond the end of Kelly's line. A portion of the Federal line had given way for want of ammunition, and Kelly sought to roll up the Federal right flank. It was now twilight, and the cartridge boxes of the Fifty-Eighth were also almost empty. The "ammunition was nearly, and in some instances quite, exhausted," Palmer testified. Once the regiment got into position, it commenced to charge up the hill into the smoke and near darkness. At the same instant, the Twenty-First Ohio came crashing down the hill. The Ohioans only had about one round of ammunition per man, which they let loose into the advancing Tar Heels. The regiment on Palmer's right had given way, or could not be found in the darkness. "The charge was abandoned and my men sought protection behind trees, such of them as had any ammunition continuing to fire vigorously."

Palmer attempted to reform the Fifty-Eighth in the darkness for yet another charge. "Fancying soon after that the enemy had discontinued firing, I ordered my men to cease firing." Palmer tried to send word to Kelly that an advance would "probably carry the enemy's position without further opposition." Kelly could not be found. The brigade commander had lost his horse in the late afternoon attack, and Palmer was informed that Kelly had been summoned by Preston to the rear for consultation. Palmer moved the Fifty-Eighth by the right flank and found the rest of the brigade. The exact order of events is not clear, but it appears that as the Fifty-Eighth found the rest of the brigade, portions of which were starting to make a final push up the hill. With Kelly still absent, command fell to Palmer, and with portions of the Fifth Kentucky, Sixty-Third Virginia, and Fifty-Eighth North Carolina, he finished routing the Federals off the ridge. Over 250 prisoners were captured, including 20 by the Fifty-Eighth.[24]

Rosecrans had quit the field earlier in the day, and by dusk he was back in Chattanooga. He issued orders for the Federal army to retreat. The Federal right on Snodgrass Hill was wrecked. As the Federal left was pulling back, the Confederates under Polk chose to charge again. Pandemonium set in among several of the Federal regiments. Many were captured before the Federal army retreated to Rossville and then back into Chattanooga.

Overall, the Federals had lost 16,170 men killed, wounded, or captured. The Confederates had lost 18,454 men in three days' worth of fighting. The rest of Kelly's brigade fell back, and the Fifty-Eighth was left alone. Palmer's men swept over the scene and "gathered a portion of the dead and all of our wounded, caused details from my regiment, assisted by the infirmary corps, to convey the latter to the foot of the ridge, and the former to the division hospital established near by." Palmer, writing just five days after the close of the battle, estimated that "every field and staff officer and one-half of the balance of the regiment [was] killed or wounded." Palmer himself had been slightly wounded during the fray. An article on October 8 in the Raleigh *Daily Progress* gave 161 men killed, mortally wounded, wounded, or missing. A further study of the records states that 57 men were killed or mortally wounded, 117 wounded, and one captured for a total of 175 men. Many of the men who were slightly wounded were probably not included in this account.[25]

For the seriously wounded, their plight was almost unbearable. Captain Bailey had advanced to the field and staff to help command the regiment after the loss of Lieutenant Colonel Kirby and Major Dula. Bailey was shot through the right side; his leg was broken; and "one ear [was] almost severed from his head." Berry Stewart, a member of Bailey's company, was wounded in the hand, neck, right arm, and left shoulder. Lt. William Austin (Company C) was struck in the right shoulder, leg, and hip. While Austin survived his wound, he never returned to duty. Pvt. Robert Patton was wounded in the head, face, and both thighs.[26]

During battle, the surgeon of the regiment often chose a position near the battle to establish a hospital. In the Confederate army, usually the surgeons from the regiments in a brigade, or at times a division, established their hospitals together. The Fifty-Eighth's hospital was located in a deserted house about three miles from Lee and Gordon's Mill. Surgeons always tried to establish the hospitals near springs or creeks to provide water for the men. The assistant surgeon of the regiment often remained near the front lines, trying to helped wounded men to the rear. If a man was wounded and able to walk or stumble along using something for a crutch, he made his way to the rear in hopes of finding a hospital. The wounded who were unable to walk simply lay upon the field, at times for hours or even days, until a friend came by to help them to the rear, or members of the infirmary corps came along with a stretcher.

At Chickamauga, like at Chancellorsville the previous May, the woods caught fire and some of the wounded who were unable to crawl to safety were consumed by the flames. There is no evidence of anyone from the Fifty-Eighth being assigned as a stretcher bearer during the Chickamauga time period. It is also unknown if Thomas Mitchell, a Griffin, Georgia, resident who is listed as assistant surgeon of the Fifty-Eighth during the battle of Chickamauga, circulated among the men. The surgeon at this time was William Harriss, who had previously served as assistant surgeon of the Sixty-First North Carolina Troops. Hospital steward was Thomas Young, a former member of Company C.[27]

Conditions at field hospitals were almost unspeakable. There were many more patients than could be properly attended. The wounded were placed in rows, possibly on a little straw if such a luxury could be found, awaiting their turn. Once on the surgeon's tables, the soldier had his wound examined. The common soldier's weapon of the day fired a large, soft lead projectile at a low velocity. The wounds that these weapons produced were horrific. One surgeon in the Army of Tennessee noted, "The shattering, splintering, and splitting of a long bone by the impact of the minié or Enfield ball were, in many cases, both remarkable and frightful, and early experience taught surgeons that amputation ... was the only means of saving life." Amputation was often the only remedy when a soldier had been struck in one of the limbs, and the common medical thinking of the time held that a soldier stood a better chance of surviving if his amputation occurred within twenty-four hours of his wounding. Once the man was on the table, the doctor probed the wound, and then, having decided upon amputation, he tied off the limb, produced a bone saw, and began to cut away. Often, stimulants used as anesthesia were not available, and surgery was performed without them. Once the limb was off, the surgeon sutured up the stump, bandaged the wound, and had the soldier placed to the side. The next wounded soldier was brought in, placed on the same table, and the doctor once again started probing the wound. Instruments, tables, and even the doctor's hands were seldom, if ever, cleaned between patients. Any disease that had already begun to set in might easily be transferred to other patients.

Since the Fifty-Eighth, with the rest of Kelly's brigade, went into the fight late in the day, care for the battlefield wounded was practiced by candlelight. As soon as transportation could be acquired, the wounded were loaded on wagons and taken to the depot, where they were loaded on trains and taken to hospitals farther south. Many were transported out of the Tunnel Hill Depot to hospitals in Ringgold, Kingston, Dalton, and Atlanta. David Lanier (Company E) was struck in the leg during the battle. He was first taken to the Floyd House and later transported to the Ocmulgee Hospital in Macon, Georgia.[28]

The Fifty-Eighth was resupplied with ammunition and spent the night camped on the field that they had won. Monday, September 21, was spent gathering the discarded arms and the wounded, and burying the dead. Private Gouge remarked in a letter home that on Monday, "All was calm only the terrible groans of the wounded which were heard in every direction." General Preston reported that his men gathered some 4,500 stands of arms "thrown away by the fleeing enemy." The burial of the dead was an unenviable task. Shovels had to be procured, and the ground was exceptionally hard and rocky. Coffins were not available, so the men were buried wrapped in their blankets. Palmer had Edmund Kirby, John Eben Childs, John Wiseman, James Morrison (Company H) and Theron Sherwood interred together. He wrote two letters to John Eben's father, informing him of his son's death, that Palmer had kept a lock of his hair, and where the grave was located so that Colonel Childs could find him. "I had his body removed to a house near by," wrote a bereaved Palmer, and

> had him buried next to Lt. Col. Kirby placing a board at the head of the grave—I directed Capt. Phillips to see to it[.] [A]t afternoon, as soon as I was able, went down & saw that it was done—The graves are in a field about one hundred fifty yards, twenty or thirty yards to the left of the upper springs & near a horse lot with black oak trees—The graves are near the lower edge of a large peach orchard. The house was a deserted one and was a temporary hospital by Genl. Prestons Division & some others—It was about 3 miles from Lees Mill.... I think but I am not certain, the former occupant had been driven out by the proximity of the army—I could not ascertain his name. Near the house building was a large pigeon house elevated on a post. It is about one mile from the Chickamauga river that two springs near it walled up with stone [sic]—Was about one half mile from where we fought which was the last & closing fight—I think the house and grave can be found from this description—Everything was done in a great hurry as we were under orders to leave.... I sympathize with you my dear friend in your bereavement—I knew Eben well—I loved him almost as a son. He was a noble boy full of promise and loved by all who knew him well.[29]

Lt. William M. Austin (Company C) was wounded in the right shoulder, leg, and hip during the battle of Chickamauga in September 1863. He did not return to the regiment (courtesy Michael Ledford).

There was many a noble boy full of promise lost on September 20.

John Eben Childs was disinterred in October

and taken to Elmwood Cemetery in Columbia, South Carolina, for burial. Edmund Kirby was taken to Richmond. His funeral was preached by the Rev. Dr. Moore at the First Presbyterian Church on October 30. His remains were re-interred in the Shockoe Cemetery in Richmond, in a plot already containing his brother. The *Daily Dispatch* had this to say about Kirby on the day after his internment: "Young, brave, of fine intellect, and with a noble disposition, he was a great favorite in the army, and had the brightest prospects in the profession he had chosen."[30]

CHAPTER 8

September–December 1863

"We had a hot time of it for awhile."—Cpl. Elijah Norris, Company D

With all the desertions, deaths by disease, and losses incurred at Chickamauga, the Fifty-Eighth North Carolina was wrecked. As the Fifty-Eighth surged up Snodgrass Hill, seventy-four men were listed as absent sick, either in a hospital or on furlough back home. Four were considered under arrest. Thirty-four men were detailed away from the regiment, serving as provost guards, nurses, coopers, or teamsters. A staggering 373 men were either absent without leave or had been declared deserters and did not return to the regiment. By October 1, approximately 205 members of the Fifty-Eighth were dead, either overcome by disease or felled by a Yankee bullet. Added to those numbers were approximately 139 for whom the records are incomplete, and the Fifty-Eighth was short almost 900 men. That was the size of some Confederate regiments when they were originally mustered into service.[1]

Time to rest and resupply did not come for the Fifty-Eighth. Just two days after the battle, the regiment moved six miles towards Chattanooga, spending the night at a creek. Some later condemned Bragg for not moving sooner to confront Rosecrans. The rest of Bragg's army was as decimated as the Fifty-Eighth. The Tar Heels covered an additional two miles on the twenty-third of September, and spent the evening under fire from Yankee shells. The following morning, the regiment fell back about a mile. Late on September 26 or early on the morning of September 27, the Fifty-Eighth was ordered to build breastworks. It took them most of the night. At 4:00 P.M., the regiment was ordered out for picket duty. Captain Harper, who was absent at home during the battle of Chickamauga, had arrived only two hours before the regiment left. The Fifty-Eighth was on picket from 4:00 P.M. on Sunday, the twenty-seventh, through 3:00 P.M. on Tuesday, the twenty-ninth. "Yankees in sight," chronicled Harper, "In sight of Chattanooga."[2]

About this time, possibly before Harper returned to the army, Colonel Palmer was granted a furlough for his slight wound and traveled back home. Since Lieutenant Colonel Kirby was dead and Major Dula was also out wounded, command of the Fifty-Eighth fell on its senior captain, Jonathan Phillips (Company G). Rank was based upon seniority. If there were enough men present to warrant additional field officers, Captain Harper (Company H) served as lieutenant colonel, and Captain Suel Briggs (Company C) as acting major. The senior lieutenants commanded their respective companies.[3]

While Palmer was away, presumably back with his family in western North Carolina, there were many championing for his promotion to brigadier general. General Heth had written to the secretary of war back in August lobbying for Palmer's promotion. Following

Palmer's heroic actions of September 20, General Buckner was the first to write on October 2. After praising Palmer and the Fifty-Eighth for their roles during the Chickamauga battle, Buckner wrote that Palmer was "an officer of marked merit as instructor and disciplinarian." Palmer's division commander, William Preston, next picked up his pen on October 4, writing to the War Department that "I have been associated with Colonel Palmer only since the commencement of the campaign this autumn. His regiment was most gallantly led [during] the battle of Chickamauga in the assault on some strong heights from which our forces had been repulsed. The 58th North Carolina was one of the regiments of Kelly's Brigade of my division [and] though suffering severely, maintained its ground nobly. Colonel Palmer though wounded remained upon the field assisting his men by his example aiding them by his composure." Last to write, on October 7, was Maj. Gen, Carter Stevenson, Palmer's former departmental commander. Stevenson praised Palmer for his previous October's campaign to capture Cumberland Gap, saying that the colonel had Stevenson's "warmest commendation." All of these letters were forwarded to James Seddon, the secretary of war in Richmond. The recommendations were brought before Jefferson Davis, and then upon his approval, forwarded to the Senate for confirmation.[4]

Following the defeat at Chickamauga, the Federal army retreated into Chattanooga and strengthened the fortifications. Bragg believe that the Federals were retreating into middle Tennessee, or even toward Burnside in east Tennessee. When Bragg himself inspected the Federal lines, he saw no retreat, only the strengthening defensive lines. Bragg had three choices: to try outflanking the Federals; to attack using frontal charges; or to starve the Federals out. Since he lacked adequate transportation and pontoons for a flanking maneuver, and since his own army was in shambles following Chickamauga, Bragg chose to lay siege to the town.

As the Army of Tennessee settled down to starve out its foe in Chattanooga, Bragg and his generals once again began to quarrel. Bragg twice asked Polk for an explanation regarding his delay in attacking on the morning of September 20. On September 29, the day after Polk submitted his account, Bragg suspended Polk and Maj. Gen. Thomas Hindman, the latter for his disobedience during the action at McLemore's Cove. Both were sent to Atlanta. Bragg was soon informed that he did not have the authority to suspend officers, and the Army of Tennessee commander promptly brought charges against the two. President Davis shortly arrived from Richmond hoping to quell the disturbance. Davis found the problems within the command structure of the army much greater than he thought. On the evening of October 9, Davis called a meeting with some of Bragg's largest detractors. For the next five days, Davis listened with astonishment to the problems within the Army of Tennessee. The Fifty-Eighth's corps commander, Simon Buckner, and then his superior, James Longstreet, were some of the loudest detractors. They even drafted and signed a petition for Bragg's removal. In the end, Davis chose to retain Bragg. Charges were dismissed against Polk, and he was traded for General Hardee and sent to Mississippi.[5]

Davis left Bragg and the Army of Tennessee on October 14. As the president rode south on his return to Richmond, Bragg set about reorganizing his army. With the blessings of Davis, D. H. Hill was ordered to report to Richmond. Buckner, the Fifty-Eighth's corps commander, lost command of the Department of East Tennessee, and also lost his corps. He remained a division commander under Lt. Gen. William Hardee. Once Bragg finished his reorganization, the Army of Tennessee contained three corps under the command of Longstreet, Breckinridge, and Hardee. Buckner's antagonism toward Bragg over the loss of his command further poisoned the Kentuckian's working relationship with Bragg.[6]

As Davis, Bragg, and the hierarchy of the Army of Tennessee quibbled away in their snug headquarters, the Fifty-Eighth was in the lines in front of Chattanooga. Every few days the regiment rotated on and off picket duty, and drill once again commenced on October 6. At times, the regiment had no tents, and the men were forced to sleep with only their blankets for coverings. Rations were in short supply. Private Dugger (Company D) wrote in his diary on the first of October, "Scarce rations of bread and no meat; but nothing strange." At least twice, the regiment was forced to move camp. The first instance occurred on October 5 as an effort to avoid Federal artillery. The second time was on October 13. The regiment was situated on a small creek. Rain fell all day, and at 11:00 P.M., the rising water forced the regiment to move out. Captain Harper recorded in his diary that the Tar Heels "waded out [in] knee deep water." The men camped in a field, and some farmer's fence was lost to become firewood to warm and dry the soggy members of the regiment. Harper was growing weary of the war, confiding in his diary on Sunday, October 18, that the communion season had started back in Caldwell County. "When shall we be permitted to praise God beneath our roof again," he wrote, "and to meet with the people of the Lord in His house on earth. May he in mercy hear and answer the prayers that may be offered up to Him this day for the spread of his Gospel and for Peace."[7]

Sometime after the battle of Chickamauga, the members of the Fifty-Eighth gathered to nominate their fellow soldiers for the Roll of Honor. This citation was established in November 1862 as a way to award medals or badges of distinction to deserving soldiers. At the first dress parade following a battle, the soldiers of each company were to, by majority vote, choose the soldier who was to receive the honor; the record was then communicated to the president. A year later, the Adjutant and General's Office issued an addendum. The October 1863 order stated that, since materials were scarce throughout the Confederacy, the soldiers who had displayed courage and good conduct, once they were chosen by their comrades, were to "be inscribed on a roll of honor, to be preserved in the office of the Adjutant and Inspector General for reference in all future time, for those who have deserved well of their country, as having best displayed their courage and devotion on the field of battle." The Roll of Honor was to be "read at the head of every regiment in the service of the Confederate States at the first dress-parade after its receipt, and be published in at least one newspaper in each State." The enlisted men and non-commissioned officers within the regiment chose First Sgt. William A. Vance (Company A); Pvt. William F. Bradshaw (Company B); Sgt. John Hughes (Company C); Pvt. Braxton Cox (Company D); Pvt. William N. Pendley (Company E); Pvt. George Y. Jarrett (Company F); Pvt. Callaway Gentry (Company G); Musc. William P. Bumgarner (Company H); Sgt. John Eggers (Company I); Pvt. Philip H. Duncan (Company K); and Pvt. Moses A. Harvel (Company L). Bradshaw, Pendley, and Eggers were killed. Duncan died of wounds on October 10.[8]

In further recognition of the role that Kelly's brigade played during the battle, General Preston ordered that eight of the Colt Revolving Rifles captured from the Twenty-First Ohio be presented to the color guards of Kelly's regiments. The Fifth Kentucky received two, as did the Sixty-Third Virginia. To the Fifty-Eighth went four of the prized repeating rifles. "I send these fine arms," Preston is reported to have said, "in the hope that they may commemorate hereafter, in the regiments, the great battle in which they were first engaged and achieved such brilliant distinction." One of the only known members of the color guard was Sgt. (later lieutenant) Green B. Woody (Company C). According to Woody's service record, Colonel Palmer assigned him the dangerous position of color bearer on October 1, 1863. It is probable that the flag issued to the Fifty-Eighth was a second national design.[9]

Colonel Palmer was back with the regiment by October 7. The regiment was mustered for pay on October 31. More needed than money were clothes. The regiment constantly seemed to be detailing men back home to procure clothing for needy soldiers. While North Carolina supplied its soldiers in the Army of Northern Virginia, the Tar Heel regiments in the Army of Tennessee were nearly forgotten. One anecdotal account compares Longstreet's fresh troops, clothed in new North Carolina manufactured uniforms, to the Fifty-Eighth's men dressed in "rags. Many had bare feet." The regiment was forbidden to cheer while going into battle or being reviewed and resorted to taking "'off their ragged old hats' and waving them silently around their heads." Many in the regiment did not even have tents. One officer reported home in a letter that he and his comrades had constructed a chimney for their fly. "If we had only a tent instead of a fly" he wrote, we "would be [out] of the weather."[10]

Sgt. Green B. Woody, pictured here after the war with his wife, Catherine, bore the flag of the Fifty-Eighth through most of the war (courtesy Michael Ledford).

The Fifty-Eighth's brigade commander, Colonel Kelly, was promoted to brigadier general and, on November 1, transferred to the cavalry. Palmer assumed command of the brigade on that date, and Captain Harper became Palmer's temporary assistant adjutant general. Harper reported on November 3 that he was a member of a "Board of Examination" for prospective officers. Through asking a series of questions, the examiners determined the competence of the candidate. Charles Moore (Company F) was elected second lieutenant on November 20. However, he failed his exam and was rejected by the board, reverting back to his rank of private.[11]

Captain Harper recorded receiving sixteen new recruits on November 8. Overall, the Fifty-Eighth received 151 new men in the months of August, September, October, and November 1863. Company A received thirteen men. Companies B and C, none. Company D got only two, while Company E received eighteen; Company F, forty-four and Company G, thirty-eight. Twelve new men joined Company H, seven in Company I, three in Company K, and fourteen in Company L. The new men averaged thirty-two years in age. Some, such as Leonard Ollis (Company A), Gilbert Hodges (Company D), and Jacob Bolick (Company H), were only sixteen years old. Many were over forty. A. N. Gibbs, Odom Gibson, and

Wright Hutchings (Company F) were all forty-three; Hile Jolly (Company L) was the oldest of the new recruits at forty-five. Some made good soldiers. Others did not. Some did not live long enough for their quality to be determined. Forty-three-year-old Andrew Clay (Company H), a Caldwell County resident, enlisted on August 24, 1863. On November 9, 1863, Clay died of disease at a hospital in Atlanta, Georgia. Harper noted in a letter home that one of the new recruits might be a "plug ugly," a problem.[12]

Seven of those new recruits came from Iredell County. Iredell resident William Goforth was recruiting for another regiment. When Goforth and his six recruits reported at Camp Holmes near Raleigh, they found themselves assigned to Company G of the Fifty-Eighth. Most new recruits for the regiment came through two conscription camps in North Carolina. The first and largest was Camp Holmes. Another, smaller, training camp was Camp Vance near Morganton, North Carolina. Once the new recruits were processed, they were shipped over the railroads through Atlanta to the Fifty-Eighth.[13]

Some of the new recruits were reporting because of the new conscript laws. The conscription age had been increased from 35 to 45. Plus, in mid–1863, Governor Vance had created the Guard for Home Defense in an effort to protect mountain counties from bands of conscript dodgers and deserters. Several of the new recruits were men who had been captured by the home guard. John W. Hilton, a wagon and buggy maker, was living in Davidson County at the start of the war. On August 28, 1862, he was arrested for "entertaining principles and sentiments in favor of the United States government" and lodged in the jail in Lexington until he could provide a $5000.00 secured bond. Hilton was made to promise that he would be "good and [keep a] peaceful behavior towards the Confederate Government." However, Hilton was no sooner released than he was making plans with other "union sympathizers to release Federal soldiers imprisoned at Salisbury." Hilton got word that the local Confederates had learned of these plans, so he fled to Forsyth County. He tried to escape north, but he was captured in June 1863 in Tennessee, not far from the North Carolina line. Hilton escaped his captors and returned to hiding out in Davidson and Forsyth counties. He soon fled again, attempting to get north to Federal lines. According to Hilton, he was "captured in west North Carolina near the Tennessee line ... and carried a prisoner to Raleigh ... and while so a prisoner in ... Raleigh was compelled by Confederate authorities to join as a private." Hilton was assigned to Company L of the Fifty-Eighth. Hilton was with the regiment by mid–November, and soon escaped to Union lines and then became a Federal prisoner. Hilton later joined the United States Navy.

Similar stories surround the enlistment and subsequent desertion of Obadiah Sprinkle from Wilkes County. Sprinkle was assigned to Company G on November 12, 1863, and was captured on November 25. Another was Felix Sluder, an Ashe County native who was also captured in Tennessee on his way to join the Federal army. Sluder was captured "on or about the last days of August 1863," taken to Camp Vance, and then assigned to Company L of the Fifty-Eighth. Sluder was also captured during the battle of Missionary Ridge. Both Sluder and Sprinkle joined Hilton in the United States Navy. Sixteen of the hundreds of deserters from the Fifty-Eighth joined the United States Navy.[14]

"Brigade changed commanders," read Harper's diary on November 12. Special Orders Number 294 came from Bragg's headquarters on that date. The orders contained a huge list of regiments and brigade shifts in the Army of Tennessee. Number fifteen (of nineteen orders) on that list read that the "Fifty-Fourth and Sixty-Third Virginia and Fifty-Eighth and Sixtieth North Carolina Regiments will constitute a brigade in Buckner's division, Brig. Gen. A. W. Reynolds commanding." The Fifty-Eighth and Sixty-Third had been serving together for some time. The Fifty-Fourth came from Trigg's brigade of Preston's division of Buckner's corps, and the Sixtieth was a member of Stovall's brigade, Breckinridge's division, Hill's corps.[15]

Alexander Welch Reynolds was known as "Gauley" to his soldiers. It was actually the name of his horse and was probably not used as a term of affection. Reynolds was born in Virginia in 1816 and graduated from West Point in 1838. His classmates included Bragg, Joseph Hooker, and Jubal Early. Reynolds saw action in the Second Seminole War and served in Iowa, Wisconsin, and Missouri. He was in Mexico during the Mexican War but did not see combat. In 1855, he was dismissed from the army due to an embezzlement charge, but was reinstated in 1858. During the secession crisis of 1861, Reynolds was in Texas and disappeared with $50,000. He never formally resigned from the United States Army, and in October 1861, was declared absent without leave. Reynolds was appointed colonel of the Fiftieth Virginia Infantry in July 1861 and was named brigadier general on September 14, 1863.[16]

For unknown reasons, Palmer's second quest for promotion to brigadier general was denied. However, Palmer's tenure as commander of the Fifty-Eighth was also coming to an end. On November 19, Palmer received orders to report to Asheville, North Carolina, and to assume command of the Department of Western North Carolina. The department was under the command of Brig. Gen. Robert Vance, brother to the governor. General Vance was ordered to report to the Army of Tennessee, but before he and Palmer could finalize the transfer, Vance was captured in east Tennessee. One of Palmer's first duties was to write the report detailing Vance's capture.[17]

Once Palmer left, the Fifty-Eighth had no field officer present. Major Dula was still absent wounded, and no one had been elected or appointed to the position of lieutenant colonel. First Lieutenant Benjamin Perry had assumed the position of adjutant on October 13. Second Lieutenant Thomas J. Coffey (Company E) was acting assistant quartermaster. The regular quartermaster, Marcus Bearden, was captured near Cumberland Gap on September 9. William Harriss was appointed surgeon for the absent Waightstill Collett. James Inglis (Company H) had served as sergeant major since May or June 1863, and William C. Coffey was quartermaster sergeant.[18]

With Palmer gone and no other field officer present, orders came to temporarily consolidate the Fifty-Eighth and Sixtieth regiments under the command of the Sixtieth's colonel, Washington M. Hardy. According to a letter that Harper wrote home to Caldwell County on November 18, each regiment kept its full complement of

Lt. Thomas J. Coffey is shown here wearing a double-breasted frock coat with buttons running up the sleeve; he served as the assistant quartermaster of the Fifty-Eighth. He relocated from Caldwell to Watauga County after the war (courtesy the Caldwell Heritage Museum).

officers, but one half of each regiment's officers were ordered to report to western North Carolina to work with Colonel Palmer rounding up conscripts and deserters. Most of the detached officers did not leave until December.[19]

Hardy was a young officer, born in 1835 in Buncombe County. His father was J.F.E. Hardy, one of the first physicians in Asheville. Washington Hardy trained for the law profession prior to the war. On April 27, 1861, he joined the Buncombe Riflemen, later Company E, First North Carolina Volunteers. Hardy was elected first lieutenant and was involved in the battle of Big Bethel, Virginia, in June 1861. The Riflemen were mustered out of service in November 1861, and he returned home and began recruiting a new company. On January 27, 1862, Hardy was elected captain of the Buncombe Light Artillery. This company was mustered into service in April 1862 as "First Company," McDowell's Battalion, North Carolina Infantry, also known as the Sixth Battalion, North Carolina Infantry. On October 8, 1862, the Sixtieth North Carolina Troops was created, and the Buncombe Light Artillery became Company A. In March 1863, Hardy was promoted to major and transferred to the field and staff; in June 1863, he was advanced to the rank of colonel.[20]

The consolidated Fifty-Eighth and Sixtieth regiments, along with the rest of Reynolds's brigade, left camp at 10:00 A.M. on Friday the twentieth and moved near General Hardee's headquarters. The regiment went into camp in a swamp. Captain Harper wrote home that he found some farmer's fence rails with which to elevate his bed as he slept under blankets out in the open. It rained that evening and Harper was glad to be out of the mud. At 6:00 A.M., the regiments moved out in the rain, heading down the LaFayette Road. After slogging through the mud for six or eight miles, the regiments halted, and about a half hour later, were ordered to "about face and they returned to Rossville." That night, they were close to their starting place. The men built large fires to dry out their clothing and blankets.[21]

Felix Sluder, a member of Company L of the Fifty-Eighth, was "captured" just a few days after enlisting. After a brief stint in a prisoner of war camp in Illinois, he joined the United States Navy. Sluder is pictured here with his wife, Celia (courtesy Jackie Sluder Grindstaff).

Orders came on November 22: Patrick Cleburne was to take his division, along with Buckner's division, to Chickamauga Station. Once at the station, the two divisions were to board the cars and travel into east Tennessee. They were to serve as reinforcements for Longstreet, who, earlier that month, had been sent to Knoxville to lay siege to the town and drive out Burnside. The twenty-second dawned clear. The Tar Heels were up early and on the road by 6:00 A.M. They crossed Missionary Ridge, in spite of the Federals, who chose to drop a few shells on the column. No one was wounded, but one shell came close to Thomas Austin (Company H). By 1:00 P.M., they were at Chickamauga Depot, awaiting transportation.[22]

In Chattanooga, the Federal command structure had recently undergone reorganization. George Thomas replaced Rosecrans as commander of the Army of the Cumberland. William Sherman was bringing his Army of the Tennessee across northern Alabama, and Joseph Hooker was arriving from Virginia with the Eleventh and Twelfth Corps. Overall command fell upon Maj. Gen. Ulysses Grant. Bragg falsely believed that part of the Federal force was trying to interpose between Longstreet and Bragg, and the latter was attempting to increase the number of operatives available to Longstreet. On November 23, a Federal corps captured part of Breckinridge's position at Orchard Knob. Bragg began reinforcing his lines. He sent orders to stop shipping troops out via the railroad. Reynolds's brigade was in the process of being loaded on the cars when the order arrived. "[T]he thunder of artillery in the direction of Missionary Ridge told us that warm work might soon be expected in that quarter," wrote a member of the Fifty-Eighth.

Cleburne received a second note, ordering him to return to Missionary Ridge with his division and whatever remained of Buckner's men. Reynolds's brigade of Buckner's division was the only body of troops that had yet to take to the rails. A third note from Bragg informed Cleburne that "we are heavily engaged. Move rapidly to these headquarters." Reynolds's brigade, without the baggage which had gone ahead, fell into line, marched back to Missionary Ridge, and went into position.[23]

Posted on the heights overlooking Chattanooga, the Confederates occupied a crescent-shaped position. The Confederate right was located at Tunnel Hill near the Tennessee River. The center was positioned along Missionary Ridge, and the left was also anchored on the Tennessee River, this time below Chattanooga on Lookout Mountain. With adequate preparation, the Confederate position was nearly impregnable. Bragg, however, failed to make those preparations until the eve of the battle. What should have been an unassailable position was left lacking adequate breastworks and artillery redoubts. Grant chose to send Hooker to attack the Confederate left at Lookout Mountain. Sherman was to attack the right at Tunnel Hill, and Thomas was ordered to apply pressure on the center, keeping Bragg from reinforcing his flanks. Grant had no confidence in Hooker, and almost none in Thomas. The main Federal point of attack was laid upon Sherman. Sending disjointed attacks on the Confederate position at Tunnel Hill held by Cleburne, Sherman failed for two days to take the position. On the other flank, Hooker easily brushed aside the Confederate defenders, capturing Lookout Mountain on November 24.

Reynolds's brigade arrived on the field and reported directly to Bragg. Bragg ordered Reynolds to take his men and report to Brig. Gen. Patton Anderson, then commanding a division on Missionary Ridge. The regiment went into position at the foot of Missionary Ridge. The Fifty-Eighth and Sixtieth consolidated was on the left of Reynolds's line, its left resting on the Seventh Florida Infantry of Finley's brigade. It is possible that the brigade was positioned, from left to right, Sixtieth, Fifty-Eighth, Fifty-Fourth, and Sixty-Third regiments.

Two days prior, Reynolds had given the strength of the brigade at 995 men. The regiments occupied breastworks made of large logs and earth. In front of these works, at a distance of three to four hundred yards, the area had been cleared, providing a clear field of fire. One company of the Fifty-Eighth was deployed as skirmishers out in front of the regiment at all times. One-fourth of the regiment was under arms all night, not being permitted to remove their accouterments or to sleep. The balance of the regiment was probably up before dawn, in position, and awaiting an attack by the Federals. Among those in the ranks were even some members of the Fifty-Eighth who had been in the guard house.[24]

Finally, on the morning of November 25, Thomas was ordered to attack. Grant believed that he saw Confederate reinforcements heading toward Tunnel Hill. Thomas, in an effort to keep the Confederates distracted, was ordered to take the Confederate rifle pits at the base of Missionary Ridge. The orders were to take that position, but to advance no further. If there was misunderstanding among Thomas's Federal troops as to where to stop the advance, there was an equal amount of misunderstanding among the Confederates in those rifle pits. Some Confederate regiments were told to hold their positions at the base of the mountain. Others were told to fire one volley, then retire to the defensive positions at the top of the mountains.

On Wednesday morning, wrote "Caldwell" for the local newspaper, "our pickets were driven in to our lines and their pursuers in turn were speedily driven back with loss by the well directed fire of our rifles." Reynolds allowed the Federals to approach to within 200 yards before ordering his men to fire. The Confederates and Federals traded volleys for about an hour before the Federals "were driven back with considerable loss." Reynolds believed that his men "conducted themselves with coolness and gallantry." The purpose of the Federal probe was completed: while the Confederates held the foot of the mountain in force, the Federals could get close to the Confederate lines. Confederate artillery, posted on the mountain above the Fifty-Eighth, dropped more than one shell on fellow Confederates. One member of Company H, who was greatly annoyed by the "premature explosion of the shells ... suggested ... that the command occupy the other side of the breast works."

Somewhere between 2 and 3 P.M., orders came for Reynolds to withdraw his brigade from its position. Reynolds pulled one company at a time out of the works, deployed them as skirmishers, and sent them up the mountain. Captain Silver, in command of the Fifty-Eighth, recorded after the war that he "gave orders for them to move as fast as possible." Later, "Caldwell" reported that his company (probably Company H) was one of the last to leave the works. As the men were vacating their positions, the Federals discovered what was happening and ordered their artillery to open fire. "The roar of the artillery and the bursting of the shells around as we ascended the ridge was heavy, to say the least of it, but providentially we suffered but little, many making narrow escapes."[25]

Capt. Samuel Silver had sent all but Company C up Missionary Ridge when he "heard a Federal officer command 'Double Quick March,' I then ordered Co. C. to move rapidly and at once notifying Capt. Briggs, its captain, that I was too weak to climb the ridge fast." Silver had been in a hospital in Newnan, Georgia, for about four weeks and had just returned to the regiment. Briggs told Silver that he would stay with him until one of them was killed. Silver wrote,

> I insisted that he go and take care of his men, but he said I can't leave you. We went slowly up the steep hill until my strength failed when I sat down and ordered Capt. Briggs to go on and join the Regiment on the top of the ridge. After a short time I moved on and reached the top ... just in front of our battery of 6 guns. The strap of my haversack which contained a slice of bacon and a small piece of corn-bread, was cut by a ball ... and

Washington M. Hardy was from Buncombe County and served as colonel of the Sixtieth North Carolina Troops. At times, he commanded both the Fifty-Eighth and Sixtieth, and at times was a brigade commander.

the haversack fell to the ground. I picked it up and carried it in my hand, passing right under those six cannons firing as rapidly as possible. I stopped the second time for a breath, a minute or two, and soon saw the flag of the 58th just in the rear of the breastworks.[26]

The Tar Heels and Virginians arrived at the top of the mountain winded, worn down, and confused. The gap at the top of the mountain left for Reynolds's men was not directly above the brigade. Some of the soldiers stumbled into the ranks of Finley's Florida brigade, causing disarray among the Floridians. These members of Reynolds's brigade, which appear to be large portions of the Sixtieth North Carolina, once reorganized, went into position behind Finley astride the Moore road. In one estimation, Reynolds had lost about half his brigade. "Caldwell" wrote, "As our companies successively arrived at the top of the Ridge, they were formed and moved into position on the brow of a hill to the right of and near Gen. Bragg's headquarters." It would appear that "Caldwell" was among those who formed behind the Floridians. It is unclear who from the Fifty-Eighth remained with Reynolds and who was reformed with the Sixtieth.[27]

Watching from the top of Missionary Ridge, Reynolds observed three lines of Federals advancing toward the foot of the mountain. A double line of skirmishers preceded the main Federal lines,

Mitchell County's Samuel Silver rose through the ranks from second lieutenant of Company E to lieutenant colonel of the regiment. He resigned just prior to the battle of Bentonville and later moved to Oregon (courtesy the North Carolina Department of Archives).

some 23,000 Federal soldiers total. Parts of the Confederate line at the bottom of the mountain did not receive orders to withdraw. This confusion led some to believe that certain portions of the Confederates in the rifle pits were cowards. Those who did stay fought valiantly, but were soon overwhelmed and forced to retreat up the mountain. A section of artillery was on Reynolds's line, and he bade the gunners to open fire. Once the Federals took the Confederate rifle pits at the foot of the mountain, General Anderson, who was with Reynolds, ordered the gunners to depress their pieces and switch to canister. "This was instantly done & so terrible was the effect of this fire on the dense lines of the Enemy, that it caused them to falter for an instant," Reynolds wrote.[28]

With shell and canister raining down upon them, the Federals were in a difficult position. Only taking the Confederate line at the foot of the mountain had been specified in their orders. Yet to remain at those works was suicidal. They were left with two choices: retreat across the field they had just advanced over, all the while exposed to Confederate artillery, or charge up the mountain. Individuals, companies, and then whole regiments chose the latter and quickly moved from the abandoned Confederate works and started to claw their way up Missionary Ridge. Many of the Federal color bearers led the way, with their regiments trailing behind on either side, forming triangular shapes. Soon, the Federals were within musket range, and Reynolds ordered his men to open fire. The fire was "so

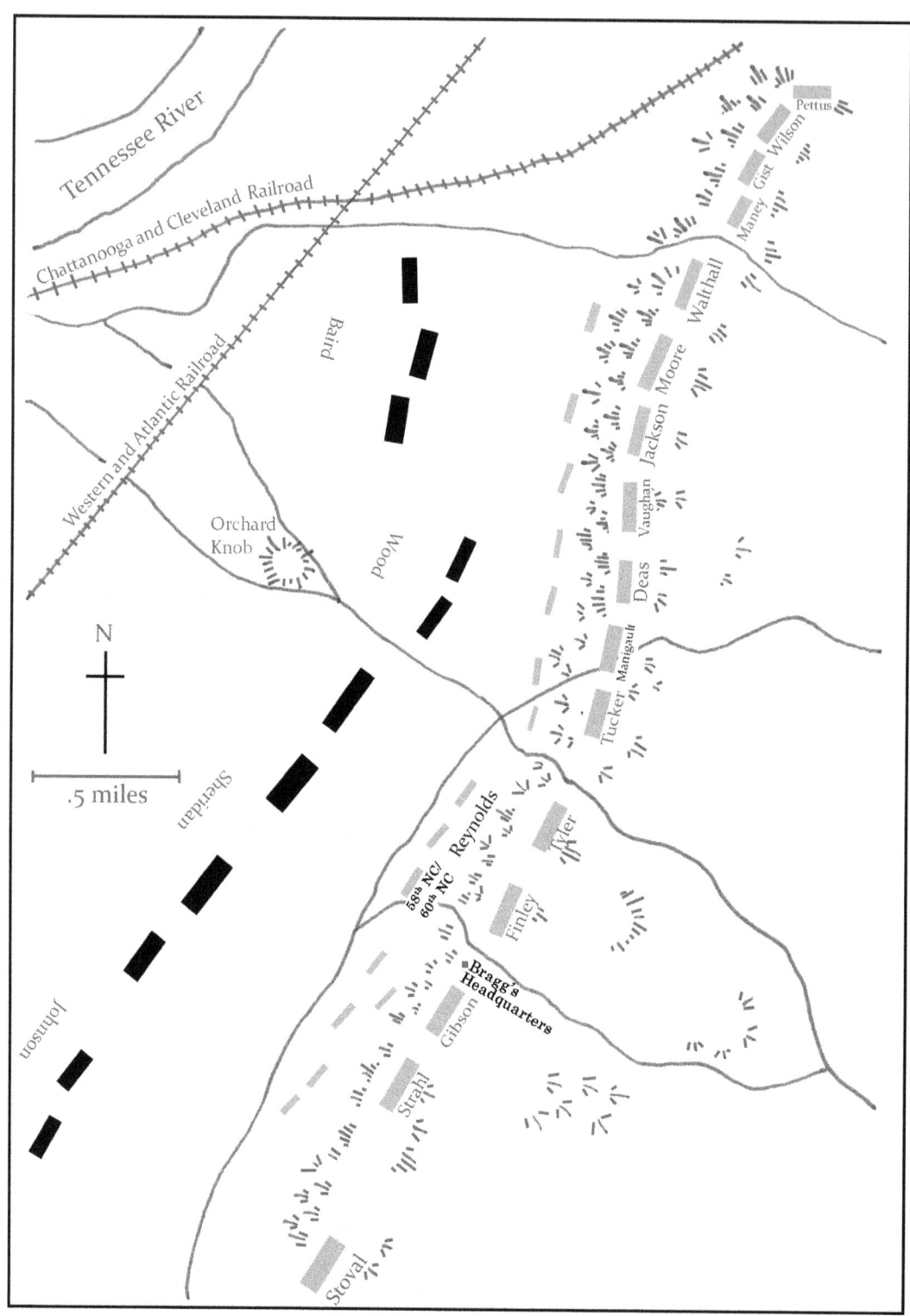

Reynolds's brigade started at the bottom of Missionary Ridge and was ordered to ascend the ridge as the Federals approached.

severe that for a time the enemy were checked." At one point, members of the Fifty-Eighth, along with other Confederate regiments, "tumbled rocks down on this vast host."[29]

Elsewhere along the Confederate line, Southern soldiers were not as fortunate. To Reynolds's right, the brigade of Col. William Tucker began to break. Reynolds wrote in his official report,

> Unfortunately at this Juncture when every heart beat high with hope, & victory was almost within our grasp, the troops posted in the rifle pits on the right of my Brigade broke & fled in the utmost disorder. The enemy seeing the advantage that must result from this disgraceful & inexplicable panic on the part of hitherto invincible troops, at once crossed the hill on my right and opened a heavy fire on my lines, completely enfilading my position; This of course rendered necessary an immediate Change of position. I therefore changed front to the rear on the left Battalion. My troops performing this delicate & dangerous manoeuver under the fire of the enemy in admirable style & without the lest confusion or irregularity.[30]

Regrettably for Reynolds and his brigade, the troops to his left were also collapsing. Unknown to Reynolds, just twenty yards to his front, a group of Federals from the First Ohio, Forty-First Ohio, and Twenty-Third Kentucky lay hidden in a "roll in the slope" resting, preparing for a final push. After fixing bayonets, the Federals surged ahead. Further adding to the pressure on the brigade, captured Confederate artillery was turned upon the few men whom Reynolds had left. Cpl. Elijah Norris (Company D) wrote that "we had a hot time of it for awhile." Reynolds called for a retreat, and according to him, the men he had left moved "by the right flank down the ridge."[31]

Portions of Reynolds's brigade were scattered to the four winds. Others retreated about a half mile down the back side of the ridge, where they made a stand with other elements of Bate's and Breckinridge's commands. "Caldwell" wrote that the "enemy again attempted a charge, but was repulsed after a brisk fight of half an hour. This last fight was made after dark, and the attack not being renewed, our troops leisurely withdrew over the pontoon bridge at Chickamauga Station." However, the retreat back to Chickamauga Station was anything but leisurely. As the sun set, a chill descended upon the worn troops as they plugged through the woods, downcast and downtrodden. Many soldiers threw away their rifles and accouterments as they made their hasty retreat. Many were also lost, not knowing where their regiments and brigades were. The remnants of the brigade with Reynolds crossed Chickamauga Creek at the Shallow Ford Bridge, remaining until 10:00 P.M., when they took up the line of march toward Chickamauga Station. "Caldwell" reported that he reached the Station at 3:00 A.M. A two-hour rest was all the men received before starting on the road south.[32]

Casualties were relatively light. Two men were killed, including Ezra DeBorde (Company G). DeBorde was from Wilkes County and had joined the regiment a month earlier. Sixteen were wounded. John H. Abbe's (Company A) right leg was fractured, and he lost part of his little finger on his left hand. John B. Coffey (Company E) was struck "slightly in the face twice and once in the ear by spent balls." Cpl. Elijah Norris (Company D) was wounded. The official report states that he was wounded in both hips. Norris wrote after the war that "I got shot in the arm, all the bones being broke to pieces." John Cox (Company K) was shot in the left leg, necessitating the amputation of that leg. One of the wounded, Solomon Roark (Company L), died of his wounds on an unknown date. Forty-three men were captured, including four of the wounded. Capt. Samuel Silver (Company K), who did not think he could make it to the top of the ridge, was loaded into an ambulance during the retreat. "I discovered about this time that a ball had passed through my hat and one

This iron tablet along South Crest Road at Missionary Ridge marks the position of the Fifty-Eighth North Carolina and Reynolds's Brigade. The Fifty-Eighth's exact position was lost when Interstate 24 was constructed in the 1960s.

through my coat." Some of those who had been taken from the guard house and placed in the front ranks "were some of the bravest."[33]

Reynolds, in his official report, praised the men under his command: "It is with no little pleasure & pride that I am enabled to say that both in the riflepits at the foot of the Ridge, & during the engagement on the ridge, all the officers & men of my Brigade acted with the gallantry & coolness of veterans." Reynolds went on to praise the actions of Capt. Alfred Stewart (Company E), who "acted with great gallantry, encouraging & setting examples of heroism to their men," and Sgt. Doctor Estes (Company E), who was noted for conspicuous bravery. Even some of the Confederate high command praised the Fifty-Eighth. As they fell back from the battlefield, the men of the regiment came across General Breckinridge, who "enquired for the regiment then filing into the road, and being told, raised his hat and complimented the 'Tar Heels' very highly on their part in the fight."[34]

Not everyone agreed with Reynolds's assessment of his North Carolina-Virginia brigade in the battle. Brig. Gen. William Bate wrote in his report that Reynolds's brigade, while at the foot of the ridge, offered only slight resistance before it "abandoned the ditches ... and sought refuge at the top of the hill, breaking and throwing into slight confusion the left of Finley's Brigade as they passed through." Once portions of Reynolds's brigade that came into Bate's line were reformed under Major James Weaver of the Sixtieth, Bate attempted to use them to drive the Federals who were gaining ground on his flank. After moving the remnant some 500 or 600 yards, they went into position on Bate's flank. Bate wanted the men to charge, but before long, more Federal flags appeared and drove "away the command under Major Weaver. This command, upon the advance of the enemy, broke and retired in disorder." The second charge came from General Bragg's report, filed on November 30, 1863. Bragg wrote that the collapse of Anderson's division began "on its left, where the enemy had first crowned the ridge.... All to the left ... except a portion of Bate's division, was entirely routed and in rapid flight." Reynolds was on the far left of Anderson's line. Bragg reiterated his charges against Reynolds and his men in 1873, when he wrote that Reynolds's men were the "first [that] gave way and could not be rallied." The report of General Anderson, and his brigade commanders, was unavailable to Bate or Bragg, and their unfounded opinions have been repeated as fact to this day. While portions of Reynolds's brigade did run or refuse to fight, the brigade was not the first to break, nor did it as a whole refuse to fight.[35]

The Fifty-Eighth passed through Graysville and Ringgold before going into camp near Catoosa Station on the evening of the twenty-sixth. "Tired and very sleepy having slept but little for three nights," wrote Captain Harper in his diary. In a letter to his wife back in Caldwell County, the writer confessed that "the men suffered those cold nights just after the battle" due to the loss of their blankets during their retreat.

The regiment was on the move again on November 27, going into camp one mile southeast of Dalton, Georgia, at 5:00 P.M. Dalton was the regiment's home for the next few months.[36]

CHAPTER 9

December 1863–May 1864

"The blood was running from his feet because he had no shoes."
— Lemuel Wilson, Company I

December 1863 found forty-five members of the Fifty-Eighth incarcerated in Federal prisoner-of-war camps. The most recent capture was Allen Butler (Company B). It appears that a group of Confederates was hiding out near Ringgold Gap. One of those was a member of Company F, Fifty-Fourth Virginia. Another was Allen Butler. Private Butler's trip was much like those of most men captured during the Missionary Ridge battle. He was first sent to Nashville, Tennessee, then transferred to Louisville, Kentucky, where he arrived on December 11. Finally, Butler was transferred via rail to Rock Island, Illinois, arriving on December 12, 1863.[1]

Once captured, a soldier gave up his rifle, cartridge box, and belt. He was also stripped of anything that belonged to the United States Army. If the soldier happened to have a Federal blanket or overcoat, then it was taken, and the Confederate soldier was left to suffer the cold. Any valuables were also taken. The captured Confederates were taken to Nashville and housed in the old Tennessee State Penitentiary. There, they were searched once again for valuables. Usually, the soldiers were loaded onto the trains and transferred to Louisville within a few days, at most a couple of weeks. Generally, within three or four days, the prisoners were transferred farther north to one of the prison camps. John Peterson (Company E) arrived in Louisville December 8, and was at Rock Island, Illinois, on December 11. John H. Miller (Company I) was in Louisville on December 17 and arrived at Rock Island on December 23. Both were captured November 25 on Missionary Ridge.[2]

Rock Island, Illinois, was the destination for most of the Fifty-Eighth's members captured during the battle for Missionary Ridge. Located on an island in the Mississippi River between Illinois and Iowa, the prison had just opened a couple of weeks prior to the arrival of Confederates captured during the battle for Chattanooga. Prisoners were housed in barracks made "in the roughest and cheapest manner, mere shanties, with no fine work about them." Each barrack was one hundred feet long, twenty-two feet wide, and twelve feet high. There were twelve windows and two doors, and the west end of each building housed a kitchen. The men slept two to a bunk, with sixty bunks in each barrack. On December 3, the first prisoners arrived, all 5,592 of them. By the end of the first month, 245 were sick and 94 had died. Josiah "Uncle Fate" Wiseman (Company A) recalled that "he got three soda crackers a day and what rats he could kill" while he was a prisoner of war.[3]

Noah Styles (Company C) was the first of the captured Fifty-Eighth men to arrive at Rock Island, landing on December 8. Styles was joined by eighteen more members of the Fifty-Eighth on December 11, two on the thirteenth, six on December 14, and three more by the end of the month. Death was quick to claim several members of the regiment. John Pipes (Company E) did not even make it to Rock Island. He died in Nashville on December 13 of chronic dysentery. At Rock Island, fellow Company E member Walter Story died of an unknown cause on January 11, 1864. He was followed by John Hawks (Company G) on January 16, who died of "variola." Of the thirty-eight members of the Fifty-Eighth who arrived at Rock Island, eleven died. The chronic dysentery of which Story died was bloody diarrhea. Cousins Alexander and Rufus Pritchard (Company E) both died on February 13: Alexander of "pneumonia" and Rufus of "bronchitis." Robert Fugitt (Company G) died on January 30 of "diarrhoea." Jesse Walker (Company G) passed on February 21. His cause of death was listed as "remitt[ent] fever." Joseph Cole and Henry Ledford, both members of Company L, died of diarrhoea, Cole on February 28 and Ledford on February 14. Diarrhoea was the leading cause of death during the war. There were more than 250 Confederate deaths in the first four months of the prison's operation on Rock Island.[4]

John Cox (Company K) hailed from Yancey County. He was wounded in the leg and captured during the battle of Missionary Ridge. His leg was amputated. Once released from prison, Cox was transferred to the Invalid Corps (courtesy Tracy Cox).

According to the family, Noah Styles and a friend, believing that they would perish in prison, devised a scheme to escape, or at least die in the process. One night, unknown to their prison mates, they took sticks from the fire and blistered their skin. They presented themselves to the guard the next morning, claiming to have contracted smallpox. The guard took one look at the men and their blisters, opened the prison door, and at a distance, ushered the two out of confinement.[5]

A few of the members of the Fifty-Eighth at Rock Island chose not to remain in prison. Flight was not their means of escape; joining the United States Army or Navy was. Apparently, a recruiter for the Navy was at Rock Island on January 25, 1864. John Miller (Company I), A. B. Merrill, Wyatt Rose, and Felix Sluder (Company L) all joined up on that date. John Hilton (Company L) joined on February 5, along with William Hampton (Company G). Obadiah Sprinkle (Company G) waited until May 23. A few joined the army over the course of 1864: Alvin Howell (Company L) on October 6; James Higgins (Company G) on October 13; Stephen Elliott (Company L) on October 31.[6]

Two of the wounded, John Cox (Company K) and Joshua Roark (Company L) were exchanged. Men could be paroled and exchanged for a man of equal rank, or one for several, depending on rank, such as fifteen privates for one colonel. The parolee was expected to not take up arms until officially paroled. This system, known as the Dix-Hill Cartel, soon collapsed, leading to overcrowded prisons on both sides of the Mason-Dixon line. John Cox was wounded in the left leg and was unable to get away from the advancing Federal army. Once Cox was in Federal lines, a doctor amputated his leg. Cox was exchanged on an unknown date, and was reported in a hospital in Atlanta in March and April 1864. On April 30, he was transferred to the Invalid Corps, a unit in which disabled soldiers could perform lighter duty. Joshua Roark was also wounded in the left leg and captured. He was hospitalized in Bridgeport, Alabama, before being transferred to Nashville, Tennessee, arriving on December 12. On January 28, Roark was taken to the "pesthouse," often a shelter used to house soldiers infected with a contagious disease, such as smallpox. Roark was exchanged on an unknown date.[7]

Three prisoners of war chose to take the oath of allegiance as soon as possible: James Molly (Company C); Serug Marcus (Company C); and William Vannoy (Company G). These soldiers were likely voluntary captures: those who chose to be captured in order to desert the Southern army. Molly's enlistment date is thought to have been the autumn of 1863. He was probably forced into the service and used the confusion of battle to desert. He arrived at Rock Island on December 9 and applied for the oath of allegiance on March 18. He disappears from the records after that. Serug Marcus enlisted in June 1862. However, he had already been sick and was declared absent without leave May through June 1863. In Nashville, he took the oath and was transferred to Louisville, where he was released on December 25, 1863. Like the other two, William Vannoy was captured on November 25. For an unknown reason, he was sent to Knoxville, where he took the oath on December 16. In most cases, oath-takers were released north of the Ohio River and required to stay north of the river until the war ended.[8]

This 1864 photograph shows Confederate prisoners at a depot in Chattanooga. Members of the Fifty-Eighth who had been captured, or even those who had deserted, would have found themselves in similar surroundings on their way to a Northern prison camp (courtesy the Library of Congress).

9. December 1863–May 1864

December passed quietly in the camp of the Fifty-Eighth near Dalton. The regiment was still without its baggage, and the men were forced to scrounge for wood and other materials to construct shelters. Captain Harper's father arrived in camp on December 2 bringing 40 boxes for the members of Company H. "Nothing to do but keep up fires and enjoy [the] contents of our boxes," Harper noted on December 7. Harper's wife, Ella, wrote to a friend that the boxes were extremely appreciated, for after the battle, "when they had lost cooking utensils, blankets, and nearly everything they were welcome visitors. They had a real feast." The regiment was inspected on December 14, and again on the December 16, this time by General Brown. It was clear on Christmas Eve, but cold, then rainy on Christmas Day.[9]

As the men tried to keep warm in their bunks inside their winter quarters, talk undoubtedly turned to the resignation of Braxton Bragg. On November 28, Bragg submitted his resignation to Davis. The following day, in a letter to Cooper, Bragg stated, "I deem it due to the cause and to myself to ask for relief from command." With swiftness unusual for Davis, he relieved Bragg of command on November 30. Bragg was ordered to turn command over to Lt. General Hardee. Bragg then made his way to Atlanta. It is hard to judge the response to the change of commanders within the Fifty-Eighth; no letters have emerged that discuss the transfer.[10]

Davis took three weeks to appoint a new commander for the Army of Tennessee. General Hardee declined the appointment. Davis preferred Robert E. Lee for the assignment, but Lee tactfully declined, bringing up the question of who would command the Army of Northern Virginia. In Davis's mind, that left Joseph Johnston and P. G. T. Beauregard, two men whom Davis despised. Johnston eventually won out, and on December 16, was appointed commander of the Army of Tennessee.

Born in Virginia in 1807, Johnston was a classmate of Robert E. Lee at West Point and a veteran of the Seminole and Mexican Wars. He attained the rank of brigadier general in the United States army before resigning to join the Confederate army, in which he was appointed brigadier general in May 1861. Johnston saved the day at First Manassas in July 1861 and was soon thereafter appointed a full general. It was Johnston who opposed the Federals near Richmond in the spring of 1862 until he was wounded at the end of May at Seven Pines. After recovering from his wounds, Johnston was appointed commander of the Department of the West in November 1862. The animosity between Johnston and Davis was unfortunate. A debate over rank seniority broke out between Davis and Johnston early in the war, and the relationship between the two never recovered. Johnston often kept his plans for military operations to himself, and Davis communicated with officers under Johnston and sent them contradictory orders, bypassing the established chain of command.[11]

Prior to Johnston's assumption of command,

Gen. Joseph E. Johnston was appointed commander of the Army of Tennessee following Bragg's loss at Chattanooga. Johnston was replaced by Hood in July 1864, but was again assigned command of the army in early 1865 (courtesy the Library of Congress).

Hardee had written to Davis, assuring him that the Army of Tennessee had recovered from its recent defeat at Chattanooga. Arriving just the evening before, Johnston set out to ride through the camps of his new command on December 27. He continued his ride for the next few days, inspecting the camp of the Fifty-Eighth on December 30. Contrary to Hardee's reports to Davis, Johnston found an army "now far from being in condition to resume the offensive. It is deficient in numbers, arms, subsistence stores, and field transportation." Cavalry was almost non-existent, and half of the artillery was worthless, with little in the way of horseflesh.[12]

Johnston set about improving his new command. He ordered two days of rations issued to the men immediately. It was a welcome addition, considering that soldiers had been on one-third or one-quarter rations for some time. Rations themselves improved, and Johnston ordered new clothing and, most importantly, shoes for his command. The descendants of Lemuel Wilson (Company I) recalled, "The blood was running from his feet because he had no shoes." Johnston also saw to a whiskey and tobacco ration. Furloughs were issued to troops. Captain Harper set out for Caldwell County on December 31. He had a furlough home for eighteen days. For soldiers who were absent without command, Johnston granted amnesty if they returned.[13]

Harper recalled his journey home when he wrote a letter to a newspaper after the war. There were ten army men in Harper's party. On the evening of December 31, they boarded a train for Atlanta, traveling "on a car without a stove and seats without cushions." The train moved so slowly that the party missed its connection in Atlanta by seven hours. About 6:30 P.M. on the first, the men boarded another train, this one bound for Augusta, Georgia. This time, the car was "comfortable but another slow train and hopelessly behind time again." The party was forced to stay overnight in Augusta. Finally, at 1:00 P.M., the group boarded a train for Columbia, South Carolina, but missed the connection to Charlotte by three hours.

By Tuesday, January 5, the men arrived in Salisbury. They could not get a train out due to a slide that blocked the lines. On January 6, they boarded a train that took them to the site of the slide, and were then forced to get off the train, walk over the slide and board another train. Harper complained that an unnamed young lady picked up the book that he had been reading, "monopolizing its contents for the balance of the ride to the next town — She, of course, did not know that I left off reading at an intensely interesting point of the story — how could she[,] or that I had no resource left me but to post up my journal."

It took nine hours for Harper's party to travel sixty miles. After disembarking at 6:00 P.M., the men commenced the walk to Lenoir, nineteen miles away. It was a "dark, cloudy night, road rough, and frozen, bad walking.... On leaving Hickory our party numbered about ten men — three only, [Sgt. Maj. James] Inglis, myself, and a negro man, reached Lenoir the same night — the others fell out at different points and sought rest and sleep by impromptu camp fires on the way side." At last, Harper reached his destination and a "tiresome tramp [was] soon forgotten in the pleasures and comforts of home."[14]

On January 8, Johnston issued General Order No. 8. General orders were issued to every regiment in the army and had to be copied into the general order book of the regiment by the adjutant. It probably took the Fifty-Eighth's adjutant, Benjamin Perry, some time to copy the eighteen points into the book. The orders largely had to do with the discipline of the army. Johnston mandated that the orders be read "at the head of each company at least once a week." And instead of just having one copy issued to a regiment, "all field, staff, and company officers" were furnished copies. The orders specified that the normal day was as follows: "Reveille at daylight; police immediately after reveille; surgeon's call fifteen minutes after reveille ... first call half hour after reveille." All of that was to take place before breakfast, which was stipulated to occur at sunrise. At 9:00 A.M. was adjutant's call, at which the regimental adjutants received the orders for the day, then came "drill from 10 to 11:30 A.M.; officer's drill from 11 A.M. to 12 P.M.; dinner at 12:30 P.M., drill from 2:30 to 4 P.M.; guard mounting at 4 P.M. ... camp and company police at 4:30 P.M.; dress parade at sunset; supper immediately after parade; tattoo at 8 P.M.; taps one hour after sunset." The first sergeant of each company was to call the roll of the company at "reveille, at morning and afternoon drill, at dress parade, and at tattoo." The men were required to be in the ranks when the drum stopped beating. Drill was suspended on Sundays, but at 10:00 A.M., brigade and division commanders were required to inspect their regiments. Once a week, regimental camps were to be inspected. Johnston asked that "whenever practicable, religious services are to be held in camp on Sundays, when the utmost decorum is to be observed."[15]

Camps were to be inspected by the commanding officer of each company twice a day: once after breakfast, and a second time at 4:30 P.M. While these two inspections occurred, the occupants stood in front of their respective tents or huts while the officer saw to their quarters, making sure that everything was "in perfect order, knapsacks properly packed, and bedding neatly folded." A non-commissioned officer and several privates were to be detailed each day to "police" or clean their respective company campgrounds. At night, once taps had been sounded, "all lights except those of commissioned officers, non-commissioned staff, and first sergeants are to be extinguished, and there is to be perfect quiet in the encampment." A single company officer was to remain "on duty in his company grounds for half an hour after tattoo, enforcing obedience to these requirements and then reporting to the adjutant of the regiment. All lights, except those of the field and staff, are extinguished at 11 P.M."

Johnston's orders went on, outlining the roles of sentinels, pickets, and camp guards, which each regiment had to furnish each day, on a rotating basis. "All orders affecting the troops," point seventeen stressed, "are to be read at the head of each company, that all may distinctly may be heard." The Articles of War, a set of 101 articles that comprised a code of military justice, was to "be read to each company immediately before or after each muster for pay."

Johnston ordered, "A spirit of courtesy is to be cultivated, and harmony, devotion to cause, obedience to superiors, and patient endurance of all hardships sought to be made the distinguishing characteristics of both officers and men. Language or conduct calculated to cause discontent among the troops is not to be tolerated, and in every instance the offender is to be put in arrest and brought before trial. This is made the duty of all officers of the command."

Captain Harper wrote home on January 25 that "all officers are now required to attend the roll call at Reveille (daylight) and tattoo (8 P.M.)." While all of Johnston's orders could be found within the official regulations for Confederate armies, he felt the need to reiterate them on taking command of the Army of Tennessee.[16]

On January 2, the Fifty-Eighth moved from its camp to the town of Dalton to serve as provost guard, or "police guard." It was not uncommon to detail regiments to serve as provosts for short periods of time. The Fifty-Eighth rotated in and out of Dalton until February 22. While serving as provost, the members of the regiment were charged with guarding prisoners; rounding up deserters and stragglers; suppressing drinking establishments, gambling houses, and brothels; and maintaining discipline. Captain Harper wrote home that once, while he was officer of the guard, he was in charge of the guardhouse containing sixty prisoners.

However, just because the regiment was stationed on extra duty does not mean that the men were excused from army life. There was a brigade review on January 25; an inspection on January 28 and a review of the corps by General Johnston the following day; and a review of the entire army on February 5. Writing after one of the reviews, Harper told his wife that it "was the finest military display I have yet seen. My Companies (E and H) marched beautifully and it was highly complimented for its appearance."[17]

Harper reported for regimental court-martial duty from Tuesday, February 2, through February 12. It appears that Harper served as judge advocate. The judge advocate was both the prosecutor for the government and the defense for the accused. He was responsible for procuring witnesses for both sides; saw that the charges and specifications were properly drawn; presented those charges to the accused; and swore in all members of the court.

Regimental courts-martial were composed of three commissioned officers, and could not be called for capital cases. Regimental courts-martial could not fine a soldier more than one month's pay, nor could they imprison or put to hard labor a non-commissioned officer or soldier for more than a month at a time. The highest ranking officer of the three was declared the president. It is unknown who the three officers were. It is known that Adkins Jefferson (Company L) and Andrew Lovelace (Company L) were fined $11.00. James Shehan (Company C) was fined $104.50 for "ordnance carried away at the time of desertion." Shehan had just deserted on February 1. John G. Barnes (Company I) related some of the other punishments handed out by the military courts, and his opinion of such matters, when he wrote home on February 19, 1864: "I do think that there is many a man that will go to hell for the way they treat men hear shaving of their heads and drumming them threw the camp stainding in the stocks standing on stumps walking of the guard line all kinds of punishment that could be put on min."[18]

On February 12, Captain Harper left for Raleigh to purchase 112 yards of cloth for uniforms. He was using the bounty monies for companies A, B, G, K, and H of the Fifty-Eighth and Company I of the Sixtieth to procure uniforms for these companies. While in Raleigh, he paid a visit to Governor Vance and attended a lecture at Common Hall, presented by the Reverend D. Lacy. Harper spent several days back in Caldwell County attending Sunday school and duck hunting before returning to the army on March 12.[19]

While Harper was absent, the Fifty-Eighth was again called out to meet the foe. Earlier in the month, a Federal force had set out from Vicksburg, heading east toward the Confederate supply depots in Meridian, Mississippi. Leonidas Polk was now in command of the Confederate forces in Alabama and Mississippi. While Polk failed to stop Sherman's blue coats, the Confederates were able to evacuate Meridian. Polk repeatedly telegraphed Johnston for reinforcements, but Johnston wrote that he had none, that the Federals in his front were double his numbers. Finally, on February 17, Polk's old friend, President Davis, stepped in and ordered Johnston to send three divisions of Hardee's corps to Polk. Grant had originally promised Sherman that he would keep the Confederates around Dalton occupied, but failed to do so until February 12, when he ordered Thomas to conduct a "reconnaissance in force" against Dalton. Ten days later, Maj. Gen. John M. Palmer led 25,000 Federal soldiers of the IV and XIV Corps south out of Chattanooga.[20]

The Federals planned a two-pronged attack. Portions of the XIV Corps, namely the first division under Brig. Gen. Charles Cruft, was to advance down the east side of Rocky Face Ridge towards Dalton. Segments of the IV Crops, namely the Second Division under Brig Jefferson C. Davis, were to advance down the west side of Rocky Face Ridge. Word reached the camp of the Fifty-Eighth near Dalton on the evening of the twenty-second: "Cook rations and be ready to march at a minutes warning." By February 23, the Federals had reached the vicinity of Ringgold, just sixteen miles north of Dalton. The Fifty-Eighth, and its fellow regiments in Reynolds's brigade, marched out that morning, taking a position in reserve in "a line of battle on the point of a mountain in front of Dalton." On the morning of the twenty-fourth, Federal skirmishers drove in Confederate pickets, and then Confederate cavalry. At 5:00 P.M., the opposing forces clashed east of Rocky Face Ridge, and the Confederates were able to drive back the Federals. On the west side of the ridge, light skirmishing also developed, but no attack was made.[21]

During the evening hours, the Confederates decided to extend their lines west of the ridge. Reynolds's brigade was called for, and about midnight, according to John W. Dugger (Company D), the brigade went into position, its right resting near the Western and Atlantic Railroad. Reynolds posted skirmishers to the front. Early the next morning, those skirmishers became engaged with their Federal counterparts. Near noon, two regiments came from Brig. Gen. Henry Clayton's brigade to bolster Reynolds's left. A third regiment, and Clayton himself, soon arrived, and Clayton took charge of that wing. Two regiments of Federals, the Eighty-Fifth and Eighth-Sixth Illinois Infantry, advanced against the left of the line and "a sharp fight took place on that wing lasting about half an hour."

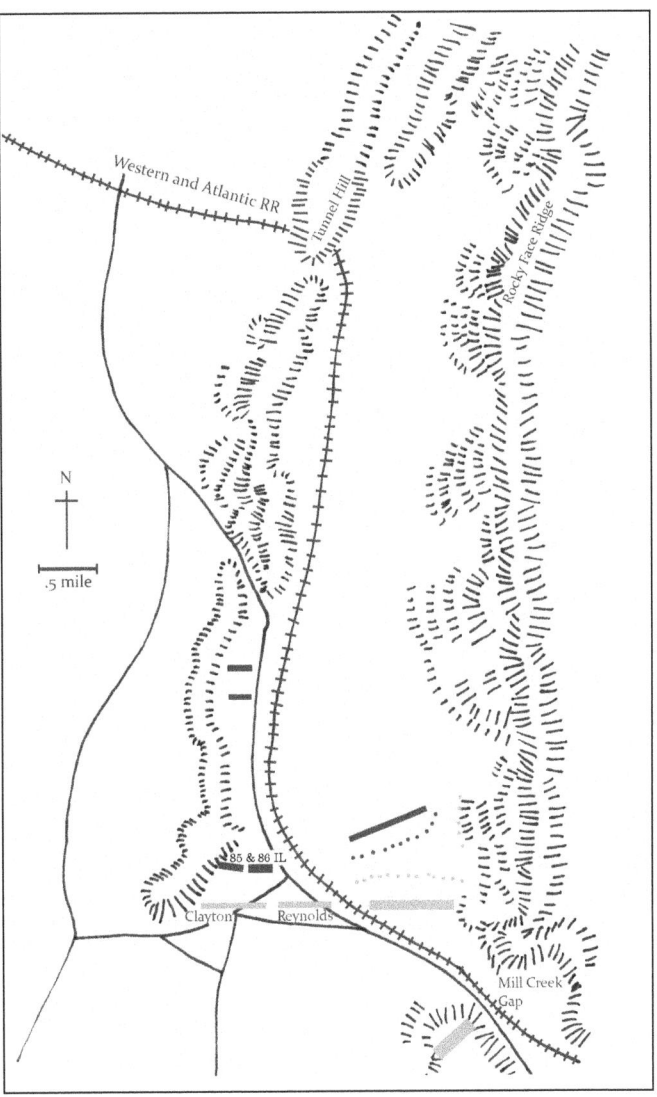

In February 1864, the Fifty-Eighth, under Reynolds, was one of the regiments called out to stop the Federal advance north of Dalton, Georgia.

Reynolds wrote that evening: "The fight was entirely successful, driving the enemy back twice." The line that the Fifty-Eighth held was not tested by infantry, even though they were "under a heavy cannonading." Jacob Wacaster (Company A) was among the wounded; an artillery round burst above him, causing "a tree to fall on him, breaking three ribs. The explosion also caused him permanent deafness, partial loss of eyesight, and vertigo." Wesley Presnell (Company D) was struck in the arm, breaking the arm and necessitating its amputation.

One of the greatest losses was the Fifty-Eighth's Scottish Sgt. Maj. James Ingles. He was mortally wounded during the fight, struck in the calf and thigh. Ingles died later that night. "Sad, sad news. Another friend gone," Captain Harper wrote when he learned of Ingles's death. Back in Caldwell County, the clerk of the Presbyterian Church in Lenoir recorded "with profound regret and yet with due submission to God the death of James Ingles ... for seven years an esteemed and respected member of this church.... The Colonel of the Regiment in announcing his death to a friend of the deceased said, 'A better and more gallant soldier never fell in defense of his country.'" Two others later died from their wounds: Third Lt. Lafayette Page (Company H) died in a hospital in Atlanta on March 9, and Lemuel Wilson (Company I) passed on March 18. The family remembered that John Bryan "captured a big horse and took [Wilson] to an old empty house where he died." In all, the Fifty-Eighth had one killed and thirteen wounded, two of whom later died.[22]

Federals also attacked that day on the east side of Rocky Face Ridge, but were driven back. That evening, they retired, and by February 27, were once again north of Tunnel Hill. The Fifty-Eighth remained on the field until February 28 before returning to camp. On the battlefield itself, the venture was a Confederate success, something that rarely happened for the Army of Tennessee. On a large scale, it was also successful for the Federals. Hardee's Corps was recalled from its trip west to join Polk. However, Sherman himself retreated away from Meridian.

John Barnes (Company I), who had just joined the army in November, wrote to his wife back home in Alexander County on the first of March: "I have bin in one battle and threw the kind [mercies] of god I came safe and I hope an trust in god that I may never be in another a person that has never bin in a battle have *no ider* how it is it don't look like any man could escape it is like the loudest thunder you ever heard in your life only there is no [cease] of it they can fire the cannons three times in a minute." Nearly any soldier's name could be given to Barnes's experience.[23]

Since the beginning of 1864, the Fifty-Eighth and Reynolds's brigade had been caught in a tug of war. Reynolds wrote Buckner on December 17, outlining the plight of the brigade:

> By accident my brigade was detained here when the rest of the division was ordered to Loudon. Since then we have been buffeted about as a brigade without friends, transferred from division to division until I am heartily sick of it. I hope you will have consideration enough for your lost and neglected children to ask or demand that we join your command immediately. All of our transportation, camp and garrison equipage is with your command; we have neither cooking utensils; all of our horses are there, and we are indeed sadly off. I am satisfied if we could get with you in Virginia we could increase our command 2,000 men. There is not a single officer or man who is not anxious to join you. Besides it is our right, and we appeal to you as our division commander to apply for us at once. We can be of little service here.

Buckner endorsed this appeal, as did Longstreet. Cooper sent it back to Joe Johnston, who wrote: "I must repeat that troops cannot be spared from this army." Johnston went further, recommending that troops with Longstreet should be returned to the Army of Tennessee.[24]

On January 26, Brig. Gen. Bushrod Johnson wrote Secretary of War James Seddon asking that Reynolds's brigade be ordered to report to its division, located with Longstreet's command in east Tennessee. The absence of Reynolds's brigade had injured "most seriously the efficiency of this division," Johnson wrote. Longstreet wrote Samuel Cooper, adjutant and inspector general of the Confederate armies, on February 1, asking Cooper to "please order Reynolds's brigade, of Buckner's division, to join this division." Even the regiment's old commander, Colonel Palmer, wrote Captain Harper the first of March, informing Harper that he had asked that the regiment be transferred to western North Carolina.[25]

Following the affair at Dalton, the Fifty-Eighth settled back down to the dull routine of camp life. Harper returned on March 18 with the cloth for officers and the bounty monies. There were brigade drills on March 14 and 15. On March 19, there was an election for the open post of third lieutenant of Company H. Joseph Stafford, an eighteen-year-old who had just joined the regiment, received 22 votes. Larkin Gilbert, a private working in the commissary department, received 29 votes. On March 22, a noticeable snow fell on the Confederate camps. Great snowball battles erupted between the men; at times whole regiments and brigades became involved. The Fifty-forth and Sixty-Third Virginia squared off against each other, but it is unclear if the Fifty-Eighth took part. The rest of April was spent drilling, reading, playing chess in Captain Harper's case, playing ball and eating poor food. A daily ration consisted of a pound of bacon or beef and 1 pound of corn meal. April 8 was set apart as a national day of fasting and prayer. "May God in his mercy hear the prayers that may be offered to Him this day and turn away his anger from us and grant us a speedy honorable and lasting peace," Harper wrote in his diary.[26]

Lt. Larkin W. Gilbert was one of just a few men left in the Fifty-Eighth at the end of the war. He joined Company H as a private in December 1862 and was paroled as a lieutenant of Company B in May 1865 (courtesy the North Carolina Department of Archives and History).

April 3 found Reynolds's brigade lined up for Sunday inspection at about 8 A.M. Captain Claiborne's diary provides a detailed glimpse of the routine. After the regiments were positioned in a column of companies,

> the officer commanding the brigade rides to the head of the column and either dismounts and, with assistance of his staff, inspects the troops in person, or selects several officers in each regiment (generally the field officers) to perform the duty, which is to examine the arms and accoutrements of each man present, to see that his gun is in good order, that his cartridge and cap box have the proper amount of ammunition (40 rounds of cartridges and 50 caps) in them, that he is properly clothed and shod, [that he is] supplied with haversack and canteen, and generally prepared for immediate service in the field.
>
> While this [is] being done, the General (or officer commanding) inspects the wagon and ambulance train which is ordered up in line nearby; [he] sees that the wagon and teams are in good condition, the harness in repair, &c., and that all is ready in the event of a sudden order to move. After the inspection is over the troops are drawn up in line, the General takes his position some forty or fifty paces in front, [and] the senior officer commands "Present Arms," which salute the General returns by taking off his hat. After the regiments are again formed in column of companies. The music is ordered to the front. The "color guard" takes its position in the center of each regiment, and the whole column passes in review a few paces in front of the General, who salutes (by taking off his hat) the head of each regiment and its colors, as it nears him. The troops are then dismissed and the camps inspected to see that the grounds are properly policed."[27]

Major Dula returned from his convalescence on April 5, and the consolidation of the Fifty-Eighth and Sixtieth came to an end. The Fifty-Eighth numbered 327 men present, with 228 ready for duty. There were 188 arms among them, and every soldier had forty rounds of ammunition. The Sixtieth North Carolina was the smallest regiment in the brigade with 141 men present. The Fifty-Fourth regiment was the largest, with 390 men present for duty, while the Sixty-Third Virginia mustered 303 men. At an inspection of the Fifty-Eighth on April 14, Captain Claiborne found that the regiment was "well armed with Austrian rifles (caliber 54) which all well kept; cartridge boxes not good, as in the other regiments, many of them too short for ammunition."[28]

The regiment received shoes and blankets from Raleigh on April 16. The boxes of shoes were inspected by a group of officers, including Capt. Caleb Conley (Company F), who reported that one of the boxes, marked "fifty pair," only contained forty-seven pairs of shoes. Two days later, the Fifty-Eighth was issued clothing. The next day, the entire Army of Tennessee was reviewed by General Johnston. On the twentieth, the Fifty-Eighth left winter camp and proceeded north of Dalton to work on fortifications. On April 25, the regiment was ordered to the area of the battle above Dalton the previous February, where the men went into camp.[29]

Desertion among the members of the Fifty-Eighth still ran virtually unchecked. One reason for all of the desertions, at least according to one member of the Fifty-Eighth, John Barnes (Company I), was the lack of furloughs back home. "You wanted me to get a furlough to come home," Barnes wrote. "I will tell you that there is no chance for a man to git a furlough heare if he gets a furlough he has to make one of his own." Approximately 91 men deserted from the Fifty-Eighth from the first of January to the end of April. Company E suffered the worst, with eighteen men leaving. Twelve of those left on the night of January 10. Only one, Simpson Kenney, ever returned, sometime prior to August 31. Company L lost twelve men, including five men on March 19. Four of them took the oath of allegiance. One of those was Linville Sheets. The forty-two-year-old Ashe County farmer had enlisted the previous October. According to a report from Brig. Gen. A. P. Campbell, Sheets poured his soul out. He told Campbell that

> Cleburne's division was at Tunnell Hill; Cheatham's division was 2 miles east of Dalton, on the railroad; Stevenson's division 2 miles west of Dalton, toward Tunnel Hill. Walker's and Stewart's divisions were at and a short distance below Dalton. Thinks that there are about 1,500 men in Reynolds'—brigade, to which he belongs, but thinks this brigade smaller than the average in Stevenson's division. A large number of new wagons were received by railroad from Atlanta; also a supply of fresh mules. Says that a great many new wagons were received, and that the talk among the soldiers was that it was intended to fix up the transportation preparatory to a movement up the East Tennessee Valley. Thinks that Johnston has from 40,000 to 50,000 men. He has been re-enforced from Alabama, and he heard that re-enforcements from Charleston, S. C., had arrived. The army gets short rations. Thinks that there is not more than two weeks supply of short rations on hand at Dalton. Artillery horses are in bad condition. They receive forage from Atlanta. Says Wheeler's headquarters are near Taylor's Bridge, and that most of the cavalry are from Tunnel Hill down via La Fayette in the direction of Rome. About four weeks since a number of cavalry horses were sent to Kingston to forage. There are no fortifications at Dalton. At Reseca, 12 miles south of Dalton, that have some fortifications. Does not know of any troops from Longstreet having joined Johnston, or vice versa. Cars run constantly between Dalton and Atlanta. Seems to be no lack of transportation.

Sheets, having been in the army for a short time, seems to have much knowledge about the Army of Tennessee. It is possible that he was used by the Confederates to plant wrong information in the minds of the Federals. Each army was known to do this and some of Sheets's information is incorrect. Sheets took the oath of allegiance at Chattanooga on March 24 and was released. He never rejoined the Confederate army.[30]

Possibly one reason for the number of desertions was the "Peace Movement" happening back in the Tar Heel state. In early 1863, James T. Leach, an eastern North Carolina planter and slave owner, ran for a seat in the Confederate States Congress. His platform was that the South needed a "just, honorable and lasting peace." Leach won his seat, which led to over 100 peace rallies across North Carolina in the summer of 1863. Soon, William Holden, a newspaper editor in Raleigh, emerged as the leader of the peace movement. Holden's newspaper office in Raleigh was sacked in September 1863, and Governor Vance broke ties with Holden and denounced the Peace Movement. Those who backed the Peace Movement platform believed that Jefferson Davis and the Confederate government had failed to secure a peace through military means. Therefore, the South as a whole, or, if no one else was willing, North Carolina, in an effort to prevent defeat, emancipation, and Federal military rule, should hold a convention to consider peace negotiations.

This led Davis to ask the Confederate Congress for the ability to suspend the writ of habeas corpus, which he was granted in February 1864. Those "advising or inciting others to abandon the Confederate cause, or to resist Confederate states, or to adhere to the enemy" could be arrested. Holden went on to run against Vance in the 1864 election and lost. Holden's loss drove many of his supporters out of the Confederate army. The role that the Peace Movement had in the numerous desertions in the Fifty-Eighth North Carolina is unclear. However, the men were aware of what was happening back in Raleigh and across the state. John Barnes (Company I) complained to his wife about the lack of news in a letter home in January 1864, writing that "we git but litel news heare any way they don't a low holden [Holden's] paper to cum heare."[31]

On March 24, 1864, the officers of the Fifty-Eighth and Sixtieth North Carolina regiments gathered together to draft a letter to Vance, thanking him for his "able and patriotic" service to the state and for working toward a "lasting peace ... in this dark hour of our country's trial"; the letter continued, "when treason shows its hideous face even in our own Capital we appeal to you with confidence ... that all private end will be sacrificed by you for the interest of our state and for the good of our common country." Eighteen officers of the Fifty-Eighth signed the letter, with Captain Harper's name at the head of the list.[32]

Around the first of May, the Fifty-Eighth received its one and only chaplain: John W. Rabey. Residing in Caldwell County, Rabey enlisted on November 30, 1861, in Company I, Twenty-Sixth North Carolina Troops. He served with the Twenty-Sixth until captured during the battle of New Bern in March 1862. Once paroled, Rabey disappeared, and on May 7, 1863, he was listed as a deserter. Rabey recorded his denomination as a "Methodist-Episcopalian." Many had been concerned about the spiritual condition of the regiment for some time. As early as July 1862, Bethel Baptist Church in McDowell County had taken a "collection of Fifteen dollars and fifteen cents to purchase testaments and religious literature" for the men in Palmer's regiment. The materials were apparently much needed, for a few months later, in October 1862, while stationed at Cumberland Gap, William Horton (Company I) had written to his sister that "this company is the worst Co to swear and gambel you ever seen in your life. They play Cards day and night."

Early in March 1863, while stationed at Big Gap Creek, twenty-three officers of the Fifty-Eighth signed a petition asking Colonel Palmer to find a minister for the regiment. Rabey arrived during one of the greatest revivals in the Army of Tennessee. "I never saw so fine a field for sowing the seeds of the Gospel," a missionary to the army around Dalton wrote to a Christian newspaper, requesting more ministers. The extent of the revival among the members is unknown. Captain Harper reported several times attending preaching and prayer meetings under the Reverend W. Wood. The discourse for March 27 was the "Parable of the sower." Harper even had the reverend to dinner. Lt. Poindexter Blevins (Company F) wrote home on March 27, voicing his displeasure at not being able to attend his church services. He wanted to be at church, "instead of being called out in the field for inspection of arms and accoutrements the deathly weapons of war." Blevins invoked the Almighty's blessing on himself and his comrades: "May the Blest Lord in his infinite Mercies cause us as a nation to humble our selves in the very dust of humility so that such may not be our fate — May His cause prosper and true Christian faith grow stronger and stronger and genuine religion may cover the whole land of America as the waters cover the chanels of the great deep."[33]

If Rabey was present in his official capacity as chaplain on May 4, a unpleasant task awaited him: the execution of over a dozen deserters by a firing squad. And the majority were from the Fifty-Eighth.

Death was the proscribed penalty for desertion. Often, deserters were given lesser punishments. At times, a blind eye might even be shown to deserters, especially those who came back of their own accord. However, desertion was so rampant in the Army of Tennessee that something had to be done. So Johnston chose some soldiers to use as examples. On May 4 and 5, 1864, twenty-two men paid the ultimate price for the crime of desertion. Thirteen men from the Fifty-Eighth were ordered to be executed by a firing squad. A few of these men, Reuben Dellinger (Company A), Joseph Gibbs, (Company C), George McFalls (Company K), and Michael Ward (Company D), had been with their companies since their inception. Gordon Morrow (Company H) had joined Vance's Legion, later transferred to Company I, Twenty-Sixth North Carolina, for a short time before joining the Fifty-Eighth. Alfrod Ball (Company G) joined the regiment in September 1862. Ball was from Wilkes County; Dellinger and McFall, from Mitchell; Gibbs from Yancey; Morrow from Caldwell; and Ward from Watauga. The others had joined later. Jacob August (Company E), enlisted in Union County on December 25, 1863. William Byers (Company G) was from Rutherford County and enlisted October 25, 1863, at Camp Holmes. Hailing from York County, South Carolina, Asa Dover (Company F), enlisted on August 20, 1863. Jesse Hase (Company A) was from Greene County, Tennessee, and joined on October 20, 1863. Also from Rutherford County was Wright Hutchings (Company F) enlisting in McDowell County on October 6, 1863. Hiram Younblood (Company F) enlisted in Rutherford County on August 14, 1863, and E. H. Younts (Company H) enlisted in Athens, Georgia, on December 16, 1863. Most of these men were in their twenties, with the exception of Hutchings, who was forty-three. Each of them had deserted just once, save Ball, who was a sergeant, and Ward, a private. They both had deserted twice. Most were court-martialed in late

Andrew Sullins, pictured here with his wife, Elmira Wiseman Sullins, joined Company A at the age of thirty-seven on October 15, 1863, and served through August 31, 1864 (courtesy Rhonda Gunter).

March or early April, save Ball, who was court-martialed on December 18, 1863. Ward was married with three children. Hase had six children; Gibbs, one; and Byers, one.[34]

Only Gibbs and Dellinger have been remembered with family stories concerning their executions. The nineteen-year-old Gibbs had a wife, Eliza, and a three-year-old son back in Yancey County. Word came to him that "Eliza was seriously ill," so Gibbs deserted on September 27, 1863, right after the battle of Chickamauga. It is unclear when Gibbs returned to the army, or if he was arrested and brought back. He was listed as present and under arrest on February 29, 1864. Dellinger is rumored to have also had a wife, whom he came home to see. On his return, he "was almost back to camp ... when he got caught." Another source on Dellinger states that he left his regiment to work with his father on the family farm.[35]

Not only were these thirteen members of the Fifty-Eighth scheduled for execution, but two members of the Sixtieth were condemned as well. An Augusta, Georgia, newspaper listed the names of twenty-one men "to be shot for desertion." All thirteen of the Fifty-Eighth's men are listed. As the story goes, on May 3, the day before the executions, "four men appealed to Johnston for the life of their brother, and he was spared." According to the record, Gordon Morrow's life was spared on May 3, and he returned to his place in his company on May 7. There are two other Morrows who served in the Fifty-Eighth. Neither, however, was present in May 1864. Daniel Morrow died in Clinton, Tennessee, on March 30, 1863, and Nathan Morrow died back in Caldwell County on August 4, 1862.[36]

For the twelve condemned men, May 4 dawned clear and cool. According to one old soldier, the firing squad was made up of men from the provost guard, possibly under the command of Lt. Robert C. Clayton of the Sixtieth North Carolina. The squad marched to General Stewart's headquarters, where they were ordered to stack arms. The detachment then marched off, and staff officers loaded some of the musket with live rounds, while others were loaded with blanks. The detachment returned, retook the arms, and marched away, not knowing who had live rounds. This was done to lessen the psychological impact upon the men who had to shoot their fellow soldiers. According to Capt. Ellis Claiborne, an officer on the staff of General Reynolds, the firing party consisted of "122 men — eighteen to each man — two out of each eight guns loaded with blank cartridges, the rest with balls."

A little before noon, the condemned men were brought into Crow Valley in a wagon. While they were unloaded and taken to the spot of execution, the drum corps beat the slow "Dead March." The entire army was drawn up into a hollow square: soldiers formed up on three sides, with the last side left open for the condemned men. An ambulance followed the men, carrying their coffins. The men were blindfolded and tied to stakes. "Words of hope [were] whispered by the minister to them so soon into eternity," recorded Claiborne. The firing squad lined up just ten paces, about thirty feet, in from of the condemned. At noon, Clayton ordered his men to fire. Three of the fourteen were not killed outright, and the reserve firing squad "of fourteen men advanced immediately up to those still living and ended their torture by blowing out their brains."

"O! what a [day] was that!" the assistant surgeon of the Sixtieth wrote. "The private soldiers were all bitterly opposed to the executions of these men.... I can never, never forget that sad scene; I was heart sick." Captain Claiborne wrote that all of the men of the division filed past the executed men, save one brigade. "The bodies of the executed men [were] put in their coffins prepared for them and buried in one common grave, with neither stone nor board to mark the spot. Such is the fate of the deserter."[37]

Back home in Yancey County, Eliza Gibbs "was doing the family 'wash' [laundry], using a huge iron pot, headed outside, as was the custom of the time, a white dove flew to the ground and fluttered around her feet. This highly unusual event she took as an omen of disaster. This turned out to be the case, since her husband died at approximately the same time the dove made its strange appearance." Eliza survived the war.[38]

Johnston's execution of deserters did little to deter other men from slipping away from the army. By the end of May 1864, an additional eighteen men had left the Fifty-Eighth.

CHAPTER 10

May–July 1864

"Great gloom fell upon the army."—Lt. Jonathan Miller, Company I

For the past five months, the Army of Tennessee had been quartered in and around Dalton, Georgia. In that five months, they had gained a new commander: Joseph E. Johnston. They had also been better fed, clothed, and otherwise supplied than during their previous time in the Confederate army. Many men had been furloughed, able to go back home and visit loved ones for the first time since enlisting. Some who had absented themselves without permission had returned and been forgiven. For those who continued to desert, executions had begun, that blow falling heavily on the Fifty-Eighth North Carolina. Overall, morale was up, and Johnston had gained about 5,000 more men than he had when he assumed command the previous December. All told, Johnston's army contained about 55,000 men in two infantry corps and one cavalry corps.

Opposing the Army of Tennessee just 30 miles to the north of Dalton were the combined Federal forces of Ulysses S. Grant. In early March 1863, Grant was ordered to Washington, D.C., where he was promoted to the rank of lieutenant general and given overall command of the Federal armies. Grant's proposed grand strategy for the campaign of 1864 was to apply pressure to several different fronts simultaneously. The Army of the Potomac in Virginia, the principal Federal army in the east, was to keep the Army of Northern Virginia within its sights. Two smaller forces also began to operate within the state: the Army of the James would drive from the coast towards Petersburg and Richmond, while a different Federal force would attack and hold the Shenandoah Valley, the breadbasket of the Confederacy. The capture of Petersburg or Richmond could cut vital rail lines, while the loss of the Shenandoah Valley could cut off supplies. A fourth column was scheduled to move from Federally controlled New Orleans towards Mobile, Alabama, cutting off that port, and then possibly toward central Alabama, destroying the munitions facility in Selma.

The final part of Grant's plan involved the Federal forces outside Chattanooga. They would drive south into North Georgia, endeavoring to destroy transportation facilities and the industrial capacity of central Georgia. All of these movements at once would keep the Confederate forces from reinforcing each other as they had done in the past. Grant originally planned to lead the operations in Georgia. However, his trip to Washington had disclosed many problems with the Army of the Potomac, and Grant resolved to make his headquarters in the field with this force. Grant choose Federal Army of the Tennessee commander and his friend, William T. Sherman, to lead the Military Department of Mississippi. Sherman had around 100,000 men in three different armies at his disposal to combat the

Confederates. Sherman vowed to make Joe Johnston and his army, not some city, his target, much as Grant did with the Army of Northern Virginia. Operations were slated to begin May 5.

The last few days of April found the Confederate army getting prepared for the upcoming campaign. The quartermaster on Reynolds's staff, Maj. W. L. McConnico, filled out a requisition asking for 2 two-horse wagons, 10 camp kettles, ink, packing boxes, 195 pairs of pants, and 1 battle flag. One of the morale-building acts of General Johnston was the issue of new battle flags for the army. While Johnston wanted the flags to resemble the square battle flags carried by the Army of Northern Virginia, those issued were a little different. These new flags for the Army of Tennessee were rectangular. Hood, who was the Fifty-Eighth's corps commander, wrote on March 11 that the "lieutenant-general commanding can well understand the pride many regiments of the corps feel in other flags they have gloriously borne in battle," but he wanted each regiment to be easily identifiable and uniform.

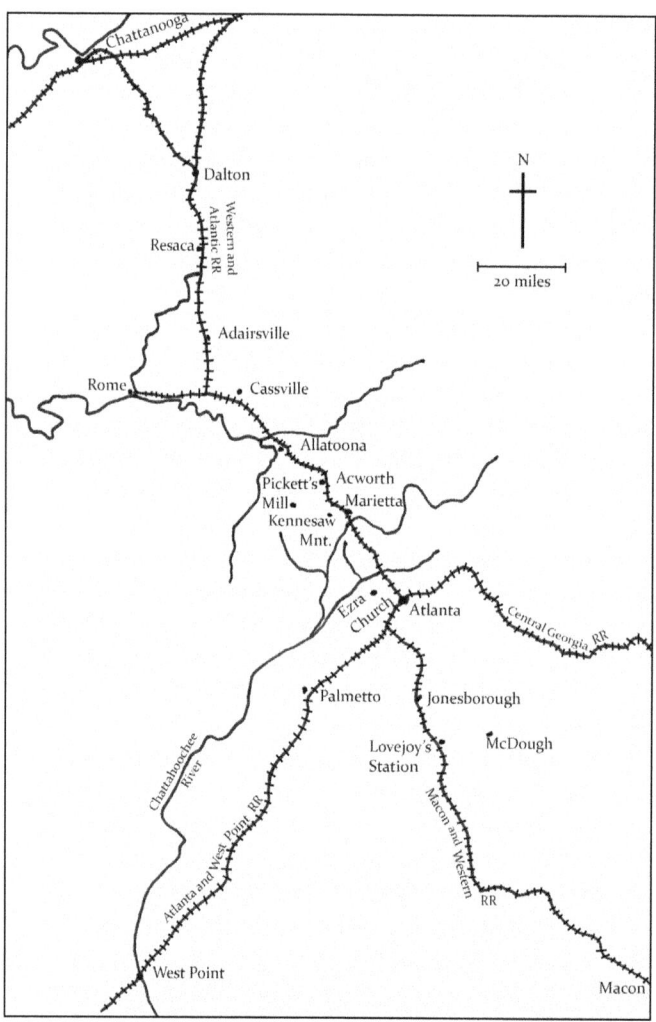

The Fifty-Eighth spent part of the winter, spring, and summer of 1864 fighting in north Georgia.

The flags the regiments currently had could "be sent for safe keeping to the capitol of the States to which the troops belong, as it will be found inconvenient to have more than one flag in a regiment."

On April 20, he issued an additional order stating that the "regiments of this corps will have their battle-flags plainly marked with their numbers and the State to which they belong." These Army of Tennessee flags were on average 35 inches on the staff by 52 inches on the fly. They, like their Virginia counterparts, had a red field, with a blue cross and white stars. The regiment number was in the top quadrant, while the state designation was in the bottom quadrant.[1]

On May 5, the Army of the Potomac in Virginia stepped off on its campaign against Robert E. Lee. At the same time, three of the other four elements of Grant's plan also stepped off. A fifth part, the march from New Orleans to Mobile, never happened. Sherman's plan was to send two of his armies, the ones under Schofield and Thomas, toward Dalton, while the third, the Army of the Tennessee under McPherson, moved under the cover of the mountains southwest to Snake Creek Gap, opposite Resaca. McPherson could then capture the thinly defended town and destroy the railroad, forcing the Confederates to abandon their position to the north. Furthermore, the Confederates would be "bottled-up" between the Federal forces. If all went well, Sherman could destroy a portion of the Confederate army as it moved south to re-establish a railroad connection. For both the Federals and the Confederates, constant contact with the railroad, their supply lines, dictated the terms for the upcoming campaign.

Johnston knew that Sherman was coming. Stevenson's division had broken camp on April 26 and was in Crow Valley working on fortifications. Hood's corps occupied the area along Crow Creek and Ault's Mill Creek, while Hardee's corps continued the line along the dominating Rocky Face Ridge to the west. Stevenson positioned Reynolds's brigade along Crow Creek, with Key's Arkansas and Goldwaite's Alabama batteries to the left, and Cumming's brigade to the right. At 8:00 A.M. on May 7, orders to "fall in" were given, and the Fifty-Eighth left its camps and moved into the breastworks, where the men spent the day working.

After spending the night in their breastworks, the Confederates were up early, waiting for the Federals. Skirmishing began that morning around 9:00 A.M. A portion of the Federal army gained the northern end of Rocky Face Ridge and gingerly made its way toward the south. One Federal general reported that sections of the top of the ridge would only hold four men abreast. The Federals ran into stiff resistance and were forced to fall back. Later that same day, Reynolds's brigade was ordered to move to the left and assigned to the eastern side of Rocky Face Ridge.

On May 10, Captain Harper was assigned brigade officer of the day and was placed over the Confederate picket line in front of Reynolds's brigade. Harper reported that at 3:00 P.M., his pickets were driven in. However, the Confederate line of Rocky Face Ridge proved impregnable. That evening, the skirmish line was retaken from the Federals. May 10 and 11 were spent in the trenches, with constant sharpshooting "slowly all day." It was unseasonably cool, with "desperately hard" rain the evening of the tenth.[2]

Reported casualties for the days spent on the line were few. On May 8, William Parsons (Company L) was captured and taken to Camp (Company H) Morton in Indiana, where he later died of "inflammation of the lungs." Richard Colman was wounded the next day in the left leg or ankle. He apparently did not return to the Fifty-Eighth. That same day, Joseph Pierce (Company I) was captured. He was also sent to Camp Morton, and he, like Parsons, died of typhoid.[3]

Sherman's front just north of Dalton was merely a diversion. On May 5, Sherman ordered the Army of the Tennessee, under James McPherson, to secure Snake Creek Gap and either attack the Confederates or occupy the railroad. McPherson, with 24,000 men, passed through Snake Creek Gap on May 8, brushing aside Confederate cavalry in the area. Resaca and the railroad were ripe for the taking, but McPherson faltered, worried that Johnston would fall back so quickly from Dalton that he would be cut off. Instead of driving off the 4,000 Confederates from Polk's corps who occupied the defensive works, McPherson pulled back to the mouth of Snake Creek Gap and dug in. The Federals destroyed a short section of the Western and Atlantic Railroad, cut the telegraph, and burned a wood-cutting station. The Federals' biggest achievement was to alert General Johnston to the danger in his rear.[4]

Johnston ordered a portion of Hood's corps to Resaca on May 10. Other forces from Polk's corps, recently stationed in Alabama, began to arrive in Resaca. Polk himself assumed

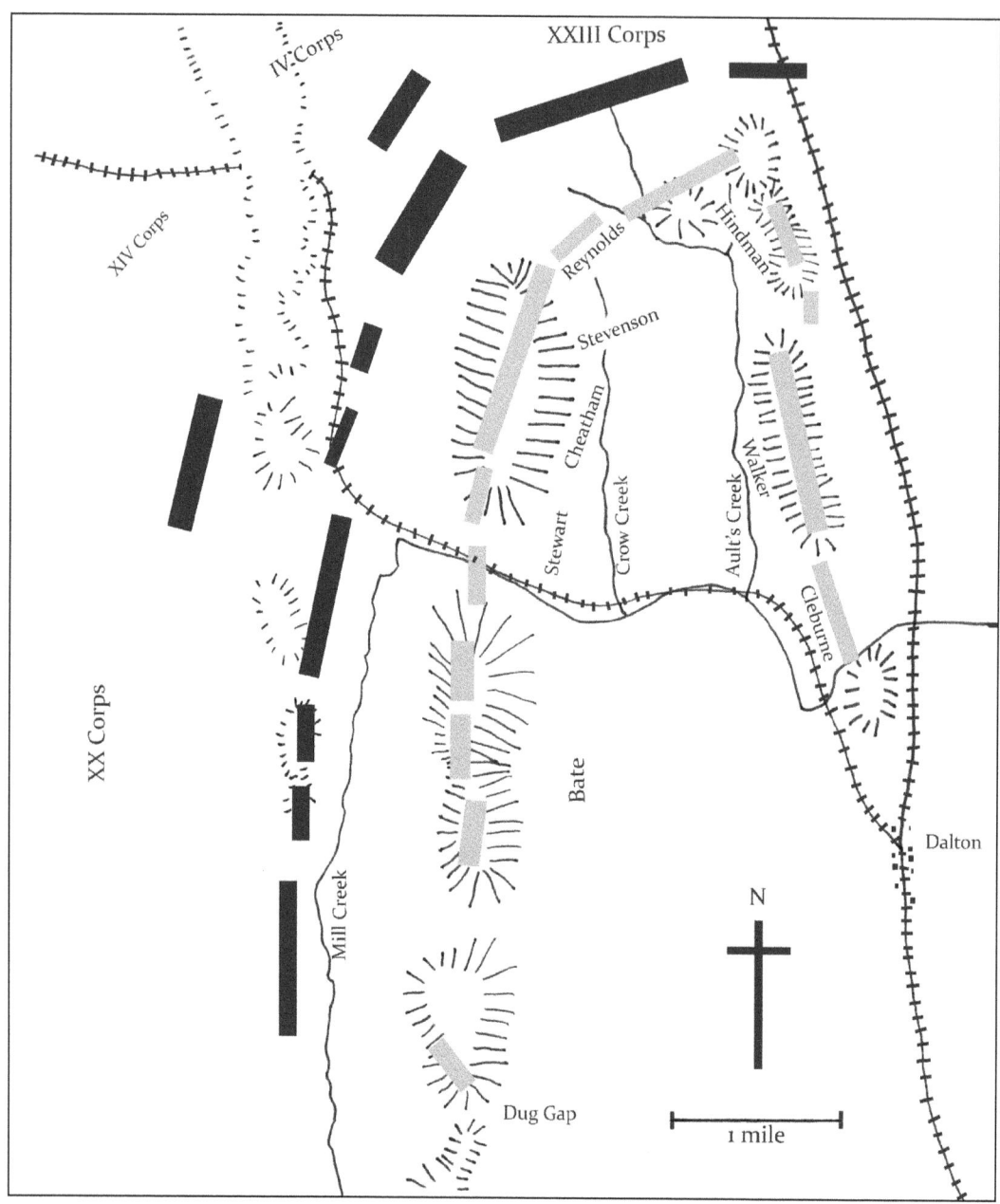

Early May 1864 found the Fifty-Eighth North Carolina in the Crow River Valley, just north of Dalton, Georgia.

command of the defenses in the area on May 11. Beginning on May 10, Sherman ordered all of his forces, save the IV Corps, to Resaca. A cavalry probe by Wheeler on May 12 showed Johnston that almost all of the Federals were gone, and Johnston began moving his Confederates towards Resaca that evening. The Fifty-Eighth quietly left its entrenchments about nine that evening and headed south, marching all night and stopping on the thirteenth of May at Tilton for breakfast. The men were soon on the road again, moving very slowly, with flankers and skirmishers out to protect them against the "enemy pressing us in rear and hovering on our flanks." That night, they stopped about two miles from Resaca, where they formed in a line of battle. Two members of Company G, Nathan Phillips and Lewis Trivett, were captured in Dalton. Phillips might have been sick, since he was in a Federal hospital in Louisville, Kentucky, on May 23. Both Phillips and Trivett died as prisoners of war.[5]

By the evening of May 13, the Fifty-Eighth and the rest of Reynolds's brigade were in entrenchments north of Resaca. Johnston placed his army in a "fish-hook" formation. The left of the line was anchored on the Oostanaula River, and ran north, paralleling the Western and Atlantic Railroad for a little over two miles. The line then bent back to the right, or east, forming a salient angle on a high point, before anchoring on the Conasauga River. Overall, the Confederate line measured a little over four miles in length. Polk's corps was on the left, followed by Hardee's, and then Hood's corps. Stevenson formed his division in two lines, with Cumming's and Brown's brigades in the front and Pettus's and Reynolds's brigades in the rear in reserve. Within Stevenson's line was a small lunette, or fort, containing Maxillian Van Corput's Cherokee Georgia Battery, consisting of four 12-pound Napoleons. Stewart's division was to the right of Stevenson, and Hindman was to Stevenson's left.[6]

Dawn broke clear on Saturday, May 14. The soldiers in both armies were up early, preparing for the day's struggle. It was Sherman's objective to cave in the Confederate right and cut the railroad. At 9:00 A.M., Sherman launched portions of the XXIII and XIV Corps in an attack that was beaten back by the Confederates. Later that afternoon, Wheeler informed Johnston that the Federal left was unprotected, and Johnston ordered Hood to launch an attack. Hood chose Stewart's and Stevenson's divisions. Stewart was on the right, and Stevenson on the left. Stevenson arranged his brigades with Reynolds, including the Fifty-Eighth, on the left; Brown in the center and Cumming on the right with Pettus in support to the rear. Stevenson's division advanced out of the works between 4 and 5 P.M. and started to half wheel to the left. This division was soon joined by Stewart's men. One Federal recalled that the Confederates "formed in admirable order, their flags floating gaily, many of their officers mounted, and a light line of cavalry riding in the rear and upon either flank." The Confederates advanced for over a mile and "charged the enemy who ran for dear life," as one member of the Fifty-Eighth recalled, "Magnificent charge." One of the Federal generals recalled that his troops were "fired into from three directions." The Confederates were able to capture the Federal works. Elijah Coffey (Company E) was one of the first over and was seriously wounded in the right hand. A portion of the Confederate advance was in a thick woods. As the brigades advanced out of the woods, the six guns—two rifled and four smoothbore cannon of the Fifth Indiana Battery located on a hill to the rear of the Union position—were turned in the Confederates' direction. The battery occupied a knoll and,

These are remnants of the two flags of the Fifty-Eighth North Carolina. The traditional portion of the flag most likely came from a Second National, while the "58" and "NC" came from an 1864 Atlanta/Dalton Depot flag. Both remnants were donated to the state by the descendants of the Harper family (courtesy the North Carolina Museum of History).

with a 400-hundred-yard-long cleared field to the front, began to drop "spherical case and shell" among the Confederates. As the Confederates attempted to work their way to the left, the Federal gunners began firing canister, which drove the Confederates back. The Confederates reformed and were pushing ahead once again towards the battery when Federal infantry, portions of the XX Corps, arrived and delivered volleys into the Confederates, who retired back to the cover of the woods. That night, the Confederates gave up their advance position in the captured Federal works and fell back into their defensive entrenchments.[7]

Earlier that day, Sherman had sent a portion of his command farther downstream looking for a way to cross the river and cut the railroad. The Federals crossed the head of Snake Creek, but thought they themselves were being cut off from the main Federal body and retreated back across the river. Johnston sent troops to the area. Prior to receiving intelligence about the Federal advance, he had ordered Hood to renew the attack early on the morning of May 15. When word reached Johnston of the Federal incursion in his rear, he called off the attack. Once Johnston knew that the Federals were not on his side of the river, he re-authorized Hood's attack. That same evening, as the men settled down for a mostly sleepless night, Sherman positioned the IV and XX Corps for a new attack upon Confederate lines, set to commence at 11:30 A.M.

Johnston sent orders to Stevenson the next morning: retake the position in the front that they had vacated the day before. Luckily for the Confederates, the Federals had not reoccupied their previous position. As soon as the Confederates moved into the position, they began constructing breastworks made of logs and rails. While working, Stevenson received orders to position one of his batteries in such a way as to apply pressure on Federal artillery that was raking General Hindman's position to the left. Stevenson was working to create a protected emplacement for his guns when other orders arrived: have the battery open fire. Stevenson moved the four guns of the Cherokee battery into position and opened fire. No sooner had the gunners begun working their pieces than the Federals appeared, driving in the Confederate skirmishers and charging with "great impetuosity. So quickly was all this done," Stevenson wrote, "that it was impossible to remove the artillery before the enemy had effected a lodgment in the ravine in front of it." The Federals had driven off the Confederate gunners, but small arms fire from the Confederates prevented the Federals from securing their prize. Stevenson found the Federal assault "in heavy force" and determined that he could not retrieve the guns but with "great loss of life." The abandoned Confederate artillery stood between the lines, each side blazing away at each other. Sherman's second assault had stalled.[8]

Johnston soon learned that the Federals were once again over Snake Creek, and he chose to cancel the planned attack. Johnston informed Hood, but the attack was already in motion, and Hood was unable to reel in Stewart.

In Stevenson's front, Brown's brigade was running out of ammunition, and Stevenson sought to replace him with the Fifty-Eighth and the rest of Reynolds's brigade. Swapping front line regiments while under fire is a dangerous move, but the regiments of Brown and Reynolds were able to accomplish the transition without being attacked. Stevenson wanted to use Reynolds, Brown, and two regiments from Cumming's brigade, along with a portion of Gibson's brigade of Stewart's division, to attack the Federals and rescue the guns. He was unable to get the regiments coordinated before Stewart called Gibson's brigade back.

The Confederates and Federals still struggled over the guns. A journalist writing for the Atlanta *Intelligencer* wrote that at a quarter from four o'clock, a fifth charge was made, the enemy throwing forward fresh troops every time. Th[i]s charge was very heavy, and was made with spirit.... With a prolonged cheer, they rushed upon our works.—A ... terrible, death-dealing volley, was poured into their ranks, and a loud ... yell of defiance rang out from the lips of the Virginians and North Carolinians. This was more than the men of Brown's and Pettus' Brigades [who were in reserve] could withstand, and though threatened with death by their officers [they] entered the pits to assist in repelling the charge. But their services were not needed. Quickly another volley [was] poured into the enemy's line of battle, and they turned and retreated in disorder to the cover of their ridge, followed by the derisive shouts of the victors....

Within half an hour ... three lines of battle, closely massed, were seen forming in front of that portion of the line held by the 58th North Carolina. There was not much time for reflection, for very soon a voice on the right of the regiment exclaimed "they are coming!" and the first column was seen to advance. "Withhold your fire until they come close to you and then aim low," ordered the officers. On came the enemy cheering loudly.... They approached within fifty yards of the line, firing rapidly upon our men—a sheet of our fire was the answer, and the dead and wounded lie piled up before our works.... Bewildered by the fierceness of our fire, they scattered through the woods and reached their lines, our sharp shooters killing and wounding them by dozens in their route down the ridge....

This sixth column was repulsed only a few minutes when the remaining two columns of Yankees marched forward, with the hope of reaching our line before our men could fire more than one volley. But their charge was not made with the same firmness as characterized ... the preceding one, and two or three well-aimed volleys from the Fifty-eighth North Carolina, assisted by a cross fire from the Fifty-fourth Virginia on the one hand and the Sixty-third [Virginia] on the other, routed the 7th attacking column of the enemy. They ... retired to their ridge, and for a few moments only the sharpshooters could be seen, their main body being no doubt engaged in reforming their broken columns.[9]

That evening, probably around 6:00 P.M., Stewart began his attack. Stevenson was ordered "to move a portion of my force ... out of the trenches. And co-operating with General Stewart, to swing around upon the enemy.... The Fifty-Fourth Virginia, on the right, leaped from the trenches and rushed bravely upon the enemy, but found there was no connection with General Stewart's left, and being thus unsupported were compelled to fall back before the rest of the brigade moved out."

However, Captain Harper related something a little different. Harper, wrote in his diary that the Fifty-Eighth also "moved over the breastworks under heavy fire and formed [and] advanced on the Enemy, our lines not connecting with Stewart (who by the way was repulsed about or before this time). We were compelled to withdraw to the entrenchments." Darkness was soon upon the combatants. Confederate skirmishers kept up a steady fire, masking the activities behind the Confederate lines. In some places, trees and shrubs burned, at times consuming the dead or badly wounded.[10]

In two days, the Fifty-Eighth was involved in two fights. In those two days, the regiment sustained five killed; thirty wounded, of whom two later died; eleven captured; and two missing in action. Many of the wounded had sustained injuries indicative of fighting behind breastworks and in trenches. Joseph Dellinger (Company A) was struck in the face, "just below the left eye." Sgt. Calvin Cottrell (Company I) was also wounded in the face with his "right eye shot out destroying also the nasal bone." Several were wounded in the act of firing their rifled muskets. Cpl. Julius Smith (Company H) was wounded in the second finger on his left hand and in his left shoulder. Jacob Bolick (Company H) was struck in the left arm, necessitating the amputation of that arm. Several of the wounds were the results of artillery shrapnel: James Parker (Company C) in the left ankle; Lt. John Norris

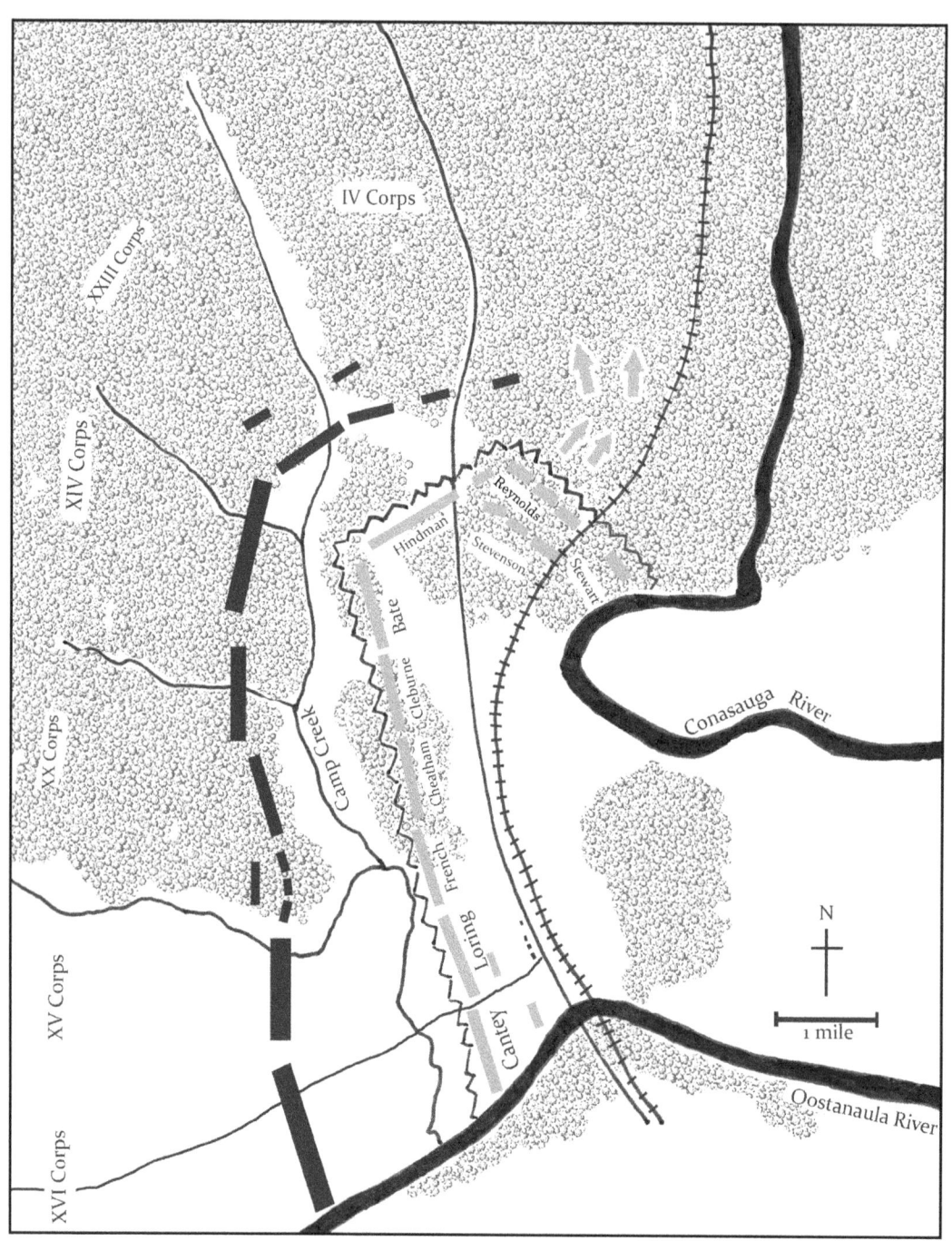

During the battle of Resaca, Georgia, the Fifty-Eighth helped turn the left flank of the Federal army.

(Company G) "shocked" by the concussion of a shell; and, Cpl. Marion Handy (Company L) by the explosion of a shell. Robert Rowland (Company C) was shot in the breast and killed, as was Aaron Reece (Company E), Robert McKissick (Company F), Charles Moore (Company F), and Austin Smith (Company H). Garrett Gouge wrote home that fellow Company K member Henry Justice was mortally wounded in the right breast. Writing a few days later, James Hurley (Company L) considered Resaca "a terrible battle" and believed that the Federals had lost "twenty thousand men in this two days of fighting."[11]

One of the wounded was Captain Harper. As the Fifty-Eighth surged over the breastworks in support of Stewart's division, Harper "received a flesh wound through the calf of the left leg." With "no ambulance being on hand," Harper "hobbled back to a surgeon." His leg wound was dressed and he was "sent on foot to the Division Hospital which I reached after dark with great difficulty about two miles southeast of Resaca on R. R." Here Harper was "refreshed with drink of spirits and lay down on my blanket on ground to rest. Slept until nearly daylight when a train was at hand to carry off the wounded." At 4:00 A.M., Harper was loaded on a train bound for Atlanta. The train stopped in Calhoun where the "Relief Committee" fed him a good lunch. Harper attempted to get a transfer to North Carolina, but was unsuccessful. That night, he was transferred to a hospital in Madison, Georgia, where he spent the next few days hobbling about on crutches, playing "droughts," attending church services, reading, and "lying about loose." He kept up a steady stream of correspondence and was quartered with a fellow officer from the Sixtieth: Capt. Edwin Clayton. Finally, on June 3, he received his furlough home and was on the 8:00 P.M. train, arriving back home in Caldwell County on June 6 at 6:00 P.M.[12]

Back out on the lines, darkness had overtaken the two sides. Under the cover of darkness, Federal soldiers tore a hole in the front of the redoubt where the abandoned Confederate artillery was located and removed the four guns. Not long after Stewart's assault, which dragged along the Fifty-Fourth Virginia and the Fifty-Eighth North Carolina, Johnston called together his corps and division commanders to explain the necessity of retreat. Federals were threatening to cut his lines of communication, and Johnston did not have enough men to fight on two fronts. That evening, the Confederates began to retreat, and

The Fifty-Eighth moved from the ground in the right of this photograph and across the hills in the center during the charge at Resaca.

around nine p.m., the Fifty-Eighth left the entrenchments, heading for the new pontoon bridge over the Oostanaula River. The Fifty-Eighth remained as a rear guard, not crossing over the bridge until the next morning. After marching about six miles, they stopped for a two-hour rest. Then they moved on for another three miles, all the while having to contend with "skirmishing ... on the flank the whole time."[13]

As the Confederates retreated, Johnston was constantly looking for a place that offered advantages for a defensive stand. He found none at Calhoun and kept his army moving south. Every half mile or so, Southern cavalry troopers threw up a log barricade across the road, forcing the Federals to stop and deploy a brigade to drive them off. This tactic seriously delayed the Federal advance. Before daylight on the morning of the seventeenth, the Fifty-Eighth was on the road again, covering six miles before stopping near Adairsville. Johnston again sought a significant defensive feature on which to anchor his forces while looking for an opportunity to attack. But the area around Adairsville was unimpressive. Regardless, as soon as the Confederate infantry halted, fieldworks were constructed. Federal forces soon began probing the Confederate lines, attacking the cavalry first. Cpl. John Dugger (Company D) recalled that the action was a "sharp ... fight." The Fifty-Eighth was formed in a line of battle but apparently remained quiet.[14]

Sherman did not believe that the Confederates would stand and fight north of the Etowah River. Hence, on May 16, he spread his forces across a wide front in pursuit of the Confederates. One group of Federals followed the Confederates, moving along the rail line. Another moved parallel to this force. A third force went farther west to capture Rome. Johnston, learning of the dispersal of the Federal forces, saw an opportunity to attack and cripple a portion of the Federal army.

The Fifty-Eighth stayed near Adairsville until the early morning of May 18. About midnight the regiment "again moved off secretly" in a dense fog, reaching Cassville about 11:00 A.M. Different roads ran south out of Adairsville, and Johnston correctly surmised that Sherman would use both. On May 19, a hot and humid day, Johnston feared that all of the recent retreating was causing a decline in morale, so he issued a general order:

> Soldiers of the Army of Tennessee, you have displayed the highest quality of the soldier — firmness in combat, patience under toil. By your courage and skill you have repulsed every assault of the enemy. By marches by day and by marches by night you have defeated every attempt upon your communication. Your communications are secured.
> You will now turn and march to meet his advancing columns. Fully confiding in the conduct of the officers, the courage of the soldiers, I will lead you in battle. We may confidently trust that the Almighty Father will still reward the patriots' toils and bless the patriots' banners. Cheered by the success of our brothers in Virginia and beyond the Mississippi, our efforts will equal theirs. Strengthened by His support, those efforts will be crowned with the like glories.

Unfortunately for Johnston, he was not about to lead his forces into battle. One of his subordinate commanders, the Fifty-Eighth's corps commander, John Bell Hood, had other ideas.[15]

Johnston's plan was to use Hardee's corps on the left and across the Adairsville Road, with Hood's corps on the right and Polk's Corps in the center to assail the Army of the Cumberland. Hood led his corps forward around 10:00 A.M. As the men advanced, they encountered no Federals. Soon, a mounted soldier rode up, informing Hood that there were Federal soldiers on his right and rear. Hood called off his attack and returned to his starting position. "It can't be!" Johnston exclaimed when the reports reached him. Still in disbelief, Johnston started to pull his men back into a defensive position on a ridge south of Cassville. Possibly the Army of Tennessee's greatest opportunity for the destruction of a portion of Sherman's command slipped through Johnston's fingers, based upon reported Federals who could not be documented.[16]

The defensive position that Johnston selected had several merits. However, the Confederate left was subject to an enfilading artillery fire. At a conference that evening, Johnston asked his corps commanders for their opinions: Hardee, whose corps was the one subjected to the artillery fire, believed that he could hold. Polk and Hood believed the position untenable, and Johnston chose to retreat across the Etowah River. Dugger recalled in his diary: "Again secretly retired about 10 o'clock." The Fifty-Eighth suffered fourteen losses, all captured. Some in the regiment believed that a few of these men, like Alfred and Bartlett Hilliard and Solomon Isaacs, all of Company I, actually deserted. Company E lost six men: Reuben Phillips, George Raby, George Goplin, John Gourley, Jesse Keener, and Warren Martin. Overall, the men of the Army of Tennessee were disappointed with no battle and downcast that they were once again retreating. The instance of straggling among the soldiers of the Fifty-Eighth was echoed throughout the army.[17]

Five miles south of Cassville was the Etowah River. The Fifty-Eighth passed through Catersville, reaching the river about 11:00 A.M. The regiment rested for an unknown amount of time before crossing the Etowah. The regiment continued about three more miles before going into camp around Allatoona. The next couple of days were spent sleeping, eating, and getting caught up on duties. "All quiet," Dugger chronicled, "except some cannonading on the left Saturday and Sunday night the 21st until Tuesday the 24th."

Sherman was also taking an opportunity to rest and refit his men. The Federals' next move was uncertain. Since the Confederate position at Allatoona Pass was a naturally strong one, a flanking movement was a surety. The question remained: right or left flank? Sherman chose the west, and early on the morning of May 24, the corps belonging to Polk and Hardee broke camp in a spring rain and moved to head off Sherman. Hood's corps was to follow later that evening. Sherman's goal was Marietta, where he believed that Confederates would make a stand. Johnston chose to position his men on a wide front between New Hope Church and Dallas, some sixteen miles from Marietta. Hood's corps moved into position at the former.[18]

Hood positioned his divisions with Hindman on the left, Stewart in the middle, and Stevenson on the right. The balance of the Federal attack was launched on Stewart's division in the middle, positioned at a crossroads, blocking the Federal army's course south. Federals in the XX Corps repeatedly attacked Stewart's lines only to be beaten back. The Fifty-Eighth saw little action and sustained only three losses on May 24 and 25. Braxton Cox (Company D) and Matthew Thompson (Company E) were captured. John Helton (Company H) was "struck on the head by a piece of shell and knocked unconscious." Fighting continued for the next three days, first at Dallas to the left, where Confederates attempted to feel out the Federals, and then at Picket Mill to the right, where the Federals attempted to turn the Confederate right.

John Cornell and Squire Presnell of Company A, and George W. Brown, James Fullwood, and Cpl. Oliver Lonon of Company F were all captured on May 26 on the Marietta Road by Federal cavalry. Lt. Milton Hampton (Company C) was wounded on May 28, and Largent Bean (Company H) had his shin fractured on May 29. George Nelson (Company E) was listed as being "accidently wounded at Lost Mountain" on May 30. Some of the captured made their way into the lines of Brig. Gen. Edward McCook, who wrote, "I don't think they want to fight this [west] side of the Chattachoochee."[19]

One of the brigade's losses during its time in the trenches around New Hope Church was Brig. Gen. Alexander Reynolds. He was wounded on May 27 and did not return to brigade command. Command instead fell upon the ranking colonel, Robert Trigg of the Fifty-Fourth Virginia. Trigg was a Virginia native and a graduate of the Virginia Military Institute. A year before the war, Trigg had organized a militia company that later became a part of the Fourth Virginia Infantry. After First Manassas, he organized the Fifty-Fourth Virginia, and later commanded a brigade at Chickamauga. With the army's reorganization, Trigg was back with the Fifty-Fourth Virginia by the first of 1864. On at least two occasions, Trigg was nominated for a brigadier generalship. While he had the necessary experience, he never attained the rank. For the foreseeable future, the brigade would be known as Reynolds's brigade, with Colonel Trigg commanding.[20]

For that entire week, the Fifty-Eighth had been moving around. Since the failed attack on the New Hope line, the regiment had taken, according to private Dugger,

> up line of march, marched sixteen miles and arrived at Dallas, Ga. Formed a line of battle in reserve near Dallas about 1 o'clock, some sharp-shooting going on in front. Hard fighting commenced about 3 o'clock and continued until dark, then ceased and remained quiet all night. Thursday the 26th skirmishing commenced very soon continued all day and night some cannonading going on through the day no regular engagement yet some vollies fired on parts of the line. Friday the 27th heavy skirmishing until about 3 o'clock brisk fighting commenced heavy cannonading going on all day skirmishing continued all night.

The Fifty-Eighth, however, was involved in little of the action.[21]

A couple of hours before daylight on May 28, Hood's entire corps was on the march in an attempted turning movement against the Federal flank. As Hood approached the Federal lines, he was dismayed to learn that the enemy had pulled back to the north side of Little Pumpkinvine Creek and entrenched. Hood was told to march his corps back and fall in on the right of Polk. The Fifty-Eighth "marched back by another route near the line of battle and arrive[d] near our old position about 2 o'clock, [halting] in a grove in reserve to rest our corps." Some time that evening, the Fifty-Eighth lined up in their battle formations for a rare night attack. Dugger recorded it in his diary, as did Lt. Jonathan Miller (Company I), who wrote after the war: "The 58th was in the charge made upon the enemy's entrenched position at New Hope Church." The outcome of this assault, along with information on other participants, appears to be lost to history.[22]

By the first of June, Sherman's army began sliding to the east, cutting the railroad at Allatoona. Johnston, believing that his army was being stretched too thin, determined to fall back to a new line. Once again, Private Dugger chronicled the Fifty-Eighth's movements. On June 1, amid constant skirmishing, the Fifty-Eighth was ordered

> to be ready to move at 12 o'clock. About 1 o'clock moved about one mile and formed the front in reserve on the right. Thursday, the 2nd, about 12 o'clock we moved further to the right slow skirmishing and some cannonading continued. An uncommon hard rain fell today. Friday, the 3rd, slow skirmishing continued. Our regiment moved about one-half mile to the left for the purpose of supporting a battery; arrived at 10 o'clock in the night and worked all night fortifying our line. Saturday slow skirmishing and some cannonading still continued. Cloudy and rainy. We moved off about 10 o'clock that night towards the right. After going about two hundred yards took position in the works as a skirmish line. Remained about one hour, and then moved off again. We waded the Georgia mud at an average depth of ten inches all night and until about 9 o'clock Sunday, the 5th, completing a march of about five miles. We rejoined our brigade and made a halt in dense woods. Drew a ration of whiskey and rested about one hour.

Johnston's first position was around Lost Mountain, about five miles north of Marietta. After receiving their ration of whiskey, the men of Company D of the Fifty-Eighth were posted about a half-mile in front of the brigade as pickets. Picket duty lasted 24 hours, and when Company D rejoined the regiment, its members helped pitch in and construct breastworks. Tuesday, June 7, Dugger noted "something strange ... no fighting in hearing today." The men had been under almost constant fire for a month.

Orders came in before daylight on June 8 to be ready to move at a moment's notice. At about sunrise the regiment was on the move, heading toward the right, marching five miles and stopping about 10:00 A.M. The men then rested for an hour and marched two more miles down the railroad. Skirmishing was reported to the regiment's front on June 9. Orders came again at 10:00 A.M. to be ready to move at a moment's notice. Near 1:00 P.M., the Fifty-Eighth, with the rest of the brigade, moved forward and deployed in a line of battle. As soon as skirmishers were posted and arms stacked, the men commenced fortifying their lines. Trees were cut down, fence rails piled up, and a ditch dug, some men having only a tin cup, plate, or bare hands as tools. The Tar Heel soldiers worked on their lines all night. Hood's corps was positioned on the Confederate right, across the Atlanta Pike. Polk's corps was in the center, with Hardee's corps on the left. The Confederate front was ten miles long.[23]

For the past several days, Sherman had held his army at Acworth while the railroad was repaired. Once the train was running, supplies and reinforcements were brought up. On June 10, Sherman commenced active campaigning once again. Unhappy with his wide front and inability to strike Sherman, Johnston chose to fall back once again. His new defensive position lined Kennesaw Mountain, which dominated the valley below. Dugger reported skirmishing and cannonading on June 15. The regiment moved a short distance to the left on the sixteenth, and immediately "commenced fortifying our position," working until 11:00 P.M. Friday was spent much the same way: strengthening breastworks. The regiment was up early on the morning of nineteenth, moving to the left of the Confederate line. "Arrived about 11 o'clock some fighting going on," Dugger chronicled in his diary. "Rained hard all day. Moved from that position at 4 o'clock and passed through Marietta, Ga. at dark. Marched on about two miles through mud, until about 11 o'clock in the night. Halted in the woods and camped. Monday the 20th, drew a ration of whiskey."[24]

Hood's new position was east of the railroad as it bent around Kennesaw Mountain. The Confederate front was seven miles long. Twice in just a couple of weeks, the men in the Confederate army were issued whiskey rations. Johnston was probably trying to add some brightness to the gloom and mud that surrounded his army. It had rained almost the entire month of June, and the mud hampered both army's movements.

Sherman could see the formidable Confederate works on Kennesaw Mountain. He chose to try to turn the Confederate left flank. The pressure on Hardee's corps forced Johnston to make changes to his line. To bolster this area, Johnston called to move Hood from his position on the right and take up a position on the left. The Fifty-Eighth left its position around daylight on June 21, passing through Marietta around 8:00 A.M. Hood's men proceeded a couple of miles down the Powder Springs Road before coming to a halt. Men from the Fifty-Eighth and Sixtieth North Carolina were thrown out as skirmishers in front of the division.[25]

Hood's corps was faced off against portions of the Army of the Ohio. About midday, several of the pickets from the Tar Heel regiments were captured, mostly from Company E: Jasper Moore, James Oxford, Samuel Parkes, Elisha Puett, James Taylor, John B. Teague, and Spenser Wood. Parkes, Taylor, and Teague all died while prisoners of war. Army of the Ohio Commander Joseph Hooker learned that these Confederates were members of Hood's corps. To Hooker, the strengthening of the Confederate left obviously meant an attack was coming, and Hooker brought up his corps, aligning it along the north side of the Powder Springs Road. The Federals immediately began building works. In front of their position was a 1,000-yards-long field, with woods containing Confederates on the other side. Several small knolls provided good artillery positions. Hooker posted two regiments, the Fourteenth Kentucky and the One Hundred and Twenty-Third New York, out in front of the main Federal line, with orders to delay the Confederates as long as possible. Hood's orders from Johnston did not include the option of attacking the enemy.[26]

Stevenson had stopped his division at the Mt. Zion Church. About 2:30 P.M., orders came for Stevenson to advance his division to the left of Hindman's division, which was in his front. Stevenson placed two brigades in front, Brown's and Cumming's brigades, followed by Reynolds and Pettus in reserve. Once on line with Hindman, Stevenson's men began to entrench their position with logs and fence rails. "Soon afterwards," Stevenson wrote in his report, "I received orders to advance from my position and drive the enemy on the road toward Manning's Mill." Hood also ordered Hindman's division to advance at the same time. "A good deal of time was occupied in getting and giving instructions," Stevenson continued, "and making the necessary preparations. About 5 P.M., we advanced and soon struck the enemy." The advancing Federals had built works to protect themselves. As the 6,000 men of Stevenson's division bore down on them, the Federals fired a few shots and

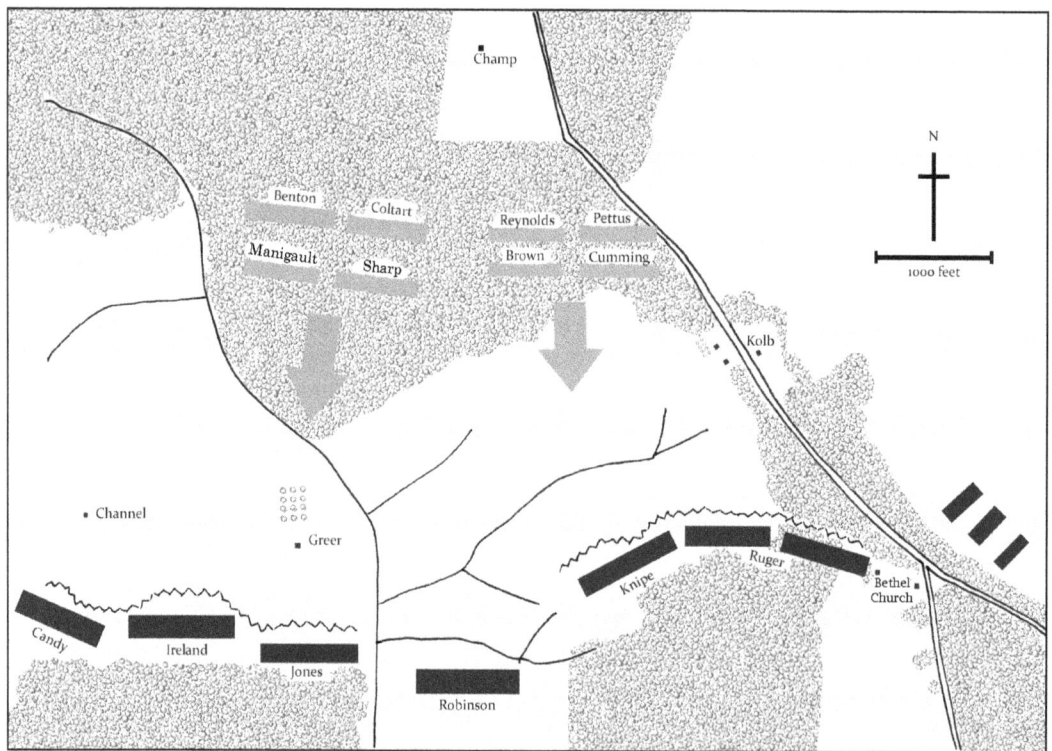

General Hood launched an unauthorized attack at Kolb's Farm in June 1864 that cost the Fifty-Eighth dearly.

quickly made for their main lines. As soon as the Federals were gone, artillery fire poured down upon the Confederates. Stevenson thought the artillery "was served with a rapidity and fatal precision which could not be surpassed."[27]

Due to the nature of the ground, the dense woods through which they traveled, and the artillery fire pouring down on them, the Confederate brigades began to fall apart. The Federal artillerymen had an open field of fire and loaded their guns with canister that created great holes in the Confederate lines. The Fifty-Eighth was caught in the open. Benoni Hobson, Jr., and Jasper Steward (Company B) were killed, while Jasper's cousin, Sgt. Barry Stewart, was wounded in the left leg. Lt. Green B. Woody, the color sergeant who had just a few days earlier been promoted to ensign, was wounded in the cheek, and John L. Blackburn (Company I) was struck in the breast and right arm. Capt. Caleb Conley (Company F) was also killed. "We got within a hundred yards of their works," Dugger recorded, before being "repulsed and compelled to fall back a few steps to a huge rock at the branch and lay under a heavy fire." Stevenson reported that the two brigades on the right, Brown's and Reynolds's, "lay in a swampy ravine within pistol-shot of the enemy's works." Many of the Confederates made their way back to the cover of the woods. Others took refuge in ravines that ran through the area. Due to the lateness of the hour when the Confederates attacked, there was no counter-attack by the Federals. The Confederates held their advanced position until 9:00 P.M., when they fell back to their original lines. One "anonymous" Tar Heel felt that the charge at Kolb Farm was "one of the most stubborn engagements since the charge at Murphreesboro Tenn."[28]

Losses among members of the Fifty-Eighth were heavy: six killed, forty-nine wounded, fourteen captured, and six declared as missing in action. Of the forty-nine wounded, seven later died of their wounds. One of the wounded was Thomas Dula, recently promoted to lieutenant colonel. Dula was struck in the thigh. Another of the wounded was Capt. Jonathan Phillips (Company G). According to a letter written by Phillips in October 1864, "A ball struck me in the forehead between the Eyes, & passed through the skull, ranging towards the back of the head & remains in the head yet. I have entirely lossed the site of my lef Eye, & partly lossed the hearing in my left Ear. I have had spasms or fits every few days since I Rec'd the wounds." Command fell upon Capt. Alfred Stewart (Company E). Total losses in Stevenson's division were 870 killed, wounded, and missing.[29]

For the Tar Heels in the Fifty-Eighth, the days after the battle at Kolb's Farm were spent in picket duty and manning the breastworks. Elsewhere along the lines, Sherman weighed his options: his army was stuck. On a map, the road appeared to be open to the south, allowing him to once again flank the Confederate army, but actually the roads themselves were nearly impassable. It had rained for most of the month of June.

James J. Laurance (Lawrence) joined Capt. Drury Harman's Company in early July 1862. He deserted from the Fifty-Eighth twice, the final time near Howell Ferry, Georgia, on July 9, 1864 (courtesy Rebecca Lawrence Wingfield).

In order to move the Federal army to the south, Sherman needed to resupply his army and then release the railroad. The only other option was to attack the Confederates at Kennesaw. Sherman surveyed the Confederate lines and chose June 27 to attack, hoping that the Confederates were weak enough at some point to permit a breakthrough. The attack was preceded by an artillery bombardment; "cannonading all day," as Dugger described it. Sherman's frontal assault failed, costing the Federals over 3,000 men killed and wounded. Finally, on July 1, the roads were dry enough for the Federal army to begin its next flanking movement.[30]

For several days, the Fifty-Eighth and the other members of Reynolds's brigade were subjected to constant enemy artillery fire. This fire slowly took its toll. William Nelson (Company E) was wounded on June 25. William Davis (Company I) was struck "in the left shoulder joint and left arm by the explosion of bombshells." Peter Eller (Company G) was wounded on July 1 when "a shell knocked a limb from a tree and struck him on the back ... and something hit him on the head at the same time and knocked him senseless ... inflicting a severe wound on the head."[31]

Johnston, aware that Sherman was once again working around his flank, informed his men that the Army of Tennessee "will change position tonight." The Fifty-Eighth went out to picket the area between the lines about 4:00 P.M. on July 2. About midnight, the regiment "secretly retired" with the rest of Hood's corps. Most of the men did, anyway. Five members of Company L — William Eller, Adkins Jefferson, Isaac Green, George McGuire, and Joseph Stikes — were either left behind and captured, or remained behind for the purpose of deserting. They were not the only members of Joe Johnston's army to do so. The Fifty-Fourth Virginia reported a loss of thirty-three men that same evening. It was rumored that the Federals had promised the surrendering Confederates that they would be able to take the oath and be released north of the Ohio River. For many in the ranks, this does not appear to be true. Eller was not released until February 25, 1865. Stikes was released on May 13, 1865, and McGuire a few days later on May 17, 1865. Jefferson died in prison on October 2, 1864, as did Green on February 13, 1865.[32]

However, it was true for some of the regiment. An anonymous officer in Company H recorded that "Lieutenant [Emanuel] Hedrick deserted and carried with him four men belonging to the company [H]" on July 1. Hedrick resided in Caldwell County when he enlisted in March 1862 in Company I, Twenty-Sixth North Carolina Troops. He was promoted to sergeant, then court-martialed and reduced back to the ranks before being elected a lieutenant of Company H, Fifty-Eighth. Hedrick was taken to Chattanooga, and then to Louisville. He was released in Louisville on July 27, 1864, after taking the oath of allegiance. Those who went with Hedrick were a musician, William Bumgarner, along with Joseph Stafford, Sgt. Julius Stafford, and Sgt. Valentine Starnes. Bumgarner and the Staffords were from Caldwell County and Starnes from Mecklenburg County. What became of Starnes is unknown. The others took the oath and were released.[33]

The Fifty-Eighth and the rest of Stevenson's division fell back, skirmishing the whole time, to a spot known as Ruff's Mill. Hood's line stretched from Rottenwood Creek on the right, along the Concord Road, almost to Ruff's Mill on Nickajack Creek on the left. The Confederate right was held by Loring's corps, the center by Hardee, and the left by Hood, with the Georgia Militia to Hood's left. Not only was the main line of the Confederates entrenched, but there was also a line of detached rifle pits in their front, which were also fortified.

The Federal Army of the Tennessee was able to cross Nickajack Creek at Ruff's Mill and drive away a group of Confederates near the mill. That evening, the Federals attacked again and captured a portion of the Confederate advance position. The Fifty-Eighth's exact role is not known. Dugger, in his diary, wrote that there was "skirmishing and cannonading occasionally all day. The enemy drove in our picket in the evening." The Federal attack almost separated the Georgia Militia from the rest of the army. Johnston, seeing that he was once again flanked out of a position, fell back farther south that evening. The Fifty-Eighth "secretly retired at 12 o'clock that night and marched until 8 o'clock Tuesday the 5th and made a halt." At least four members of the regiment were captured, either in the works, or along the retreat route. They included Bryant Gibbs of Company F, and Bryant Tilman, Elisha Decker, John Lingle, and James Raby of Company H.[34]

John Wesley Styles was a member of Company C of the Fifty-Eighth. He served as a provost for Maj. Gen. Simon Buckner in September and October 1863. Styles later rejoined the Fifty-Eighth, but was listed as a deserter on September 10, 1864 (courtesy Michael Ledford).

Johnston's new line, according to Sherman, was "the strongest pieces of field fortifications I ever saw." The defensive position was designed by Brig. Gen. Francis Shoup, chief of artillery for the Army of Tennessee. Shoup's line contained 36 small forts, named "Shoupades" in his honor. "Each fort," according to a later historian, "was diamond shaped in plan with its two outer faces pointing in the direction of the enemy ... the forts were constructed ... using double walls of logs filled with compacted earth. The exterior face walls were 10 to 12 feet thick at the base and extended to a height of 10 to 12 feet — surmounted by an infantry parapet." Artillery fire inflicted little damage, and each fort could contain up to 80 infantrymen. In between each Shoupade was a wall of vertical logs, eight feet high. At a point in between each Shoupade was an artillery emplacement for two guns. The Shoupades were positioned in such a way as to cover the entire Confederate front in a crossfire. It would be futile to attack such a position, and Sherman, for once, refrained from a large-scale operation.[35]

Members of the Fifty-Eighth had little time to inspect their new entrenchments. As soon as the regiment arrived, the men were placed out in front of the division as pickets. Stevenson's division was on the left of Johnston's line, near the Turner's Ferry Road. Dugger recalled that the Federals advanced skirmishers that afternoon, and a "hot little skirmish fight [was] conducted till dark." An anonymous officer in Company E recorded that the regiment "was thrown on picket and charged by a skirmish line, and in line of battle, but we held our position." The Fifty-Eighth rotated off picket at nine the next morning. Three members of Company F were reported captured: Julius Conley, John Morrow, and Marion Sisk. Both Conley and Morrow later died in prison. The regiment was back on picket on July 6.[36]

At noon on July 6, the Fifty-Eighth rotated off picket duty and headed for the breastworks. At 1:00 that afternoon, the regiment crossed over the Chattahoochee River "and

During the siege of Atlanta, the Tar Heels in the Fifty-Eighth daily looked out on this barren landscape (courtesy the Library of Congress).

marched a country road down the river five miles" before coming to a halt and going into camp for the evening. It is not clear if only the Fifty-Eighth moved, or the entire brigade, or possibly the entire division. Nor is it clear why they moved. It could be simply to relieve the overcrowding of the Chattahoochee River line, or to reinforce some picket post guarding one of the fords over the river.[37]

The regiment alternated between inactivity and short movements for the next few days. Corporal Dugger chronicled in his diary that the regiment was immobile for much of the seventh. Near sundown, it moved "two miles down the river and camped." Friday, July 8, was quiet, with a little sharpshooting at the river. At midnight, the Fifty-Eighth "marched five miles toward Atlanta ... and halted at day-light." Sunday was quiet, along with Monday, "except some cannonading on the right." The same was true on the twelfth and thirteenth. On July 13, the regiment "moved and arranged camp." The next day was quiet. It was not until July 15 that the Fifty-Eighth got back into the war. The men left camp at four in the morning and marched four miles to go on picket duty. It was a common practice for the outer line of pickets, when in the presence of the enemy, to be rotated on and off duty at night. The Fifty-Eighth went on duty that evening, and rotated off duty at two in the morning on Sunday, July 17. The regiments then "marched about six miles down the Atlanta road, halted at dark, and camped for the night."[38]

Much had happened during the regiment's "quiet" time. On July 9, Johnston chose to withdraw from the defensive position on the Chattahoochee River. The Federals had once again crossed the river at a point away from the Confederate lines. Johnston, in order to preserve his lines of communication and supply, was forced to retreat. His next retrograde stop was the defenses of Atlanta. On July 17, a courier handed General Johnston a telegram from Samuel Cooper in Richmond:

> Lieutenant-General J. B. Hood has been commissioned to the temporary rank of general under the late law of Congress. I am directed by the Secretary of War to inform you that as you have failed to arrest the advance of the enemy to the vicinity of Atlanta, far in the interior of Georgia, and express no confidence that you can defeat or repel him, you are hereby relieved from command of the Army and Department of Tennessee which you will immediately turn over to General Hood.[39]

No one in the Fifty-Eighth, just then coming off picket duty, made any mention of the change of commanders at the time. After the war, Lieutenant Miller (Company I) wrote, "By placing Hood in command at Atlanta, great gloom fell upon the army." This outlook was not to brighten.[40]

CHAPTER 11

July–December 1864

"There are more or less men killed and wounded every day."
— Garrett Gouge, Company D

Writing from his headquarters in Petersburg, Virginia, Robert E. Lee said he thought replacing Joseph Johnston mid-campaign was a bad idea. The Army of Northern Virginia commander thought that Johnston's replacement, John Bell Hood, was "a bold fighter," but doubted his abilities to actually lead the army. Lee believed that General Hardee was a better choice. However, Hardee had already been offered the position once and had declined.[1]

Hood was born in Kentucky in 1831 and graduated from West Point in 1853. He served in Texas and California before resigning his commission in April 1861. At the start of the war, he was elected colonel of the Fourth Texas Infantry and, in March 1862, was promoted to brigadier general, head of the famous Texas brigade. He later commanded a division in the Army of Northern Virginia and was part of the force that Longstreet brought to Tennessee in September 1863. At the rank of lieutenant general, Hood commanded one of the Army of Tennessee's corps. Hood was wounded at Gaines Mill in June 1862; at Gettysburg in July 1863, where he lost the use of his left arm; and at Chickamauga in September 1863, necessitating the amputation of his right leg. Many have argued that his extensive wounding should have disqualified him from any command. Now he sat at the head of one of the two principal Confederate armies.[2]

It was not that his promotion should have come as a shock. For months, Hood had been writing to Jefferson Davis about the conditions and his missed opportunities while serving under Johnston. General Bragg, now serving as Davis's chief of staff, arrived from Richmond on July 13. His mission was to "confer with Genl Johnston in relation to military affairs." Bragg met with Johnston, but also with Johnston's corps commanders, including Hood. When Bragg sent his report back to Davis, a personal

John Bell Hood served as the Fifty-Eighth's corps and Army commander from February 1864 until January 1865 (courtesy the Library of Congress).

letter from Hood was enclosed. Bragg believed that having Hood as commander of the Army of Tennessee would "give unlimited satisfaction." However, Bragg warned Davis that Hood was not "a man of genius, or a great general, but as far better in the present emergency than any one we have available."[3]

Hood met with Johnston at the latter's headquarters the morning of July 18. Hood, and later the other two corps commanders, Hardee and Stewart, telegrammed Richmond protesting Johnston's removal. Davis did not rescind the order. Command of Hood's corps temporarily passed to Maj. Gen. Frank Cheatham.

The reaction to Hood's appointment among the rank and file of the Fifty-Eighth is unknown. Overall, the men of the Army of Tennessee were not happy. Pvt. James Wysor of the Fifty-Fourth Virginia, in the same brigade as the Fifty-Eighth, wrote home that "the whole army placed the most implicit confidence in Gen Johnston which they do not in Hood." Yet another member of the brigade, Capt. James Clark, Company F, Sixty-Third Virginia, said, "The army was very much out of fire about Gen. Johnston being released from his command of the army. There never was a General that was more confident in his men more than Gen. Johnston."[4]

After Hood's promotion to commander of the Army of Tennessee, Benjamin Cheatham temporarily served as the Fifty-Eighth's corps commander (courtesy the Library of Congress).

While Johnston had rebuilt the Army of Tennessee and restored morale in his men, the Army was still in shambles. A return submitted on July 10 listed 35,856 effective infantry present, with a total of 51,707 present with the army. An additional 48,747 men were absent without leave. Stevenson's division reported just 4,008 men present for duty. It was estimated that an additional 40,000 men were sick in one of the many hospitals in Georgia. Men also continued to slip away from the Fifty-Eighth. In June, eight men had deserted. The number more than tripled in July, with twenty-five men slipping away from the army. Another nineteen men were captured or wounded in July prior to July 20.[5]

Hood knew that he had to do something to save Atlanta. On July 18 and 19, scouts reported a gap between two of the three Federal armies in Hood's front. Hood chose this gap in an effort to destroy, or at least drive back, a portion of the Federals. The plan was for his old corps, under Cheatham, to hold the enemy to the east at bay while Stewart's and Hardee's corps launched attacks to the north into the gap. Once the Federals to the north were destroyed, then those to the east could be likewise attacked.

The Fifty-Eighth spent July 19 marching "from place to place arranging our lines and building breast-works." The orders had come to build a defensive work about a mile and a half in front of the Atlanta defenses, with Peachtree Creek, which the Federals had to cross, just to the front. Stewart's corps was on the left, Hardee in the center, and Cheatham on the right. Cheatham's line extended towards, but not quite to, the Georgia Railroad. Cheatham was also ordered to shift most of his artillery to the left of his line so that he could "command the entire space between his left and Peach Tree Creek," preventing the different Federal corps from linking up. The work on fortifications continued all night.[6]

Farther to the east was Joseph Wheeler's cavalry, about 2,500 men, with one four-gun battery. Behind them, actually in the Atlanta defenses, was part of the Georgia Militia. These men were charged with holding those lines of approach. Hood was aware that there were Federals to the east but did not realize that McPherson's Army of the Tennessee was as close as Decatur. The Federals continued their advance on the morning of the twentieth. By 10:00 A.M., Wheeler had sent a note to Hood, informing him that the Federals were just two-and-a-half miles from Atlanta and that he needed reinforcements. Hood, sizing up the situation, ordered Cheatham to shift one division front to the right, or south. A division front occupied one third to one half of a mile. Instead of moving merely that distance, Cheatham moved nearly two miles. At the same time, Hood ordered Hardee and Stewart to move one half a division front to the right. Hardee was ordered to keep in contact with Cheatham's left.

The unplanned movement caused considerable delay. Cheatham started shifting, halted, deployed battle lines, and then re-formed to continue his movement to the right. The attack slated to begin at 1:00 P.M. was not actually launched until 4:00 P.M. and was beaten back by Federals, who had been given ample time to entrench. Cheatham's troops were badly strung out. The men between Cheatham and Hardee were no more than a picket line. The men in Cheatham's center, which he estimated was one mile in length, were "deployed in [a] single line" and he had been forced to take a brigade from his left to bolster his right. While Dugger reported "heavy skirmishing and cannonading all day and the night following," the exact position of the Fifty-Eighth and their role is unknown. There were two reported losses for the regiment: Pvt. Jason Finley (Company F) was wounded in the left temple, and Pvt. Sanders Fowler (Company L) was captured.[7]

Pictured here with his wife, Mahala, Levi Townsend was a miller prior to enlisting in Company D of the Fifty-Eighth in July 1862. He was sick and furloughed back home to Watauga County in December 1863. He never returned to the regiment (courtesy Wanda Hodges).

Much of the daytime of July 21 was spent in the same position. That evening, at 8:00 P.M., the regiment pulled back about two miles, closer to Atlanta. A line of new works was laid out, and Hood instructed division and brigade commanders to inspect the sites assigned to their respective commands before dark. As soon as it was dark, the men moved to the new line and began to fortify their position. Cheatham rotated men on and off the work parties all evening. While not working or on picket duty, they were resting. Cheatham's line stretched from the Georgia Railroad to Bald Hill.[8]

While the Fifty-Eighth was not actively engaged on the Twenty-First, other parts of the Army of Tennessee were. Part of Wheeler's cavalry and Patrick Cleburne's division were driven off Bald Hill. Cleburne tried to retake the hill, renamed Leggett's

Hill in honor of the Federal division commander whose men took the high ground there. As soon as the hill was taken, the Federals began bringing up artillery to shell Atlanta. While Cleburne fought, Hood was devising another battle plan. Stewart and Cheatham would pull back closer to the city, while Hardee's men marched through the streets of Atlanta, and then to the east, in an attempt to flank McPherson. Once the attack opened, Cheatham was to join in the fray.

Hardee's attack was set to begin at daylight. However, he was not in a position to commence the plan until after noon. Had he attacked earlier in the day, he would have found the left flank of the Federal line unprotected, and could have "rolled up" that flank. However, there were now entrenched Federals to his front, and while his Confederates were able to break through the line in places, capturing enemy soldiers, pieces of artillery, and stands of colors, he was not able to capitalize on his achievements. Around 3:00 P.M., Hood ordered Cheatham to demonstrate against the Federals in his front, hoping to pin them down while keeping reinforcements from Hardee's front. About an hour later, when Hardee renewed his attacks, Hood ordered Cheatham to assault the Federal works.

Joseph Taylor Ollis claimed in his pension application to have served in the Fifty-Eighth. A clerical error placed him in the Eighty-Eighth North Carolina (courtesy Doyle Ollis).

Cheatham sent orders to his division commander to attack in echelon. Stevenson went in first, but several volleys and artillery fire from the Federals on Bald Hill stopped his attack before he could even dislodge Federal pickets. Stevenson fell back to his starting point. Further to Stevenson's left, the Confederates were more successful, capturing portions of the Federal works. Toward dark, the Confederates were ordered to fall back into the defenses they had constructed the night before. One hundred members of the Fifty-Eighth went on picket duty that night in front of the works. The Fifty-Eighth reported no wounded or killed for either the twenty-first or the twenty-second. However, they did report twelve captured, a few of whom they suspected of desertion, though they could not prove so.[9]

At dark on the evening of July 23, the Fifty-Eighth rotated off picket duty and returned to the breastworks. Sgt. Jesse Mace (Company A) and Pvt. Martin Moore (Company E) were both wounded on the twenty-fourth, Mace in the right wrist and left hand and Moore in the left arm. The Fifty-Eighth stayed in position until 1:00 P.M. Wednesday, July 27, when the regiment was ordered out of its works and into the works around Atlanta. Work on the fortifications around Atlanta had begun following the fall of Vicksburg in July 1863. Five redoubts were constructed on prominent hills for artillery, which were connected with a line of rifle pits. The area in front of these lines was cleared of timber for 900 to 1000 yards. There were additional artillery emplacements, along with five additional redoubts not within the works. Many thought these works unassailable.[10]

On the previous day, Cheatham returned to his division, and the new corps commander took over the job. Stephen D. Lee was born in Charleston, South Carolina, in 1833 and graduated from West Point in 1854. He resigned from the Army in 1861 and became an

The Fifty-Eighth would have seen many of the Confederate forts surrounding Atlanta, like this one photographed in 1864 (courtesy the Library of Congress).

aide-de-camp to General P.G.T. Beauregard. He was commissioned a captain in the artillery, rising to the rank of colonel under Lafayette McLaws. Lee was promoted to brigadier general in November 1862 and commanded the artillery in and around Vicksburg. In August 1863, Lee was promoted to major general and placed in command of the cavalry of the Department of Mississippi, Alabama, West Tennessee, and East Louisiana. In June 1864, he was promoted to lieutenant general and, in July, was assigned command of Hood's corps. Lee was the youngest lieutenant general in the Confederacy.[11]

The corps that Lee took numbered just 11,900 effectives. Another 4,653 men were present, but were reported unfit for duty. An incredible 21,334 men of Lee's corps were declared absent without leave. Almost sixty percent of Lee's soldiers had slipped off, and most were back in their home communities.[12]

Lee barely had time to meet with division commanders before orders came from Hood. Part of the Federal army had been detected moving toward the west side of Atlanta, attempting to completely cut off the city from the outside world. Furthermore, Sherman had authorized cavalry raids as far south as Macon. While the majority of the troopers were captured by the Confederates, the Federal infantry met with more success. Lee took two of his divisions west. His orders were to find a position near Ezra Church, along the Lick Skillet Road, and to dig in, effectively blocking the path of the enemy. Then, according to Hood's orders, General Stewart was to bring two of his divisions and roll up the Federal flank. Unfortunately for Lee, the Federals only just beat him to the important juncture. Lee believed that a quick attack could drive away the Federals before they had time to entrench. Lee's attacks were disjointed, and while some of his men were able to gain the Federal works, others did not, and all were driven back. Stewart brought up his two divisions, but met with the same unsatisfactory results.[13]

The Fifty-Eighth was not involved in the battle of Ezra Church. The regiment was left in the trenches to hold the Federals at bay. Dugger reported that on July 27, the regiment, at 1:00 P.M., moved from its former position and "formed behind in the suburbs of Atlanta and remained until dark. We moved back to the front works on the left of Kowan's battery." Dugger is probably referring to Cowan's company of the First Mississippi Light Artillery, posted north of Atlanta, between Bouanchard's Louisiana Battery and Peachtree Fort. The Fifty-Eighth stayed near the battery until midnight, when the regiment "rallied and went on picket." The men were on picket until 9:00 P.M. on July 28, when they were relieved and returned to the breastworks. The next night they were back on picket duty. The month ended with "all still today; raining in the evening." Pvts. William S. Cook and Alfred Eller (Company I) were captured on July 28. Callaway Gentry (Company G), who was nominated for the Badge of Distinction for gallantry at Chickamauga, deserted on July 29. He took the oath of allegiance on August 27 and was released. Pvts. Alexander Osborn and William Wood (Company L) also deserted on July 29. Wood took the oath on August 29 and Osborn on October 10. Both were released.[14]

William S. Cook, who served in Company I, moved from Watauga to Caldwell County after the war. He is shown here wearing his iron cross, a medal given to former Confederate soldiers by the United Daughters of the Confederacy.

Stevenson's division was detached from Lee's corps for most of the month of August. Duty in the trenches and in picket out in front of the trenches was to be their lot for the next couple of weeks. The brigade moved to the left about dark on August 1. The following day, the Fifty-Eighth was out on picket duty in front of the Georgia Militia. They were relieved that evening, and "returned to the Brigade at the front works on the Marietta Road," chronicled Dugger in his diary. The next day, August 3, there was "some sharp-shooting in front, the enemy in two hundred yards of our works. A close place for 'Rebs.'" Those words were the last thoughts penned by Cpl. John Dugger of Company D. He was killed the following day. The circumstances regarding his death remain unknown.[15]

Typically, a regiment rotated on and off picket duty every three days. The men normally spent a whole twenty-four hours on picket. If the enemy attacked, the pickets provided a warning for the troops back in the main trenches. Pickets typically fought while falling back, giving the other troops time to prepare for assault.

Sherman chose to give his men a rest for the next couple of weeks. In the interim, he bombarded the city of Atlanta. For the next few days, shells rained down on the troops and civilians still in the city. "We are still in our entrenchments" Garrett Gouge (Company D) wrote home that month, "and a lively skirmish and cannonading going on every day and night. There are more or less men killed and wounded every day." Thomas Alexander (Company F) was wounded in the left foot on August 5. He was sent to a hospital in Macon. Lt. Robert Sisk of the same company fractured his right hand on August 9. He too was sent to Macon and was apparently retired from the army in February 1865. Isaac Sherrill (Company E) was wounded the same day when an artillery projectile accidentally exploded. It could be that Sherrill's accident was like that of one Georgia militiaman who had picked up an apparently exploded shell and was foolishly striking it with a rock when it went off. Sherrill was lucky; the militiaman was killed. Sherrill rejoined the regiment by the end of the month.

On August 10, the Confederate and Union artillery engaged in a day-long, massive bombardment. Reuben Isaacs (Company D) was wounded in the left hip. Desertions also continued. Moses Byrd (Company G) left for the third and final time on August 12. The three Fox brothers of Company C—James, Moses, and Skelton—crept off on August 15. The following day, Willis Bailey (Company G), while on picket duty, deserted. Finley Teaster (Company D) slipped away on August 17.[16]

Sometime around August 23, or possibly as late as November 18, Reynolds's brigade was consolidated with Brown's brigade. Colonel Trigg, who had been in command of Reynolds's brigade, was furloughed home to southwest Virginia on August 23 and did not return to the Army of Tennessee. Next in command was Col. Washington M. Hardy of the Sixtieth. But he too was furloughed home on August 23. Reynolds's old brigade numbered just 984 men. The brigade was consolidated with Brown's brigade, composed of the Third, Eighteenth, Twenty-Sixth, Thirty-Second, and Forty-Fifth Tennessee Regiments, and placed under the command of Col. Joseph B. Palmer. Palmer was born in Tennessee in 1825 and orphaned at an early age. He attended Union University in Murfreesboro, Tennessee, and was admitted to the bar in 1848. Palmer served two terms in the Tennessee house, and for four years he was the mayor of Murfreesboro. At the start of the war, he was elected colonel of the Eighteenth Tennessee, before being captured at Fort Donelson. He was wounded three times at the battle of Murfreesboro and again at Chickamauga. Several times Palmer had been in brigade command. This new brigade of North Carolinians, Tennesseans, and Virginians later bore his name: Palmer's Brigade. "A gallant officer" is how the Fifty-Eighth's Lt. Jonathan Miller (Company I) referred to Palmer after the war. Col. Joseph B. Palmer appears to have no family relationship to the Fifty-Eighth's old commander, Col. John B. Palmer, still in western North Carolina.

Ephraim Harmon served in Company D of the Fifty-Eighth, volunteering in July 1862. He was listed as a deserter on August 31, 1863 (courtesy Jackie and Dawn Peters).

Joseph Palmer's brigade continued to be a part of Stevenson's division, Lee's corps, Army of Tennessee.[17]

Just a couple of days prior to Palmer's taking over the consolidated brigade, the Fifty-Eighth reported 336 men present (with twenty-two sick and four under arrest). The regiment was armed with .54-caliber rifles, probably the Austrian Lorenz. The Lorenz was the second-most-imported rifle, behind the British Enfield, during the war. In this report, the clothing of the Fifty-Eighth's members was described as bad, but the men had a soldierly bearing. Their discipline was good, but their drill was indifferent. They treated their animals well, and their personal cleanliness was rated as good.[18]

Cpl. Gilbert Hodges (Company D) picked up John Dugger's diary about three weeks after Dugger's death and began making his own notes. He wrote that the Fifty-Eighth was on picket duty on July 22 and again on July 25.[19]

The Federals soon grew tired of lobbing shells into Atlanta. It was once again Sherman's plan to slide past the Confederate defenses and cut Hood's last railroad link into Atlanta. During the night of August 25, the Federals began preparations to withdraw. "I well remember the night that Sherman evacuated his fortification," Lt. Jonathan Miller (Company I) wrote after the war. "I was on guard duty between the two lines, about midnight they commenced cannonading, and throwing shells into the city. We expected every moment that they were going to charge our lines, but the cannons all stopped firing, and when daylight came, to our surprise there was not a 'Yankee' in our front." Sherman had earlier ordered his cavalry to break up the rail line between Macon and Atlanta, which they had done, but the Confederates had quickly repaired the damage. Sherman then decided to move his entire army, save the XX Corps, which was left to guard the bridges over the Chattahoochee River, to destroy the line. Hood sought to counter the movement even though he was not sure of Sherman's final destination. On August 27, the Georgia Militia was ordered to replace Stevenson's division on the front lines, and Stevenson was ordered to a reserve position. Hodges recorded that the men of Fifty-Eighth passed through Atlanta and halted at 12 o'clock "on the extreme left," rejoining their former comrades in Lee's corps.[20]

Hardee's corps was positioned at East Point, south of Atlanta. On August 28, Hardee was ordered farther south to the intriguingly named village of Rough and Ready, while Lee's corps was ordered to East Point. Hodges recorded a move of just one mile to the left, possibly on the orders from Hood for Stevenson's division to replace Brown's division. Monday brought another "short move to the left." At two in the morning on August 30, the regiment moved out, covering three miles farther to the left. The previous evening Hood had come to the conclusion that Sherman's objective was Jonesboro, Georgia. Hood already had sent reinforcements to the town, and on August 30, ordered Hardee and Lee's corps to the area. Hood believed that there were perhaps two Federal corps in the area and was unaware that the entire Federal army, save one corps, was nearby. Hardee's corps was to move at 4:00 P.M. to be in position to attack early the next morning. Lee was to follow at 9:30 P.M. According to Hood, once Hardee successfully attacked the Federals, Lee was to attack, helping to drive the Federals back across the Flint River.[21]

However, things rarely go as planned. Hardee might have gotten his soldiers started at 4:00 P.M., but the last of his corps did not pass until 11:00 P.M., putting Lee one-and-a-half hours behind schedule. In his diary, Hodges recalled leaving at 11:00 P.M. At some point, Hardee's advance found Federals blocking their path, and Hardee was forced to make a detour. The Confederates found the evening muggy, and the heat was oppressive. Because of the delays, Hardee's advance did not reach Jonesboro until daylight, about the time the

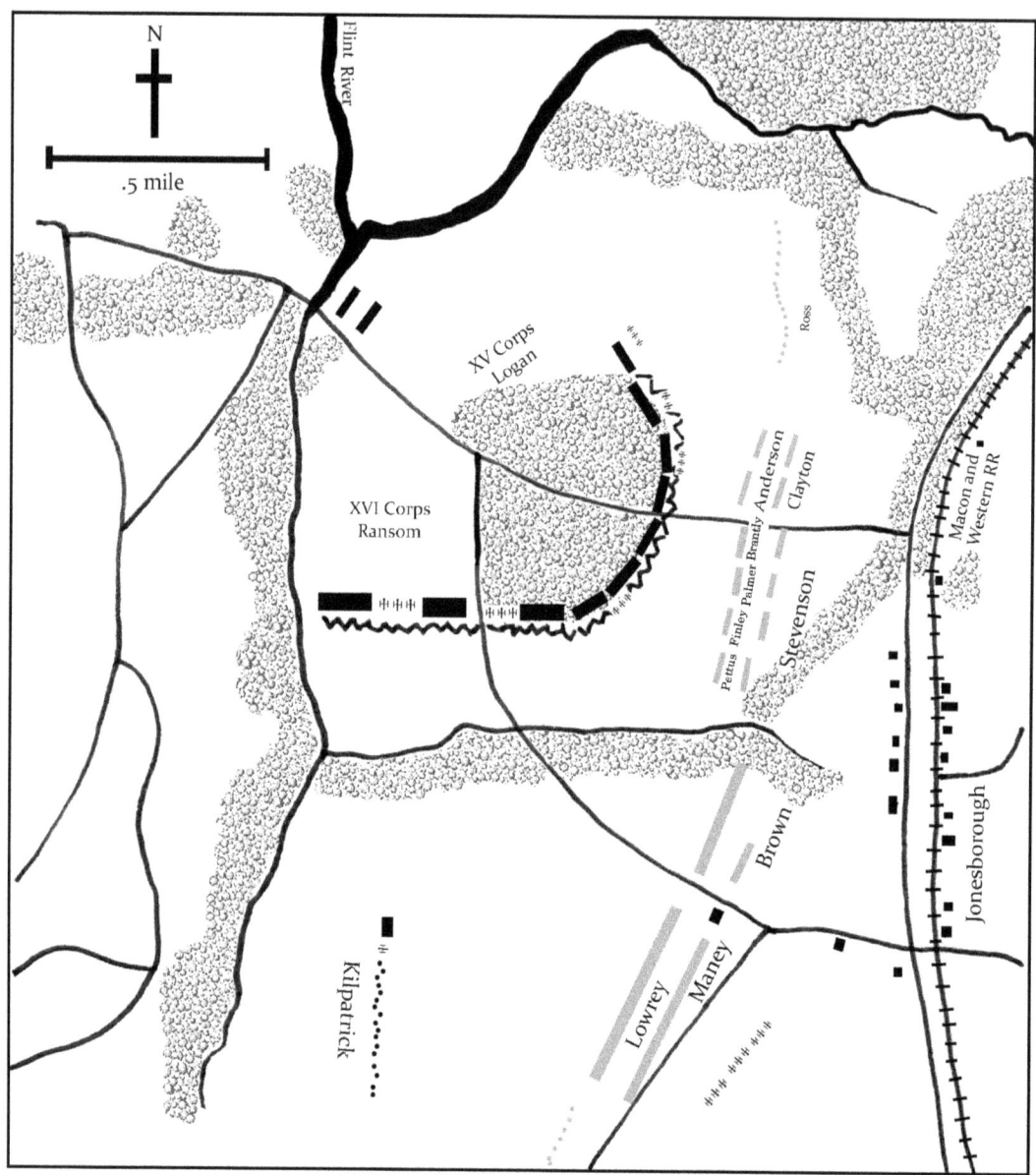

The attack at Jonesboro, where the Fifty-Eighth was serving in Palmer's brigade, was poorly planned.

attack was scheduled to step off. The first of Lee's corps did not reach Jonesboro until 10:00 A.M. Hodges recorded arriving in Jonesboro at noon.[22]

A disagreement soon arose among the field and staff of the regiment. Capt. Alfred Stewart, a veteran of the Twenty-Sixth North Carolina and captain of Company E of the Fifty-Eighth, had been in command of the regiment since July 10, though at times he shared that responsibility with Capt. Samuel Silver of Company K. Lt. Col. Thomas Dula resigned on August 3 due to the fact that he had been elected solicitor of Caldwell County. There is a good chance that Dula never rejoined the regiment since his wounding at Kolb's Farm on

June 22. There had been a fair amount of competition for the post, dating back to the time that the promotion of Dula occurred. Colonel Palmer, writing from western North Carolina, had recommended that Silver be promoted to major, over Stewart. On August 5, Stewart wrote to both brigade commander Col. Joseph B. Palmer and the secretary of war in Richmond, claiming "the position of major of said regiment." Stewart wrote that even though he and Silver had been promoted to captain on the same day, Stewart was

Pictured here post-war with his wife, Allie, Moses Fox served in Company C of the Fifty-Eighth. He deserted on August 15, 1864 (courtesy Charles Seibert).

actually a first lieutenant, while Silver was a second lieutenant, thus making Stewart senior in rank to Silver. Stewart asked Palmer to recommend him to the secretary, while in his letter to the War Department, he requested that his commission to major be dated back to June 16, "at which time the commission of Lt. Col. T. J. Dula" was dated. On August 31, as the men were preparing for battle, Capt. Alfred Stewart's promotion to major came through.[23]

The delay gave the Federals time to entrench. At this point in the war, formidable defenses could be constructed in just 15 minutes. The Federals had not only all morning, but part of the afternoon. By 2:00 P.M., most troops were on line, with Lee's corps parallel to the railroad, and Hardee's corps on the left at a right angle to Lee's line. Lee had positioned Anderson's division on his right, with Clayton's division in reserve. Stevenson was on the left, in two lines. Palmer's brigade was in the front of Stevenson's line, on the right. The battle plan was thus: Hardee's men, under Cleburne, were to start the attack, working to the right. Once they were well and truly engaged, Lee was to join in. Yet, once again, Hood's plans flew apart.

Lee was ordered to await heavy firing from Hardee's front. However, not long after the first shots of the skirmishers, Lee launched his attack. Hardee's men were not actually engaging the main Federal line, but driving off cavalry that was attempting to flank them. Lee's attack was largely unsupported. Once they came out of the woods where they had formed, Lee's men crossed into an area where trees had been felled, creating a serious obstacle that broke apart the Confederate alignment. The Confederates were

Brig. Gen. Joseph B. Palmer, who was not related to Col. John B. Palmer, served as the Fifty-Eighth's brigade commander through the battle of Bentonville, North Carolina.

able to drive off the Federal skirmishers and to advance to within a dozen yards of the Federal works before artillery and small arms fire caused them to stop. Soon, men started streaming towards the rear, and nothing the officers did could inspire them to advance again. "[A]ll the wounded fell into the hands of the Enemy that could not walk off," Drum Major Blair wrote home on September 5.[24]

Losses in the Fifty-Eighth amounted to thirteen men. Maj. Alfred Stewart was mortally wounded in the attack, possibly never knowing of his promotion. He was "one of the best men of our regiment," Sgt. Elijah Norris of Company D wrote after the war. Cpl. James Hurley (Company L) was also killed, as was Lt. Doctor Estes (Company E). James Sisemore and Samuel Weatherman, both of Company A, were each struck in the left arm. Sisemore's arm was amputated. William Anglin and Henry Metcalf, both of Company C, were wounded. Anglin had a compound fracture of the left thigh, and Metcalf was struck in the head, left arm, and left thigh. Anglin was taken to a hospital in Macon, where he succumbed to his wounds on September 18. Two more men were wounded in Company F: Alnay Bright and William Gibbs. Bright was struck in the right leg by an artillery shell. Gibbs lost the index finger on his right hand. Like William Anglin's, Bright's wounds proved mortal. He passed away in a hospital in Macon on September 16.[25]

It is unlikely that Hood ever planned for Lee to be as involved as he was in the attack on Jonesboro. Hood, writing after the war, stated that he had told Hardee that if the attack was not successful, "to send Lee's Corps, at dark, back to or near Rough and Ready, in order to protect our retreat to Lovejoy Station." To reiterate this, at 6:00 P.M., Hood sent orders to Hardee to have Lee's corps move to Atlanta, as Hood believed the city to be under imminent attack by the Federals. Hood had yet to grasp the fact that Hardee faced the entire Federal army at Jonesboro. Those orders did not reach Lee until 1:00 A.M. on September 1, and the corps marched out an hour later. "[S]tarted to Atlanta and march hard all day," was all that Hodges recorded in his diary.[26]

Because of the Confederate loss at Jonesboro, Hood lost his last railroad link to the rest of the Confederacy. He could no longer receive supplies. Since he had no way to feed and otherwise provision his men and animals, he had to abandon Atlanta, one of the most important of all Southern cities. On September 2 and 3, Hood did what he had to do: he abandoned the city. All munitions still within the city were destroyed, and the warehouses containing food for the military were opened to the citizens.

Sometime the next day, one of Hood's staff officers found Lee about six miles from Atlanta and ordered him to stop and cover the retreat of the elements of the Army of Tennessee still in Atlanta. Lee's corps was on the McDonough Road, which leads south out of Atlanta. What steps Lee took to accomplish his orders are unknown. Later that day, Lee was ordered to rejoin Hardee near Lovejoy Station. Hardee had established a line about a mile north of Lovejoy Station. Earlier that day, Sherman had ordered one of his generals to "feel for" the McDonough Road. Had more than just a few small patrols been sent out, Lee's entire corps could have been caught with no support and captured or wrecked beyond repair.[27]

Lee ordered his corps deployed on the march as such: Clayton's division in the lead, followed by Stevenson's division, and lastly, Johnson's division, with each division followed by artillery. Johnson had replaced Anderson due to the latter's wounding at Jonesboro. Throughout the day, Lee's corps must have been under fire. James Turbyfield (Company B) was wounded in the back and hip when an artillery round went off nearby. It could have been the shrapnel from the same round that struck Sgt. John Autry (Company G) in the groin and right testicle, "necessitating removal of gland." Lt. David Baird (Company D) was struck in the breast, and fellow Wataugian Lorenzo Miller (Company I) was "hit with spent ball — and struck senseless." Johnson Craige (Company H) and James Howell (Company H) were both captured. Craige later died as a prisoner of war, and Howell took the oath of allegiance and joined the Federal army.[28]

On September 2, Hardee, who had fought again at Jonesboro on the previous day, established new lines to the south at Lovejoy Station. Stewart's corps took its place within the new lines first on September 3, followed by Lee's Corps that evening. The Fifty-Eighth lost four men captured on September 2. Sgt. Maj. Drury Coffey was captured on September 4. Sgt. Elijah Norris (Company D) was also wounded around that time. As the regiment neared Lovejoy Station, "just as the sun was setting," Norris "was shot down.... I [thought] I was killed, a big bullet lacking only about an inch of going through me. This was on September 4, one day before I was 21 years old." Norris was sent home and never did heal enough to return to the army.[29]

Another interesting event occurred at the same time that Norris was wounded. George Mullis (Company G) was captured near Jonesboro, or near Stockbridge, on September 4. He was sent to Nashville and then on to Louisville. By November 1, he was at Camp Douglas near Chicago. On January 10, 1865, the thirty-four year old Mullis drafted a letter to commissar of prisons, stating that he was conscripted into Confederate service in September 1863, and had been 'forced to bear Arms against the government of the United States" against his will. He stated that he had "always maintained the principles of a tried and true Union man." Mullis asked that he not be exchanged but requested "that permission be granted to take the Oath of Allegiance to the United States and [regain] the privileges of an American citizen." The United States government was slow to act upon Mullis's petition, not granting his request until May 12, when he took the oath and was released.[30]

Sgt. Maj. Drury D. Coffey was appointed to the field and staff on February 25, 1864. He was captured September 3, 1864, and was not released from prison until May 18, 1865 (courtesy the Caldwell Heritage Museum).

Sherman soon came to the realization that Hood had abandoned Atlanta, and on September 6 he withdrew from Hardee's front and occupied the city. On September 15, a general ten-day truce was installed. The truce was for exchanging prisoners and for clearing the city of all civilians. Drum Major Blair sat down on September 5 and penned a letter home, informing his mother that he was "still among the living and enjoying good health." Blair told her that he was "nearly worn out marching" and that he had been "on the march for a week." Showing some disappointment in Hood, Blair wrote, "We have lossed more men and property in ... the las few days than Johnston lossed in the whole campaign." On a personal note, Blair complained that he "had not had but one letter from home in two months."

On September 8, the Fifty-Eighth left its works on the front lines and went into camp. Garrett Gouge (Company K) wrote home on September 12, "I have nothing of interest to write to you at present.... I was proud to get a few days' rest for we have lost a great many good soldiers ... I am tired of the war and long to see it end. I would like to get home and fid you all well to enjoy peace one time more." Gouge's words could have been written by any member of the Fifty-Eighth.[31]

Captain Harper returned to the regiment on Tuesday, September 13, a day he recorded as "Clear, Hot." On September 17, the regiment was mustered to be paid. Hood had recommended on September 7 to Confederate authorities that the men needed to be paid, "a good portion of which has not been paid for ten months." On a cloudy and rainy September 18, portions of the Army of Tennessee began to move. Their destination was the town of Palmetto, on the Atlanta and West Point Railroad. The Fifty-Eighth and the rest of Palmer's brigade moved to the north of the railroad, formed in a line of battle, and fortified their position. It was the goal of Hood to take his entire army north and cut Sherman's line of supplies.

On September 25, President Davis arrived to confer with Hood and to review the army. On September 26, according to Hood, the president and the general rode out on "an informal review of troops. Some brigades received the President with enthusiasm; others were seemingly dissatisfied and inclined to call out, 'give us General Johnston.'" The reaction by Palmer's brigade is unknown. Private Gouge simply chronicled in a letter home on September 26: "We were reviewed by Jefferson Davis, our president, today. I got to see him for the first time." The Fifty-Eighth had almost two weeks to continue its rest.[32]

While meeting with Davis, Hood laid out his strategy for wrecking Sherman's lines of communication and supply, hoping to force Sherman out in the open where he could be attacked, or where Sherman would attack Hood in a defensive position.

Lee's corps crossed the Chattahoochee River at Moore's Ferry on pontoon bridges on September 29. On October 1, the Army of Tennessee was near Powder Springs. Stevenson had orders to move his division out at 6:00 A.M., followed by Clayton and Johnson. On October 2, the Army was near Flint Hill. On October 3, Lee's corps "took position near Lost Mountain to cover the movement of Stewart's corps." Hodges recorded their position as "in the Yankee works north west of Marietta." Stewart's men set out to destroy parts of the railroad and to capture Big Shanty and Allatoona. Big Shanty, known today as Kennesaw, fell on October 4, as did Ackworth. A small group of Confederates assaulted the Federals at Allatoona and had victory within their grasp, when reports arrived that there were Federals coming up in the rear, and the Confederates disengaged and moved off. On October 4, the Fifty-Eighth moved toward Ackworth, stopping to build breastworks. That evening the men left their works, moved three miles, and encamped for the night. Again on October 5 they were on the road, moving four miles, and again that evening they were able to occupy the abandoned Federal works. The next morning, the regiment had orders to move off as quietly as possible with Stevenson in the lead. The men marched another ten miles and passed through Dallas. They covered another sixteen miles on the seventh and fourteen miles on the eighth, passing through Van Wert. Orders had gone out on the morning of the eighth that after reveille, "All playing of bands, beating of drums, and sounding of calls will be suspended" until further notice. On October 10, the Fifty-Eighth crossed over the Coosa River, marched another fifteen miles, and went into camp for the evening. Hood ordered Lee to capture Reseca on October 10, and his corps moved off to the east, marching ten miles. The following day, Hodges recorded that the Fifty-Eighth covered eighteen miles.[33]

Hood ordered Lee to move "upon Resaca" and to "display his forces and demand the surrender of the garrison, but not to attack, unless, in his judgment, the capture could be effected with a small loss of life." The Fifty-Eighth arrived on the outskirts of town around 3:00 P.M. Lee sent an order to the commander of the garrison, signed by Hood, demanding the surrender of the town, which was refused. Lee chose not to assault the works, which were strong and well manned, "believing that our loss would have been severe." Stevenson asked Lee if skirmishers could be deployed, which Lee allowed, with the directive that no demonstrations or large-scale fights be brought on. Hodges recorded that "a sharp skirmish commenced and continued until after dark." The Confederates spent the night before Reseca and the next morning moved toward the north, traversing seven miles. They covered another ten miles on October 14, and a whole twenty miles on the fifteenth, finally arriving at Snake Creek Gap. At Snake Creep Gap, Lee was forced to deploy a couple of his brigades, those commanded by Deas and Brantley, of Johnston's division, to hold off the Federals while the rest of the Army of Tennessee passed through Mattox's Gap.[34]

Johnson L. Craige was only twenty years old when he enlisted in May 1862. He was a member of Company H of the Fifty-Eighth and was captured at Jonesboro, Georgia, around September 1, 1864. Craige eventually found himself at Camp Douglas in Chicago, Illinois, where he died on December 2, 1864, of "chronic diarrhea" (courtesy the North Carolina Department of Archives).

Sherman had been following Hood. He had left one corps in Atlanta and set out with 41,000 men in pursuit. Sherman wanted to overtake and then destroy Hood's army. However, Hood's forces were always about a day ahead of Sherman. The Federal general did not wish to continue following Hood, believing that it would take more than one Federal army to corner the Confederates. Hood had advanced to a position where he was blocked by the Federals in Nashville. If Hood chose to bypass Nashville, then those Federals could set out for the industrial centers in Montgomery and Selma, Alabama. Instead of following Hood, Sherman wanted to head south and march his army to Savannah. The federal government, even while Sherman was in north Georgia, granted his request.

On October 15 and 16, Hood rethought his strategy. While the morale of his troops had improved since taking the offensive, he still believed that they were unprepared to fight a pitched battle. Neither could Hood dig in and wait for the Federals. They could build equally daunting field works, bring reinforcements, and then leave a portion of these men to entrap Hood while they went elsewhere. Hood had to maintain the initiative that he had held for the past month. So Hood chose to keep moving and sought to destroy the railroads in northeast Alabama and to possibly even regain the area between Nashville and Chattanooga, central Tennessee, Kentucky, maybe as far north as the Ohio river. Sherman had to chose between a march across Georgia or following Hood, and Hood hoped to get into Tennessee and Kentucky and recruit more men. After defeating Sherman, probably in Kentucky, Hood would send reinforcements to help in Virginia.[35]

Directives soon came from Hood's headquarters: the Army of Tennessee was going to continue on the offensive. Hood ordered, among other things, that twenty days' worth of rations be prepared, some going into the men's haversacks, and others into the wagons. Lieutenant Miller recorded after the war that the men in the Fifty-Eighth had been on "less than half rations" and in the evenings, "were compelled to make their ration for the day following by parching corn which continued all night, each mess taking it by turns, keeping the pans hot all night." The men were poorly clothed and equipped. On October 13, while near Resaca, Lee had ordered officers, from the divisional level down to the company level, to make sandals out of "green beef-hides" for men without shoes.[36]

The next week proved wearisome for the members of the Fifty-Eighth. They took up the line of march on October 16, covering eight miles. The following day, they covered another twelve miles, crossing over the Chattahoochee River. They had no sooner stopped than they were ordered to march back two miles in the direction they had just come to go on picket duty. On October 18, they crossed over into Alabama, covering ten miles. Twelve more miles followed the next day with another river crossing. Fifteen miles on October 20 were followed by six miles the next day as the regiment moved through Gadsden, Alabama. Drum Major Blair took the time to pen a letter home to his father. The regiment had gotten "a large mail bag unexpected." Blair thought the Army of Tennessee was "in good health & fine spirits and I think will make a good fight if an opportunity affords." Toward the end of his letter, Blair wrote that he "would like very much to be at home to help you eat some of youre sweet potatoes but I dont expect to be there soon."[37]

A lucky break followed on October 22: the regiment "remained in camp and drew shoes and clothing." The regiment moved at five that evening, covering another mile before halting for the evening. At sunrise on the twenty-third, the men shook off the frost and took to the road again, this time covering between twelve and sixteen miles. At 7:00 A.M. on the twenty-fourth, the regiment was on the road again, crossing a "barren country called Sand Mt.," and then fording the Black Warrior River. "Feet badly blistered," Captain Harper recorded that day. In a letter home, Harper blamed his blistered feet on wearing socks that were too tight. Frost once again greeted the Fifty-Eighth on the morning of October 25. Again they made about twenty miles, and again Harper wrote that his feet were "blistered and very sore." That night, he recorded "pumpkin bread for supper." It started to rain on the twenty-sixth, yet Lee's corps made twelve miles. "Road very muddy," Harper wrote, "Slosh, slosh. Passed through the shabby looking town of Summerville." That night, Harper and the other members of the Fifty-Eighth pitched what shelter they had managed to carry. Harper's was just a blanket, yet he "slept soundly ... not withstanding the rain." The rain extinguished a fire that he had tried to build to warm himself.[38]

There was reasoning, albeit vague, regarding their wanderings. Hood's original goal had been to cross over into Alabama and destroy the railroads and depots around Stevenson and Bridgeport. Hood wrote that the cavalry command of Nathan Bedford Forrest, who had been ordered to join Hood while Hood's own cavalry remained behind to watch Sherman, had been delayed by the high waters of the Tennessee. Truthfully, Forrest was conducting a raid in western Tennessee and did not know of the orders to join Hood. For some unknown reason, Hood chose to strike through northern Alabama, crossing the Tennessee River at Florence. For Sherman, it did not really matter: he had given up chasing Hood. On October 26, Sherman had returned to Atlanta. He soon torched the city, and on November 16, commenced his infamous March to the Sea.[39]

It was much the same for the next couple of days: up early and on the road. The regiment marched for three quarters of an hour, and then stopped for a fifteen-minute rest. The weather was mostly pleasant. Captain Harper thought it "high living — potatoes, apples, peaches, etc. bought." He recorded a "fine camping place and a big rabbit hunt" on October 29. On that day, orders came through promoting Capt. Samuel Silver (Company K) to lieutenant colonel. It is likely that Silver, who is recorded as being in charge of the regiment from May to August 1864, had again assumed command after Major Stewart was killed at Jonesboro. Silver was the only field-grade officer on staff. Brigade Commander Col. Joseph Palmer had recommended Silver for promotion in September, writing that Silver had "proven to be very attentive and efficient. I feel satisfied from his character upon my knowledge of him as an officer to recommend him for promotion to the lieutenant colonelcy" of the Fifty-Eighth. Palmer respectfully urged that his "promotion be made without delay."[40]

Around 6:00 A.M. on Sunday, October 29, the regiment struck the road again. After marching about twelve miles, the men halted and stacked arms. They were within a mile or so of the Tennessee River and the town of Florence, Alabama. Lee was ordered to cross some of his men over the Tennessee River the next day. He took two brigades of Johnson's division and ferried them across the river in pontoon boats. Two brigades of Clayton's division crossed at another point farther to the west. There were some Federal cavalry in the town, which Lee's men drove out.

The last day of October broke clear and warm. The Fifty-Eighth broke camp and marched around 4:00 A.M., taking a position opposite Florence. Hodges estimated they had covered twelve miles. The pontoon bridges across the Tennessee River were finished later that afternoon. The regiment stayed in camp on the first of November. On that day, Captain Harper was appointed acting major of the Fifty-Eighth. Another captain with seniority to Harper was present, but the identity of that captain is unclear. The regiment crossed the Tennessee River on the pontoons in the rain the next morning. The men moved about a mile past town and started to work on fortifications. At six the next morning, they rotated off the line. On November 5, the Fifty-Eighth, with the rest of the brigade, moved back across the river and towards Huntsville. A skirmish was fought about five miles down the road near Shoal Creek. Afterwards, the brigade went into camp.

The next morning many men were in church when the bugle called them back into line. They marched back toward Florence, and according to Elijah Coffey (Company E), they "had a little fight with the caveldry" and went into camp on the banks of the river. It rained the nights of the sixth, seventh, and all day on the eighth, finally clearing off on November 9. The rain hampered Hood's planned movement back to the east. Also delaying Hood was the unfinished railroad. He expected to find supplies when he got across the Tennessee River, but was forced to wait almost three weeks for the railroad to be fixed and for supplies to be brought up.[41]

For the men of the Fifty-Eighth and the rest of Palmer's brigade, the routine over the next two weeks was about the same: short moves, short rations, and work on the fortifications. The monotony was unpleasantly interrupted on Friday, November 11, at 10:00 A.M., when a deserter from the Fifty-Fourth Virginia was executed.[42]

Hood thought that if he moved into central Tennessee, Sherman might be forced to return north to stop the Confederate advance. Hood also sought to recapture Tennessee and possibly Kentucky. Accordingly, Hood ordered his men north on November 19. The Fifty-Eighth left camp on the twentieth and marched between eight and ten miles in a cold rain with the "roads exceedingly muddy." The army was moving on two different roads. Lee's and Stewart's corps were on the road to Lawrenceburg, marching northeast. Lee's corps was in the lead.

Instead of rain, the twenty-first brought snow and winds. The march this day led the men across the state line into Tennessee. This march was also short, about ten miles. Tuesday, November 22, also brought snow. The regiment marched at 8:00 A.M. and passed through the town of West Point, covering four miles before bivouacking for the night. "Night bitter cold," Harper recorded. "Slept well before large hickory log fire." The twenty-third was cold, but clear, and the regiment marched at 11:00 A.M. After covering about five miles, the soldiers went into camp at 3:00 P.M. On the twenty-fourth, the regiment was on the move at 7:00 A.M., marching on a frozen road. While the road was easier for artillery and supply wagons, it was hard on the men's feet, especially for those who did not have shoes. In all they covered about fifteen miles, striking the Columbia and Waynesboro Pike and passing through Henryville and crossing the Buffalo River. Another fifteen miles was covered on November 25.[43]

Rain greeted the men on the twenty-sixth. Stevenson's division was in the lead, and the Fifty-Eighth and the Sixtieth were thrown out in front of the corps. While on the march, the very front of the marching column was covered by cavalry, usually at least two miles ahead. Then came an infantry screen. If the cavalry was attacked, the troops could fall back on their infantry support. The advanced infantrymen were expected to check, or slow down, the enemy, giving the main infantry behind them time to form in some defensive position, or form for an offensive movement.[44]

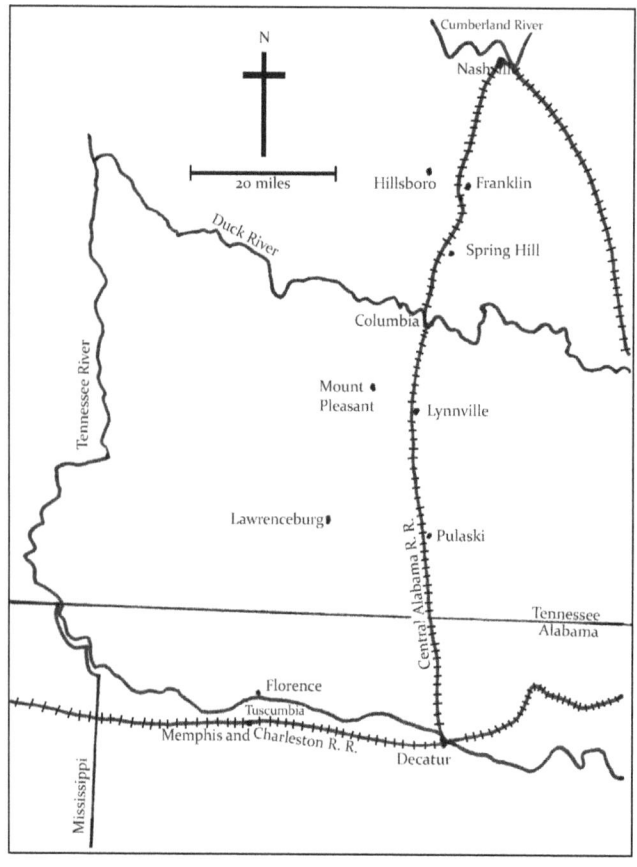

The Fifty-Eighth started north on Hood's Franklin-Nashville campaign, but advanced no farther than Columbia. The regiment was then detailed to guard prisoners back into Mississippi.

On the evening of the twenty-sixth, the Fifty-Eighth went on picket duty, relieving a part of Nathan Bedford Forrest's cavalry. Harper reported some "slight skirmishing." Hood was confronting two Federal divisions under John Schofield at Columbia, Tennessee. Schofield had his back to the Duck River and was afraid that Hood might cross the river at another point and cut off his line of retreat. So, on the night of November 27, Schofield abandoned his works and crossed the river. The Fifty-Eighth's division commander was warned by some of his scouts, possibly members of the Fifty-Eighth, that the Federals were abandoning their defenses. Stevenson strengthened his scouts, and sent them forward, where they soon discovered empty Federal breastworks. Stevenson dispatched two Tennessee regiments to take the town and later moved most of his division forward.[45]

Hood's plan had been thus: Stephen Lee, with two-thirds of his corps and most of the artillery, would hold Schofield's attention to the front with threatening attacks and an artillery bombardment. While Schofield was occupied, Hood would cross the rest of the Army of Tennessee, Stewart and Cheatham's corps, and Lee's other division, over the river to trap Schofield. However, Schofield beat them to the draw and was already across the river. With the Fifty-Eighth and Sixtieth in advance, Palmer's brigade entered Columbia about daylight, skirmishing with the Federals across the river. Harper reported finding a "hat, boots, coat etc.," all items the men desperately needed. Unlike the soldiers in the Army of Northern Virginia, the Army of Tennessee rarely had the opportunity to acquire captured Federal gear. While the Sixtieth North Carolina was ordered to move up the river and provide a flanking fire against the Federals on the other side, the Fifty-Eighth was ordered to act as provost marshal for the town.[46]

Like some other members of the Fifty-Eighth, Joel Trivett (Company D) used the confusion following the battle of Chickamauga in September 1863 to desert (courtesy Jackie and Dawn Peters).

Confederate cavalry crossed the Duck River on November 28, followed by infantry the next day. Schofield, finding himself outflanked, moved his command back to Spring Hill. On the evening of the twenty-ninth, Hood found the Federals. But darkness came before the Confederates could get into position to launch a full-scale attack. All throughout the night, the Confederates could hear the Federals retreating north along the Columbia-Franklin Pike. While Hood ordered the road to be blocked both above and below town, his orders were not carried out. Even worse, Hood retired for the evening without seeing that his orders were fulfilled. Thus, Schofield escaped, and Hood lost his best chance to seriously damage a portion of the Federal army in Tennessee. The Federals took up a new position just south of Franklin and strengthened existing works or constructed new works. Schofield wanted to retreat over the Harpeth River, but the bridge had been destroyed, and the ford was almost impassable. Furthermore, Schofield's pontoon boats had not yet come up. Hood's Confederates advanced slowly, skirmishing with Federals at Thompson's Station and elsewhere. By 4:00 P.M., the Confederates were in position and Hood launched his much-disputed frontal assault. The Confederates were able to push back two Federal brigades in advance of their front lines. And, they were able to penetrate the Federal works near the Carter House. Even though the Confederates tried repeatedly to widen the breach, they were unable to do so and were driven back. At times, only the Federal works separated the lines. The Confederate assault became known as "Picket's Charge of the West."

In actuality, the Confederate charge at Franklin was the larger of the two. At Gettysburg, 12,500 Confederates charged over a mile in an assault that lasted just under an hour. At Franklin, 19,000 Confederates charged over two miles in an assault that lasted five hours. The Confederates at Franklin lost 6,252 men, including fifteen generals, six of whom were killed or mortally wounded. Patrick Cleburne, one of the best generals in the Army of Tennessee, was among those killed. Hood's generals had tried to persuade him not to attack. He had ignored their advice and virtually destroyed the Army of Tennessee. After holding off the Confederates, Schofield continued to retreat north. He abandoned his works at Franklin the night of the battle and began moving into the defensive works at Nashville on the first of December. Hood was left with Franklin. He buried his dead and then moved north.

At Nashville, instead of Schofield's two isolated divisions, Hood found extensive works protecting the city and 66,000 Federal soldiers. The Confederates, numbering around 21,000 men, began to arrive on the afternoon of December 2 and quickly constructed works south of town. Ultimately the Confederate line was four miles long. Under pressure from the authorities in Washington, D.C., the Federal army ventured out of the works before daylight on December 15. With the Confederate right pinned down, another Federal assault on the left overran Hood's lines. Hood's men fell back and took up another defensive position. The following day, the Federals overwhelmed this line, and Hood was forced to retreat. Hood lost another 4,400 men. The Army of Tennessee had started the campaign with an estimated 38,000 men. Losses for the entire campaign came to 23,500 men. The remnants of the Army of Tennessee made their way south, first to Tuscumbia, then west to Iuka and Corinth, and finally, to Tupelo, Mississippi, where they went into camp on January 10.

Providentially, the Fifty-Eighth was not a part of Hood's ruinous Tennessee campaign. While the Army of Tennessee marched north, the Fifty-Eighth stayed in Columbia, guarding prisoners and performing garrison duty. On December 5, the Fifty-Eighth reported 246 effective men, with 311 present. The difference probably included men sick, on detail, or possibly under arrest. Lieutenant Colonel Silver was placed in command of the entire post, and on December 6, Harper was in command of the garrison and captured prisoners. Harper's headquarters were in a cabin that had formerly belonged to a Yankee officer. It is not known if the rest of the Fifty-Eighth was likewise quartered, but just about anything was better than what their fellow soldiers were enduring. Even though the Tar Heels were not on the front lines, it was still cold with two inches of snow and sleet falling on December 9.

Orders came on the morning of December 12: the regiment was ordered to cook rations and prepare to move about 1,200 Federal prisoners. With the snow melting, the Fifty-Eighth, along with the "Fourth and the Twenty-Fifth," marched out of Corinth about noon on December 14. Harper was the only one to record this December journey.

> [December 15] Cloudy, Warm Slight rain. Marched at 8 A.M. on Lawrenceburg road. Road muddy. Camped at Carethers 6 miles north of Lawrenceburg.—14 [miles].
> [December 16] Cloudy, Night rain. Marched at & A.M. Passed thro' Lawrenceburg. Made 18 miles. Marched on the old "Military road."
> [December 17] Rain all day. Warm. Took country road, west of Military road, made, say 15 [miles] and camped on small creek near burnt factory on Shoal Creek 10 miles [North] of Florence.
> [December 18] Forded Shoal Creek—Roads very muddy. Left old Military road 4 miles [north] of Florence and took road for G. Ferry. Camp on Cypress Creek at burnt factories, made say—12 miles. Road very bad.
> [December 19] Heavy rain all day. P.M. Cold and windy. Marched at 8 A.M. through rain and mud. Camped on North bank at Garners Ferry 9 miles. Night—Cold and disagreeable. Blankets wet.
> [December 20] A.M. Cloudy. P.M. Rain and cold. Crossing the river in ferry boats all day. Camped on south bank. Disagreeable day....
> [December 21] Snow and sleet. Windy Marched at 10 A.M. to Bartons Station on R. R. 2 miles and camped. Bridge down and could get no transportation on R. R.

On December 22, those who were barefoot or sick were left behind. And at 8:00 A.M., Lieutenant Colonel Silver took half of the prisoners, along with the Fourth and Twenty-Fifth, and boarded a train for Corinth, leaving Harper with the Fifty-Eighth and the other prisoners. Harper recorded a "hard freeze" on the twenty-third and spent the day waiting in vain for rail transportation. At 10:00 A.M., a train finally returned, and some of the prisoners and the Fifty-Eighth climbed on board. They were in Corinth by 4:00 P.M., and Harper was billeted in a hotel.[47]

Christmas Day 1864 was cold and cloudy. The rest of the prisoners arrived that day, and later that afternoon, the Fifty-Eighth moved from town to a camp. News came the following day that the Federals were raiding to their south along the Mobile and Ohio Railroad, near Okolona. This was the third raid in the Okolona area in 1864. A force of Federal cavalry left LaGrange, Tennessee, and moved south, damaging portions of the railroad. At 10:00 A.M. on the morning of the twenty-seventh, the Fifty-Eighth boarded trains and headed south. After trailing most of the day, the unit encountered a burned bridge near Tupelo. The regiment moved back a short distance to the community of Saltillo and went into camp. The following day, the regiment once again boarded the trains, disembarking north of Tupelo. The men then commenced marching down the railroad tracks on the crossties. Harper complained about not having his horse, which he had been unable to transport. His feet were sore, as he was having to march "with heavy boots that are too large for me." That evening they camped about six miles north of Okolona.

Harper and the rest of the Fifty-Eighth awoke on December 29 with the ground frozen hard beneath them, and with a cold wind upon them. At 8:00 A.M., they set out and were in the burned-out town of Okolona before lunch. The Federals had torn up the railroad tracks, burned trestles, and plundered homes in the area. Near Okolona, Harper found some distant kin of the Lenoirs, who promised to take care of him in the event of his wounding. These distant Caldwell County cousins had seen their gin house and cotton burned, while "white and negro soldiers ransacked the house but did steal comparatimly little from them." The thirtieth and thirty-first found the regiment quartered in the hotel building and a few churches that had survived the burning of the town. It was a good thing to be quartered inside, as Elijah Coffey recorded "a dredful storm" on the night of the thirtieth. In the afternoon, the Fifty-Eighth moved a mile and a half outside of town and went into camp.[48]

January 1 dawned clear and cold. The Fifty-Eighth was ordered back to town, and by January 4 was quartered once again in local churches. The next few days continued for the most part cold, with periods of rain. Finally, on January 13, orders came for the Fifty-Eighth to rejoin what was left of the Army of Tennessee.[49]

CHAPTER 12

January–May 1865

"and won for themselves a merited fame."—Brig. Gen. Joseph B. Palmer

A new year usually brings high hopes. Unfortunately for the Confederacy, 1865 dawned bleakly. All across the South, the Confederate armies had been fought to the breaking point. In Virginia, Robert E. Lee's army held to its entrenched lines north and south of the Confederate capital by the slimmest of sinews. Lee and his Confederates had fought valiantly, blocking the flanking movements of Grant's soldiers as they constantly tried to insert themselves between Lee and the capital. But Lee was the master of Grant, and tens of thousands of Federal soldiers were lost charging numerous Confederate defensive positions. At last, Grant laid siege to Petersburg, and slowly, methodically, began cutting the railroad that supplied the Confederates in his sector. On the Gulf Coast, Mobile Bay, one of the major entryways for supplies from abroad, was closed by the Federal navy on August 5. Farther west, the Confederates in the Trans-Mississippi theater of the war tried to mount an invasion of Missouri in September 1864. While meeting with initial success, they were later defeated and forced to retreat to Texas. Finally, Atlanta, the great Southern manufacturing center, had fallen to Sherman's masses in the summer of 1864. Sherman chose not to keep the crown jewel of the South, but burned most of it to the ground. Instead of following Hood into Tennessee, Sherman chose to strike off in a different direction entirely.

Without a glance over his shoulder, Sherman marched south with his battle-hardened veterans. It must have seemed like a holiday for many: no breastworks to charge, no large group of Confederates nipping at their flanks, no supply lines to protect. The Federals were going to live off the land, and in the words of Sherman, "make Georgia howl." Save for a small November battle at Griswoldville and isolated cavalry actions, Sherman's march toward Savannah was largely unopposed. It took the Federals twenty-six days to cover 250 miles. Fort McAllister, on the Ogeechee River, had held off numerous attempts by the Federal navy to shell it into submission. On December 13, the fort fell to Sherman's infantry after a quick assault. The Confederates evacuated Savannah on the night of December 20, and Sherman's army was in control of the city by the next morning. Sherman sent word to Lincoln of the city's capture, presenting the president Savannah as a Christmas present.[1]

Around 8:00 A.M. on January 14, 1865, the Tar Heels of the Fifty-Eighth shouldered their rifles and began marching up the railroad towards Tupelo. Some of the horses of the field and staff had caught up with the regiment, and the officers rode alongside the marching men. They made twelve miles that day. The next day was clear and pleasant as the regiment once again took to walking on the crossties of the railroad. After two-and-a-half miles, Captain

Harper traded places with Lieutenant Colonel Silver, allowing Silver to ride while Harper walked. They caught up with Palmer's brigade two miles west of Tupelo. Palmer's brigade numbered just 1,027 men. The Fifty-Eighth brought an additional 310 men to the ranks, making Palmer's brigade the largest in Stevenson's division. The Fifty-Eighth was also the largest single regiment present, according to a return filed on January 19, 1865. The Sixtieth North Carolina had been consolidated with the Sixty-Third Virginia, for a total of 340 men present, and all six of the Tennessee regiments within the brigade had been consolidated into one regiment with 471 men present. The Fifty-Eighth was also the largest regiment in the division. The Forty-Sixth Alabama of Perrus's brigade mustered just 174 soldiers. In all, on January 20, the Army of Tennessee, excluding the cavalry, could only muster 16,913 men present for duty. Their aggregate, or the number of men they should have had present, was 77,366.[2]

Lt. William H. Wiseman (Company A) had served in the Sixth North Carolina State Troops prior to transferring to the Fifty-Eighth. He is last reported on April 21, 1865, in a hospital in Macon, Georgia, but did live to return home to the mountains of western North Carolina (courtesy Tense Banks).

Lieutenant General Hood, who had been connected with the Fifty-Eighth for almost a year, asked to be re-assigned on January 13. He was relieved of command and ordered to report to Richmond on January 15, but that was order was not made permanent until January 23. Lt. Gen. Richard Taylor was assigned to command the Army of Tennessee, along with his own department. However, the Army of Tennessee was soon broken up, with two corps going to South Carolina in an attempt to combat Sherman, while the remaining corps was left in the west with Taylor.[3]

Tupelo was home for the Fifty-Eighth for about a week. Orders had come down on January 15 for daily drills to begin again, when the weather permitted. On January 18, more orders came: Lee's corps was ordered to make preparations to move east. The men of the regiment were to prepare three days' rations and to have at least twenty rounds of ammunition in their cartridge boxes. At Montgomery and at Macon, an additional three days' rations would be available, and at Milledgeville, four days' rations were to await the troops. On the twentieth, the Fifty-Eighth drew new clothing in Tupelo, and on the twenty-first, the men were waiting for the train. Finally, about dark on the twenty-second, with rain intermingled with sleet, the Fifty-Eighth boarded the heatless freight cars, bound for Meridian, Mississippi. The regiment reached Meridian at 9:00 A.M. on Tuesday, January 24. They continued on to McDowell's Bluff, Alabama, where the men boarded boats that ferried them across the Tombigbee River to Demopolis; here they again boarded a train to Selma, Alabama, arriving at 11:00 P.M. on the twenty-fifth. At Selma, they boarded another boat, which took them to Montgomery. At Montgomery, they once again boarded trains, arriving in Columbus, Georgia, on Sunday, January 29. They made good time the following day and were in Macon by 4:00 P.M., and then near Milledgeville, where the railroad had been destroyed by Sherman, at 11:00 P.M.

"Sandy country" full of "long leaf pine" greeted the men on January 31. The regiment marched about sixteen miles, passing through Milledgeville during the day. Captain Harper paid someone twenty-five dollars for a ride in a carriage on the first of February. At 9:00 A.M. on February 2, the Fifty-Eighth was in Mayfield, where the men boarded a train for Augusta, arriving at 4:00 P.M.; another two miles was covered that evening before going into camp. Several men were furloughed home on February 3, including Lieutenant Colonel Silver. This left Captain Harper in command of the regiment. That evening, under orders from General Beauregard, Harper moved the Fifty-Eighth back to Augusta to board another train. By the next evening, the regiment was in Branchville, South Carolina. The trip from Tupelo to Augusta was 500 miles and had taken nine days.[4]

One officer of the Fifty-Eighth provided this description after the war.

> The men thinly clad, carrying each a single blanket, and most of the time with scant rations, passed the severe winter of 1864-'65 in active field service. In the prime of life, active, cheerful and full of fun, living in the open air the year round, a great part of the time on the march, the men became inured to hardships and the winter's cold, and complaints of suffering from exposure to the weather were rarely heard. The question of rations gave them more concern. All of this applied also to the field and company officers, who were equally exposed with the private soldiers."[5]

One of the first lines of Confederate defense was set up on the north bank of the South Fork of the Edisto River. The Fifty-Eighth, along with the rest of Palmer's brigade, was ordered to move via New Bridge and Midway to Cannon's Bridge. Confederate cavalry skirmished with Federals on the South side of the river under cloudy and rainy skies. On February 7, Cannon's Bridge was burnt. While the weather remained disagreeable, Harper recorded eating "sweet potatoes, turnips, pork and so on." On February 9, the Edisto River line was broken at

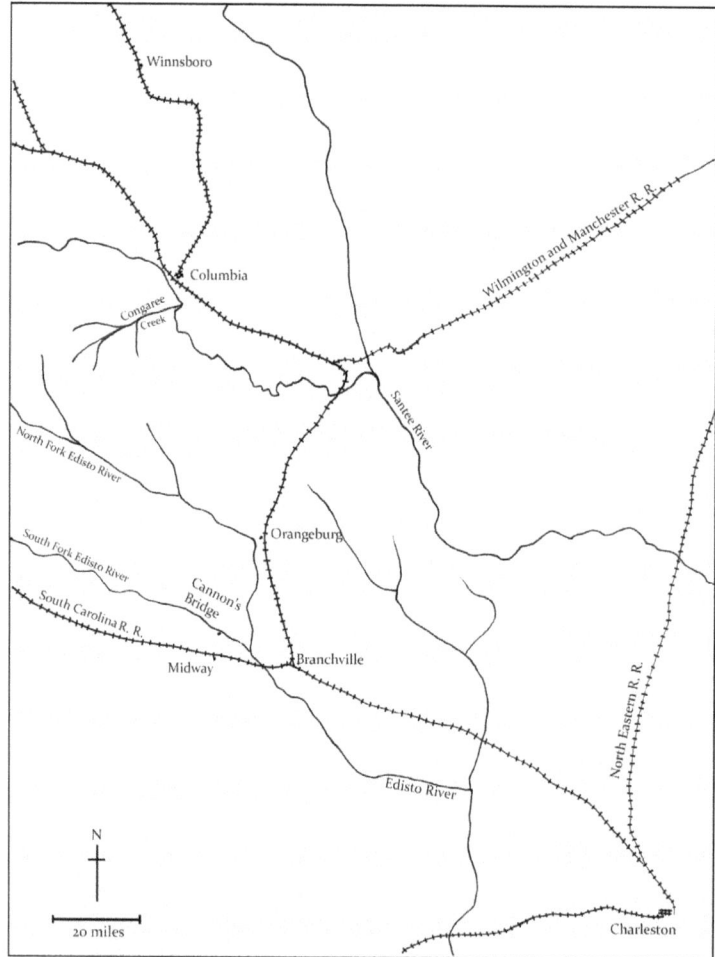

In February 1864, the Fifty-Eighth debarked at Branchville, South Carolina. They attempted to slow the Union advance through the state.

Binnacker's Bridge, seven miles to the north of the Fifty-Eighth's position at Cannon's Bridge. Palmer's brigade was in danger of being cut off and soon abandoned its position, moving north towards Orangeburg. Two men were captured: Thomas Ford (Company B) and William Crisp (Company H). A "blowing snow" pelted their faces as they marched.[6]

Sherman had once again divided his army into two wings, with one feinting towards Charleston and the other towards Augusta, Georgia. His real intent was the capital of South Carolina: Columbia. On February 10, the Fifty-Eighth stopped short of Orangeburg and threw together breastworks. Later that evening, the regiment moved seven miles farther northeast. After another cold night, they were back on the road, "tired and footsore." They were soon in "short breastworks" at Shilling's Bridge on the North Fork of the Edisto River in a line of battle that stretched for three miles. There was "slight skirmishing" that evening.

On February 12, the Federals occupied Orangeburg. That same day the war almost came to an end for the remnants of the Fifty-Eighth. Toward evening, the Federals were able to cross the river both above and below the position of the Confederates. One Federal officer recalled laying a pontoon bridge across the river and then advancing on the Confederates, who offered token resistance with "one field piece and feeble musketry." With both of the flanks threatened, and with the possibility of the line of retreat being cut off, Palmer, still in command of the division, called for a withdrawal. Major Harper was in charge of the works at the bridge. "The courier sent to Maj. Harper with orders to retire," Jonathan Miller wrote after the war, "having been captured, caused the Maj. to keep up the fight at the bridge, which we held and prevented the enemy from crossing. Keeping up an incessant fire in our front, they extended their line up the river and beyond our right and, crossed the river in considerable force, and advanced on our right, and had nearly cut off from the Columbia road, the only line of retreat. By the skillful maneuvers of Major Harper he got out of the trap with the loss of only two of his men, who were captured." There were actually more than two men captured. On February 12, the Fifty-Eighth reported a loss of approximately seventeen men captured.[7]

Monday, February 13, was clear and cool. The regiment had marched until 9:00 o'clock the previous evening and had gone into camp about sixteen miles northeast of Orangeburg. The men were on the road again at daylight and covered seven miles, camping five miles away from Columbia. On the fourteenth, Palmer's brigade marched to within two miles of Columbia and constructed breastworks on Congaree Creek. Much of the fifteenth was spent within these works, which were between six and twelve feet high. Part of the brigade was witness to the skirmishing between the Confederate and Federal forces, but apparently the Fifty-Eighth was not in such a position. Harper simply recorded that the skirmishing took place below their position. One officer of the regiment wrote that the Confederates "had hoped to meet important re-enforcements—probably a division from Lee's army—but none appeared." That evening the order was given to evacuate their position. According to Harper, the Fifty-Eighth was in the rear guard and the last to cross over the river, burning the bridge as they went.[8]

Orders were given for the evacuation of Columbia. The Fifty-Eighth was in a line of battle in the streets of the city for much of February 16. "The citizens offered," Jonathan Miller wrote after the war, "and insisted on the Confederate soldiers taking all their substance they could make use of." During the day, the Federals shelled the town intermittently. That evening, Palmer's brigade marched out of town and crossed the Broad River three miles north of Columbia. Some members of Palmer's brigade claimed to be some of the last infantry in the city. A member of the Eighteenth Tennessee claimed that the brigade left "the city just before the entrance of Sherman's vanguard." The Fifty-Eighth had one loss, Cpl. John Morritt (Company F), who was captured on the seventeenth as the Federals entered the city.[9]

Soon thereafter, Columbia burned. Sherman blamed the Confederates. The Confederates, and later generations of South Carolinians, blamed Sherman and his men. None of the men in the Fifty-Eighth recorded anything about the event as they were leaving. After the war, Jonathan Miller chronicled his thoughts: "After the evacuation of Columbia by our small force, Sherman burned the city on the 17th of [February]."[10]

Following the evacuation of Columbia, the Fifty-Eighth retreated north toward the Tar Heel state. On February 19, the regiment moved through Winnsboro, covering another estimated twenty-one miles the next day. Harper wrote that evening that it had been a "tiresome march" with his "feet blistered." Finally, on February 22, the regiment crossed into North Carolina, passing through Waxhaw, and camped that evening seventeen miles from Charlotte. The next day the regiment moved another thirteen miles closer to the city. Palmer reported on the twenty-third that his brigade had an aggregate of 855 men present for duty. It was the largest brigade in Lee's Corps, which contained just over 2,000 men.[11]

Captain Harper walked to Charlotte on February 24. It was probably there that he learned that Gen. Joseph Johnston had been re-assigned command of the army by Robert E. Lee. Lee himself had only recently been appointed commander-in-chief by the Confederate Congress, a move that stripped Jefferson Davis of the position. It was a little too late for Lee to do much. Davis had resisted appointing Johnston for over a month, but was finally compelled to move Johnston back into a command situation. Johnston was charged with concentrating "all available forces" in an attempt "to thwart the designs of the enemy." Writing from Charlotte on February 25, Johnston sent out his first general order, exhorting "all absent soldiers of the Army of Tennessee to rejoin their regiments and again confront the enemy they so often encountered in Northern Georgia, and always with honor." Jonathan Miller wrote, "The presence of Gen. Johnston in command, inspired the fullest confidence in the small army."[12]

Rain began falling on the evening of February 23, effectively slowing the advance of the Federals to a crawl. The Federals were stalled about 60 miles south of Charlotte. In order to keep the Confederates off balance, Sherman ordered his cavalry to head toward Charlotte, while he attempted to prod his army across swollen creeks, moving northeast. While parts of the Federal column were on the move by February 26, they continued to experience rising streams and endless mud through the first of March. By March 1, the Confederate high command knew that Charlotte was not Sherman's objective.[13]

John A. Mast served in Company D until July 1864, when he went over to the enemy. He was taken to Louisville, Kentucky, where he took the oath and was released in September 1864 (courtesy Terry Harmon).

On February 27, General Johnston reviewed Lee's entire corps, at which time Johnston reported that 2,100 men were present. A couple of days before, when reviewing just part of Lee's Corps of the Army of Tennessee, Johnston received three cheers from each brigade as he rode past. It is unclear if "old Joe" received the same adulation from the Tar Heel remnant in Lee's Corps.[14]

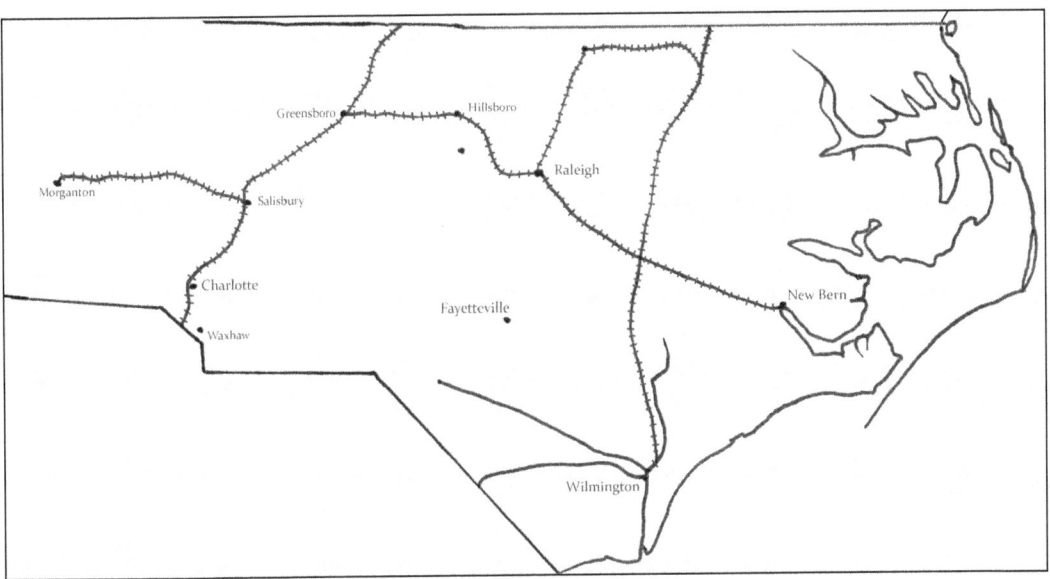

The Fifty-Eighth entered the state of North Carolina at Waxhaw on February 22, 1865. The men were transported by rail through Salisbury and Greensboro to the eastern part of the state.

Word came on Friday, March 3, "to be ready to move at a moments notice." Also on that date, Maj. Gen. Daniel Harvey Hill arrived in Charlotte and assumed command of Lee's Corps. Major General Stevenson returned to the command of his division, and Brigadier General Palmer, to his brigade. Hill was a native of South Carolina, a West Point graduate, and brother-in-law to Stonewall Jackson. Hill was teaching in Charlotte at the beginning of the war and was colonel of the First North Carolina Volunteers, later reorganized and known as the Bethel Regiment. Hill had commanded brigades and divisions in the Army of Northern Virginia and later a corps in the Army of Tennessee. When the Army of Tennessee was reorganized after the battle of Chickamauga, Hill, due to his disagreement with Bragg, was left without a command and was relegated to backwater districts.

At 2:00 A.M., a whistle sounded, and everyone hurried back to camp and formed ranks. The alarm proved to be a false one, and the men returned to their slumber. Orders did come later that day for the men to prepare three days' rations and to board trains as they became available. The Fifty-Eighth waited the rest of the fourth, and the fifth, with no transportation in sight. One of the problems stemmed from the backlog of men and materials waiting in Salisbury. In that town, the gauge of the railroad changed, and everyone and everything had to be unloaded, and then reloaded to continue their journey.[15]

Finally, on March 11, the Fifty-Eighth was near Salisbury, bound for the eastern part of the state. On the twelfth, the regiment passed through Lexington, and by the evening of the fifteenth, were marching through Smithfield. The evening of the next day the men crossed over a river, probably the Cape Fear, and moved about five miles from Smithfield toward Bentonville in the "rain and slosh." That same day Captain Harper applied for the position of major of the regiment. A day later, Lt. Col. Samuel Silver resigned from his position as commanding officer of the Fifty-Eighth. Silver claimed that he was not "sufficiently educated to perform the executive duties of the office" he was in, and that the situation of his family in western North Carolina, subjected to "tories and deserters," necessitated his presence. Silver's "unconditional resignation" was rejected by Lieutenant General Stewart. For some unknown reason, and by some unknown hand, the resignation of Silver was accepted on April 9, 1865.[16]

The regiment spent the next day in camp, and on March 17 marched back toward Smithfield. That afternoon the rain stopped and the skies cleared. While in camp that evening, the men attempted to wash some of their clothes. The next morning, the regiment took to the road again, moving south and passing through the town of Bentonville at 8:00 P.M. "A forced march" was the way one member of the regiment described the tramp that day. The tired troops then went into camp.[17]

Johnston had been unclear as to the objective of the Federals after taking command. Raleigh, Fayetteville, or someplace along the coast could be the Federals' goal. Fayetteville fell on March 11. Johnston realized that his only chance was to attack a portion of the Federal army and beat this portion before the other wing of the Federal army could attack. This had to be done before the enemy advancing west from Wilmington and New Bern could effect a juncture with Sherman's forces. Since Johnston was still unclear as to the destination of Sherman, he chose to concentrate his newly christened "Army of the South" at Smithfield. From this position, he could attack a portion of Sherman's command or the Federals advancing from New Bern. The Army of the South was composed of the remnants of the Army of Tennessee, about 4,000 men under Lt. Gen. Stewart; 6,500 men under Braxton Bragg who were left from the Wilmington garrison; 7,500 men under General Hardee; the remnant of the garrison in and around Charleston; and, about 4,000 cavalry in two small divisions. In all, it had about 22,000 men. This small group of men would be going up against the left wing of Sherman's forces, the XIV and XX Corps. Hardee fought a successful delaying action at Averasboro on the March 16, allowing Johnston time to concentrate his forces.

With his forces gathering, Johnston formed his battle plan. The cavalry was to continue slowing down the advancing Federals. Johnston would then move one division, under Maj. Gen. Robert F. Hoke, to block the Federals on the road. Johnston's other forces would form in the woods to Hoke's right, at an angle. When the Federals deployed to battle Hoke, Johnston would start his attack, his concealed right wing catching the Federals in the flank and sweeping them from the field.

There were no warm fires to greet the morning of Sunday, March 19. The men had also been admonished to keep quiet during the night. Thankfully, the day dawned clear, free from the troublesome rains that had plagued the troops during the past week. The Fifty-Eighth was still three miles from the spot chosen for the attack. By 10:00 the men had started moving into their assigned positions. "Old Joe" seemed to be everywhere that morning, and as the men passed him, they began to cheer, even though they had been ordered to keep quiet. Hill placed Coltart's division on the left, Stevenson's division was positioned in the center, and Clayton's division was on the right. Stevenson deployed his men in two lines. The first contained Palmer's brigade, while Brig. Gen. Edmund W. Pettus's brigade fell in 250 yards behind Palmer. Palmer's brigade had 708 men present, and Pettus's brigade numbered 472 men, giving Stevenson's division a total of 1,181 men. Upon reaching their assigned position, the veteran soldiers began "to construct temporary breastworks," dragging in trees and digging trenches with whatever tools could be found. They only had time to erect the works, topped with logs, to a height of about 18 inches before the Federals tested them. The terrain in which the brigade deployed was wooded, but not as thick as in other places. While the majority of Palmer's men were entrenching, Palmer sent out the Forty-Fifth Tennessee as skirmishers.[18]

As was customary, the forage details of the Federal army were up early, ahead of the main army, looking for supplies. They soon ran into Confederate cavalry blocking their path, and the Federal bummers skirmished with the Confederates, waiting for the infantry to come up. The XIV Corps was in the lead that day. No one on the Federal side, including Sherman, believed that the Confederates were in force in front of the left wing. Believing that the bummers only faced cavalry, the lead division commander told the officer in charge of the bummers, "Get your d---ed [sic] bummers out of the way, and I will drive the rebels out with a skirmish line!"

The lead Federal brigade deployed and had no trouble driving the Confederate cavalry off the field. Soon, however, they tangled with Hoke's entrenched position, which forced them to drop to the ground and start digging breastworks while Minié balls and artillery shells zinged overhead. At noon, the Federals advanced, with a portion striking Hoke's line, and another portion attacking the position of the Army of Tennessee. The attack landed a little to the right of Palmer's line, even though his right wing was able to get in a few shots. The Confederates were able to repulse the attack "with ease, killing and wounding a number without any loss on my part," Palmer later wrote in his report. The Federals fell back and once again commenced fortifying their position.[19]

Mustered in as a private in Company F of the Fifty-Eighth, Jasper Elliott was promoted to drummer in the spring of 1863. While he survived the war, he disappears from records after August 1864 (courtesy John Elliott).

Hardee and his men began arriving on the field during this time, and Johnston placed Hardee in command of all of the troops in the right wing, including the Fifty-Eighth and Palmer's brigade. The Confederate high command saw an opportunity to attack the disorganized Federals and planned to launch the attack at 2:15. However, most of Hardee's command was still not in position. Just minutes before the Confederates were to step off, couriers went out postponing the attack until 2:45. The thirty-minute delay was intended to allow Taliaferro's division time to get into position on the far Confederate right. Since Hardee was extending his line, he chose to designate Stevenson's division as the "division of direction." Palmer's brigade was on the front line, so his brigade would be the center of the attack, and all other regiments, brigades, and divisions in the attack formed on Palmer's brigade.

"My experience with this army," Stevenson wrote not long after the battle, " has convinced me that one of the greatest obstacles in the way of our success in assaulting the fortified position of the enemy has been caused by a failure to keep the commands properly aligned, and to move them straight to the front." Accordingly, Stevenson placed mounted guides between his main line and his skirmishers.[20]

Not long thereafter, orders came for the advance. It was 2:45, and Palmer's brigade stepped out and "advanced with a yell." The last grand charge by a Confederate army was underway, and the battle torn-banner of the Fifty-Eighth, along with those of the other North Carolina, Tennessee, and Virginia regiments under Palmer's command, had the honor of leading the way. Confidence was high. According to a Tennessee member of the brigade, "We could take the [enemy's] works or old Joe would not order it."[21]

"This brigade moved steadily forward," Palmer proudly chronicled after the battle, "for about 400 yards in common time, preserving its alignment almost as if on parade, although for a part of that distance under considerable fire." Harper wrote after the war that the troops moved forward "with great spirit and dash." Pettus's brigade was following Palmer at a distance of 300 to 400 yards. One Federal soldier recalled, "There was neither halt nor pause, only when they came within 50 or 60 yards they began firing." Palmer's men had to scale a fence and then quicken their pace to the double-step.

The Confederates slammed into the Federal works, and the Federals quickly gave way. A swampy ravine was to the rear of the Federal position, into which they were quickly pushed back. The Confederates stopped on the edge of the ravine and poured a hot fire into the enemy soldiers, who were trying to scramble up the other side. Soon the Confederates were in the ravine themselves, clambering up the other side. General Hardee took the lead and rode his horse into field on the other side, encouraging his men onward. Palmer's brigade surged ahead, moving ahead at the double-quick. A section of a Federal artillery was trying to limber up and make a speedy escape. "In running down and taking the guns," according to Harper, "some of the artillery men were shot while on the chest throwing out shells to lighten the load." Palmer's brigade was credited with capturing one of the enemy guns. Once again, the Federal infantry in front of the Confederates under Hardee's command was forced to give way.[22]

At the end of the war, when the Fifty-Eighth and Sixtieth regiments were consolidated, Capt. Benjamin F. Baird transferred from Company D to Company A. He returned to Watauga County at the close of the war, where he died in 1901 (courtesy the North Carolina Department of Archives).

The gallant charge of the Fifty-Eighth and the other Confederate regiments was not without loss. Lt. David Baird (Company D) was struck in the breast and left arm. Cpl. Benjamin Presnell, of the same company, was mortally wounded in the abdomen. His date and place of death are unknown. William C. Coffey (Company E) was struck in the left finger and right thumb. Elisha Fox (Company H) was also struck in the right hand, losing his middle finger. James McKinney (Company K) was wounded in the head. Augustus Green (Company E), who the day before the battle had returned to the regiment from leave, was killed.[23]

As the regiment advanced, the men found "the old pine field ... strewn with blankets, provisions and plunder of all sorts thrown away by the flying foe." General Hardee, as his command reached the Goldsboro Road, called for a halt. "The rapid pursuit over fence and a deep ravine," Harper wrote after the war, "so scattered our men that a halt was made to reform." Just as damaging to Palmer's alignment were the "woods thickly set with troublesome undergrowth." Part of Palmer's brigade was on one side of the road, while part was on the other side of road. Pettus's brigade passed through to the front of Palmer's men, and Palmer was told to stay in reserve. Palmer "immediately sent a staff officer to throw my left wing back on a line with my right."

Before Palmer could get his command redressed, he was ordered forward again. However, it would appear that the order reached only those troops on the far side of the road. As they surged ahead, the remainder of the brigade on the other side of the road was left behind. This included the Fifty-Eighth, and possibly the Sixtieth, regiments. Palmer's brigade pushed ahead through a swamp and came out on the right of Baker's brigade, in an area known as the "bull pen." They were actually in the rear of another part of the Federal line. While the position might have been advantageous, Federal reinforcements soon arrived in the Confederate rear, and Palmer and the others were forced to retreat.[24]

Before Palmer's command reached the Goldsboro Road to reform, General Hill found the Tar Heels in reserve, and, through a staff officer, sent them farther to their right to help protect the Confederate line. The Fifty-Eighth, and possibly the Sixtieth, according to Captain Harper,

> moved up in support of and close to the front line, here facing south, and at the time hotly engaged. Firing was also going on on the right, extending partly to the rear, but not so near, and a battery of artillery kept up a most aggravating enfilade fire over the regiment, which would have made the position extremely uncomfortable if the gunners had slightly depressed their pieces. As it was, very little could be seen for the smoke which filled the woods, and the ground gently rising toward the battery, their shells for an hour flew

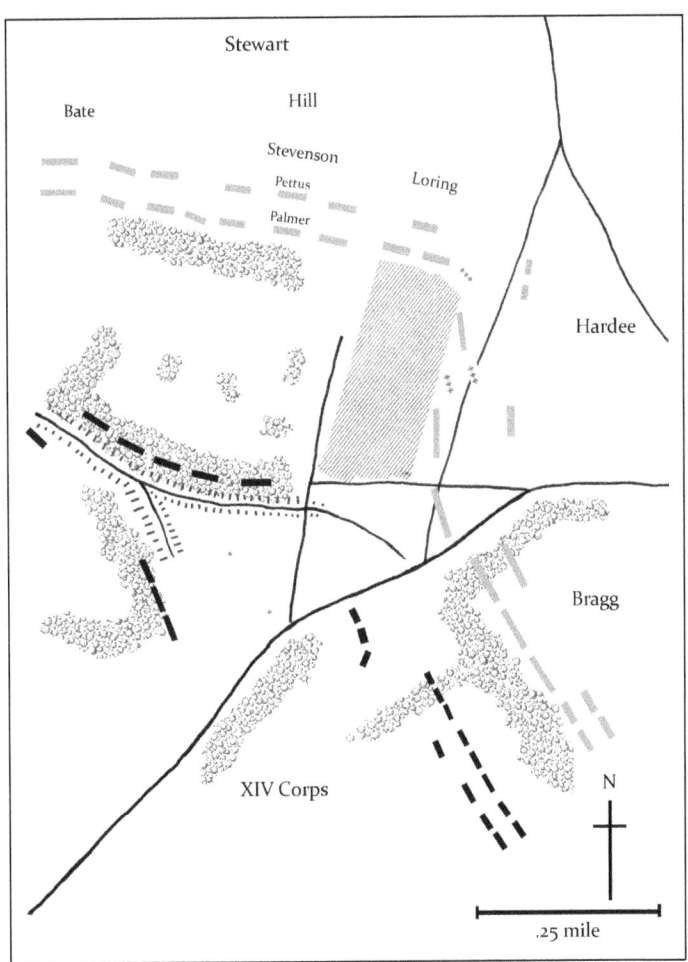

At Bentonville, the Fifty-Eighth and other regiments of Palmer's brigade were able to push the Federal lines back.

almost harmlessly through the timber some ten feet or more overhead, and most of them burst in [the] rear.

All of the shells did not fly over the heads of the Tar Heels. Lt. William C. Coffey (Company E) was wounded in the breast by the "contusion [of a] shell" that afternoon.[25]

The arrival of Federal reinforcements on the Confederate right was cause for concern. Soon, orders came: the Fifty-Eighth was to countermarch, moving from their current position to a new one. "It seemed just a little unnecessary to remind him that the regiment was already facing the enemy," Harper wrote after the war,

> who was close at hand, and being heard to that effect in a most convincing sort of way. The Major, however, did presume to say as much, only to hear, "Yes, I know, but I want you to look after these fellows over here," pointing over his shoulder to our rear and right. The regiment was accordingly countermarched, halted on the spot and fronted — this time facing north, or opposite to the direction we had just before faced — dressed on a line of guides a little oblique to the original line and the men ordered to lie down for shelter.

General Palmer was with the regiment for a while, "seated on his horse apparently unconscious that anything unusual was going on, though the musket balls were flying pretty thick, and some of the enemy's shells must have passed near his head." He soon rode away to tend to the rest of his brigade.[26]

Fighting for the day slowed down about eight that evening. All through the night, both members of the infirmary corps and regular soldiers sought out their wounded comrades and buried their dead. About midnight, the Fifty-Eighth rejoined Stevenson's division, and the Confederate army retired to its former positions on the field. The Fifty-Eighth was positioned in the front ranks with Pettus's brigade, while the rest of Palmer's brigade was in reserve behind them. The reasoning was probably because the Fifty-Eighth had not participated in the third charge of the day and was not as drained as the remainder of the brigade.[27]

March 20 found the opposing armies unusually quiet. There was skirmishing on the Confederate left, but the Confederate line was reinforced, and the armies were content to

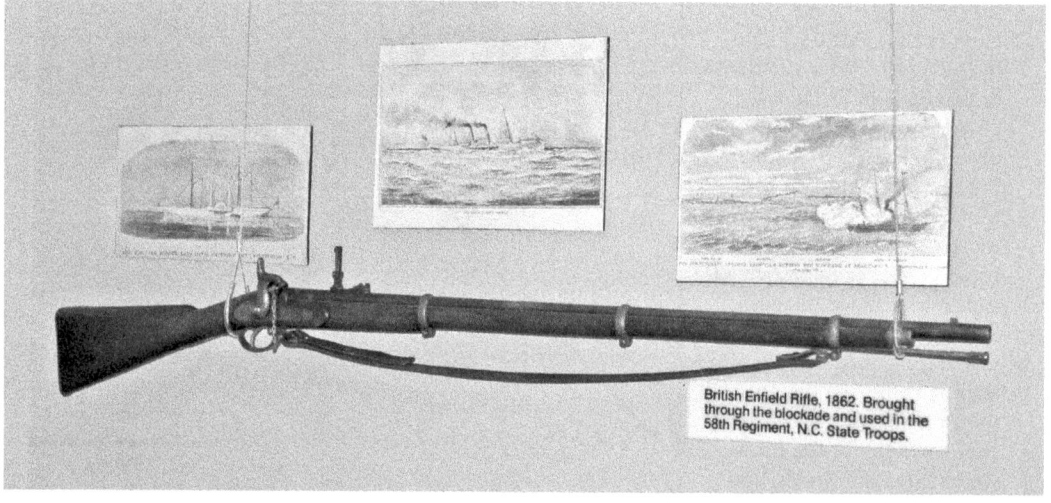

This British Enfield rifle, on display at the Bennett Place State Historic Site, is thought to have been carried by Maj. G.W.F. Harper at the battle of Bentonville.

wait out one another. Johnston wisely determined that the Federal lines were too strong to attack, but did not withdraw from his own position. He offered two reasons for his decision. The first was to recover his wounded, transporting them to Smithfield to be loaded onto waiting trains and off to hospitals in Raleigh and Greensboro. His second reason he tendered to Robert E. Lee: "We held our ground in the hope that [the enemy's] greatly superior numbers might encourage him to attack." Sherman had done as much before, including Kennesaw. At one point during the day, as Hoke was shifting his command to better cover the bridge in the rear of the Confederate lines, General Hill ordered Stevenson's division to support Hoke, but General Stewart countermanded the order. The Fifty-Eighth remained in the front line of breastworks, not seeing any action.[28]

Cloudy skies greeted the soldiers on the morning of Tuesday, March 21. It started to drizzle about mid-morning, with rain, at times hard, by noon. During the day, General Johnston ordered Palmer and Baker's brigades of Lee's corps to redeploy to the Confederate left, with Palmer eventually being held in reserve. It would appear that the Fifty-Eighth remained in the trenches next to Pettus's brigade and did not move during the day. The Federals had attacked the far Confederate left flank during the day, and, for a time, had cut off the Confederate army from their only line of retreat. The Federals chose not to exploit their advantage and partially withdrew from their position, a decision that Sherman would later regret. With his lines stretched so thin, Johnston had no choice but to retreat and issue the necessary orders.[29]

Palmer's brigade and the Fifty-Eighth were praised by others following the battle. General Stevenson wrote on March 23: "Never was more dash and gallantry displayed than was exhibited by Palmer's Brigade in their successful assaults upon the breastworks of the enemy." Writing on March 29, Palmer praised the Fifty-Eighth: "Capt. G.W.F. Harper, commanding Fifty-Eighth North Carolina ... handled [his] command with ability and bore [himself] handsomely through the day." In 1888, Palmer, in writing to Harper, continued to extol the regiment: "The orders published by me at the time will show and it now gives me great pleasure to repeat that the Fifty-Eighth and Sixtieth North Carolina Regiments in this engagement behaved with distinguished gallantry, and won for themselves a merited fame, which will last as long as the historic fields of Bentonville, will appear on the pages and in the annals still to be written of this grand old State, on whose soil her native sons have achieved such splendid distinction."[30]

Due to the scarcity of detailed records after August 1864, losses in the Fifty-Eighth during the battle of Bentonville are difficult to ascertain. Captain Harper reported that three men had been killed, with twenty-three wounded. Palmer's brigade lost a total of 14 killed, 121 wounded, and 42 missing. Overall, combined Confederate losses were placed at 1,527, which is probably a low number.[31]

Orders came to Captain Harper, still in command of the Fifty-Eighth, to pull out of his works at 2:00 A.M. on Wednesday, March 22. Harper led the regiment through the mud, at times knee-deep, across the creek and into bivouac on the north side of Bentonville. Instinctively, the tired Confederates erected breastworks and waited for Billy Yank, who, according to Harper, "failed to make his appearance." Their rest was short lived, and by noon they were on the road again, marching to within six or seven miles of Smithfield and going into camp after dark. "Tiresome and disagreeable march," Harper wrote in his diary. But he was able to add, "Peach trees in bloom." The next few days were not much better. The regiment stayed in camp on March 23, but on the following day, moved through Smithfield, camping about four miles on the other side. Saturday, March 24, found the men

The Fifty-Eighth North Carolina charged across this field toward the Union lines at Bentonville.

in a "camp miserably smokey and dirty." General Johnston, according to returns prepared by the adjutants of his army, had just 13,900 men present for duty that Saturday. On Sunday, the day inspections were normally held, General D. H. Hill looked over his men. The regiment changed camps again on March 27, to one that regimental commander Harper thought "pleasant." For the next few days, the men were able to rest, wash, and even fish for shad.[32]

Even though the end was truly in sight, Johnston was still concerned for the welfare of his men. On March 27, he asked his commands to ascertain how many men were without shoes and how many were without weapons. On March 29, Stevenson reported that just sixty-eight of men were unarmed. That same day, Hill reported that his corps had 361 men barefoot, with 884 men whose shoes could not withstand any hard marching. On the last day of March, Johnston was able to report that his consolidated command had grown to 25,011 men present for duty.[33]

Sunday, April 2, was a clear and pleasant day spent in camp. Some men chose to go to church. Mail had begun arriving, and some worked on getting caught up on their correspondence. None seemed to be aware that the Virginia cities of Petersburg and Richmond had collapsed, and Robert E. Lee's Army of Northern Virginia was moving toward the west, with hopes of combining forces with Johnston's Confederates still in and around Smithfield. News did arrive in camp the following day that a raid being conducted by Federal cavalry in western North Carolina had arrived in Lenoir. "Much troubled for the loved ones at home," Harper recorded in his diary. Finally, on April 5, he heard of the "fall of Richmond."

Harper, whose diary is the sole source of firsthand information regarding the Fifty-Eighth at this point in the war, turned to his faith in Christ during this period of "much trouble." "All things work together for good to them who love God," he wrote on April 4.

"The Lord executed righteousness and judgment for all that are oppressed," he wrote on April 6, and "Remember not the sins of my youth nor any transgressions," on April 12, two days after the Army of the Northern Virginia surrendered at Appomattox, Virginia.[34]

Johnston reviewed the remnants of the Army of Tennessee on April 4. One member of the army penned these lines about the review:

> The review of the skeleton Army of Tennessee, that but one year ago was replete with men, and now filed by with tattered garments, worn out shoes, bare-footed and ranks so depleted that each color was supported by only thirty or forty men.... The march was so slow—colors tattered and torn with bullets—that it looked like a funeral procession. The countenance of every spectator ... was depressed and dejected, and the solemn, stern look of the soldiery was so impressive—oh! It is beginning to look dark in the east, gloomy in the west, and like almost a lost hope when we reflect upon the review of to-day!

Johnston held another review of Hardee's corps a few days later. Governor Vance was present at this occasion. On that same day, April 7, Johnston reported that his Army of the South now mustered 30,424 men.[35]

By April 8, Johnston had rallied all of the soldiers he could have expected. He then set about reorganizing the Army of the South. General Order Number Thirteen went out on April 9 announcing many changes. The Army of the South was no more. Johnston chose to go back to the former designation of the Army of Tennessee. Hardee, Stewart, and Lee were corps commanders, and Wade Hampton commanded the cavalry. Palmer's brigade was broken up. His new command was now made up of thirty-nine Tennessee regiments consolidated into four new regiments. Palmer's brigade was transferred to Cheatham's division of Hardee's corps.[36]

The two North Carolina regiments in the old Army of Tennessee were also consolidated; the new organization was known as the Fifty-Eighth North Carolina Regiment (Consolidated) or the Fifty-Eighth North Carolina Battalion. The new commander of the consolidated regiment was Lt. Col. Thaddeus Charles Coleman. Born in 1837 in Asheville, Coleman was a graduate of the University of North Carolina and a civil engineer. Coleman first joined the service as a lieutenant in Company C, First North Carolina Artillery, in July 1861. He later served as an engineer at the rank of captain on the staff of Lt. Gen. John B. Hood. On April 9, he was appointed lieutenant colonel and assigned to command the consolidated regiment. Captain Harper also received his long-awaited promotion that day. The Caldwell County resident was now Major Harper.

The Fifty-Eighth's adjutant, Benjamin Perry, had been absent on detached duty, then absent without leave since March 1864; and Orville Ewing, Jr., adjutant of the Sixtieth, took over the responsibilities. Capt. Marcus Bearden, appointed assistant quartermaster back in July 1862, probably still held the post. Both William Toxey of the Twenty-Fifth Alabama and Hamilton Griffin, who was from the Sixtieth, were listed as surgeons, while J. F. Dunn, assistant surgeon of the Sixtieth, filled the same role in the new regiment. John Medaris of the Fifty-Eighth was quartermaster sergeant. John Hensley of the Fifty-Eighth was ordnance sergeant. John Blair, who held the position of drum major in the Fifty-Eighth since October 31, 1863, kept his position in the new consolidated regiment. There was apparently no chaplain, no ensign (color-bearer), nor a sergeant-major or commissary sergeant.[37]

While some of the remnants of the Fifty-Eighth went to companies A, B, D, and G, the remnants of the Sixtieth were assigned to Companies C, E, and H. Supernumerary officers simply tagged along without commands, or like Lts. William Davis and Jordan McGee of Company I, were dropped. The new commander of Company A was Capt. Benjamin Baird, formerly of Company D, who was "one of the few men that never dodged when a ball whizzed by him." William C. Coffey, formerly of Company E, was Baird's first lieutenant. Albert Davis, formerly of Company D, was second lieutenant. Capt. Suel Briggs, former commander of Company C, took over command of Company B. Larkin Gilbert of Company H was Brigg's first lieutenant, and Jonathan Duncan of Company K became second lieutenant of Company B.

Edwin Clayton, formerly captain of Company K, Sixtieth North Carolina, became captain of Company C, Fifty-Eighth. John Sales, also formerly of Company K, Sixtieth, was Clayton's first lieutenant, and Stephen Brooks, formerly a private in Company H of the Sixtieth, became Clayton's second lieutenant. Capt. Frederick Tobey, who had been in the Fifty-Eighth since December 30, 1861, transferred from command of Company A to Company D. James Conley of Company B, Fifty-Eighth, became first lieutenant of Company D; and the company's second lieutenant, David Baird, was hospitalized in a facility in Greensboro. Company E was now captained by William Alexander, former commander of Company I, Sixtieth North Carolina. Robert Clayton of Company B, Sixtieth, was his first lieutenant, and George Lindsey, former color bearer of the Sixtieth, was Clayton's second lieutenant. It is possible that Clayton carried the banner of the consolidated regiment.

Poindexter Blevins, who transferred from Company L to Company F, was promoted captain of Company F subsequent to August 31, 1864, and retained command of his company. His first lieutenant was Leander Hurley, also formerly of Company L. Levi Silver, formerly of Company K of the Fifty-Eighth, was second lieutenant. Companies G and I of the Fifty-Eighth were consolidated into Company G. Hamilton Long, formerly a lieutenant of Company K, Fourth North Carolina State Troops, became commander of Company F. Jonathan Miller, formerly a lieutenant in Company I, Fifty-Eighth, became first lieutenant of Company G. Theodore McGimsely, also a former lieutenant of Company I, became second lieutenant of Company G. Robert W. White transferred from Company F, Sixtieth, to take command of Company H, Fifty-Eighth. His lieutenants were Eli Jackson, formerly of Company G, Sixtieth, and Henry C. Fagg, formerly of Company B, Sixtieth.[38]

The consolidated Fifty-Eighth Regiment was then placed in the brigade of William F. Brantley, a member of D. H. Hill's division, S. D. Lee's corps. The other regiments in the brigade were the Twenty-Fourth Mississippi Consolidated, made up of the Twenty-Fourth, Twenty-Seventh, Twenty-Ninth, Thirtieth, and Thirtieth-Fourth Mississippi Infantry Regiments; the Twenty-Second Alabama Consolidated, consisting of the Twenty-Second, Twenty-Fifth, Thirty-Ninth, and Fiftieth Alabama Infantry Regiments; and the Thirty-Seventh Alabama Consolidated Regiment, composed of the Thirty-Seventh, Forty-Second, and Fifty-Fourth Alabama Infantry Regiments.

Brantley was born in Alabama in 1830, but moved to Mississippi as a child. He was a lawyer prior to the war, an officer in the militia, and a representative in the Mississippi secession convention. Brantley rose through the ranks, becoming a captain in Twenty-Ninth Mississippi, followed by promotions to lieutenant colonel and then colonel. He was wounded at Shiloh and Stones River and was commissioned brigadier general in July 1864, leading the brigade formerly under Samuel Benton.[39]

Johnston's new Army of Tennessee would have no time to shake out its alignment. Word reached Johnston that the Federals were beginning to move out of their camps, and accordingly, on April 10, the Confederates once again took to the roads. The Fifty-Eighth left camp at 10:00 A.M. and moved in the rain toward Raleigh. The men camped that night near Battle's Bridge. The regiment was up early the next morning and at 7:00 A.M. was on

This marker, which sits near the graves of some of the Confederates killed during the battle of Bentonville, was dedicated in March 1895.

the march again. Around three that afternoon, the men passed through Raleigh, continuing west out of the state capital and camping three miles from the city on the Hillsboro Road. Wednesday, April 12, dawned clear with the march resuming at 6:00 A.M. According to Harper, the Fifty-Eighth was in the lead and marched to within two and a half miles of Hillsboro.[40]

Rain greeted the soldiers on April 13. The Fifty-Eighth was on the march at 6:00 A.M., and Harper was serving as brigade officer of the day. As the Fifty-Eighth moved through the colonial town of Hillsboro, Federal soldiers entered Raleigh for the first time during the war. The Fifty-Eighth went into camp a mile past Hillsboro around 3:00 P.M. The rain cleared out that afternoon. Friday, April 14, was Good Friday. The regiment was on the road at 5:30 P.M. and covered about twenty miles, camping near the Haw River Railroad bridge. Good Friday is the day that Christians remember the death of Christ. For Joseph Johnston, the day became one he would remember for the death of his army. On the evening of April 14, the Federal command's headquarters received the letter that Jefferson Davis had written the day before, suggesting to Sherman that arrangements needed to be made "to terminate the existing war."[41]

At 6:00 A.M., on the fifteenth, the Fifty-Eighth was again on the road, this time in a heavy rain. The rank and file soldiers marched on the railroad tracks, while the mounted officers rode alongside on the roads. After having made "8 or 9 miles," the regiment went into camp about fifteen miles from Greensboro. "Report of Lee's surrender confirmed," Harper recorded in his diary as the first paroled Confederate soldiers from the Army of Northern Virginia began passing through to their homes. A few days later, Harper wrote that the "Paroled Prisoners from Lee's Army passing for days past in a constant stream." They were up early again the next morning and on the road at 6:00 A.M. By 1:00 P.M., they were in Greensboro, where they went into camp near the railroad depot.[42]

April 17 was clear, pleasant, and warm. With all of the parolees from the Army of Northern Virginia, refugees from other parts of the Confederacy, and soldiers from the Army of Tennessee, law and order was difficult to maintain. Several times local citizens had attempted to break through the guards into the government warehouses in the city. A few times they succeeded, only to be driven out by reinforcements. Governor Vance, one of the refugees in the city, ordered the clothing and other stores in the warehouses issued to North Carolina soldiers. Major Harper reported that his men drew new clothing that day. It is possible that the Fifty-Eighth received some of the new charcoal gray jackets manufactured by Peter Tate in Ireland and shipped through the blockade.[43]

That same day, Joseph Johnston and William Sherman met at the Bennett Place, a small farmhouse located between Raleigh and Greensboro. Once they were alone together, Sherman let Johnston read a telegraph he had received earlier announcing the death of Abraham Lincoln. Terms for surrender were presented, terms that surrendered not only all of the remaining Confederate armies in the field, but also the civil government of the Confederate States. Johnston and Sherman met again on April 18 and agreed to the terms, as long as they were acceptable to Jefferson Davis and Sherman's superiors in Washington, D.C. A truce was declared between the Confederates and the Federals until news regarding the terms of surrender was received. The Fifty-Eighth was on guard duty in Jamestown on April 18, but appears to have returned to Greensboro the next day. Major Harper reported on the nineteenth that he had a "fine morning bath."[44]

While the Fifty-Eighth received new clothes and the men were able to bathe, Johnston's Army of Tennessee was disintegrating. Hundreds of men began slipping away from their ranks, heading home to their farms. Harper noted in his diary on Sunday, April 23 that there was "demoralization in the army," and on the following day a large portion of what remained of the Sixtieth "left for home."⁴⁵

Sherman and Johnston's terms reached Washington, D.C., on the evening of April 21 and were quickly overturned. The terms to which the generals had agreed went far beyond the terms proffered to General Lee at Appomattox, which were to be Sherman's guidelines. Johnston was attempting to surrender not only the Army of Tennessee, but all other Confederate armies in the field. The terms stated that the president of the United States "would recognize the various Southern state governments" and that a general amnesty would be granted to all Southern people, including "President Davis and his cabinet." New United States President Andrew Johnson, and his cabinet, including Secretary of War Edwin Stanton, quickly dismissed Sherman's proposals, stating that Sherman had overstepped his boundaries.

Sherman learned on April 24 that his proposed, all-encompassing peace plan had been rejected and sent word to Johnston that the truce would end and hostilities would resume. Johnston began preparing his troops, with orders for his corps commanders to proceed to Salisbury. At the same time, Sherman began preparing his men to follow the Confederates. President Davis wanted his remaining mounted men to proceed toward the west into Texas to continue the war. Those who were not mounted, or could not secure horses, were to disband, with orders to meet at some predetermined location to continue the war. Johnston wrote that the Confederate high command should save "the people, spare the blood of the army, and save the high civil functionaries. Your plan, I think, can only do the last." Johnston chose to ignore Davis's plan and sent another letter to Sherman.⁴⁶

The Fifty-Eighth had gone into camp at Jamestown, a few miles to the southwest of Greensboro, and along the North Carolina railroad. On April 26, the regiment was ordered to return to Greensboro.

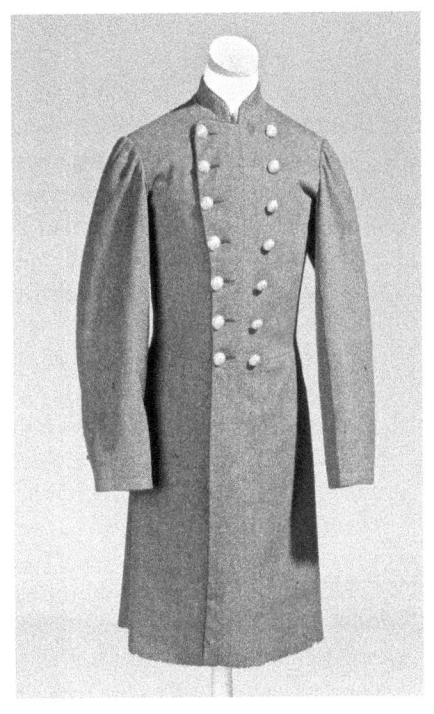

Top: George W. F. Harper was a Caldwell County native who rose through the ranks to become major of the Fifty-Eighth. The rank is noted by the single star on his collar (Courtesy the Caldwell Heritage Museum). *Bottom:* A jacket worn by Harper through the war (jacket courtesy the North Carolina Department of Archives and History).

That same day, Johnston and Sherman met again at the Bennett Place. This time, Sherman presented the terms that Grant had offered Lee at Appomattox. These terms stipulated that Johnston and his men had to stop fighting, and had to deposit all weapons and public property in Greensboro. Two sets of rolls were to be prepared, one to be given to an officer whom Sherman designated and the other to the commander of the troops. Each officer and enlisted man had "to give his individual obligation in writing not to take up arms against the Government of the United States until properly released from this obligation." Officers were allowed to retain their sidearms and private horses, and once all of the above was accomplished, "all officers and men will be permitted to return to their homes, not to be disturbed by the United States authorities so long as they observe their obligation and the laws in force where they may reside." Sherman signed the document, as did Johnston.

Unlike the terms offered to Lee, a second set of accords was reached between Johnston and Maj. Gen. John Schofield, who stayed in North Carolina after Sherman left. These supplemental terms decreed that transportation would "be loaned to the troops for their march to their homes, and for subsequent use in their industrial pursuits." Each brigade got to keep one-seventh of its arms, and transportation was to be furnished by the navy to those living in Texas and Arkansas.[47]

At last, for the common soldier in the ranks, the war was over. "This ship of state well neigh foundered," Harper wrote in his diary. On April 27, General Johnston issued General Order No. 18: "The object of this convention is pacification to the extent of the authority of the commander who made it. Events in Virginia, which broke every hope of success by war, imposed on its general the duty of sparing the blood of this gallant army and saving our country from further devastation and our people from ruin." Johnston then asked his corps commanders to see that the requested returns were completed. That same day, General Sherman ordered 250,000 rations distributed to the soldiers under Johnston's command, enough to see most of the Confederate soldiers home, to keep them from living off the land.[48]

Johnston also took this opportunity to pay his men. Davis had entrusted $39,000 in silver specie to Johnston. Davis asked for the return of the silver coins, but once again, Johnston ignored the president and chose to pay his men. Johnston had been asking for money to pay his soldiers ever since returning to command, and had always been told that the money simply did not exist. Each soldier, officer, and enlisted man received approximately $1.17 in silver. Harper recalled after the war that the men received "one dollar and fourteen cents" in "Mexican silver dollars." "There being no means of making change for the cents, the men, in groups of seven, drew for the surplus dollar." Johnston also gave his soldiers cloth, thread, and yarn to use for themselves, or to barter for food.[49]

On Monday, May 1, the Fifty-Eighth North Carolina Troops was paroled and began making preparations to march home. Unlike their fellow soldiers in Virginia, the men of the Army of Tennessee did not march among the Federals and surrender their arms. They simply stacked their weapons where they were. Many flags were furled and left with the rifles. Harper took it upon himself to take home all, or at least part, of the flag of the Fifty-Eighth. On Tuesday, the men of the Fifty-Eighth received their paroles. Also that day, General Johnston issued his farewell address in General Order No. 22. He implored his former comrades to adhere to the terms of the recent convention and to

> discharge the obligations of good and peaceful citizens at your homes as well as you have performed the duties of thorough soldiers in the field. By such a course you will best secure the comfort of your families and kindred and restore tranquility to your country. You will return to your homes with the admiration of our people, won by the courage and noble devotion you

have displayed in this long war. I shall always remember with pride the loyal support and generous confidence you have given me. I now part with you with deep regret, and bid you farewell with feelings of cordial friendship and with earnest wishes that you may have hereafter all the prosperity and happiness to be found in the world.[50]

At 1:00 P.M., the former soldiers lined up once again and started marching southwest. Despite orders to retain one-seventh of the arms, one officer of the regiment estimated that they kept one-third of their arms, with forty-rounds per weapon. "A small wagon carried a chest of reserve ammunition, a few rations, and ... the blankets of the men." They had covered twelve miles before going into camp. The cool and pleasant weather continued the next day, and they covered about sixteen miles. On May 4, they passed through Mocksville, and on May 5, were in Statesville. "No excess or depredations were committed, and the men cheerfully responded to the orders of their officers, to whom, as all knew, respect and obedience could no longer be enforced," Harper wrote after the war. "On returning to their wasted homes, with rare exceptions, they proved themselves to be model citizens." Those men from Ashe County were discharged and began their way home. The rest boarded a train at Statesville, and by 3:00 P.M. were in Hickory Station. Harper wrote in his diary that he was at home in Lenoir by 9:00 P.M., and added as a post-script, "My Connection with the Army closed here." Those from Watauga County continued through Lenoir. Capt. Benjamin Baird had secured a wagon at Greensboro to transport those too sick to walk. Once the remnants of Companies D and I reached Boone, they too were disbanded. Jonathan Miller's concluding remarks were: "Thus ends the war between the two sections."[51]

Isaac Bailey, former Captain of Company B, wrote in 1901 a fitting epilogue to the Fifty-Eighth's service. The regiment was "paroled on 2 May 1865, the fragment of noble, battle-scarred veterans who breasted the storm in each of these battles, and intervening skirmishes. Now and hereafter the question may be asked, why we did not succeed? The answer is: They who justly deserve success, do not always win it. Braver men never fought or died, but overpowering numbers and munitions of war were against us."[52]

Chapter 13

1865–Present

"that you fought like the legions of Caesar"—*Watauga Democrat*, 1917

It was a hard trip back up the mountain for the Baird cousins. Jonathan Miller related how Capt. Benjamin Baird secured a wagon to transport the sick and wounded, but Miller did not record that one of those wounded was Benjamin's cousin, Lt. David Baird (Company D). During the battle of Bentonville, David "took a bullet through the chest." He was hospitalized in Raleigh and Greensboro and went home after the surrender with the rest of the regiment. According to the family, David was met by "Little Liza" Baird, another Baird cousin, in Lenoir. Little Liza placed David on her horse with her and took off for the Globe community of Caldwell County, spending the night with some relatives. The next day, they started up the winding mountain road toward the Valle Crucis community. The trip was fraught with danger, as bushwhackers frequented the area, and horses were a rare and valuable commodity. "Liza kept both ears constantly alert for the saddle noises and conversation of riders ... and each time she heard such sounds she quickly turned into the woods" to avoid detection. They eventually made it back to the Valle Crucis community of Watauga County.[1]

The Bairds, and scores of other men, returned to land devastated by the hand of war. Western North Carolina had given thousands of men to the Southern armies. These men had left their farms and families and had marched away to far-off places. Many did not return. Those farms and families suffered profoundly as a result. Women and children often went hungry. Local governments had appointed men to help the destitute wives and families, and there were food distribution programs, but these efforts were often inadequate.

Citizens all across the Tar Heel State felt the hard hand of war. Along the coast, the Federal army and navy had captured sections of the Outer Banks in late 1861. They made numerous landings and raids, and several pitched battles were fought in the area. The central portion of the state, which was a bread basket for the Confederacy, largely escaped the Federals until the very end of the war, when Sherman's forces arrived. However, the central portion of state had to contend with its fair share of dissidents. The western portion of the state also escaped the movement of large federal armies until the very end. In March and April 1865, Gen. George Stoneman led a raid through Watauga and Caldwell counties before continuing east. After taking Salisbury and burning the Confederate supplies there, he returned by that same route. Numerous skirmishes were fought along the route of the raid, including one in Boone on March 28. Elijah Holder, a corporal in Company I, was in

Watauga County when the raid occurred. He claimed that he was in command of "seventy-two recruits" in Boone when he was struck in the left hip. Two other members of the Fifty-Eighth were captured that day, both members of Company D: Pvt. Reuben Isaacs and First Sergeant Finley Mast. Isaacs was taken to Louisville, where he took the oath of allegiance and was released on June 17. Mast was taken to Camp Chase, Ohio, where he took the oath on June 10 and was released.[2]

However, it was not the impact of large Federal armies sweeping through the countryside that caused the majority of the problems for the families of the soldiers of the Fifty-Eighth. The war had gone well for the first year and a half. While many men had left the communities where they had grown up, neighbors had been willing to help those left behind. This changed in the fall of 1863, when the Confederates abandoned east Tennessee. Technically, the back door was open to western North Carolina. This was stemmed to a degree when General Longstreet arrived with his forces in Knoxville, but by the spring of 1864, Longstreet was gone. Events escalated in 1864,

In this post-war image, Riley Hodges is pictured with his wife, Violet Moody Hodges. Riley enlisted in Company D in July 1862 and served through August 1864 (courtesy Barbara Kelly).

plunging western North Carolina into a true civil war. Local governments simply broke down. The state tried to counter with the creation of the home guard in July 1863. Each county had a company or two of men who were too young, too old, or exempt from regular military service. These men were responsible for rounding up deserters and conscript evaders, and maintaining law and order.

Leander Pyatte was one of the outliers sought by the home guard. He became liable for Confederate service when the conscriptions laws were changed in September 1862 to include those up to age 45. Pyatte was born ca. 1826, and according to the family, saw soldiers approaching his home, coming to force him to serve in the army. Pyatte slipped out of the back of the house and was "hiding out in Pyatte's laurels [in present-day Avery County] when he returned one night to repair the children's shoes. Soldiers who were watching the house took him by force. He told Tilda [his wife] that he would not live long as he was suffering from a fever.... Tilda was left with nine children clutching to her skirts as they watched their father dragged away." Pyatte was mustered in as a private in Company A on December 10, 1863. He died in a hospital in Atlanta, Georgia, on January 10, 1864.

In Yancey County, the home guard was out looking for Thomas Bryant, who had enlisted in June 1862. Bryant had deserted, possibly even before his company had been mustered into Confederate service, and joined the Union army. Bryant was at home, and according to the family, was "sitting on a fence near the house, when he spotted a group of Confederate soldiers ... approaching.... They shot him dead from atop the fence." Or, according to another story, he spotted the Confederates and tried to escape by running into a nearby holler, where he was "shot in the back as he tried to scale a large rock." Regardless of the exact circumstances of his death, Bryant was killed in 1865.[3]

While many residents in western North Carolina sided with the Confederacy or with the Union, many were simply indifferent. Numerous atrocities were committed by those operating outside the realm of either government. Moses Miller served briefly in Company G before being declared absent without leave. His wife, Nancy, had a neighbor lady who "begged Nancy to go with her to Big Rock Creek to try and get some meal at a grist mill." Nancy refused to go with this woman. As the unknown woman was returning home, "a bushwhacker shot her down about a half mile" from the Tipton Hill community in Mitchell County. "She was found with about a half a gallon of meal still under her arm." Lt. Jackson Stewart was fifty-eight years old when he enlisted in what became Company B in May 1862. He served until April 1863, when he resigned due to "ill health & old age[,] having been unable for duty for the last three months." He returned to Mitchell County, where he was elected sheriff, charged with protecting those like Nancy Miller and her neighbor. Stewart "would not stand down from nor step aside for any man." Since he stood at 6'3" and weighed over 200 pounds, it is easy to see why. However, Stewart was bushwhacked in November 1864 by some federal soldiers while he was on the road between Bakersville and Roan Mountain. On his way back to Watauga County after the surrender at Greensboro, William Cook (Company I) was told, as he passed through Lenoir at war's end, "not to go to his home; that the bushwhackers were in the woods in great numbers and were stealing, robbing, and carrying off everything they could get. Even the bed clothes were taken off the beds." Cook's mother "sent him to a pine thicket, and to that place she would make a daily pilgrimage, carrying him things to eat." Cook later said, "I was so discouraged I went out in the thicket and wept." James Rankin, who had briefly served as quartermaster of the Fifty-Eighth in 1863, came home from the war, and felt it necessary, about midnight one night, to climb "through the kitchen window ... like a thief.... As a reception for me and other returning soldiers, we were arrested soon after our return by the notorious Colonel Kirk."[4]

The deplorable conditions found in western North Carolina were the same throughout the Tar Heel State. Governor Vance was arrested in Statesville on May 13 and sent to a military prison in Washington, D.C. Federal General John M. Schofield was technically in charge of the state, with Gen. J. D. Cox in charge of the western portion of North Carolina. Since Congress was not in session when the war ended, it was up to President Andrew Johnson to determine how the Southern states should be re-admitted to the Union. Johnson believed that since the right of secession did not exist, all a state had to do was repeal its ordnance of secession, adopt a new constitution, and emancipate its slaves. A state could then be re-admitted to the Union. On May 29, Johnson appointed Raleigh newspaper editor William W. Holden provisional governor of the state and issued an amnesty proclamation, pardoning all who would swear their allegiance to the United States. Holden was widely disliked across the state for his promotion of a peace movement during the war.

Holden called for an election on September 21 for the purpose of electing delegates to a convention to be held in Raleigh. At that meeting in October, the act of secession was repealed, slavery was abolished, and a date in November was set for the election of a new governor and representatives to the General Assembly. Jonathan Worth was elected governor; the Thirteenth Amendment was ratified; and "Union men" were elected as the state's representatives to Congress.

North Carolina should have been set for re-admission to the Union. However, problems soon arose. Congress met in December 1865 and the representatives from the Southern

Finley Patterson Mast (Company D) entered the service in 1862 as a thirty-year-old private. He quickly advanced to the rank of sergeant, then first sergeant. Mast was captured in Boone during Stoneman's Raid and sent to Camp Chase, where he took the oath and was released in June 1865. He is pictured here with his wife, Rhoda (courtesy John Terry Harmon).

states were not seated, based upon the grounds that only the Congress, and not the president, could determine a state's re-admission to the Union. The Republicans in Congress feared an alignment between Southerners and Northern Democrats that could offset the advantages gained during the war. In 1866, Congress adopted the Fourteenth Amendment, which gave every citizen due process and equal protection under the law. The amendment also barred from office state and federal government officials who had acted in support of the Confederacy during the war. The amendment was quickly ratified, although there were no representatives from Southern states present to vote upon it.

In May and June of that year, representatives met in Raleigh and prepared a new constitution. In August 1866, that constitution was put to a vote and defeated. These two events led many in Congress to believe that the Southern states were not yet ready to be re-admitted to the Union. Accordingly, in March 1867, the Congress passed the Reconstruction Act, over the veto of President Johnson. The new act re-instituted government control over the states; placed an appointed United States general in control of each state; charged the commander with maintaining peace and with the protection of rights and property, using force if necessary; made existing state governments provisional and subject to modification or abolition by the powers of the military commander; and required each state to follow a program to qualify it and its representatives for readmission to Congress. North Carolina and South Carolina constituted the Second Military District and were placed first under the command of Maj. Gen. Daniel E. Sickles, and then later, under General Edward R. S. Canby. Governor Worth was allowed to remain as governor, but with limited powers.

Between January 14 and March 17, 1868, a Constitutional Convention met in Raleigh to produce a new state constitution. This constitution imitated the constitutions of Northern states in that it abolished slavery; repudiated the debt created by the war; created a bill of rights that forbade the suspension of the writ of habeas corpus; upheld the freedom of the press; abolished property and religious qualifications for voting; fixed the voting age at twenty-one; and provided for a public school system with a statewide superintendent of public instruction. One month after the close of the convention, North Carolinians ratified their new constitution and elected state and county officers as well as representatives to the lower house of Congress. Holden became the new governor on July 1, 1868, and soon thereafter, the General Assembly convened. The Republican-controlled legislature ratified the Fourteenth Amendment and elected two Republican senators. On July 20, 1868, those two senators and several elected representatives took their seats in Congress, and North Carolina was officially back in the Union.[5]

So the former members of the Fifty-Eighth returned to a lawless, broken land, controlled by a hostile government. Many returned sick. Curtis Higgins (Company G) recalled the long walk back to the mountains: "Some of us were barefoot, a lot of us were sick and hurt, we were all tired out and half starved. A lot of the boys never did get home, just lay down and died along the way." Another member of Company G, John B. Cook, recalled that when he "arrived at home, his shoes were worn off his feat." Asa Brown started off in Company I, but later transferred to the Fifth Battalion, North Carolina Cavalry. At some point during the war, Asa contracted typhoid fever. "He had no bedding," according to the family, "so [he] was laid on a church bench. He laid there so long that his hip bones cut through his skin."[6]

Others carried visible reminders of their wounds. Ashe County's Jonathan Phillips, a former captain who was struck in the head in battle in June 1864, died of his wounds on January 24, 1865, and was buried in his native Ashe County. His cousin, Payton Phillips, who was struck in the forehead at Chickamauga, "lived the rest of his life with only a little skin over a part of his brain tissue as a result of his wound." Samuel Riddle (Company C) lost a leg due to a wound at Kolb's Farm and was known as "Peg Leg Sam" for the rest of his life. Jacob Ayers (Company B) was struck in the left thigh at Chickamauga and was forced to use a wheelchair for much of the rest of his life as he operated a general store in the Glen Ayer community in Mitchell County. After his brief stint in Vance's Legion and the Fifty-Eighth, Walter W. Lenoir was transferred to the Thirty-Seventh North Carolina Troops. Six weeks after his transfer, he was struck twice in the leg during the battle of Ox Hill, Virginia. Lenoir's leg was amputated and he was forced to wear a prosthetic limb, which he ordered from Philadelphia. Walter thought his artificial leg was "as good as they make 'em, but ... a wretched substitute for the one that I left in Virginia."[7]

North Carolina actually took the lead in supplying veterans with prosthetic limbs after the war. On January 23, 1866, the North Carolina General Assembly passed a resolution asking the governor to contract with a manufacturer to supply limbs. Those who wanted to purchase their own, or who opted not to use a prosthetic, were given a payout. Eleven members of the Fifty-Eighth received some type of compensation from the state for their loss of limbs during the war. Those receiving legs were Thomas Alexander, Michael Mitchell, and Samuel Riddle. Those who received arms were J. A. Bolick, Jacob Eller, Jesse Mace, Samuel McLeod, Martin Moore, Wesley Presnell, and John Tipton. Mac Williams, whose company designation is unknown, received compensation for the loss of his eyesight during the war.[7]

A few men did not survive the journey back to their homes. William Tolley (Company

A) was wounded at Chickamauga. He died in January or February 1864 while trying to return home and is buried someplace along the Toe River. Emanuel Haas (Company H) was sick and sent to the hospital, first in Clinton, and then to Knoxville. Alfred Guy was bringing him home when he died while in Kingsville, South Carolina, on May 25, 1863. According to the family, Lynville Edwards and his brother John (Company G) were on their way home after the end of the war when Lynville took sick. They stopped in an abandoned cabin in Kentucky, where Lynville died. John had to bury him and then continue on back to Yancey County with his sad news.[8]

Some families never knew what happened to their husbands, fathers, and sons who had marched off. Burril Anderson (Company F) was among them. His family believed that he died in the hospital to which he was sent in September 1863. James B. Bailey's (Company C) wife was killed in 1863 when a neighbor struck her in the head with an iron skillet. Bailey came home, remarried, and then left for the war again. In January 1865, he was admitted to a hospital in Meridian, Mississippi, with pneumonia. He was furloughed for sixty days on March 7 and simply disappeared from history. According to the family, he was never heard from again. Leander Pyatte, who slipped in to work on shoes for his family and was promptly captured by the home guard, "was never heard from again," according to his family. There is a good chance that his wife and nine children never knew what became of him. Isabella Jarrett, wife of Levi Jarrett (Company B), did not learn the fate of her husband until 1901.[9]

For many soldiers, the war-time wounds that they bore left no outward physical traces. While post-traumatic stress disorder was not formally diagnosed until 1980, many veterans of both the Blue and the Gray suffered nonetheless. During the war, those soldiers who experienced the disorder were labeled as cowards, possibly charged with desertion, and at times, imprisoned or even executed. After the war, many veterans simply refused to talk about their experiences, not wanting to re-live the trauma; these men tried hard to avoid traumatic stimuli. They did not want to attend the annual veteran reunions or visit former battlefields on which they fought, as many of their comrades in arms frequently did.[10]

The majority of the members of the Fifty-Eighth actually did make it back home to their farms in the mountain valleys and hollers. They returned to pick up the pieces of their lives. Lieutenant Colonel Keener returned to the Ingalls sections of present-day Avery County, where he operated a store, served as a postmaster, and was a leader at Pine Grove Methodist Church. Carson Byrd (Company B) was traveling back through Watauga County when he spent the night with Harrison Aldridge. He met Aldridge's daughter, Martha Everline, and they were later married. Ramulus Brown (Company A) farmed 200 acres in

Eli G. Harmon was from Watauga County and served in Company D until September 5, 1863, when he deserted. After the war, he moved to Van Buren County, Arkansas (courtesy Vanessa Grindstaff).

McDowell County with five recently freed slaves whom he hired. He also worked a grist mill on the North Fork of the Catawba River and ran a licensed distillery, besides being a magistrate. Cpl. John Moffitt (Company F) was a teacher and chair maker who farmed in McDowell County on the side. Ensign Green B. Woody returned to the Toe River Valley, where he was a deacon at the Pleasant Grove Baptist Church, a justice of the peace, and a postmaster; he also ran a store and made furniture and caskets.[11]

For some, the homecoming was bittersweet. William Banks (Company C) found that his land had been sold during the war and he had to fight in court to get it back when he returned home. John Autry (Company G) found upon his return that his wife had gone to Tennessee with a younger man.[12]

Some chose not to stay in the Old North State following the war. Capt. James Marler (Company E) went to Missouri around 1868. Matthew Thompson (Company E) moved to Texas not long after the war. Orlando Collett (Company A) joined Thompson in Texas in 1869. John W. Clark (Company D) first moved to Mitchell County, then, about 1900, to Whitman County, Washington. Edmund Silver (Company K) relocated to Oregon, where he taught school and preached. Lt. Col. Samuel Silver also moved to Oregon, where he farmed, serving as postmaster at Grouse and as a Sunday school superintendent.

Eli Harmon (Company D) moved to Copeland, Arkansas. Oliver Lonon (Company F) also went to Arkansas, living in Baxter County. Hospital steward James Riddle took his family to West Virginia, while James A. White (Company E) moved his family to Otoe County, Nebraska. Zephaniah Kanipe (Company F) went to Texas, where he was a Methodist minister, millwright, carpenter, and distiller. Thomas McHargue (Company D) moved to Greene County, Tennessee. Lawson Peterson (Company G) went to Unicoi County, Tennessee, along with John A. Hensley (Field and Staff), Swinfield D. Howell (Company C), Eli Jarrett (Company B), George Loyd (Company C), Thomas Randolph (Company G), and Joseph Waldrope (Company A). Sgt. Maj. Drury Coffey went to Kansas in 1892, but was back in Caldwell County by 1907.[13]

The story of Curtis Higgins (Company G) is a good example of the experiences of those who went west. According to the family, Higgins

> hung around Yancey County ... for several years. Stories of the prosperous west now being opened up by the Union Pacific Railway, made their way back to the Southland. Curtis and several other young Southerners, hooked up with Dick Sparks, a stockman of some means who was taking livestock across country to California to show in the 1869 State Fair in Sacramento. Curtis was responsible for driving twelve head of cattle, twelve hogs and a small bunch of chickens in return for an interest in the livestock. The small group was well armed and rode horseback across the plains from the Missouri River to Sacramento but the entire group won a total of only $10.00 in cash prizes in the showing of their livestock, which was mostly in poor flesh from their long journey. The chickens, which survived the trip, proved almost worth their weight in gold, since most of the poultry in California at that time were of the scrubby ... variety.

Higgins would go on to settle in Modoc County, California, in 1874 and operated a stagecoach line and postal route in the area. He did not pass on until 1932 and was one of the last living veterans in his county.[14]

Others chose to remain in the state but felt a change of scenery was necessary. Greenberry Buchanan (Company B) resettled near Cades Cove in the present-day Smoky Mountains National Park. Alfred Carpenter (Company A) went to Cherokee County until 1880, when he returned to Mitchell County. Carson Byrd moved from Mitchell to Watauga

County, settling in the Valle Crucis community. Jesse Mace (Company A) left Mitchell County and moved to Madison County, settling on the headwaters of Bee Tree Creek.[15]

William C. Coffey, a former lieutenant in both companies E and A, had left his native Caldwell County prior to the war, moving to Butler, Tennessee, where he operated a store. A flood in 1861 destroyed his business, and he soon enlisted in the Twenty-Sixth, later being transferred to the Fifty-Eighth. After the war, he came to Boone where he and his brother started a new store. William went to Zionville in Watauga County in 1866, where he opened a branch of the store. After a couple of years, William returned to Boone and helped his brother run the store and a new hotel. Thomas Coffey was both a teacher in Valle Crucis and a store operator prior to war. He later became captain of Company E. Besides being active in the hotel and mercantile business in Boone, Thomas helped pass legislation that resulted in a turnpike between Blowing Rock and Boone.[16]

Others changed professions at the close of the war. William Austin (Company C) went to Raleigh to study medicine. He later served as superintendent of public health. Jacob Bowman (Company B) studied law under Judge Richmond Pearson and was admitted to the bar in 1868. In 1898 he was appointed judge of the Superior Court. Capt. Fredick Tobey was just nineteen years old when the war began. He was found by the 1860 census as a student living with his grandparents. After the war, Tobey moved to Lincoln County, North Carolina, where he operated a boarding house, and later, a store. Tobey died on November 24, 1924, and is buried in Hollybrook Cemetery. His widow, Mattie Lester Tobey, who was born in 1864 and lived until 1961, was the sole surviving Confederate widow in Lincoln County and possibly the last remaining widow of a member of the Fifty-Eighth North Carolina.[17]

Some veterans chose to become involved in politics. Capt. James Marler (Company E) represented Burke County in the state house in 1867. William Austin (Company C) represented Yancey County in the state house in 1881 and 1889. Moses Young (Company K) served in the state house in 1874. Besides running his store, Thomas Coffey served as chairman of the board of education for Watauga County. Lt. Col. Thomas Dula, prior to the war, worked as a lawyer and represented Caldwell County in the state house. In 1864, he was elected solicitor of Caldwell County. He later moved to Wilkes County, which he represented in the United States House and in the North Carolina Senate. He also served as a United States commissioner before passing away in 1906. Capt. Isaac Bailey (Company B) represented Mitchell County in the state senate from 1887 to 1893. Capt. Suel Briggs (Company C) represented Yancey County in the state senate from 1889 to 1897. Sgt. Maj. Drury Coffey served as a Caldwell County representative in Raleigh in the state house prior to war. After the war, he served eight consecutive terms as a Caldwell County commissioner. Quartermaster sergeant James E. Rankin served as mayor of Asheville from 1872 to 1874, 1876 to 1877, 1897 to 1898, 1911 to 1919, and 1915 to 1919.[18]

A few individuals met tragic ends. During a card game in 1879, James Higgins (Company G) was stabbed and killed by Cornelius Edwards. Edwards felt remorse for his act and paid a man who was bonded to him $100 to marry Higgins's widow and help raise their nine children. Meredith Burleson fell into a mica mine in 1886. Johnson McKinney (Company E/K) was delivering a load of apples in Rock Hill, South Carolina, in 1915 when he fell ill and died far from home. Cornelius R. Wallace (Company K) was killed when he fell off a mill dam and broke his neck. Alexander Wilson (Company C) died in poverty in 1906. The Rev. Edmund Silver (Company E/K) was in Hilliard, Florida, in March 1918, dealing in real estate, when a passing mule startled the mule he was riding. The mule threw Silver into a tree stump, breaking his neck. His remains were returned to Yancey County.[19]

Silver was not the only former member of the Fifty-Eighth to venture south and into Florida. Col. John B. Palmer spent the rest of the war in western North Carolina, serving as a commander of the Department of Western North Carolina, and, toward the close of the war, as commander of a small field force composed of infantry, artillery, and cavalry. According to his service record, Palmer was captured, and then paroled in Athens, Georgia, on May 8, 1865. Palmer had no home to which he could return: his "Grasslands" estate was burned during a raid in June 1864. By August 1865, Palmer had relocated to Lincoln County, North Carolina.

Not long after the suspension of hostilities, President Johnson had issued a general amnesty for Confederate soldiers. However, several classes of men who had served in high ranking positions, such as civil or diplomatic agents, former governors, former officers in the United States Army, or those above the rank of colonel, were exempt from the general amnesty. These individuals had to apply for a special presidential pardon. Palmer, writing from Lincoln County, applied for his pardon on August 23, 1865. As dictated by law, Palmer's application was recommended to the president by Governor Holden, and on September 2, Palmer was pardoned by the president. By May 1866, Palmer and his family were living in Columbia, South Carolina. The colonel was working for the Childs family at their textile factory.

It did not take long for Palmer to climb back into the business world. In 1870, he was director of the Farmer's Fertilizer Company, and in 1871, was on the board of directors of the new National Bank of Newberry, South Carolina. He also served as president of the Central National Bank in Columbia. Before long, Palmer was involved in rebuilding railroads in the South. He was president of the Charlotte, Columbia, and Augusta railroad. In 1876, Palmer moved to Richmond, Virginia, and became president of the Petersburg Railroad. By 1890, he was vice president of the Atlantic Coast Line, a railroad that would eventually link most of the East Coast. In 1889, Palmer finally sold his property in western North Carolina. Prior to this, in 1879, he bought about 80 acres of orange groves in Central Florida in a new community known as Winter Park. Palmer and his wife, Fannie, split their time between Florida, Columbia, and Richmond, with occasional trips to Europe. He had little contact with his former soldiers in the Fifty-Eighth, even though he penned a letter outlining the regiment's experiences in the battle of Chickamauga. Palmer died in Winter Park on December 10, 1893, and was laid to rest in Elmwood Cemetery in Columbia. "Col. Palmer was a noble hearted man, whose friendship was an honor to those who possessed it," lamented one South Carolina newspaper.[20]

Major Harper spent his first couple of days back

Edmund Silver began his military service in Capt. John C. Keener's company, but about the time of the formation of the Fifty-Eighth, transferred to Samuel Silver's command, which became Company K (courtesy Michael Ledford).

After the war, John B. Palmer lived in Columbia, South Carolina, Richmond, Virginia, and Winter Park, Florida, where he died in 1893. Palmer is buried with his wife and son in Elmwood Cemetery in Columbia.

from the Confederate army resting and attending church. He made no entry in his diary from May 8 until May 31, when he recorded that he was "working on farm and garden [and] occasionally hunting squirrels." Prior to the war, Harper had been educated at Davidson College. Upon his return to Caldwell County, he took his education, both from the college and from the military, and applied himself to the problems of an impoverished community. Harper started a store. In 1894, he established the Bank of Lenoir and served as its president. He also helped with the building of the Chester and Lenoir Railroad and later served as its president, as well. Harper was very active in the United Confederate Veterans until his death in 1921. Papers across the region lamented his death. The *Statesville Landmark* considered Harper "a good man, one who walked uprightly, feared God and eschewed evil." The *Charlotte Observer* called Harper "one of the strong men of the mountains."[21]

Just two years after the war, North Carolina had already started looking after the veterans of the state. Even though the state was impoverished, veterans who had lost limbs or their eyesight were compensated. In March 1885, North Carolina enacted its first pension for the benefit of Confederate veterans who were not capable of earning a living or who had an income of less than $250 a year. An applicant had to go before a county official, at times a justice of the peace, or a pension board, and a doctor, before he could receive his allowance. Frequently, certain men, sometimes in the community and sometimes in Raleigh, could be called upon to help the veterans and their widows with their applications. In 1895, the eligibility was expanded to include all veterans or their widows over the age of 60 who had an income of less than $100 a year. The state continued to broaden the scope of its benefits to veterans and their wives as time progressed. In 1900, disabled veterans were able to receive $150 per year. In 1919, all veterans, as well as widows over the age of 60 and who had married veterans before 1890, were eligible. In 1923, pensions were approved for black Confederate soldiers who had served at least six months. The age of eligibility for widows was dropped to fifty-five in 1920, to fifty in 1921, and to forty-five in 1930. The last pension paid out by the state to a Confederate widow occurred in 1990.

While pensions helped veterans with some level of financial support, another movement helped heal some of the fractured lives of the veterans themselves. Beginning in the early 1880s, the former Confederate veterans started to assemble together. In 1881, North Carolina's Society of Ex-Confederate Soldiers and Sailors was formed. Other states had similar organizations; in 1889, many of these veterans' groups joined together to form the United Confederate Veterans (UCV). Georgia's John B. Gordon was the first national commander. In January 1893, a monthly magazine was begun by Sumner Archibald Cunningham, entitled *Confederate Veteran*. The *Confederate Veteran* later became the official publication of the United Confederate Veterans. Articles found within the pages of the *Confederate Veteran* were largely penned by the veterans themselves.

By 1901, there were 70 chapters, or "camps," in the North Carolina Division of the United Confederate Veterans. Many of the camps were named in honor of fallen comrades from the areas where the camps were formed. The Nimrod Triplett (Camp 1273) was established in Boone in Watauga County. Triplett was a member of the First North Carolina Cavalry and had been killed during the war. The General Pender Camp 1154 was located in Burnsville, Yancey County, with N. M. Wilson and W. A. McLelland as commanders. In Caldwell County there was the Col. John T. Jones Camp 952. The camp in McDowell, simply known as the Confederate Veteran Camp 914, held a recruiting drive in 1897, in which thirty-seven men joined the fifteen already enrolled in the camp. The new and old members of the camp met at the courthouse and paid their yearly dues of ten cents. The "object of the organization is historical, literary, social, educative upon the rising generation to appreciate and honor the reasons that guided and the conduct of those who lost in the 'great internecine strife.'" Among the new members were A. N. Gibbs, Lt. Robert Sisk, and Jason Finley, all of Company F of the Fifty-Eighth. Pvt. John A. Seagle was one of the officers in the camp.[22]

These camps often hosted local reunions once a year. In August 1891, veterans gathered at Blowing Rock, on the border of Caldwell and Watauga counties. The event was scheduled to last for three days, and while the rain kept some away, hundreds gathered. They lined up on Wednesday at 10:00 A.M. and marched from the Watauga Hotel to a stand erected near the Blowing Rock Hotel. The crowd was then entertained by a band "rendering some very fine music." Next, Major Harper, "after a few brief remarks," introduced other speakers. A dance was held that evening. More speeches followed the next day, but the rain soon caused the reunion to come to a close. It seemed for a while that the reunions in Watauga and Caldwell counties rotated between the two places. In 1899, Lorenzo Miller (Company I) was trying to organize a drum and fife band for the reunion. "Mr. Miller was considered the best fifer in Gen. Johnson's army," the newspaper reported.

Sgt. Calvin Cottrell (Company I) related attending a reunion in Lenoir in 1899. They had traveled to Lenoir the day before. The next morning, September 26, they were up early, and after feeding their livestock, ventured into town. Cottrell estimated that there were "five or six thousand people gathered together." Orders were issued about 11:30 for the men to fall into ranks with their old comrades. "Then the old Confederate Veterans fell into line led by Maj. G.W.F. Harper. Then the mounted Veterans moving in columns of four; and carriages containing Veterans less able to march, the sons of Veterans commanded by John K. Moore, moving in double file, and a bicycle parade, and all led by the Lenoir Cornet Band." The line of men and boys marched through the streets and by Davenport College, and then back to the courthouse "from whence we started, then gave the old rebel yell that was almost deafening, and march up in front of the hotel where the speaking was to be." After the speeches were delivered, the veterans marched back to the grounds of the college "where there were three of the longest tables I had ever seen, loaded down with all the good things any man, women, or child could desire. And further, the good ladies from all over Caldwell county, it seemed were there, trying to wait on the people." At the end of the day, there was "much hearty hand shaking" and the veterans started back towards their homes. Cottrell believed that many of his "fellow comrades will never meet again on earth. They are fast ripening for the grave and the resurrection."[23]

Besides local reunions, there were also state and national reunions held once a year. The first national reunion was held in Chattanooga, Tennessee, July 3–5, 1890. Wesley Presnell (Company D), William Davis (Company I), and Elijah Norris (Company D), along with three others, were elected by other Watauga County veterans in 1900 to attend the national reunion in Louisville, Kentucky, that year.[24]

Some of the veterans of the Fifty-Eighth were involved in marking the spot where the regiment fought at the battle of Chickamauga. At first, "the advanced point reached by North Carolinians [was] marked only by a wooden board nailed to a telegraph pole." A commission was appointed to go to the battlefield and examine and document just where the regiment had fought. Veterans of the Fifty-Eighth who served on the commission included Capt. Benjamin F. Baird (Company D), Lt. David F. Baird (Company D), both of Watauga County, and Capt. Isaac H. Bailey (Company B) of Mitchell County. Another member of the commission was Clinton Cilley, a Union veteran who settled in western North Carolina at the close of the war, and for a time, served as mayor of Lenoir.

David Baird and another Fifty-Eighth veteran, William S. Davis (Company I), who might have replaced Benjamin Baird, went to Chickamauga in the fall of 1893. They examined the field and located the position where the Fifty-Eighth fought thirty years earlier. "They say the grounds," recorded the *Watauga Democrat*, "are still natural and that they had no trouble to locate the place occupied in the fight. They brought with them some relics from the battle ground."

In 1895, the Chattanooga National Park was dedicated and opened to the public. Memorial services and other events were held across the battlefield, and numerous veterans gathered on the field. There were an estimated 60,000 to 100,000 people in attendance, including Capt. Isaac Bailey (Company B). It was another ten years before the state of North Carolina completed granite markers for some of its regiments that had fought at Chickamauga. On November 10, 1905, Gov. Robert Glenn gathered with "a small party of North Carolinians" to dedicate the Tar Heel markers. The marker to the Sixtieth was dedicated first, followed by the marker to the Fifty-Eighth. Among the Tar Heels present were Major Harper and Sgt Elijah Crump. Harper told the party of the role played by the Fifty-Eighth in the battle.[25]

Two organizations which still survive and are related to the United Confederate Veterans are the United Daughters of the Confederacy and the Sons of Confederate Veterans. The origins of the United Daughters of the Confederacy can be traced back to the war-time enterprises of women all across the South. These women organized hospital associations, knitting circles, and sewing organizations that helped the Southern war effort. After the

Sgt. Elijah J. Norris was just eighteen when he enlisted in Company D in August 1862. He was wounded three times and was at home convalescing when the war ended. He is pictured here in his post-war United Confederate Veterans uniform (courtesy Wayne Brown).

war's conclusion, cemetery, memorial, monument, auxiliaries to Confederate veteran camps, and Confederate home associations were all formed. The United Daughters of the Confederacy was formally organized on September 10, 1894, in Nashville, Tennessee. By 1912, the Daughters had 800 chapters and 45,000 members. Many of the monuments that grace the courthouse lawns of most Southern towns and cities can be traced to the work of the United Daughters of the Confederacy.[26]

On June 3, 1910, over 6,000 people gathered in Lenoir in Caldwell County to dedicate their Confederate monument. Lt. Gov. William C. Newland, Jr., was present, along with North Carolina Supreme Court Justice Walter Clark. Maj. George W. F. Harper of the Fifty-Eighth led about 200 old veterans in a parade (courtesy the Caldwell Heritage Museum).

Not many counties in western North Carolina could afford to erect monuments immediately after the war. The veterans in Watauga County tried to erect a monument in 1905, but for unknown reasons, never succeeded. In June 1910, the citizens of Caldwell County gathered to dedicate their monument in Lenoir. The crowd was estimated at 6,000 people. Four marshals led the parade, followed by a carriage containing Lenoir Mayor Wakefield, Lt. Gov. William Newland, and Supreme Court Judge Walter Clark. Another carriage bore Mrs. F. R. Williams, president of the North Carolina Division of the United Daughters of the Confederacy (UDC). Next came a carriage with elderly members of the UDC, along with Delight Harper Benfield. Then came the band, followed by "the veterans marching in columns of fours to the number of 200, commanded by Maj. G.W.F. Harper who was the ranking officer present. The old warriors looked somewhat grizzled and some of them walked with perceptible stoop and limp, but to the stirring music of the band their faces and eyes showed the fire and vim of the sixties. Many citizens bared their heads as the grand old men passed them and felt that the debt of honor due to them by their country could never be paid."

After parading through town, the group reached the monument and grandstands. Numerous speakers addressed the crowd, including Judge Clark, "who delivered an able and scholarly address of about an hour's length." Numerous veterans were presented with

Left: Sam Bennett was reported as both a member of Company K, Fifty-Eighth North Carolina, and North Carolina's last surviving Confederate soldier until his death in 1951. *Above:* After serving in Company E, Elijah L. Moore returned to Caldwell County, where he died in 1903 (courtesy the North Carolina Department of Archives and History).

crosses of honor and awards given by the UDC. "Then came the unveiling, which was done skillfully by a cord from the speaker's stand" by Benfield. "As the veil fell a round of applause went up from the assembly." This was followed by the singing of the Doxology, and then "the veterans were served a splendid dinner on the court house campus, [then] greetings and hand shakings of the 'Old Boys'.... The closing number of the day's program was an automobile ride for the veterans which every one seemed to enjoy to the fullest extent."[27]

The old veterans slowly passed over the river. There were still a few left in the 1940s when the United States entered into World War II. Moses J. Byrd (Company G) passed away in Arkansas in September 1941. Yancey County's Moses J. Peterson (Company H) also died in September 1941. William Moretz (Company I) passed in 1942 and is buried in Watauga County. Phillip Greer (Company M/G) passed in May 1947 in Watauga County.

Probably the last member of the Fifty-Eighth to depart this life was Sam Bennett (Company K). Bennett died in 1951 and was recognized as being the last Confederate soldier in North Carolina. However, the records are not very clear. He was born on May 4, 1850. He claimed in a 1930 pension application to have enlisted on October 15, 1864, in Company K of the Fifty-Eighth. Unfortunately, as the Yancey County resident grew older, the stories that he told about his war-time service do not give credence to the claim. Bennett claimed to have served in the home guard in Yancey County before enlisting in 1863 in the "Black Mountain Regiment with his grandfather, Pittman Williams, and four of Williams sons." Bennett recalled being sent to Virginia, "where he served under General John B. Gordon."

When asked about being wounded "by a Yankee bullet," he responded by saying that he was "injured by dynamite set off by our own troops while preparing earthworks near Richmond. I know the charge was going off and I ran but I didn't know anything afterward until I woke up in an Army hospital." Afterwards, Bennett claimed that he was an orderly in the hospital "and I waited on the sick and wounded." There are numerous problems with Bennett's story. There was not a "Black Mountain Regiment" for starters. Company C of the Sixteenth North Carolina, which did come from Yancey County, was known as the Black Mountain Boys. And there was a soldier named Pittman Williams. However, Williams and his sons served in Company I of the Twenty-Ninth North Carolina, which was a part of the Army of Tennessee. They were never in Virginia. We will probably never know in just what regiment that Sam Bennett served.[28]

The work of remembering the Fifty-Eighth North Carolina Troops continues today. On several occasions, members of the regiment have received grave markers provided by the Veterans Administration. Of special note is the 2002 rediscovery of the Delap Family Cemetery in Campbell County, Tennessee. This is the site of the burial of more than sixty members of the Fifty-Eighth who died in the area while stationed there in the winter of 1862–1863. The cemetery was cleaned, grave markers were installed, and a special ceremony remembering those soldiers was held in June 2005. In the Toe River Valley area of western North Carolina, a Sons of Confederate Veterans camp is named the Col. John B. Palmer Camp (1946) in honor of Colonel Palmer. In 2008, this camp placed a monument on the grounds of the Yancey County Courthouse in Burnsville commemorating the lives of 148 Yancey County men who died during the war. For many of these men, like Robert Rowland

Yancey County's Confederate Monument bears the names of 140 men from the county who died during the war. Numerous members of the Fifty-Eighth are honored on the stone.

Dozens of members of the Fifty-Eighth perished while in east Tennessee in 1862–1863. Many of them were buried here at the Delap Family Cemetery in Campbell County, Tennessee.

(Company C), killed during the battle of Reseca, the monument is their only marker. Yet another marker has recently been installed in Marion, in McDowell County, by the McDowell Men, Camp 379, Sons of Confederate Veterans.

Part of a speech delivered at a veterans' reunion in Watauga County in the 1910s is a fitting epitaph to the story of the Fifty-Eighth North Carolina Troops: "Oh! it is said that Napoleon's hosts fought no harder when France and her lilies were crushed that you fought for your own southern lilies whose petals dropped blood for the hearts that were hushed — that you fought like the legions of Caesar with more than a Rome to defend. It is said that wherever brave men are mentioned the lips of love whisper your names."[29]

CHAPTER 14

The Fifty-Eighth North Carolina in Perspective

North Carolina provided over seventy regiments for Confederate service. The Fifty-Eighth was unique in several ways. The members of the Fifty-Eighth were not fighting for some grand notion of state's rights, nor for any attachment to the South's "peculiar institution." They joined the Confederate army when it became law for them to do so. Someone came around with a piece of paper informing them that they were compelled to serve. Some were even forced into the army at the point of a gun. These unwilling volunteers left their mark upon the regiment.

The Fifty-Eighth was one of the largest regiments to come from North Carolina. A total of 2,036 men served in the ranks. In comparison, the Thirty-Seventh Alabama Infantry, organized in the spring of 1862, had 1,767 men within its ranks. The Thirty-Seventh also served in the Army of Tennessee. The Eighth Florida Infantry, mustered into service in May 1862, contained 1,134 men within its ranks. This regiment served in the Army of Northern Virginia. One reason for the size of the Fifty-Eighth was that the regiment contained twelve companies instead of the standard ten. Company L, from Ashe County, contained 149 men. Company M was comprised of men from Ashe and Watauga counties and contained 91 men. Most of the companies in the regiment had more men than the standard company did. This was due in large part to the conditions under which the regiment was created: voluntary enlistees received a bounty, plus the opportunity to enlist in a company of their choosing; those who were forced into service received no bounty and were sent to a regiment of the government's choice. The majority chose to volunteer, save the members of companies L and M, who were true conscripts.

With so many men in service who had no real desire to be there, desertions quickly became problematic. Determining the exact number of deserters within in the Fifty-Eighth is impossible; there are just too many missing records. Cpl. Samuel W. Blalock enlisted in the Mitchell Rangers on February 11, 1862, at the age of sixteen. He never again appears on the records of the company. Others appear in the records until August 31, 1864, when the last known muster roll for the Fifty-Eighth was compiled. Sometime between this date and the surrender at Greensboro, these men go missing from the records. They might have died of disease, been killed, been detailed away from the company, or simply slipped away during the final months or days of the war. Some may have been present at the surrender but for some reason do not appear on the Greensboro surrender rolls. Major Harper is such a soldier. He was undoubtedly present, as attested to by his diary, but is not listed as having received a parole.

There were 707 men reported as deserters from the Fifty-Eighth North Carolina

Troops. An additional 114 men came back to the army but later deserted again. Ten of these men returned, but then deserted for a third time. In all, there were 821 reports of desertion in the Fifty-Eighth. However, the information available is far from complete. In comparison, the Twenty-Fifth North Carolina Troops, which numbered 1,670 men, had only 255 desertions. This regiment, while recruited from the same mountains in western North Carolina, albeit a little farther south, was mustered into service on August 15, 1861, and fought in the Army of Northern Virginia. The Sixtieth North Carolina, which was brigaded with and at times consolidated with the Fifty-Eighth, had a regimental strength of 1,054 men. Of these, 351 deserted, giving the Sixtieth a desertion rate of 33 percent. The Fifty-Eighth's desertion rate was 34 percent.[1]

Every conceivable reason, and probably a few inconceivable reasons, caused the men to desert. Some were concerned about conditions at home, especially as the war progressed, and in 1864, as Confederate forces left east Tennessee. Some felt that their service in the Fifty-Eighth was a hardship on their families because they were not home to protect them or to put in crops, cut firewood, and hunt. Many of the men came from large families. Forty-one-year-old George Troutman (Company B) deserted twice, once on May 24, 1863, while the regiment was stationed near Clinton, Tennessee, and again from camp near Charleston, Tennessee, on September 1 of that same year. He had "about 10 children to take care of" back in Mitchell County. Later his son, James Troutman, served in the Thirteenth Tennessee Cavalry (U.S.). It has often been written that many soldiers left when it came time to plant or to harvest and later returned to service. In May 1863, the incomplete records of the Fifty-Eighth tell us that thirty-one men deserted. Fifteen returned to the regiment. In September 1863, 107 men deserted; sixty-one returned.[2]

A few who deserted were actually cowards. Between September 17 and September 20, right around the battle of Chickamauga, the Fifty-Eighth lost twenty-six men. Some might have lost their nerve on the eve on an imminent battle, or they might have simply been looking for an opportunity to desert and found the pre-battle confusion an opportune time.

Many who deserted left as a way to make a political statement. Some were truly more supportive of the old Union than of the new Confederacy. According to William Younce's memoir, when once questioned about where his loyalties lay, he responded that he owed his "allegiance to that country only that is represented by that beautiful emblem of the free, the Stars and Stripes." While it might be said that the vast majority of deserters who left the Fifty-Eighth had no fondness for the Confederate government, neither were they found of the Federal government. Had they been pro–Union, then more of them would have joined the Federal army. The vast majority of the deserters saw it as a "political act, devoid of grand scope and drama, of relatively powerless men seeking to limit the power of others over them."[3]

In the end, 135 of the approximately 707 deserters joined the Union army or navy. The majority joined either the Third North Carolina Mounted Infantry or the Thirteenth Tennessee Cavalry. Both organizations were made up of "home yankees" or galvanizers, former Confederates who had crossed over the lines and joined the enemy. The Thirteenth Tennessee Cavalry was organized in Strawberry Plains, Nashville, and Gallatin, Tennessee, in October 1863. In the month prior to the regiment's formal organization, twenty-two former members of the Fifty-Eighth joined. They did not enlist in one single company, or, maybe they were assigned to different companies to keep the former Confederates separated. All told, there were forty-five former members of the Fifty-Eighth in the Thirteenth Tennessee. The Thirteenth saw action in Kentucky, Southwest Virginia, Tennessee, and North

Carolina. The regiment was mustered out of service on September 5, 1865. The largest number of Fifty-Eighth deserters joined the Third North Carolina Mounted Infantry. This regiment was organized in Knoxville, Tennessee, in June 1864, and saw action in Tennessee and western North Carolina. These men were mustered out on August 8, 1865. Fifty-three former Fifty-Eighth members served in this regiment. Many joined in 1864, but a few did not join until March of 1865, leading to speculation that these men might have been pressed into service.

There were several in the Third who found serving in the Union army as distasteful as serving in the Confederate army. Jordan Church enlisted in the Third on January 1, 1865, and deserted in April 1865 once the regiment reached Boone. Josiah Davis enlisted on March 25, 1864, and deserted November 17, 1864. Hugh Phillips enlisted on January 25, 1865, and deserted April 17 while stationed in Boone. Other members of the Fifty-Eighth joined other Tennessee cavalry regiments, the United States Navy, or one of the United States Volunteer regiments. Most of the Navy recruits were men in Confederate prisons, as were the members of the United States Volunteers. The latter were sent out West to help with the numerous Indian uprisings that took place during the war.[4]

However, even some of these soldiers were not true Unionists. On July 18, 1862, Hezekiah Thomas enlisted in what became Company D of the Fifty-Eighth. He was just sixteen years old. He was captured on September 5, 1864, during the battle of Jonesboro, Georgia, and eventually landed in Camp Douglas in Chicago, Illinois. On May 5, 1865, a recruiter for the Federal army came through the prison camp and Thomas enlisted in Company C, Sixth United States Volunteers. He wrote after the war that he and "thousands" of other Confederates enlisted in the Federal army because "we were all about to starve to death ... we did it to save life, Lee had surrendered at this time and Johnson had not, but he disbanded his men soon after." After enlistment, Thomas was "taken out to Fort Kerney, in Nebraska and from there I was taken to Grand Island (Nebraska) to make hay for the Government and while there some of the Government horses was stolen and ... (I was detailed with a corporal) to go ... hunt for the horses; so we followed the horses for about 400 miles, and after we got there we decided to come home and we never went back to get our discharge." Just how many whose reasons for joining the Federal army were similar to Hezekiah Thomas's motivation is unknown.[5]

Even with the mass desertions, there were still enough men left to make contributions to several of the battles in which the regiment fought. At Chickamauga, the regiment was a factor in the Confederate victory with their late afternoon attack on the Federal position. Their "baptism of fire" led to 50 percent casualities in the regiment. In May 1864, outside Resaca, the unit was able to drive the Federals from their works. At the end of the war at Bentonville, the regiment again rendered great service, helping to break several Federal lines.

Nevertheless, the regiment, like most in the Army of Tennessee, suffered from the leadership problems higher up in the chain of command. At Missionary Ridge the men were rushed from the train platform and onto the battlefield, being placed under unfamiliar commanders. During the actual battle, conflicting orders were sent to different commanders, causing confusion. They saw limited action at the first and second battles of Dalton and at Rocky Face Ridge. At Resaca, they drove the Federals from their works and maintained their position against repeated Federal assaults on May 15, even though they did attack later unsupported, thanks to Hood's not sending out the timely orders to cancel a planned assault. At the battle of Kolb's Farm on June 22, General Hood launched an unauthorized attack that failed, costing the Fifty-Eighth many men. The regiment spent time in the trenches during many of the battles around Atlanta. The regiment was slightly involved in the battle of Jonesboro, but details are sketchy. The Fifty-Eighth missed most of the Nashville campaign, along with the battle of Averasboro. All told, out of 2,021 men who joined the Fifty-Eighth North Carolina Troops, 355 died during the war. Fifty-five were killed on a battlefield, with 36 dying of wounds. Approximately 104 died of diseases, 13 were executed, and 158 died of unknown reasons.

The regiment itself suffered from a lack of commanders. Following the battle of Chickamauga, the regiment had no field officers present. The assignment of Colonel Palmer to western North Carolina did not help. Palmer never gained his promotion to brigadier general, and hence was always listed as colonel of the Fifty-Eighth. Since he occupied the position, no one else could be promoted to colonel. As other field and staff officers were often absent for a variety of reasons, command often fell upon the captains of the regiment. When a position among the field and staff became vacant, the captains fought among themselves for the promotion.

While the Fifty-Eighth North Carolina Troops was able to fight well, it will never be considered a "bedrock" regiment of the Army of Tennessee. It was plagued by desertion and by a lack of competent commanders, in addition to the almost total abandonment by its home state, which led to shortages in clothing and other munitions, to leading in turn to further declines in morale. Had the Fifty-Eighth been sent farther away, northern Virginia, or farther west, and had then been given competent commanders, an A. P. Hill, or Stonewall Jackson, or Cleburne, it might have been able to achieve more. But even then the stigma of being "unwilling volunteers" might have persisted. Regardless, some of those unwilling volunteers did turn out to be good soldiers.

CHAPTER 15

Looking for the Fifty-Eighth North Carolina Today

While some of the fields where the Fifty-Eighth camped and fought have been lost to development, many others still exist today as parks and can be visited. Here are a just a few of those places.

Cumberland Gap National Historical Park—The Fifty-Eighth was stationed in Cumberland Gap for just a short amount of time, basically September and October 1862. They occupied the Federal works and worked on cleaning up the debris the Federal army left. In 1940, Congress authorized the establishment of the Cumberland Gap National Historical Park. It took another nineteen years for the surrounding states to purchase the property, which today contains 20,000 acres. The visitor center has information on the war in Cumberland Gap, there are two forts with cannons, and several historical markers denote the locations of other forts in the area. Nothing marks the sites of the camps, nor have the graves of the thirteen members of the Fifty-Eighth North Carolina who died while stationed in the area ever been definitively located.

Delap Family Cemetery, Campbell County, Tennessee—From September 1862 until late summer 1863, the Fifty-Eighth North Carolina was stationed at different points in east Tennessee, mostly at Big Gap Creek, now called Lafollette, and Jacksboro. Dozens of members of the Fifty-Eighth, and of other regiments, died while in the area that winter. Their places of burial were lost until 2002, when a descendant of a Fifty-Eighth soldier asked the right person at the local historical society. That person remembered hearing a story from an elderly lady in the community about soldiers being buried in a family cemetery. The cemetery was found, with numerous graves marked with plain field rocks. The cemetery was cleaned, stones were ordered from Veterans Administration, those stones were erected, and a memorial service was held in June 2005. It is believed that there are 119 Confederate graves within the cemetery. This cemetery is located in a housing development off Jacksboro Pike on Ellison Road.

Chickamauga and Chattanooga National Military Park—In September 1863, the Fifty-Eighth was rushed to Chickamauga, Georgia, to bolster the ranks of the Confederate Army of Tennessee. Not long after arriving, the regiment was involved in its first large battle, fought September 19 and 20. The Fifty-Eighth played a key role in driving off the Union defenders on the evening of the last day of the battle. Chickamauga became the first national military park authorized by Congress in 1890. Just about all of the positions occupied by the Fifty-Eighth are preserved within the park. There is a granite monument to the regiment on Snodgrass Hill, and several iron plaques denote the different positions of the

The Fifty-Eighth North Carolina's final position at Chickamauga is marked by this monument.

regiment during the three days of fighting. Several miles to the north is the Chattanooga section of the park. The Fifty-Eighth was also heavily involved in this battle fought in November 1863. However, the position was lost to development when Interstate 24 was constructed in the 1960s. An iron plaque is located on South Crest Road beside the Interstate near where the regiment fought. Not far away is a monument marking the site of Bragg's headquarters. A portion of the Fifty-Eighth rallied around Bragg's headquarters after retreating up the mountain. The visitor center, with its collection of firearms, is well worth a visit. This park is the largest battlefield park in the United States and contains 666 monuments, 659 markers, and 257 cannons.

Dalton, Georgia— The Fifty-Eighth spent the winter of 1863–1864 in the Dalton area, at times actually pulling provost duty in town. The regiment was involved in the February 1864 battle just north of town. In April 1864, the men broke winter camp and proceeded north of Dalton, and it was along Crow Valley Road that the mass execution of May 1864 took place. The graves of these twelve men remain unmarked. In early May 1864, the regiment was in position north of town. There are several markers in the area that indicate the positions of the Confederate and Union armies, including one for Crow Valley Road that mentions Stevenson's division. There is also a pavilion describing the battles in the area in front of the Highway Patrol Post off U.S. 41, on the north side of Dalton. In town is the Westview Cemetery. This cemetery contains the graves of several members of the Fifty-Eighth.

Reseca, Georgia— In mid–May 1864, the Fifty-Eighth was redeployed to Reseca, where it was involved in the battle there. Much of the property that saw the Blue and Gray battle each other has been preserved by the state and may one day be open to the public. Those who attend the annual re-enactment of the battle held each May should take notice of the road into the site. This is the area over which the Fifty-Eighth charged, moving from south of the dirt road to the north side, near where the house sits on a hill. The Confederate Cemetery in Resaca contains the graves of more than 420 unknown Confederates. The cemetery is near the Reseca/Atlanta Campaign Pavilion on U.S. 41.

Kennesaw Mountain National Battlefield, Georgia— The battle of Kennesaw was fought on June 27, 1864. The Fifty-Eighth was not involved in the June 27 defensive battle, but had fought a few days earlier at Kolb Farm. Kolb Farm is a part of the Kennesaw Battlefield Park. The Fifty-Eighth made an ill-fated charge on June 22. The battlefield was acquired by the federal government in 1917. While the Fifty-Eighth's position off Power Springs Road is preserved, it is not easily accessible.

Marietta, Georgia— Following the battle of Chickamauga, the town of Marietta became a vast hospital. The size of the hospital facility increased as the Atlanta campaign grew in intensity. Many of the dead from these hospitals were buried in the Marietta Confederate Cemetery. In 1866, the Georgia Memorial Association began re-interring bodies of Confederate soldiers buried on battlefields like Chickamauga and Kolb Farm. There are undoubtedly numerous members of the Fifty-Eighth buried at the Marietta Confederate Cemetery, which includes a marker to the North Carolinians buried within. The cemetery is off Power Springs Road.

Atlanta, Georgia— Nothing is really left of the entrenchments and battlefield sites in Atlanta. The Fifty-Eighth's position at the July 22, 1864, battle has long been paved over more than once. It is worth the time to visit the Atlanta Cyclorama, the largest oil painting

Numerous members of the Fifty-Eighth North Carolina Troops, including those killed during the battle of Chickamauga, lie buried in the Confederate Cemetery in Marietta, Georgia.

in the world, which depicts part of the fighting on July 22, 1864, and Oakwood Cemetery, final resting place of 6,900 Confederate soldiers who died in the massive hospitals at the Georgia Fairgrounds and during the battles around Atlanta. There are undoubtedly a few members of the Fifty-Eighth, like Leander Pyatte (Company A), who died in an Atlanta Hospital, interred within its hallowed grounds. The cemetery is located at 248 Oakland Ave.

Columbia, South Carolina— No big battle was fought between the Blue and Gray in Columbia. The Federals did lob a few shells at the capital, and a large portion of the city burned during the Federal occupation. There is not much to see related to the Fifty-Eighth and the war. However, Elmwood Cemetery in Columbia has the graves of Col. John B. Palmer and Pvt. John Eben Childs. After entering the cemetery, visitors should bear to the left to get to Palmer's grave. John, Fannie, and their son Edmund are buried not far from the Confederate section, under a huge magnolia tree. John Eben Childs's body was interred on the Chickamauga battlefield and later reinterred at Elmwood. On entering the cemetery, one should bear to the right to locate the family plot where he is buried. As Elmwood is a large cemetery, it is advisable to stop at the office and get a map. The cemetery is at 501 Elmwood Ave.

Bentonville Battlefield, North Carolina— The Confederate army under Gen. Joseph E. Johnston fought the Federal army under Gen. William T. Sherman at Bentonville March 19–21, 1865. The Fifty-Eighth fought valiantly and helped in driving the Federals from their works. However, fortune was not with the Confederates and the battle ended essentially as a draw, with the Confederates retreating. The site of the battle of Bentonville became a North Carolina Historic Site in 1957, and the area preserved has expanded in the past sixty years. The Fifty-Eighth's position is well preserved. Visitors should stop by the park office and acquire a map to help them get around. Bentonville Battlefield in located in Johnston County, about an hour southeast of Raleigh.

Bennett Place, Durham, North Carolina— Generals Johnston and Sherman met here, on the grounds of the Bennett Farm, to discuss the surrender of Johnston's command in April 1865. The Fifty-Eighth was never actually at the Bennett Place. It was stationed in Greensboro and Jamestown. However, a visit to the Bennett Place is great way to learn about the surrender negotiations. Plus, the museum at the Bennett Place has an Enfield rifle thought to have been carried by Major G.W.F. Harper during the battle of Bentonville. The Bennett Place is off Bennett Memorial Road.

Local history museums— Some of the counties that provided men who made up the Fifty-Eighth have fantastic local history museums. The Caldwell Heritage Museum has a wall of photographs of local soldiers and several artifacts related to the time period, including a day dress belonging to Mrs. Harper. Lt. Walter Lenoir was born and later died at Ft. Defiance, also in Caldwell County. He is buried on the grounds in the family cemetery. The Avery County Historical Museum in Newland also has a military room with information about the Fifty-Eighth, and the museum staff can provide directions to Grasslands in Altamont so visitors can see where Colonel Palmer's home once stood.

Appendix A:
Fifty-Eighth North Carolina Troops Roster

Below is a list of members of the Fifty-Eighth North Carolina, along with each soldier's dates of birth and death, with place of burial, when known. A roster containing individual service records, derived from their Compiled Service Records, can be found in Jordan, *North Carolina Troops, 1861–1865: A Roster*, Volume 14.

Key to Abbreviations

1st Lt.	First Lieutenant
2nd Lt.	Second Lieutenant
3rd Lt.	Third Lieutenant
ACS	Assistant Commissary Sergeant
1st Sgt.	First Sergeant
Adj.	Adjutant
As. Quart.	Assistant Quartermaster
As. Surg.	Assistant Surgeon
Capt.	Captain
Cem.	Cemetery
Co.	County
Col.	Colonel
Cpl.	Corporal
Drum. Maj.	Drum Major
F&S	Field and Staff
Hos. Ste.	Hospital Steward
Lt. Col.	Lieutenant Colonel
Maj.	Major
Misc.	Miscellaneous
Musc.	Musician
Pvt.	Private
Qsgt.	Quartermaster Sergeant
Sgt.	Sergeant
Sgt. Maj.	Sergeant Major
Surgeon	Surgeon

Name; Rank; Company; Place of Enlistment; Date of Birth–Date of Death; Place of Burial

Abee, Andrew; ---; A; ---; 22 Oct. 1829–before 1876
Abee, James E.; Pvt.; A/D; Mitchell; 12 June 1838–9 May 1901
Abee, John H.; Pvt.; A; Mitchell; 21 April 1833–28 June 1913
Adams, David; Pvt.; D; Watauga; 1 March 1828–31 Dec. 1913; Allan Adams Cem., Watauga Co.
Adams, Zachariah; Pvt.; D; Watauga; 4 Jan. 1835–4 May 1902; Allan Adams Cem., Watauga Co.
Alexander, Benjamin Julius; Pvt.; E; 10 Jan. 1831–5 Dec. 1907
Alexander, Randolph; Pvt.; E; Wilkes; b. ca. 1827
Alexander, Thomas M.; Pvt.; F; Camp Holmes; ---; Hopewell Presb. Ch., Mecklenburg Co.
Alexander, William R. Capt.; E; Buncombe; 1841–7 March 1923; Buncombe Co.
Allen, Paschal; Pvt.; F; McDowell; 4 Feb. 1830–16 July 1892; Centennial UMC, Rutherford Co.
Allis, G.; ---; A
Allison, Alexander; Pvt.; F; McDowell; ca. 1840–13 Jan. 1863; Jacksboro, Tenn.
Allison, Elisha A.; Pvt.; F; McDowell; ca. 1834–20 Feb. 1863; Jacksboro, Tenn.
Allred, John L.; Sgt.; F; McDowell; 1831–24 March 1915; McDowell Co.
Anderson, Burril; Pvt.; F; Burke; b. ca. 1810
Anderson, George W.; Pvt.; F; Camp Vance; ---; Drucilla Presb. Ch., McDowell Co.
Anderson, Enos, Jr.; Pvt.; G; Camp Holmes
Anderson, Holder; Pvt.; K; Mitchell; d. 1 Jan. 1864; Atlanta, Ga.
Anderson, Hosea Pinkney; Cpl.; E; Caldwell; 5 July 1839–1916; Cedar Valley Cem., Caldwell Co.
Anderson, Jasper Newton; Pvt.; A; Mitchell; b. ca. 1836
Anderson, John Marcus; Pvt.; E; ---; 10 April 1842–20 Aug. 1892; Union Bapt. Ch. Cem., Caldwell Co.

Anderson, John P.; ---; A
Anderson, Lorenzo D.; Pvt.; B; Mitchell; b. ca. 1835
Angel, James G.; Pvt.; C; ---
Anglin, James Jackson; Cpl.; C; Yancey; 25 March 1844–16 Aug. 1938; Anglin Cem., Yancey Co.
Anglin, Raborn Brankenridge; Pvt.; G/C/B; Yancey; 11 Oct. 1832–21 Aug. 1917; R.B. Anglin Cem., Yancey Co.
Anglin, William; Sgt.; C; Yancey; 1844–18 Sept. 1864; Macon, Ga.
Anglin, William; ---; D
Anglin, William, Jr.; Pvt.; G; Yancey; 1826–5 Oct. 1863; Ga.
Armstrong, M. T.; Pvt.; H; Yadkin; b. ca. 1817
Arnett, John B.; Pvt.; A; Mitchell; b. ca. 1829
Arrowood, Elijah M.; Cpl.; B; Camp Jackson
Arrowood, James A.; Pvt.; B; Yancey/Mitchell; b. ca. 1843
Arrowood, James P.; Pvt.; B; Mitchell; b. ca. 1824
Arrowood, Levi; Pvt.; F; McDowell; 25 June 1821–31 Dec. 1905; Arrowood Cem., McDowell Co.
Arrowood, M. H.; Pvt.; B; Dalton, Ga.
Ausburn, Jacob; Pvt.; A; Hamilton Co., Tenn.
Austin, A. Webb; Pvt.; H; Caldwell
Austin, Jacob A.; Pvt.; E; Union; ca. 1838–4 May 1864; Dalton, Ga.
Austin, Thomas J.; Pvt.; H; Caldwell; 8 Feb. 1825–27 Feb. 1909; Harpers Chapel Cem., Caldwell Co.
Austin, William M.; 2nd Lt.; C; Yancey; 5 May 1832–24 March 1912; Academy Hill Cem., Yancey Co.
Autery, Jasper A.; Pvt.; G; Yancey; ca. 1843–15 March 1898; Autrey Cem., Yancey Co.
Autry, Hiram Avery; Pvt.; A; Mitchell; 29 Feb. 1844–4 Jan. 1917; Autery Cem., Yancey Co.
Autry, John Patton; Sgt.; G; Yancey; ca. 1835–12 Dec. 1921; Autrey Cem., Yancey Co.
Autry, Joseph Patrick; 1st Sgt.; A; Mitchell; 1837–7 Jan. 1878; Brinkley-Gillespie Cem., McDowell Co.
Ayers, Jacob M.; Pvt.; G/B; Yancey; 29 Aug. 1840–31 Jan. 1938; Roan Mtn. Cem., Mitchell Co.
Ayers, Wilburn; Pvt.; C; Yancey; 11 May 1834–8 July 1914
Bailey, Curtis; Pvt.; B; Mitchell; b. ca. 1844; Yellow Jacket John Bailey Cem., Yancey Co.
Bailey, Ezekiel H.; Pvt.; G; Yancey; 31 March 1833–1 March 1917; Phillips Cem., Yancey Co.
Bailey, Isaac Hutsel; Capt.; B; Mitchell; ca. 1841–2 Feb. 1926; Riverside Cem., Buncombe Co.
Bailey, James Bave; Pvt.; C; Yancey; ca. 1836–1860s
Bailey, James W.; ---; C; 1822–27 Nov. 1882; Old Bakersville Cem., Mitchell Co.
Bailey, Jefferson; Pvt.; B; Mitchell; b. ca. 1842; Yancey Co.
Bailey, Jesse; Pvt.; G/C; Yancey; 1834–1902; Bailey Hill Cem., Yancey Co.
Bailey, Jesse W.; Pvt.; C; Yancey; b. ca. 1845; Oklahoma
Bailey, John; Pvt.; G; Yancey; b. ca. 1836
Bailey, John Wesley; Pvt.; C; Yancey; 30 Oct. 1833–20 March 1914; Nebo Cem., McDowell Co.
Bailey, Neal; ---; H
Bailey, Thomas; Pvt.; B; Mitchell; b. ca. 1830; Yellow Jacket John Bailey Cem., Yancey Co.
Bailey, Thomas C.; Pvt.; B; d. 1 July 1863; McInturff Cem., Mitchell Co.
Bailey, Thomas L.; Pvt.; F; McDowell; b. ca. 1841
Bailey, Tom; ---; K
Bailey, William M.; Pvt.; C; Yancey; 18 Feb. 1831–5 Nov. 1904; Bailey Hill Cem., Yancey Co.
Bailey, Willis; Pvt.; G; Yancey; b. ca. 1843; Bailey Cem., Yancey Co.
Baily, Charles; Pvt.; A; Yancey; ca. 1843–prior to 1 March 1863
Baird, Abram; ---; D; ---; b. ca. 1830
Baird, Andrew Jackson; Pvt.; D; Watauga; ca. 1842–26 Jan. 1897; Baird Cem., Watauga Co.
Baird, Benjamin Franklin; Capt.; D/A; Watauga; 8 Jan. 1832–21 June 1901; Baird Cem., Watauga Co.
Baird, David Franklin; 2nd Lt.; D; Watauga; 11 June 1835–17 April 1919; Baird Cem., Watauga Co.
Baird, Finley P.; Pvt.; H; Caldwell; b. ca. 1813
Baird, John H.; Pvt.; D; Watauga; ca. 1833–prior 2 March 1863; Jacksboro, Tenn.
Baird, Joseph C.; Pvt. E; Caldwell; b. ca. 1830
Baird, Julius; Sgt.; E; Caldwell; ca. 1841–prior to 26 Sept. 1862
Baird, William; Pvt.; H; Caldwell; b. ca. 1827
Baird, William Carson; Pvt.; H; Caldwell; ca. 1841–23 May 1862
Baird, William Julius; Sgt.; E; Caldwell; 28 Feb. 1841–9 Nov. 1862; Baird Creek Cem., Caldwell Co.
Baker, Elijah W.; 1st Sgt.; B; b. ca. 1834
Baker, J. A.; Pvt.; K
Baker, John; Pvt.; F; Mitchell
Baker, Newton A.; Pvt.; B; Mitchell; 22 Sept. 1836–24 March 1863; Jacksboro, Tenn.
Baker, Robert Flournoy; Pvt.; B; 19 Jan. 1820–1912; Fitzhugh Fem., Collins Co., Texas
Baker, W. B.; ---; C
Baker, Wash; ---; B
Baker, William; Pvt.; A; Mitchell; b. ca. 1836
Baker, William R.; Pvt.; E; Caldwell; 1832–23 Dec. 1863 or Feb 6, 1864; Atlanta, Ga.
Ball, Alford T.; Sgt.; M/G; Wilkes/Watauga; d. 4 May 1864; Dalton, Ga.
Ballow, Thomas H.; Pvt.; C; Yancey; d. 21 Jan. 1863; Jacksboro, Tenn.
Banks, Joseph M.; Pvt.; G; Yancey; ca. 1839–7 Feb. 1863
Banks, William Burton; ---Pvt.; C; Yancey; b. 8 Feb. 1820; Banks Cem., Yancey Co.

Barber, Thomas M.; Pvt.; E; Caldwell/Mitchell; b. ca. 1839

Barger, Samuel; Pvt.; E; Burke

Barker, Calvin; Cpl.; L; Ashe; ca. 1841–11 April 1863; Clinton, Tenn.

Barker, Eli C.; Pvt.; L; Ashe; b. ca. 1823; Scott-Blevins Fam. Cem., Ashe Co.

Barker, James Monroe; Pvt.; L; Ashe; 28 Aug. 1842–4 Feb. 1924; James M. Barker Fam. Cem., Ashe Co.

Barker, M.; ---; F

Barker, Montgomery; Pvt.; L; Ashe; b. ca. 1838

Barker, Thomas C.; Pvt.; L; Ashe; b. ca. 1837

Barker, William Poindexter; Pvt.; L; Ashe; 17 Dec. 1844–6 May 1932; Grassy Creek Com. Cem., Ashe Co.

Barlow, Hamilton; Pvt.; H; Caldwell; 25 July 1821–13 Nov. 1882; Caldwell Co.

Barlow, Smith; Pvt.; E; Caldwell; June 1844–10 Feb. 1912; Lower Creek Cem., Caldwell Co.

Barnes, John G.; Pvt.; I; Alexander/Watauga; ca. 1829–5 May 1864; Dalton, Ga.

Barnes, Solomon; Pvt.; I; Alexander/Camp Holmes; ca. 1820–6 July 1864; Nashville, Tenn.

Barnett, Simon; Pvt.; B; Mitchell; b. ca. 1830

Barnett, Thomas H.; Pvt.; E; Caldwell; 8 Dec. 1845–23 April 1921; Barnett Cem., Caldwell Co.

Barrier, Samuel; Pvt.; E; Caldwell; 1831–13 Sept. 1906; Jonas Ridge Cem., Burke Co.

Bartlett, Joseph Henry; Pvt.; B/K; Mitchell; ca. 1842–29 Sept. 1863; Chickamauga, Ga.

Bartlett, Samuel D.; Pvt.; B/E/K; Mitchell; ca. 1840–4 July 1864; Mitchell Co.

Baugus, Richard; Pvt.; G; Camp Holmes

Beach, John W.; Pvt.; D; Watauga; b. ca. 1844

Beam, John; Pvt.; B; Dalton, Ga.; d. 14 April 1864; Dalton, Ga.

Bean, Henry Newton; Pvt.; H; Caldwell; May 1831–29 March 1918; Bean's Cem., Caldwell Co.

Bean, John; Pvt.; H; Caldwell; ca. 1845–prior to 1 Jan. 1865

Bean, Largent; Pvt.; H; Caldwell; 10 March 1835–10 April 1919

Bean, Mathias; Pvt.; H; Caldwell; 4 May 1826–26 March 1914

Bean, Thomas; Pvt.; H; Caldwell; 12 Nov. 1843–13 Sept. 1929; Belleview Cem., Caldwell Co.

Bearden, Marcus J.; As. Quar.; F&S; b. ca. 1831

Beaver, Charles R.; Pvt.; C; ---; Feb. 1842–prior to 23 March 1865; Greenwood Cem., Barnesville, Ga.

Beaver, George L.; Pvt.; G; Yancey; ca. 1843–9 March 1919; Wake Co.[1]

Beaver, J. T.; ---; C

Beaver, William H.; Pvt.; D/C; Yancey; 12 June 1835–ca. 1910; Sullivan Co., Tenn.

Belton, Pleasant H.; Pvt.; E; Rockingham

Benfield, Adolphus L.; Pvt.; A/K; Burke; 1832–16 Nov. 1913; Patton Simmons Cem., Carter Co., Tenn.

Benfield, Alfred; Pvt.; F; McDowell; b. ca. 1831

Benfield, Byard Henry; Pvt.; A; Mitchell; 22 Jan. 1837–13 Aug. 1909; Daniels Cem., Avery Co.

Benfield, Harrison; Pvt.; F; McDowell; b. ca. 1841 ---[2]

Benfield, John Jackson; Pvt.; F; McDowell; 18 June 1830–25 Jan. 1906

Benfield, W. A.; Pvt.; F[3]

Benfield, W. John; Pvt.; F; McDowell; b. ca. 1830

Benfield, Weightstill Alexander; Pvt.; F; McDowell; 6 Aug. 1842–29 Dec. 1921; Burke Co.

Benfield, William Harrison; Pvt.; F; Burke; 25 Jan. 1841–30 Oct. 1912; North Catawba Bapt. Ch. Cem., Burke Co.

Bennet, Jason; Pvt.; G; Yancey

Bennett, Archibald; Pvt.; B; Mitchell; ca. 1833–23 April 1916; Haun Cem., Unicoi Co., Tenn.

Bennett, Gaines; Pvt.; G; Yancey; d. 9 April 1863; Clinton, Tenn.

Bennett, Guilder; Pvt.; G; Yancey; b. ca. 1831

Bennett, Jeremiah; Pvt.; G; Yancey; b. ca. 1841; Huntdale Cem., Mitchell Co.

Bennett, John; Pvt.; B; Mitchell; b. ca. 1841

Bennett, John; Pvt. G; Yancey; ca. 1836–20 April 1865; Yancey Co.

Bennett, Samuel M.; ---; K; 4 May 1850–9 March 1951; Mitchell Co.

Bennett, Uriah; Pvt.; G; Yancey; 10 May 1829–1 July 1909

Bennett, William J.; Pvt.; G; ca. 1835–1 June 1924; Mitchell Co.

Bentley, James; Pvt.; I; Alexander/Camp Holmes; b. ca. 1830

Bentley, William; ---; I; Alexander/Camp Holmes; b. ca. 1814

Berleson, William P.; Pvt.; C

Berry, Pinkney; Pvt.; F; McDowell; b. ca. 1844

Bevill, George; Pvt.; F; Yadkin; b. ca. 1831

Biddix, Charles; ---; A

Biddix, Francis A.; Pvt.; A; Mitchell; b. ca. 1815

Biddix, James A.; Pvt.; A; ---; d. 8 June 1865; Hart's Island, N.Y.

Bingham, William G.; 1st Sgt.; I; Watauga; 20 Oct. 1834–24 Nov. 1872; Cove Creek Cem., Watauga Co.

Bishop, Elbert; Pvt.; D; Watauga; b. ca. 1833

Bishop, Samuel J.; 1st Sgt.; M/G; Watauga; 18 Sept. 1839–27 Jan. 1933; Fairview Cem., Watauga Co.

Bishop, William P.; Pvt.; H; Polk; b. ca. 1841

Black, Jesse; Pvt.; L; Camp Holmes; d. 10 May 1864; Mecklenburg Co.

Blackburn, Edmond; Pvt.; M/G; Watauga; 3 July 1825–1906; Blackburn Cem., Watauga Co.[4]

Blackburn, John L.; Pvt.; I; Watauga; 3 May 1831–13 Feb. 1916; Ashe Co.

Blair, E. C.; Wagon Mast.; F&S
Blair, John Caldwell; Drum Maj.; E/F&S; Caldwell; 20 Feb. 1840–12 Feb. 1886; Montgomery, Newland, and Bell Cem., Alexander Co.
Blalock, John; Pvt.; B; Dalton, Ga.
Blalock, Samuel Woodfin; Cpl.; A; 20 March 1845–24 Dec. 1917; Academy Hill Cem., Yancey Co.
Blanchard, T. C.; Pvt.; E; Buncombe Co.
Blankenship, Govan M.; Pvt.; G; Yancey; 6 April 1837–24 March 1898; Govan Blankenship Cem., Yancey Co.
Blaylock, Albert N.; Pvt.; G/K; Johnson's Depot
Bledsoe, J. Macon; Pvt.; F; Camp Stokes, Tenn.
Blevins, Edward; 3rd Lt.; L; Ashe; ca. 1819–11 March 1884
Blevins, George Douglas; Pvt.; L; Ashe/Saltville; 21 Oct. 1844–2 April 1918; Testerman Fam. Cem., Ashe Co.
Blevins, George W.; Pvt.; L; Ashe; d. 1 Feb. 1915; Watauga Co.
Blevins, John; Pvt.; L; Ashe; b. ca. 1835
Blevins, Morris; Pvt.; L; Ashe/Dalton, Ga.; b. ca. 1825
Blevins, Poindexter; Capt.; L/F; Ashe; 2 May 1836–2 Feb. 1922; Baptist Chapel Church Cem., Ashe Co.
Blevins, William Harrison; Sgt.; L
Bolick, Jacob Anthony; Pvt.; H; Caldwell; 6 May 1845–29 Nov. 1925; Bolick Cem., Caldwell Co.
Bolick, Joseph B.; Pvt.; A/K; Burke; 5 Sep. 1837–28 Aug. 1922; Fairview Cem., Yancey Co.
Bolick, Rufus; Pvt.; E; Caldwell; b. ca. 1843; Caldwell Co.[5]
Boon, Berton; Pvt.; C; Yancey; b. ca. 1843
Boon, James; Pvt.; A
Boone, William R.; Pvt.; A; Mitchell; b. ca. 1837
Bowling, Joel; Pvt.; F; Guilford
Bowman, Ambrose; Pvt.; A; Mitchell; b. ca. 1836
Bowman, Jacob Weaver; Capt.; B; Mitchell; 31 July 1831–8 June 1905; old Bakersville Cemetery; Mitchell Co.
Brackens, John; Pvt.; B; b. ca. 1838
Bradley, James; Pvt.; F; McDowell; b. ca. 1838
Bradshaw, Elijah E.; Cpl.; H; Caldwell; b. ca. 1824; Bradshaw Cem., Caldwell Co.
Bradshaw, William; Pvt.; H; Caldwell; ca. 1839–1863; Chickamauga, Tenn.
Bradshaw, William F.; Pvt.; B; Mitchell; ca. 1844–20 Sept. 1863
Branch, Ephraim; Pvt.; E
Branch, S. C.; Pvt.; F; Camp Stokes, Tenn.
Branch, Sidney E.; Pvt.; F; McDowell; ca. 1840–13 July 1864
Brand, John; Pvt.; E; Forsyth; ca. 1824–29 July 1864; Knoxville, Tenn.
Braswell, Thaddeus; ---; E; Burke; 19 Jan. 1838–6 Aug. 1923; Avery Co.
Brendle, Logan G.; Pvt.; F; Forsyth

Brewer, John A.; Pvt.; G; Wilkes/Camp Holmes; b. ca. 1833
Brewer, Riley; Pvt.; D; Watauga; b. ca. 1829
Briggs, Alson; Pvt.; C; Yancey; 16 July 1834–20 Jan. 1896; Briggs Cem., Yancey Co.
Briggs, Harvey J.; Pvt.; C; ca. 1830–29 Sept. 1862; Big Springs, Tenn.
Briggs, Jackson; Pvt.; C; Yancey; b. ca. 1830; Zion Church Cem., Yancey Co.
Briggs, John E.; Pvt.; A; Yancey; ca. 1835–16 March 1865; Chicago City Cem.
Briggs, Melvin W.; 3rd Lt.; C; 1838–6 Jan. 1921; Briggs Cem., Yancey Co.
Briggs, Suel Brown; Capt.; C/B; Yancey; 1836–1900; Briggs Cem., Yancey Co.
Bright, Alnay; Pvt.; F; McDowell; ca. 1834–16 Sept. 1864; Macon, Ga.
Bright, Davis; Pvt.; F; Camp Vance; ca. 1822–20 Nov. 1863; Confederate Cem., Dalton, Ga.
Bright, Merritt; Pvt.; F; McDowell; b. ca. 1834; Sugar Hill Bapt. Ch., McDowell Co.
Brinkley, Alexander; Pvt.; A; Mitchell; 6 Jan. 1815–26 Sept. 1898; Bear Creek Cem., Mitchell Co.
Bristow, Samuel; Pvt.; E; Randolph; 1 April 1823–3 March 1900; Cedar Falls, Randolph Co.
Brooks, Alfred; Pvt.; B/D; Mitchell; b. ca. 1841
Brooks, J. A.; Pvt.; H; Buncombe
Brooks, John; Pvt.; B; b. ca. 1819; Fishery Union Ch. Cem., Unicoi Co., Tenn.
Brooks, Martin; Pvt.; B/E; Mitchell; b. ca. 1840
Brooks, Stephen; 2nd Lt.; C; Cooke Co., Tenn.
Brookshire, Benjamin Franklin; Pvt.; L; Wilkes/Tazewell, Tenn.; 18 Sept. 1830–02 March 1907; Bethel Bapt. Ch. Cem., Buncombe Co.
Brookshire, Thomas Patterson; Cpl.; H; Buncombe; 27 July 1839–5 May 1915; Bethel Bapt. Ch. Cem., Buncombe Co.
Browes, James W.; Pvt.; F
Brown, Alfred; Pvt.; I; Watauga; ca. 1835–17 April 1863; Clinton, Tenn./Jont. Brown Cem., Watauga Co.
Brown, Asa; Pvt.; I; Watauga; 29 Oct. 1837–29 Jan. 1921; Brown Fam. Cem., Ashe Co.
Brown, Elisha; Pvt.; H; Caldwell; ca. 1836–9 Nov. 1862; Jacksboro, Tenn.
Brown, George W.; Pvt.; F; Macon
Brown, John J.; Pvt.; L; Ashe; 24 June 1826–20 Jan. 1893; John Brown Cem., Ashe Co.
Brown, John Wesley; Cpl.; I; Watauga; 28 April 1842–22 Sept. 1917; Critcher Cem., Watauga Co.
Brown, Julius A.; Pvt.; H; Caldwell; b. ca. 1846
Brown, Richard E.; Pvt.; I; Watauga; b. ca. 1843
Brown, Romulus W.; Pvt.; A; Burke; 10 June 1843–20 July 1905; Brown Cem., McDowell Co.
Brown, William L.; Pvt.; I; Watauga; d. 18 March 1863; Jacksboro, Tenn.
Broyles, H.S.; ---; Misc.; Huntsville, Ala.; b. 25 June 1847; Knox County, Tenn.

Bryan, John Gibson; Cpl.; I; Watauga; 1 March 1833–17 Feb. 1914
Bryant, Bethel Allen; Pvt.; G/B; Yancey; b. 1835; Beans Creek Cem., Mitchell Co.
Bryant, John H.; Pvt.; H; Caldwell
Bryant, John Wesley; Pvt.; G; Yancey; 1 July 1841–24 April 1913; Bryant-Hampton Cemetery, Yancey Co.
Bryant, Peter; Pvt.; H; Caldwell; b. ca. 1838
Bryant, Robert M.; Pvt.; H; Caldwell; b. ca. 1846
Bryant, Thomas; Pvt.; C/D; Yancey; 1829–1865; Witson Cem., Yancey Co.
Bryant, Tilman L.; Pvt.; H; Caldwell; 1841–19 March 1927; County Home Cem., Caldwell Co.
Bryant, William; Pvt.; C; Yancey; b. ca. 1838
Buchanan, Abram Johnson; Pvt.; B/E/K; Mitchell; ca. 1838–ca. 1884; Bean's Creek Bapt. Ch. Cem., Mitchell Co.
Buchanan, Adam; Pvt.; B; Camp Jackson; 24 Jan. 1834–12 Feb. 1910; Green Young Cem. Mitchell Co.
Buchanan, Alexander; Pvt.; B; Mitchell; b. ca. 1836
Buchanan, Allen; Pvt.; A; Mitchell; b. ca. 1826
Buchanan, Arter T.; Pvt.; C; Yancey; 25 Feb. 1823–28 June 1917; Snow Creek, Mitchell Co.
Buchanan, Eli; Pvt.; E/K; Mitchell; ca. 1824–1 Jan. 1864; Atlanta, Ga.
Buchanan, Ephraim; Pvt.; E/K; Mitchell; b. ca. 1844
Buchanan, Greenbury Young; Sgt.; B; Mitchell; 8 Oct. 1845–21 Jan. 1925; Grandview Cem., Maryville, Tenn.
Buchanan, James C.; Pvt.; C/E; Yancey; 3 Dec. 1844–8 Nov. 1919; Liberty Hill Bapt. Ch. Cem., Mitchell Co.
Buchanan, James G.; Pvt.; B; Big Creek Gap; Buchanan Cem., Mitchell Co.
Buchanan, James S.; ---; B
Buchanan, James S.; Pvt.; E/K; Mitchell; 6 March 1835–16 Dec. 1911; Buchanan Cem.
Buchanan, James W.; Pvt.; B; Clinton, Tenn.; 11 March 1827–19 April 1916; Buchanan Cem., Mitchell Co.
Buchanan, Jasper N.; Pvt.; B; Mitchell; b. ca. 1843
Buchanan, Joel; Pvt.; E/K; Mitchell; ca. 1834–Oct. 15 or Nov. 6, 1863; Atlanta, Ga.
Buchanan, John B.; Pvt.; E/K; Mitchell; ca. 1829–prior to 1 March 1864
Buchanan, Joseph M.; Pvt.; E/K; Mitchell; b. ca. 1842
Buchanan, Leonard M.; 2nd Lt.; B/E/K; Mitchell; 24 Oct. 1809–15 June 1881; Avery Co.
Buchanan, Marion; Pvt.; B/E; Mitchell; 6 Oct. 1832–28 Nov. 1909; Buchanan Cem., Avery Co.
Buchanan, Merritt; Pvt.; E/K; Mitchell; b. ca. 1829
Buchanan, Molton; Pvt.; B/E/K; Mitchell; 28 Nov. 1848–30 July 1897; Pannell Cem., Mitchell Co.
Buchanan, Newton; Pvt.; E/B; Camp Jackson; 26 July 1842–27 Dec. 1926; Pleasant Gardens Bapt. Ch., McDowell Co.
Buchanan, Reuben; ---; K; ---; 1847–1910; Robinson Cem., Mitchell Co.
Buchanan, Robert; Pvt.; E/K; Mitchell; ca. 1835–ca. 1870
Buchanan, Thomas; ---; E; Mitchell
Buchanan, Thomas; Pvt.; B; Mitchell; 1819–1900
Buchanan, Waightsville; Pvt.; B/E/K; Mitchell; ca. 1835–1 March 1863
Buchanan, William Arthur; Pvt.; B; Camp Reynolds; 23 Feb. 1823–7 April 1917; Grindstaff Cem., Graham Co.
Buchanan, William Marion; Pvt.; E/K; Mitchell; 6 Oct. 1832–28 Nov. 1909; Buchanan/Hicks Cem., Avery Co.
Buchanan, William W.; Pvt.; E/K; Mitchell; b. ca. 1833
Buchanan, William W.; Pvt.; K; Mitchell; b. ca. 1823
Buckner, Nimrod; Pvt.; E; Buncombe Co.; b. 14 Feb. 1840
Bumgarner, George W.; Pvt.; H; Caldwell; b. 14 Oct. 1863
Bumgarner, George W.; Pvt.; L; Ashe; b. ca. 1833
Bumgarner, William P.; Musc.; H; Caldwell; ca. 1838–21 July 1923; Centre Grove Cem., Caldwell Co.
Burchfield, John; Pvt.; K; Clinton, Tenn.
Burchfield, Nathan; Pvt.; B; Mitchell; b. ca. 1842
Burchfield, Wilson; Pvt.; B; Mitchell; b. ca. 1840
Burchfield, Thomas; Pvt.; B; Mitchell; b. ca. 1837; Mitchell Co.
Burgin, Charles; Pvt.; F; McDowell; ca. 1844–ca. 1864[6]
Burleson, Aaron; ---; K; ---; 25 Jan. 1838–9 Sept. 1921; Minn. Comm. Cem., Avery Co.
Burleson, Jason C.; Pvt.; E; Mitchell; ca. 1836–5 Feb. 1863; Jacksboro, Tenn.
Burleson, Meredith; Pvt.; K; Mitchell; ca. 1834–1886
Burleson, Reuben P.; Pvt.; B; Mitchell; 30 July 1841–1883; Burleson Cem., Mitchell Co.
Burleson, William P.; ---; Misc.; ca. 1844–15 Sept. 1862; Cumberland Gap, Tenn.
Burleson, Wilson M.; Pvt.; B; Mitchell; 7 Feb. 1833–3 July 1872; Burleson Cem., Mitchell Co.
Burlison, Joseph M.; Pvt.; B/A; Camp Jackson; 1843–1917
Burlison, William, Jr.; Pvt.; A; Yancey; b. ca. 1844
Burlison, William A.; Pvt.; A; Mitchell; 1834–1888
Burlison, William A.; Cpl.; I
Burnett, Daniel; Pvt.; K/C; Buncombe Co.; b. ca. 1838
Butler, Allen; Pvt.; B; Camp Jackson
Byers, William R.; Pvt.; G; Rutherford/Camp Holmes; ca. 1841–prior to 1 Sept. 1864
Byrd, Carson; Pvt.; B/E; Mitchell; 3 May 1842–12 May 1928; Watauga Co.

Byrd, Charles; Pvt.; G; Yancey; b. ca. 1839
Byrd, Charles; ---; K
Byrd, Charles, Jr.; ---; H
Byrd, Cornelius R.; 3rd Lt.; G; Yancey; ca. 1842–2 Nov. 1863; Kingston, Ga.[7]
Byrd, Joseph Y.; Cpl.; G; Yancey; ca. 1844–prior to 1 July 1863
Byrd, Mitchell Taylor; Pvt.; B; Mitchell; 13 Aug. 1846–4 July 1923; Byrd Cem., Yancey Co.
Byrd, Moses Jefferson; Pvt.; G; Yancey; 15 Nov. 1848–26 Sept. 1941; Ark.
Byrd, William D.; Pvt.; C; Yancey; b. ca. 1843; George Byrd Cem., Yancey Co.
Byrd, William J. C.; Pvt.; G; Yancey; b. ca. 1841
Byrd, William P.; Pvt.; B; Mitchell; b. ca. 1836
Calaway, William Henderson; Pvt.; D; Watauga; b. 27 Aug. 1845
Calhoun, Barnabas Bass; Pvt.; L; Ashe; 13 April 1834–12 Dec. 1930; Fork Mountain Cem., Avery Co.
Calhoun, James; Pvt.; L; Ashe; 1833–1926; Calhoun Cem., Carter Co., Tenn.
Calloway, Benjamin; Pvt.; A; Mitchell; b. ca. 1840
Calloway, Elijah; Pvt.; M/G; Ashe/Watauga
Calloway, Jacob A.; Cpl.; L/F; Ashe; 9 March 1843–19 Nov. 1928; Jefferson Mun. Cem., Ashe Co.
Calloway, James; Pvt.; M/G; Ashe
Calloway, James M.; Sgt.; L; Ashe; d. 5 June 1864; Atlanta, Ga.
Calloway, James N.; Pvt.; L; Dalton, Ga.; ca. 1844–after 1930; Jefferson Mun. Cem., Ashe Co.
Calloway, Marshall; Pvt.; M/G; Ashe; 19 Aug. 1827–3 Feb. 1906; Marshall Calloway Fam. Cem., Ashe Co.
Calloway, Miles B.; Pvt.; L; Ashe; b. ca. 1842
Calloway, William; Pvt.; M/G; Ashe/Watauga
Cameron, George; Pvt.; E; Burke; d. 10 Jan. 1864; Marietta, Ga.
Campbell, Mabin; ---; G
Campbell, Rufus; Sgt.; I; Watauga; 17 Nov. 1844–27 April 1921; Union Cem., Watauga Co.
Canipe, William; Pvt.; B; Camp Jackson; 1837–13 Jan. 1923; Mitchell Co.
Cannon, George; Pvt.; F; McDowell; b. ca. 1833
Cannon, Robert M.; Cpl.; F; Big Gap Greek, Tenn.; b. ca. 1839
Cannon, Stephen; Pvt.; C/G; Yancey; ca. 1841–28 Jan. 1926; Yancey Co.
Cannon, Wesley W.; Pvt.; H; Caldwell; 24 Sept. 1830–14 March 1911; Littlejohn UMC., Caldwell Co.
Cantrell, Thomas; ---; Misc.
Caraway, Elisha; Pvt.; A; Mitchell; b. 1839
Caraway, William H.; Pvt.; G; Yancey; b. 1837
Carlton, Cornelius M.; Musc.; I; Watauga; b. ca. 1844
Carlyle, James H.; Pvt.; H; Polk; ca. 1844–1911
Carpenter, Alexander L.; Pvt.; A; Mitchell; 5 Nov. 1834–9 Dec. 1906; Pisgah Meth. Ch. Cem., Avery Co.
Carpenter, Alfred Andrew; Pvt.; A; Mitchell; 31 Oct. 1838–25 Feb. 1925; Carpenter Cem., Avery Co.
Carpenter, David L.; Pvt.; A; Yancey; ca. 1840–12 Oct. 1864; Point Lookout, Md.
Carpenter, Erwin L.; Pvt.; A; Mitchell; b. ca. 1844
Carpenter, Jacob; Pvt.; A; Mitchell; 4 Jan. 1833–10 March 1920
Carpenter, James A.; Pvt.; A; Mitchell; ca. 1841–prior to 14 July 1863
Carpenter, Jonathan Nell M.; Pvt.; A; Yancey; b. ca. 1843
Carpenter, Joseph; Pvt.; A; Mitchell
Carpenter, Reuben H.; Pvt.; A; Yancey; 15 Oct. 1842–7 Feb. 1898; Pisgah UMC, Avery Co.
Carpenter, William; Pvt.; A; Dalton, Ga.
Carpenter, William N.; Pvt.; A; Mitchell; 12 Aug. 1837–12 May 1899; Pisgah UMC, Avery Co.
Carrell, William G.; Cpl.; E; Caldwell; b. ca. 1843
Carroll, James; Pvt.; C; Yancey; b. ca. 1833; Pisgah UMC, Avery Co.
Carroll, James M.; Pvt.; E; Mitchell; Caldwell/Burke; b. ca. 1839; Pisgah UMC, Avery Co.
Carroll, John P.; Pvt.; E; Caldwell; ca. 1834–9 Aug. 1864; Atlanta, Ga.
Cartwell, John; ---
Carver, William; Pvt.; A; Mitchell; b. ca. 1843
Casner, Levi; Pvt.; G; Camp Holmes; d. 11 April 1864; Rock Island, Ill.
Cauble, Daniel Webster; Pvt.; C; Buncombe; 1 Jan. 1843–8 June 1921; Riverside Cem., Buncombe Co.
Caudill, James F.; Pvt.: G; Camp Holmes; ca. 1845–17 Dec. 1920; Mecklenburg Co.
Cearly, William; Pvt.; I; Camp Holmes
Chambers, F. M.; Pvt.; L; Dalton, Ga.
Chandler, David A.; 1st Lt.; A/K; Mitchell; ca. 1834–31 March 1863; Jacksboro, Tenn.
Chapman, Nathan; Pvt.; A; Mitchell; ca. 1841–29 March 1863
Chebbs, Joseph R.; Pvt.; E; Caldwell
Childs, John Eben; Pvt.; H; Mitchell; ca. 1844–20 Sept. 1863; Columbia, SC[8]
Church, Eli M.; Pvt.; I; Watauga; 1838–1930; Watauga Co.
Church, Jordan; Pvt.; M/G; Watauga; b. ca. 1837
Church, Marion; Pvt.; M/G; Watauga; ca. 1832–8 Sept. 1863
Clark, Cornelius Washington; Pvt.; E; Caldwell; b. ca. 1838
Clark, Deaston C.; Pvt.; A/E/K; Caldwell; ca. 1842–23 Sept. 1863; Chickamauga, Ga.
Clark, Doran F.; Pvt.; A; Caldwell; b. ca. 1842
Clark, James Wilburn; Pvt.; D; Watauga; 23 Nov. 1824–4 July 1890; Carter Co., Tenn.
Clark, John Wesley; Pvt.; D; Watauga; 14 Dec. 1828–23 June 1907; Whitman Co., Wash.

Clark, Robert P.; Pvt.; D; Watauga; ca. 1846– prior to 1875
Clarke, Andrew; ---; A
Clarke, Thomas A.; Pvt.; E; Caldwell; 10 Oct. 1843–28 April 1911; Forest Hills Cem., Burke Co.
Clay, Andrew; Pvt.; H; Caldwell; ca. 1820–9 Nov. 1863; Atlanta, Ga.
Clayton, Edwin M.; Capt.; C; Buncombe; b. Feb. 1837
Clayton, Robert Morris; 1st Lt.; E; Buncombe; 31 March 1845–4 July 1931
Cloer, Caney W.; Pvt.; K; Caldwell; b. ca. 1838
Clontz, R. Nelson; ---; Misc.
Cloud, Terrell C.; Pvt.; A; Mitchell; ca. 1842–12 Feb. 1916; Burke Co.
Cobb, Newton; Pvt.; H; Caldwell; b. ca. 1843; Ebenezer Meth. Ch., Caldwell Co.
Coche, John W.; Pvt.
Coffee, Thomas; Pvt.; K; Caldwell; b. ca. 1835
Coffey, Armstead N.; Pvt.; H; Caldwell; b. ca. 1843
Coffey, Barlett; Pvt.; E; Caldwell; Feb. 1842–10 Oct. 1912; Harper Chapel UMC, Caldwell Co.
Coffey, Charles L.; Pvt.; E; Caldwell; 1830–23 Dec. 1916; Caldwell Co.
Coffey, Drury Dobbins; Sgt. Maj.; E/F&S; Caldwell; 23 April 1838–16 Aug. 1913
Coffey, Edmond; Pvt.; E; Caldwell
Coffey, Elbert; Pvt.; E; Caldwell; ca. 1837–15 May 1863; Big Gap Creek, Tenn.
Coffey, Elijah; Pvt.; E; Caldwell; 20 Aug. 1838–6 Oct. 1891; Harper's Chapel, Caldwell Co.
Coffey, Harvey N.; ---; E; Mitchell; b. ca. 1838
Coffey, Irvin; Pvt.; H; Caldwell; b. ca. 1842
Coffey, Israel B.; Pvt.; E; Caldwell; 19 April 1845–10 July 1902
Coffey, J. B.; Pvt.; E
Coffey, J. H.; Pvt.; E
Coffey, J. P.; ---; E; Caldwell; 6 Nov. 1845–2 May 1924; Reformed Church Cem., Watauga Co.
Coffey, Jesse F.; Pvt.; E; Caldwell; ca. 1842–7 March 1863; Big Gap Creek, Tenn.
Coffey, John; Pvt.; E; Caldwell; 29 July 1844–5 June 1923; Mt. Pleasant UMC, Burke Co.
Coffey, John Bunyon; Pvt.; E; Caldwell; b. 1839; McMinn Co., Tenn.
Coffey, Larkin; Pvt.; E; Caldwell; ca. 1834–1862; Cumberland Gap, Tenn.
Coffey, Levi L.; Pvt.; D; Watauga; 30 May 1833–11 Feb. 1925; Coffey Cem., Watauga Co.
Coffey, Patterson Vance; Pvt.; E; Caldwell; 19 Sept. 1845–2 March 1911; Drain, Ore.
Coffey, Shuford; Pvt.; E; Caldwell; b. ca. 1837
Coffey, Silas C.; 1st Sgt.; E; Caldwell; ca. 1835–July 1898
Coffey, Thomas Jefferson; As. Quar.; F&S; Caldwell; December 1828–11 June 1901; Watauga Co.
Coffey, William C.; Pvt.; E; Caldwell; 1838–27 Jan. 1919; Watauga Co.
Coffey, William Columbus; QSgt.; F&S/A/E; Caldwell; 3 April 1839–10 March 1920; Boone City Cem., Watauga Co.
Coffey, William Elbert; 3rd Lt.; E; Caldwell; July 1839–16 Feb. 1912; Forest Hills Cem., Burke Co.
Cogdill, Fidella P.; Pvt.; E
Coggins, James; Pvt.; F
Cole, David Flemming; Pvt.; L; Ashe; 6 March 1840–24 March 1925; Ashe Co.
Cole, James; Pvt.; L; Ashe; ca. 1834–20 Sept. 1863; Chickamauga, Ga.
Cole, Joseph; Pvt.; L; Ashe; ca. 1837–28 Feb. 1864; Rock Island, Ill.
Cole, Lorenzo D.; Pvt.; L; Ashe; 24 March 1843–16 Feb. 1914; Meat Camp, Watauga Co.
Cole, Wilborn; Pvt.; L; Ashe; 20 April 1831–22 Jan. 1917; Mt. Zion UMC, Alleghany Co.
Coleman, Richard A.; Pvt.; H; Caldwell; 14 Aug. 1843–24 Oct. 1913; Burke Co.
Coleman, Thaddeus Charles; Lt. Col.; F&S; Buncombe Co.; 16 Jan. 1837–21 Jan. 1896; Buncombe
Collett, Orlando Columbus; Sgt.; E/A; Caldwell; 31 Aug. 1837–15 Jan. 1920; Roaring Springs Cem., Motley Co., Texas
Collett, Waightstill Avery; Surg.; F&S; 28 Jan. 1830–9 July 1880
Combs, Meredith; Pvt.; L; Ashe; 1844–25 Feb. 1927; Comers Creek Cem., Grayson Co., Va.
Conley, Alfred L.; Pvt.; F; McDowell; ca. 1829– prior 9 May 1863; Cumberland Gap, Tenn.
Conley, Caleb O.; Capt.; F; McDowell; ca. 1833–22 June 1864; Kolb's Farm, Ga.
Conley, James; QSgt.; F&S
Conley, James; Pvt.; A; Rochester, NY; b. ca. 1838
Conley, James C.; 1st Lt.; B/D; Lincoln; b. ca. 1838
Conley, Jason; Capt.; F; McDowell; ca. 1832–31 Oct. 1862; Big Gap Creek, Tenn.
Conley, John F.; Pvt.; F; McDowell; b. ca. 1830
Conley, Julius G.; Pvt.; F; Camp Reynolds; ca. 1840–19 Aug. 1864; Camp Douglas, Ill.
Cook, A.; Pvt.; E
Cook, Calvin Harrison; Cpl.; A; Mitchell; b. ca. 1840
Cook, Isaac; Pvt.; A; Mitchell; b. ca. 1834
Cook, John; Pvt.; M; Watauga; 23 Oct. 1828–15 Sept. 1917; Cook Cem., Watauga Co.
Cook, John A.; Pvt.; D; Watauga
Cook, John Butler; ---; G; ---; 23 Oct. 1827–1916; Cook Cem., Watauga Co.
Cook, John Massey; Pvt.; A; Yancey; 8 Dec. 1842–16 Sep. 1918; Pineola Cem., Avery Co.
Cook, Johnson; Pvt.; G; Watauga
Cook, Lewis D.; Pvt.; A; Yancey; b. ca. 1841
Cook, Thomas; Pvt.; A; Mitchell; ca. 1828–27 Jan. 1864; Atlanta, Ga.
Cook, William; Pvt.; E
Cook, William S.; Pvt.; I; Watauga; 29 April 1843–16 March 1926; Cook Cem., Caldwell Co.

Coombs, Calvin; Pvt.; G; Wilkes
Cooper, James M.; Pvt.; I; Watauga
Cooper, John; Pvt.; G; Yancey
Corn, N.P.M.; ---; Misc.
Cornell, Alfred; Pvt.; D; Watauga; b. ca. 1840
Cornell, Benjamin; Pvt.; D; Watauga; b. ca. 1842
Cornell, John; Pvt.; D; Watauga; ca. 1839–20 June 1864; Rock Island, Ill.
Cornell, Joseph; Pvt.; D; Watauga; ca. 1845–5 May 1900; Danner Cem., Watauga Co.
Cornett, Isaac; Pvt.; I; Watauga; 28 May 1839–11 March 1913; Avery Co.
Cornett, John C.; Pvt.; I; Watauga; b. 22 Sept. 1835
Cornutt, William A.; Pvt.; L; Ashe; 14 June 1833–after 27 June 1864
Cosby, Joseph; Pvt.; F; McDowell; b. ca. 1836
Cottrell, Calvin J.; Sgt.; I; Watauga; 13 May 1843–8 July 1923; Boone City Cem., Watauga Co.
Councill, John H.; Pvt.; I; Ashe; ca. 1837–18 Oct. 1862; Lee Co., VA
Cox, Braxton; Pvt.; D; Watauga; ca. 1843–1919; Higginsville, Mo.
Cox, John; Pvt.; K; Mitchell; b. ca. 1843; Cox Cem., Yancey Co.
Cox, Nathan; Pvt.; L; Ashe
Cox, William R. Pvt.; D/K/G; 31 Jan. 1846–26 July 1865; North Catawba Cem., McDowell Co.
Craig, Alfred Holland; Pvt.; H; Caldwell; 25 Dec. 1840–30 May 1920; Smith/Grove Cem., Caldwell Co.
Craig, J. R.; Pvt.; H
Craige, A. Coleman; Sgt.; H; Caldwell; 31 Jan. 1839–5 March 1919; Craig Cem., Caldwell Co.
Craige, Alfred Harrison; Pvt.; H; Caldwell
Craige, Johnson Lafayette; Pvt.; H; Caldwell; 1841–2 Dec. 1864; Camp Douglas, Ill.
Craige, Sidney Isaac; Sgt.; H; Caldwell; b. 1834
Craunch, Samuel; ---; F
Crawford, Henry T.; Pvt.; C; Yancey
Crawford, James M.; Pvt.; C; Yancey; ca. 1838–21 Jan. 1863; Jacksboro, Tenn.
Crawley, Albert E.; Sgt.; F; McDowell
Crawley, Ambrose E.; Pvt.; F; McDowell; 25 Sep. 1827–28 April 1901; Pinnacle UMC, McDowell Co.
Creasmon, Berry C.; Pvt.; C/D; Yancey; b. ca. 1828; Collegeville Cem., Saline Co., Ark.
Crisenbury, James M.; Pvt.; D; Watauga
Crisp, Hiram H.; Pvt.; H; Caldwell; ca. 1846–20 Sept. 1863; Confederate Cem., Marietta, Ga.
Crisp, J. P.; Pvt.; H
Crisp, John; ---; E; Mitchell; b. ca. 1831
Crisp, William L.; Cpl.; H; Caldwell; b. ca. 1827
Crowder, Isaac T.; Pvt.; G; Yancey
Crump, Elijah H.; 1st Sgt.; H; Caldwell; ca. 1838–28 Dec. 1909
Curlee, John W.; Pvt.; E; Union; b. ca. 1826
Curtis, Merrit B.; Pvt.; F; McDowell; 1826–20 Oct. 1862; Cumberland Gap, Tenn.
Curtis, Stanford; Pvt.; F; McDowell; b. 1836
Curtis, William Walter; Pvt.; E; Caldwell; 10 Nov. 1833–6 Dec. 1907; Curtis Family Cem., Caldwell Co.
Cuthbertson, David H.; Pvt.; A; Mitchell; ca. 1832–prior to 1 March 1864
Cuthbertson, Nathan M.; Pvt.; A; McDowell; b. ca. 1835
Cuthbertson, Samuel T.; Pvt.; A; Mitchell; ca. 1829–ca. 1892; Cuthbertson Fam. Cem., McDowell Co.
Dale, Martin L.; Pvt.; A; Mitchell
Dale, Silvanus; ---; A
Dancy, Samuel; Pvt.; E/A
Daniel, Martin V.; Pvt.; A; 1842–29 June 1905; Daniels Cem., Avery Co.
Danner, Anderson A.; Pvt.; D; Watauga; March 1845–17 June 1921; Flattop Cem., Watauga Co.
Danner, John; Pvt.; D; Watauga; 6 June 1828–15 April 1905; Danner Cem., Watauga Co.
Davenport, Gilson B.; Pvt.; I; Watauga; ca. 1843–prior to 1 March 1863
Davidson, William F.; Pvt.; E; Buncombe; b. ca. 1836
Davis, Albert F.; 2nd Lt.; I/D/A; Watauga; 2 Oct. 1834–30 Nov. 1896; Old Bethany Lutheran Cem., Watauga Co.
Davis, Asa; Pvt.; I; Watauga; ca. 1842 between 14 and 20 Sept. 1862
Davis, Elbert; Pvt.; I; Watauga; b. ca. 1834
Davis, George W.; Pvt.; D; Watauga; b. ca. 1842
Davis, Henry; Pvt.; Misc.; Adams Co., Miss.
Davis, Isaiah I.; Pvt.; H
Davis, Joseph L.; Pvt.; E; Caldwell; d. 6 Nov. 1863; Dalton, Ga.
Davis, Josiah; Pvt.; E/K; Mitchell; b. ca. 1829
Davis, Lewis; Pvt.; I; Alexander/Camp Holmes; ca. 1835–29 May 1864; Chattanooga, Tenn.
Davis, Nicholas; Pvt.; E; Surry
Davis, William Sidney; 3rd Lt.; I; Watauga; 24 July 1831–1 July 1917; Hopewell Meth. Cem., Watauga Co.
Day, Harvey; ---; H
Dean, Alexander C.; Pvt.; A; Burke; b. ca. 1838
Dean, George W.; Sgt.; A; Mitchell; b. ca. 1836
Dean, George Washington; Pvt.; K; Mitchell; b. ca. 1835
Dean, Noah; Pvt.; K; Yancey; 1829–1905; Franklin/Oaks Cem., Avery Co.
Deborde, Ezra; Pvt.; G; Wilkes/Camp Holmes; 3 Feb. 1825–25 Nov. 1863; Missionary Ridge, Ga.
Decker, Elisha; Pvt.; H; Caldwell; b. ca. 1831
Dellinger, Henry T.; Pvt.; A; Mitchell; 28 April 1845–6 Jan. 1916; Pisgah UMC, Avery Co.
Dellinger, John C.; Pvt.; A; Mitchell; 12 April 1843–20 April 1889; Pisgah UMC, Avery Co.
Dellinger, Joseph F.; Pvt.; A; Lincoln; ca. 1822–6 May 1904
Dellinger, Reuben A.; Pvt.; A; Mitchell; b. ca. 1839

Denney, Samuel; Pvt.; E/K; Mitchell; b. ca. 1846
Denny, James H.; Pvt.; L; Ashe
Dent, Isaiah; Pvt.; H
Deyton, Charles P.; ---; K
Deyton, David M.; Pvt.; B; Camp Jackson; b. ca. 1834; Woody Cem., Yancey Co.
Deyton, William; Pvt.; C; Yancey; 13 Aug. 1836–3 March 1905; Bailey Hill Cem., Yancey Co.
Dickson, James D.; Pvt.; L/F; Ashe; b. ca. 1847
Dickson, Joseph Harvey; Pvt.; E
Dobson, John Lafayette; 1st Sgt.; F; McDowell; 13 Jan. 1833–24 May 1911; Gardin-Haney Cem., McDowell Co.
Dobson, Patrick Henry O'Neal; Pvt.; F; Burke; b. 28 Oct. 1828; Obeth Cemetery, Burke Co.
Dollar, Alexander Monroe; Pvt.; L; Ashe; Aug. 1838–14 Aug. 1908; Tenn.
Dollar, William Henry; Pvt.; L; Ashe; 4 July 1839–28 July 1907; W. H. Dollar Fam. Cem., Ashe Co.
Done, Morgan; Pvt.; C/D; Yancey; b. ca. 1825
Dotson, Allen S.; Pvt.; I; Watauga; 4 Oct. 1838–3 Feb. 1888; Upper Beaver Dams Bap. Ch., Watauga Co.
Dotson, George W.; Pvt.; I; Watauga; b. 24 March 1863
Dougherty, Michael; Pvt.; L; Ashe; b. ca. 1831
Dover, Asa; Pvt.; F; York District, S.C.; ca. 1843–4 May 1864; Dalton, Ga.
Dover, John H.; Pvt.; F; York District, S.C.
Dover, Robert A.; Pvt.; F
Dowell, Joshua; Pvt.; G; Wilkes/Camp Holmes; 6 June 1816–17 April 1911; Moravian Falls Cem., Wilkes Co.
Duff, David C.; Pvt.; M/G; Johnson Co., Tenn./Watauga; b. ca. 1840
Dugger, Benjamin Franklin; ---; D; 4 Oct. 1837–10 May 1921; Howell Cem., Watauga Co.
Dugger, Joel; Pvt.; I; Dalton, Ga.
Dugger, John Wesley; Cpl.; D; Watauga; ca. 1843–4 Aug. 1864; Atlanta, Ga.
Dula, Thomas Joshua; Lt. Col.; F&S; Caldwell; 22 April 1831–18 Jan. 1906; Wilkes Co.
Dun, Callaway; Pvt.; L; Ashe
Duncan, John Calvin; Pvt.; G; Yancey; 1836–1868; Hicks Chapel Cem., McDowell Co.
Duncan, Jonathan A. W.; 2nd Lt.; K/B; Mitchell; 7 Aug. 1832–15 Dec. 1915; Bear Creek Cem., Mitchell Co.
Duncan, Philip H.; Pvt.; E/K; Mitchell; ca. 1838–10 Oct. 1863; Dalton, Ga.
Duncan, William F.; Sgt.; G; Camp Palmer
Dunn, J. F.; As. Surg.; F&S
Dyer, Drury Calvin; Pvt.; D; Watauga; 14 May 1841–12 May 1918; Zion Hill Bapt. Ch., Watauga Co.
Eastridge, Barnabas; Pvt.; L; Ashe; 26 April 1840–1922; Sinking Creek, Tenn.
Eastridge, Henry; Pvt.; L; Ashe; 1833–18 Feb. 1918; Hampton-Jones Cem., Johnson Co., Tenn.
Eastridge, John; Pvt.; L; Ashe; b. ca. 1833
Edmisten, Abram Shuford; Comm. Sgt.; E/F&S; Caldwell; b. ca. 1844
Edmisten, Alexander Henderson; Sgt.; E; Caldwell; b. ca. 1836
Edmisten, James M.; Pvt.; E; Caldwell; 1 June 1824–27 Sep. 1898; Joe Bryant Cem., Caldwell Co.
Edmisten, John; Pvt.; E; Caldwell; b. ca. 1828
Edmisten, Milas; Pvt.; E; Caldwell; 1832–1901; Forest Hills Cem., Burke Co.
Edmisten, William H.; Pvt.; E; Caldwell; b. ca. 1821
Edmisten, William Harrison; Pvt.; E; Caldwell; b. 30 Jan. 1832
Edmiston, A. H.; Pvt.; H; Caldwell
Edmiston, A. S.; Pvt.; H; Caldwell; b. ca. 1845
Edwards, Alex; Pvt.; E/H; Surry
Edwards, James N.; Pvt.; G
Edwards, John Rouse; Pvt.; C; Yancey; ca. 1815–20 April 1863; Knoxville, Tenn.
Edwards, John Wesley; Pvt.; G; Yancey; 31 Jan. 1833–26 April 1916
Edwards, Lynville; Pvt.; G; Yancey; ca. 1846–1865; Kentucky
Edwards, Sanders; Pvt.; B; Camp Jackson; b. ca. 1839; Greenlee Cem., Mitchell Co.
Edwards, Stephen; Pvt.; C/G; Yancey; 29 Nov. 1842–24 April 1863; Clinton, Tenn.
Edwards, Thomas; Pvt.; A; Hamilton Co., Tenn.
Eggers, Adam; Cpl.; D; Watauga; 23 July 1831–2 Jan. 1863; Jacksboro, Tenn.
Eggers, Hugh M.; Pvt.; I; Watauga; 26 Dec. 1826 ---
Eggers, John; Sgt.; I; Watauga; 2 Dec. 1835–20 Sept. 1863; Chickamauga, Ga.
Eggers, Landrine; ---; I; Watauga; 18 Nov. 1830–21 April 1916; Watauga Co.
Eggers, Riley; Pvt.; I; Watauga; b. 6 Feb. 1836
Eggers, Washington; Pvt.; I; Watauga; 21 Aug. 1829–21 Jan. 1872
Eldreth, John; Pvt.; L; Ashe
Eldreth, Zachariah; ---; L; ---; d. prior to 8 Dec. 1863
Elkins, Albert; Pvt.; G; Yancey; ca. 1835–prior to Oct. 1867
Elkins, Berton; Pvt.; C
Elkins, Joseph; Pvt.; B; Camp Jackson; ca. 1841–10 Sept. 1913; Stanton, VA
Elkins, William; Pvt.; E; Burke; b. ca. 1839
Eller, Alfred P.; Pvt.; I; Watauga; 3 May 1843–14 April 1921; Boone City Cem., Watauga Co.
Eller, Calvin; Capt.; L; Ashe; b. ca. 1830
Eller, Calvin, Jr.; Pvt.; L; Ashe; 1844–1924; Calvin Eller Cem., Ashe Co.
Eller, Jacob; Pvt.; L; Ashe; 19 May 1832–23 July 1899; Jacob Eller Cem., Ashe Co.
Eller, Peter; Pvt.; G; Wilkes/Camp Holmes; 1828–1898; Baker-Eller-McNeill Cem., Ashe Co.

Eller, William; Pvt.; L; Ashe; b. ca. 1836
Elliott, Alney B.; Pvt.; F; McDowell; August 1828–after April 1910; McDowell Co.
Elliott, Charles M.; Pvt.; F; McDowell; ca. 1832–18 Oct. 1863; Atlanta, Ga.
Elliott, Hiram; Pvt.; F; Camp Holmes; d. 29 Dec. 1863; Kingston, Ga.
Elliott, James Crawford; Pvt.; L; Ashe; 5 April 1841–24 Jan. 1912; Reuben Elliott Cem., Ashe Co.
Elliott, Jasper Marion; Musc.; F; McDowell; 1831–1922; Turkey Cove Cem., McDowell Co.
Elliott, John G.; Pvt.; F; McDowell; 10 June 1824–8 Oct. 1899; Neals Fam. Cem., McDowell Co.
Elliott, Rufus; Pvt.; L; Ashe; ca. 1837–3 April 1864; Rock Island, Ill.
Elliott, Shelly; ---; A
Elliott, Spencer; Pvt.; F; McDowell; b. ca. 1825
Elliott, Stephen; Pvt.; L; Ashe; 27 June 1830–6 June 1908; Reuben Elliott Cem., Ashe Co.
English, Aden; Pvt.; A/K/F; Mitchell; 1829–1917
English, David Jackson; Pvt.; A; McDowell; 1818–ca. 1881
English, James Henry; Pvt.; F; McDowell; 1 Feb. 1833–3 Feb. 1907
English, John Milton; Pvt.; A; Mitchell; 1820–1893; Phillips Cem., Avery Co.
English, Josiah Harvey; Pvt.; A; 1840–May 1862; Ashland, Va.
English, Samuel W.; Sgt.; A; Mitchell; 5 June 1823–6 Aug. 1910; Gibbs Cem., Yancey Co.
English, William Creasenberry; Pvt.; A; Mitchell; 1825–1864; Knoxville, Tenn.
Ensley, Alfred; Pvt.; E; Buncombe; b. ca. 1832
Epley, David; Pvt.; F; McDowell; ca. 1835–20 Sept. 1863; Chickamauga, Ga.
Epps, Thomas P.; 1st Lt.; F; McDowell; b. ca. 1828
Erwin, Arthur D.; Pvt.; A; Mitchell; 1 May 1836–3 April 1868
Estepp, Samuel; Pvt.; G; Yancey; b. ca. 1829
Estes, Amos; Pvt.; E; Caldwell; b. ca. 1843
Estes, Doctor W. T.; Bvt. 3rd Lt.; E; Caldwell; ca. 1845–31 Aug. 1864; Jonesboro, Ga.[9]
Estes, General Correll; Pvt.; E; Caldwell; ca. 1843–29 March 1863
Estes, Henderson D.; Drum Maj.; E/F&S; Caldwell; ca. 1838–4 Feb. 1864; Cassville, Ga.
Estes, James Monroe; Pvt.; E; Caldwell; b. ca. 1829
Estes, John H.; Pvt.; E; Caldwell; ca. 1843–22 June 1864; Kolb's Farm, Ga.
Estes, John Jackson; Pvt.; E; Caldwell; --- 10 Dec. 1863; Kingston, Ga.
Estes, Lance F.; Pvt.; E; Caldwell; 6 Oct. 1834–31 Aug. 1908; Crisp Cem., Caldwell Co.
Estes, Langston Lorenzo; Pvt.; E; Caldwell; 14 March 1844–11 Sept. 1923; Estes Cem., Caldwell Co.
Estes, William; Pvt.; E; Caldwell; b. ca. 1836
Ewing, Orville, Jr.; Adj.; F&S; Davidson Co., Tenn.

Fagg, Henry Clay; 2nd Lt.; H; Madison Co.; ca. 1846–7 Jan. 1913; Riverside Cem., Buncombe Co.
Faircloth, John W.; Pvt.; L; Ashe; b. ca. 1843
Faircloth, M. L.; Pvt.; A; Sampson Co.
Faircloth, Michael M.; Pvt.; L/F; Ashe; b. ca. 1845
Fardow, W.; Pvt.
Farecloth, William; Pvt.; A; Hamilton Co., Tenn.
Farrington, Mumford; Pvt.; L; Ashe; b. ca. 1829; Senter Primitive Bapt. Ch., Ashe Co.
Farthing, Elijah H.; Pvt.; I; Watauga; b. ca. 1830
Feaster, T. P.; ---; D
February, Mordecai; Pvt.; B; Mitchell; ca. 1835–20 Sept. 1863; Chickamauga, Ga.
Fender, William; Pvt.; G; Yancey; b. ca. 1844
Fergerson, William; Pvt.; C; Yancey; b. ca. 1842
Fincannon, Henry; Pvt.; H; Caldwell; ca. 1830–20 Sept. 1863; Chickamauga, Ga.
Fincannon, James A.; Pvt.; H; Caldwell; ca. 1843–ca. 1863
Fincannon, John Wesley; Pvt.; H; Caldwell; 18 June 1830–1 May 1905; Sardis Cem., Caldwell Co.
Fincannon, Wesley W.; Pvt.; H; Caldwell
Finey, Franklin; Pvt.; A; Dalton, Ga.
Finley, Jason C.; Pvt.; F; McDowell; b. ca. 1839; Nebo Cem., McDowell Co.
Fleming, David; Pvt.; H; Caldwell; ca. 1845–17 April 1863; Clinton, Tenn.
Fleming, James; Pvt.; H; Caldwell; ca. 1840–prior to 1 Jan. 1863; Johnson's Depot, Tenn.
Flemming, Thomas J.; Pvt.; F; McDowell; 9 April 1833–26 Jan. 1921; Carson's Chapel Cem., McDowell Co.
Flemming, William J. B.; Pvt.; E
Fletcher, James; Pvt.; H; Caldwell; ca. 1839–22 Jan. 1863; Jacksboro, Tenn.
Fletcher, Spencer; Pvt.; I; Watauga; ca. 1834–prior to 1874
Fletcher, Thomas Burt; Pvt.; I; Watauga; ca. 1842–12 Sept. 1917
Forbes, Robert; Pvt.; C; Yancey; ca. 1842–6 June 1863; Knoxville, Tenn.
Ford, Squire John; Pvt.; M/G; Watauga; 5 April 1840–9 April 1910; John Ford Cem., Watauga Co.[10]
Ford, Thomas; Pvt.; B
Forney, James Abram; Pvt.; F; McDowell; 20 April 1844–9 Oct. 1863; Jacksboro, Tenn.
Fowler, James A.; Hos. Ste.; L/F&S; Ashe; 29 Jan. 1840–1 Sept. 1910; Brown-Fowler Cem., Ashe Co.
Fowler, Sanders M.; Pvt.; L; b. Ashe; b. ca. 1843
Fowry, Edward; ---; F
Fox, Alexander; Pvt.; E; Caldwell; b. ca. 1845
Fox, Alexander; Pvt.; K; Caldwell; ca. 1847–11 May 1863; Caldwell Co.
Fox, Elisha Calvin; Pvt.; H; Caldwell; b. 11 Feb. 1847; Cedar Valley Cem., Caldwell Co.

Fox, Henry; Pvt.; K; Caldwell; ca. 1848–3 June 1926; Alexander Co.
Fox, James Austin; 1st Lt.; F; McDowell; b. ca. 1837
Fox, James T.; Musc. C; Yancey; 24 Sept. 1835–9 April 1923; Holcombe-McCracken Cem., Yancey Co.
Fox, Moses James; Pvt.; C; Yancey; 18 May 1844–21 May 1926; Sid McCorry Cem., Yancey Co.
Fox, Nathan Franklin; Pvt.; D; Watauga
Fox, Noah; Pvt.; K; Caldwell; b. ca. 1841
Fox, Skelton; Pvt.; C; Yancey; 7 May 1838–29 Dec. 1927; Milt McCourry Cem., Yancey Co.
Francom, Solomon; Pvt.; E; Caldwell; ca. 1835–prior 26 Sept. 1862
Francum, William; Pvt.; E; Caldwell; ca. 1836–27 Nov. 1864; Camp Chase, Ohio
Franklin, Albert Johnson; Pvt.; A; Yancey; 8 Dec. 1843–28 Feb. 1917; Pisgah UMC, Avery Co.
Franklin, David S.; Pvt.; A; Yancey; 24 Aug. 1845–16 July 1891; Pisgah UMC, Avery Co.
Franklin, George W.; Pvt.; A; Mitchell; b. ca. 1828
Franklin, J. S.; ---; A
Franklin, Jacob A.; Pvt.; A; Mitchell; b. ca. 1843
Franklin, James A.; Pvt.; A; Mitchell; b. ca. 1842
Franklin, James M., Jr.; Pvt.; A; Mitchell; b. ca. 1822
Franklin, Levi Alexander; Pvt.; A; Mitchell; 3 Feb. 1844–1886
Franklin, Samuel D.; Pvt.; A; Mitchell; ca. 1826–prior to 20 March 1863; Big Gap Creek, Tenn.
Franks, William; ---; Misc.; Madison Co.
Frasier, John W.; Pvt.; B; Mitchell; b. ca. 1821
Freeman, John; Pvt.; B/K; Mitchell; 1829–ca. 1875; Scott or Wise Co., Va.[11]
Freeman, Littleton; Pvt.; B/E/K; Mitchell; 14 Feb. 1819–5 Jan. 1892; Mitchell Co.
Freeman, Samuel; Pvt.; B/E/K; Mitchell; 1827–ca. 1913; Carter Co., Tenn.
Freeman, W. Larcan; Pvt.; A; Mitchell
Freeman, William; Pvt.; F; Haywood; b. ca. 1823
Frisbee, Daniel; Pvt.; H; Buncombe; b. ca. 1843
Frizzle, Albert; Pvt.; F; McDowell; b. ca. 1839
Frizzle, Thomas; Pvt.; F; McDowell; b. ca. 1841
Fry, John H.; Pvt.; G; Iredell/Camp Holmes; 14 Aug. 1844–9 Sep. 1906; Stoney Point Cem., Alexander Co.
Fugitt, Robert; Pvt.; G; Wilkes/Camp Holmes; ca. 1841–30 Jan. 1864; Rock Island, Ill.
Fullwood, James Madison; Pvt.; F; McDowell; 13 Feb. 1841–2 Oct. 1883; Crawfordsville, Ark.
Fullwood, Samuel B.; Pvt.; F; McDowell; 3 May 1832–18 Oct. 1863[12]
Gaddy, James; Pvt.; A; Mitchell; b. ca. 1824
Gaddy, Jesse A.; Pvt.; A; Mitchell; b. ca. 1840
Gaddy, Samuel H.; Pvt.; A; Anson; b. ca. 1843
Gardner, Elisha M.; Pvt.; B/D; Mitchell; 31 March 1844–20 May 1909; Red Top Cem., Blount Co., Tenn.
Gardner, George; ---; K; 1823–ca. 1880s; Slagle Cem., Mitchell Co.
Gardner, James W.; 2nd Lt.; G; Yancey; b. ca. 1843
Gardner, Thomas; Pvt.; B; Mitchell; ca. 1821–1890s; Beans Creek Cem., Mitchell Co.
Garland, Crisenbery; Pvt.; B; Mitchell; 4 June 1825–ca. 1895
Garland, Elisha M.; ---; E; Mitchell; ca. 1845–13 Feb. 1920
Garland, Ezekiel; Pvt.; B; Camp Jackson; ca. 1845–ca. 1890
Garland, Gibbs; Pvt.; B; Camp Jackson; b. ca. 1815
Garland, Hodge Rayburn; Pvt.; B; Mitchell; 10 June 1810–30 Jan. 1863; Jacksboro, Tenn.
Garland, John Calvin; 3rd Lt.; B; Mitchell; ca. 1841–1866; Red Hill Cem., Mitchell Co.
Garland, John Samuel; Pvt.; B; Mitchell; 4 March 1833–16 Oct. 1916; Red Hill Cem., Mitchell Co.
Garland, William; 1st Lt.; B; Mitchell; 2 April 1826–24 Feb. 1871; Beans Creek Cem., Mitchell Co.
Gates, James A.; Pvt.; B; Clinton, Tenn.
Gentry, Benjamin; Pvt.; M/G; Ashe/Watauga; b. ca. 1836
Gentry, Callaway; Pvt.; M/G; Ashe/Watauga
Gentry, Jesse; Cpl.; M/G; Ashe/Watauga; ca. 1840–25 Sept. 1863
Gentry, Joseph C.; ---; M
Gentry, Robert P.; Pvt.; A; Mitchell; b. ca. 1839
Gentry, William H.; Capt.; L; Ashe; 3 July 1828–1 Dec. 1907; Jefferson Mun. Cem., Ashe Co.
Gentry, William P.; Pvt.; M/G; Ashe/Watauga
George, James R.; Sgt.; C; Yancey; 8 July 1840–11 July 1903; John F. Reams Cem., Laurel Co., Ky.
German, William; Pvt.; E; Caldwell; ca. 1840–23 Oct. 1863; Kingston, Ga.
Gheen, James; Pvt.; B; Dalton, Ga.
Gheen, Thomas; Pvt.; B; Dalton, Ga.
Gibbs, A. N.; Pvt.; F; McDowell; b. ca. 1820
Gibbs, Bryant Conley; Pvt.; F; Camp Vance; b. 1827
Gibbs, Joseph A.; Pvt.; C/D; Yancey; ca. 1844–4 May 1864; Dalton, Ga.
Gibbs, Joshua F.; Pvt.; F; McDowell; b. ca. 1830
Gibbs, William Fulwood; Pvt.; F; McDowell; 1834–1901
Gibson, Henry F.; Pvt.; F; McDowell; ca. 1829–20 Sept. 1863; Chickamauga, Ga.
Gibson, Odom; Pvt.; F; McDowell; 4 July 1820–20 Jan. 1908; Carson's Chapel Cem., McDowell Co.
Gilbert, Larkin W.; 1st Lt.; H/B; Caldwell; b. ca. 1836
Giles, James B.; Pvt.; C
Giles, James Boneparte; Pvt.; H; S.C./Polk; 3 Nov. 1839–13 June 1902; Green Creek Bapt. Ch., Polk Co.
Gilkey, Augustus Bechtler; Pvt.; F; McDowell; 7

Jan. 1831–1 May 1922; Oak Grove Cem., Mc-Dowell Co.
Gillespie, Henry; Pvt.; A; Mitchell; b. ca. 1838
Gilliland, Joseph J.; Pvt.; H/B
Gilliland, Robert; Pvt.; H/B
Gillispee, Francis M.; Pvt.; A; Mitchell; ca. 1843–1 April 1863
Gilly, Alfred; Pvt.; L; Ashe; Hill Co., Mitchell Co.
Gilly, James; ---; L
Gilly, John; Pvt.; L; Ashe; ca. 1830–6 Aug. 1864; Ashe Co.
Glazebooks, John; Pvt.; H; Caldwell; 21 June 1842–31 May 1905; North Catawba Cem., Caldwell Co.
Glenn, Dudley G.; Pvt.; D; Watauga; ca. 1841–Oct. 1862; Tennessee
Glenn, Simeon; Pvt.; D; Watauga; ca. 1842–ca. 1865; North Carolina
Goforth, J.; ---; E
Goforth, William; Sgt.; G; Iredell/Camp Holmes 3 Oct. 1832–21 Jan. 1911; New Prospect Bapt. Ch. Cem., Iredell Co.
Goodwin, J. J.; As. Quar. F&S;
Goplin, George J.; Pvt.; E
Gorenflo, J. F.; 1st Sgt.; E; Madison; b. ca. 1844
Gouge, Garrett D.; Pvt.; K; Mitchell; 25 Feb. 1825–19 Sep. 1892; Sam Gouge Cem., Mitchell Co.
Gouge, John Wesley; Pvt.; C; 24 Dec. 1833–6 Jan. 1908; Gouge Cem., Unicoi Co., Tenn.
Gouge, William; Pvt.; E/K; Mitchell; 15 April 1828–1862 or 1863
Gourley, John; Pvt.; E; Guilford; b. ca. 1819
Gragg, Alexander; Pvt.; D; Watauga; 22 March 1834–5 June 1863; Knoxville, Tenn.
Gragg, Daniel; Pvt.; E; Caldwell; ca. 1838–18 Sept. 1864; Camp Douglas, Ill.
Gragg, Edward P.; Pvt.; M/G; Watauga
Gragg, Empsey; Pvt.; D; Watauga; 23 Oct. 1829–20 June 1922; Watauga Co.
Gragg, Harvey H.; Pvt.; D; Watauga; 23 Oct. 1829–20 Jan. 1864; Cassville, Ga.
Gragg, James Osmond; Pvt.; E; Watauga; 1833–1907; Gragg Cem., Avery Co.
Gragg, William Smith; Pvt.; D/I; Watauga; ca. 1845–2 May 1863; Knoxville, Tenn.
Graham, Daniel; Pvt.; M/G; Ashe/Watauga; b. ca. 1827
Gray, McKinsey M.; Pvt.; M/G; Watauga
Graybeal, John; Pvt.; L; Ashe; 27 May 1837–2 Oct. 1928; John Graybeal Sr. Cem., Ashe Co.
Green, Adam; Pvt.; D; Watauga; ca. 1843–5 March 1863; Clinton, Tenn.
Green, Alexander; Pvt.; I; Watauga; b. ca. 1839
Green, Alfred; Pvt.; D; Watauga; b. ca. 1844
Green, Amos, Jr.; Pvt.; I; Watauga; b. 8 Sept. 1834
Green, Archibald B.; Pvt.; E; Caldwell; b. ca. 1834
Green, Augustus F.; Pvt.; D/E; Watauga; ca. 1838–19 March 1865; Bentonville, N.C.
Green, Benjamin; Pvt.; E; Watauga/Caldwell; 1 Aug. 1844–10 May 1921; Reform Ch. Cem., Watauga Co.
Green, David; Pvt.; I; Watauga; d. 22 Dec. 1863; Caldwell Co.
Green, Edmund; Pvt.; E; Caldwell; b. ca. 1844
Green, Edmund; Pvt.; D/E; Caldwell; b. ca. 1828
Green, Fergerson; Pvt.; M/G; Watauga; b. 10 June 1838
Green, Isaac; Pvt.; M/G; Watauga; b. ca. 1841
Green, Isaac S.; Pvt. L; Ashe/Dalton, Ga.; ca. 1846–13 Feb. 1865; Camp Morton, Ill.
Green, Jacob; Pvt.; D; Watauga; b. ca. 1834
Green, James M.; Pvt.; A; Yancey; b. ca. 1841
Green, James Madison; 1st Sgt.; K; 29 Jan. 1841–10 April 1936
Green, Jeremiah; Cpl.; D; Watauga; 8 June 1843–27 Feb. 1927; Squire Adams Cem., Watauga Co.
Green, John C.; 1st Lt.; B; Mitchell; ca. 1830–28 Jan. 1863; Jacksboro, Tenn.
Green, Jonathan; Pvt.; D/E; Caldwell; ca. 1833–18 March 1863; Greeneville, Tenn.
Green, Joseph; Pvt.; D/B; Watauga; b. ca. 1828
Green, Joseph H.; Pvt.; E; Caldwell; ca. 1843–24 Sept. 1862; Cumberland Gap, Tenn.
Green, Larkin; Pvt.; D/E; Watauga; ca. 1839–18 Nov. 1862; Cumberland Gap, Tenn., or Big Stone Gap, Tenn.
Green, Levi; ---; D
Green, Patterson; Pvt.; A; Mitchell; b. ca. 1840
Green, Samuel P.; Pvt.; A; Mitchell
Green, Smith F.; Pvt.; E; Caldwell; d. 24 Nov. 1863; Salisbury, N.C.
Green, Smith P.; Pvt.; M; Watauga; b. ca. 1837
Green, Stephen M.; Musc.; A; Yancey; ca. 1844–17 Oct. 1864; Macon, Ga.
Green, Stewart; Pvt.; H; Polk; b. ca. 1840
Green, Wiley; Pvt.; E; Watauga; d. 13 Nov. 1863; Asheville, N.C.
Green, William; Pvt.; K; Mitchell; 25 Dec. 1838–13 Jan. 1923
Greene, Solomon, Jr.; Pvt.; D; Watauga; 25 Feb. 1822–26 March 1910; Laurel Springs Bapt. Ch. Cem., Watauga Co.
Greer, David; Pvt.; D; Watauga; ca. 1839–10 March 1863
Greer, Isaiah; Pvt.; M/G; Ashe/Watauga
Greer, Jefferson; Pvt.; M/G; Ashe/Watauga
Greer, Jesse; Pvt.; L; Ashe
Greer, Noah; Pvt.; M/G; Ashe/Watauga; May 1840–24 July 1913; Watauga Co.
Greer, Phillip; Pvt.; M/G; Watauga; 20 Nov. 1843–9 May 1947; Zionville Bapt. Ch. Cem., Watauga Co.
Greer, Riley; Pvt.; D; Watauga; Dec. 1840–1870; Simmons Cem., Watauga Co.
Greer, Solomon; ---; L
Greer, Thomas; Pvt.; M/G; Ashe/Watauga; 1844–5 Sept. 1928

Gregory, Isaac; Pvt.; C; Yancey; b. ca. 1844
Griffin, David Amos; Pvt.; H; Caldwell; 8 Nov. 1842–5 May 1925; Bellview Cem., Caldwell Co.
Griffin, Hamilton; Surg.; F&S; Louisville, Ky.
Griffin, Stephen R.; Pvt.; H; Caldwell; ca. 1838–1 April 1863; Jacksboro, Tenn.
Griffis, W. H.; Pvt.; E; Guilford
Grindstaff, Jake; ---; E; Mitchell
Grindstaff, John; Pvt.; E/K; Mitchell; b. ca. 1844
Grindstaff, Joseph "Jobe"; Pvt.; E/K; Mitchell; January 1824–15 Aug. 1925; Pleasant Gardens Bapt. Ch., McDowell Co.
Grogan, Anderson; Pvt.; D; Watauga; ca. 1834–12 Feb. 1865; Camp Morton, Ind.
Grogan, Elijah; Pvt.; M/G; Ashe/Watauga; 1833–1914; Zionville Bapt. Ch. Cem., Watauga Co.
Grogan, Henry; Pvt.; M; Watauga; ca. 1839–2 Nov. 1886; Zionville Bapt. Ch. Cem., Watauga Co.
Grogan, Jordan; Pvt.; M/G; Watauga; 15 Nov. 1845–6 April 1931; Old Lawrence Fam. Cem., Ashe Co.
Grubb, George W.; Pvt.; I; Watauga; 19 Nov. 1828–3 April 1902; Bethany UMC, Ashe Co.
Grubb, Phillip H.; Pvt.; D; Watauga; d. 27 Feb. 1863; Jacksboro, Tenn.
Gurley, Harvey M.; Pvt.; A; Burke; ca. 1837–13 April 1863; Clinton, Tenn.
Guy, John C.; Pvt.; D; Watauga; b. ca. 1838
Guyer, Isaac S.; Pvt.; A; Mecklenburg; b. ca. 1828
Haas, Emanuel Hosea; Pvt.; H; SC/Caldwell; d. 25 May 1863; Kingsville, S.C.
Hagaman, Hugh; Pvt.; D; Watauga; 2 Nov. 1837–30 June 1911; Hagaman Cem., Watauga Co.
Hagaman, Isaac Jr.; Pvt.; I; Watauga; b. ca. 1834
Hagaman, Martin G.; Pvt.; D; Watauga
Hagey, William; Pvt.; F; Camp Holmes; d. 30 June 1864; Atlanta, Ga.
Halcomb, B.W.; ---; C
Halifield, Alfred; Pvt.; E; Mitchell
Hall, David S.; Com. Sgt.; F&S; Yancey; b. ca. 1837
Hall, Elijah; Pvt.; A; Mitchell; b. ca. 1829
Hall, Elijah Y.; Cpl.; F; McDowell; 30 Oct. 1836–15 Oct. 1917; Halltown Cem., McDowell Co.
Hall, Joshua; ---; F; McDowell; ca. 1834–25 April 1863
Hall, Marcus; Pvt.; K; Mitchell; 1845–1894; Blue Rock Bapt. Ch., Yancey Co.
Hall, Moses; Pvt.; A; Mitchell; 11 March 1833–24 March 1916; Oak Grove Cem., McDowell Co.
Ham, Alfred; Pvt.; L; Ashe; Jan. 1841–16 May 1922; Dave Sullivan Cem., Ashe Co.
Ham, Gideon; Pvt.; L; Ashe; ca. 1842–6 Sept. 1928
Ham, Joshua, Sr.; ---; L; 3 Jan. 1826–7 Jan. 1930 or 9 April 1902
Ham, Thomas; Pvt.; L; Ashe; 20 Jan. 1839–29 April 1893; Thomas Ham Cem., Ashe Co.
Hamersar, Jackson; ---; E; Mitchell

Hamlett, Oliver Merritt; Pvt.; M/G; Watauga; 26 Feb. 1821–3 Dec. 1915
Hammond, G. C.; ---; Misc.; Watauga
Hampton, Milton Pinckney; 1st Lt.; C; Yancey; b. 1841
Hampton, Thomas N.; Sgt.; C; Yancey; b. ca. 1837
Hampton, William F.; Pvt.; M/G; Watauga; 1833–1 April 1929; Watauga Co.
Handy, F. Marion; Cpl.; L/F; Ashe; b. ca. 1836
Hanes, Marion M.; Pvt.; G; Wilkes/Camp Palmer; ca. 1846–10 Feb. 1863
Haney, Daniel Wesley; Pvt.; F; McDowell; b. 11 Nov. 1839; Gardin-Haney Cem., McDowell Co.
Haney, S. C.; ---; C; ca. 1838–1862 or 1863; Cumberland Gap, Tenn.
Harbin, Milton G.; Pvt.; Misc.
Haremon, Crisp; Pvt.; E; Person
Harman, Drury Calvin; Capt.; D; Watauga; 17 April 1826–23 Dec. 1904; Old Harmon Cem., Watauga Co.
Harmon, Andrew J.; Pvt.; D; Watauga; 16 July 1833–16 Nov. 1904; Zion Hill Bapt. Ch. Cem., Watauga Co.
Harmon, Andrew J.; Pvt.; I; Watauga; 20 Oct. 1839–15 Nov. 1913; Meredith/Daniels Cem., Avery Co.
Harmon, Eli George; Pvt.; D; Watauga; b. April 1835; Salem Cem., Van Buren Co., Ark.
Harmon, Ephraim Council; Pvt.; D; Watauga; 6 Oct. 1842–5 Sept. 1930; Old Harmon Cem., Watauga Co.
Harmon, Goulder Carroll; Pvt.; D; Watauga; 1838–1908; Zion Hill Cem., Watauga Co.
Harmon, John Wiley; Pvt.; D; Watauga; 7 April 1838–24 March 1926; Beech Creek Cem., Watauga Co.
Harmon, Wiley A.; Pvt.; D; Watauga; 5 Feb. 1827–2 April 1910; Old Harmon Cem., Watauga Co.
Harp, Calvin; Pvt.; M/G; Watauga
Harper, George Washington Finley; Maj.; F&S; Caldwell; 7 July 1834–1921; Bellview Cem., Caldwell Co.
Harrel, Claton C.; Pvt.; E; Mitchell
Harrell, Thomas C.; Pvt.; B; Mitchell; b. ca. 1844
Harrill, D. L.; Pvt.; E; Surry
Harris, John P.; Pvt.; E; b. ca. 1844
Harrison, Benjamin Calvin; Pvt.; E; Caldwell; 2 May 1844–9 May 1894; Harrison Fam. Cem., Caldwell Co.
Harrison, Joseph W.; Pvt.; M/G; Watauga; b. ca. 1842
Harriss, William White; Surg.; F&S; 1823–6 Dec. 1901; Oakdale Cem., New Hanover Co.
Hart, Andrew; Pvt.; L; Ashe; ca. 1845–2 Sept. 1863; Fort Delaware, Del.
Hart, Joseph; Pvt.; L; Ashe; ca. 1844–26 Aug. 1863; Fort Delaware, Del.
Hart, Riley; Pvt.; L; Ashe; ca. 1835–14 July 1863; Fort Delaware, Del.

Hartley, Joseph H.; Pvt.; E; Caldwell; b. ca. 1829
Hartley, Nathan; Pvt.; E; Caldwell; ca. 1834–ca. 1862; Big Gap Creek, Tenn.
Hartzog, William H.; Pvt.; L; Ashe/Dalton, Ga.; ca. 1846–15 June 1864; Columbus, Ga.
Harvel, Moses Alex; Pvt.; L; Ashe; Jan. 1844–ca. 1910; Pike Co., Ky.
Harvel, William; Pvt.; A; Yancey; b. ca. 1843
Harvey, George B.; Pvt.; F; McDowell; ca. 1838–20 Sept. 1863; Chickamauga, Ga.
Harvey, John L.; Pvt.; F; McDowell; b. ca. 1825
Harvey, Samuel S.; Pvt.; F; McDowell; b. ca. 1845
Hase, Jesse; Pvt.; A; Hamilton Co., Tenn.
Hass, John; Pvt.; E; Caldwell; d. 14 May 1865; Camp Douglas, Chicago, Ill.
Hatley, John F.; Pvt.; D; Watauga; 9 Jan. 1838–15 April 1925; Johnson Co., Tenn.
Hatley, Lafayette; Pvt.; D; Watauga; ca. 1841–23 March 1864; Dalton, Ga.
Hatley, Riley Burton; Pvt.; D; Watauga; 24 Nov. 1839–20 Feb. 1921; Hatley Cem., Whitman Co., Wash.
Hatley, Wiley Smith; Pvt.; D; Watauga; 15 March 1843–21 March 1919
Hatton, Warren A.; Pvt.; M/G; Watauga; 30 May 1839–4 July 1920; Nelson Chapel Cem., Caldwell Co.
Havener, Alexander G.; Pvt.; A
Havener, Joseph F.; Pvt.; A; Lincoln; b. ca. 1838
Hawkins, Jesse D.; Pvt.; E; Caldwell County; b. 1 Aug. 1831
Hawks, John; Pvt.; G; Camp Holmes; d. 16 Jan. 1864; Rock Island, Ill.
Hayes, Calvin; ---; F; ---; d. 28 March 1865; Wake Co.
Hayes, Jacob S.; Pvt.; D; Watauga; ca. 1844–4 Feb. 1863; Tennessee
Hayes, Jefferson M.; Pvt.; E; Caldwell; ca. 1838–ca. 1862
Hayes, Joseph, Sr.; Cpl.; I; Watauga; 23 Oct. 1828–28 April 1907; Gragg Cem., Watauga Co.
Hayes, Joseph Washington; Pvt.; G; Iredell/Camp Holmes; b. ca. 1825
Hayes, Robert Skyles; Pvt.; D/I; Watauga; b. 1831
Hayes, William; Pvt.; I; Watauga; ca. 1838–1900; Oregon
Hays, Hugh; Pvt.; E; Mitchell
Hedrick, Emanuel M.; 1st Lt.; H; Caldwell; b. ca. 1828
Helton, John Nelson; Pvt.; H; Caldwell; 1838–1908
Hendrick, William H.; Cpl.; C; Cocke Co., Tenn.
Hendricks, James; Pvt.; E; Randolph; d. 22 Oct. 1864; Macon, Ga.
Henline, Henry; Pvt.; A; Mitchell; b. ca. 1834
Hensley, Erwin H.; ---; C; ---; 23 Oct. 1848–12 June 1934; Hensley Cem., Yancey Co.
Hensley, John A.; Or. Sgt.; A/F&S; Mitchell; b. ca. 1827
Hensley, John E.; Pvt.; G; Yancey; ca. 1837–14 Aug. 1864; Yancey Co.
Hensley, John H.; Pvt.; G; Yancey; b. ca. 1826
Hensley, John M.; Pvt.; F; McDowell; b. ca. 1835; Richmond Hill Cem., Rutherford Co.
Hensley, Samuel F.; ---; C
Hensly, Henderson; Pvt.; C; Yancey; b. ca. 1825
Henson, Jordan; Pvt.; D; Watauga; ca. 1830–10 May 1863; Knoxville, Tenn.
Henson, Jourdon J.; Pvt.; D; Watauga; 20 June 1847–23 Jan. 1919; Henson Chapel UMC, Watauga Co.
Herndon, Harrison; Sgt. Maj.; F&S; b. ca. 1826
Herrill, Henry C.; Pvt.; B; Mitchell; b. ca. 1846
Hethwood, M.; ---; B
Hicks, Andrew; Pvt.; D; Watauga; ca. 1829–1893; Hicks Family Cem., Watauga Co.
Hicks, Carroll; Pvt.; D; Watauga; ca. 1839–23 Sept. 1862; Cumberland Gap. Tenn.
Hicks, Harmon; Pvt.; D; Watauga; d. prior 22 March 1863; Jacksboro, Tenn.
Hicks, James Young; Pvt.; F; McDowell; 21 June 1828–7 Feb. 1882; Providence UMC, McDowell Co.
Hicks, John N.; Pvt.; E/H; Watauga; b. ca. 1835
Hicks, Levi; Pvt.; D; Watauga; b. ca. 1830
Hicks, Patterson; Pvt.; D; Watauga; ca. 1843–2 March 1863; Cumberland Gap, Tenn.
Hicks, W. W.; ---; D
Higgins, Charles; Pvt.; G; Yancey; b. ca. 1834
Higgins, Curtis Alexander; Pvt.; G; Yancey; 30 Dec. 1846–27 Nov. 1932; Adin, Modoc Co., Calif.
Higgins, David C.; Pvt.; G; Yancey; b. 29 March 1838; Academy Hill Cem., Yancey Co.
Higgins, James Erwin; Pvt.; G; Yancey; ca. 1830–prior to 22 Nov. 1879
Higgins, John; Pvt.; G; Wilkes/Camp Holmes; John Higgins Cem., Yancey Co.
Higgins, Thrower; Musc.; G; Yancey; 27 March 1835–1 Oct. 1904; W. E. Higgins Cem., Yancey Co.
Hileman, Jacob; Pvt.; B/D/E; Mitchell; b. ca. 1844
Hileman, John C.; Pvt.; B/E; Mitchell; b. ca. 1832
Hill, Levi; Pvt.; G; Camp Holmes
Hilliard, Alfred Jr.; Pvt.; I; Watauga; b. ca. 1842; Montana
Hilliard, Bartlett Young; Pvt.; I; Watauga; Aug. 1832–7 Jan. 1914; Hilliard Cem., Watauga Co.
Hilton, John W.; Pvt.; L
Hine, Eli; Pvt.; F; Forsyth
Hinson, Joseph; Pvt.; B; Mitchell; b. ca. 1842
Hipps, Phillip Marcus Benton; Sgt.; H; Madison/Buncombe; 23 Aug. 1844–24 Dec. 1915; Iron Plains, Haywood Co.
Hobbs, Caleb A.; Pvt.; E; Caldwell; b. ca. 1844
Hobbs, Wallace; Pvt.; E; ---; b. ca. 1845
Hobson, Benoni, Jr.; Pvt.; E/B; d. 22 July 1864; Bald Hill, Ga.
Hockings, Jesse D.; Pvt.; E; Caldwell
Hodges, Callaway; Pvt.; I; Watauga; ca. 1844–7 March 1890; Watauga Co.

Hodges, Edward; 1st Sgt.; D; Watauga; ca. 1831–1881
Hodges, Gilbert W.; Cpl.; D/A; Watauga; 25 July 1845–11 Nov. 1910; Oklahoma
Hodges, John Wesley; Pvt.; D; Watauga; 1 May 1845–28 March 1924; Jont. Brown Cem., Watauga Co.
Hodges, Larkin Gilbert; Sgt.; D/A; Watauga; 15 Nov. 1841–13 Oct. 1933; Maney Cem., Buncombe Co.
Hodges, Riley; Pvt.; D; Watauga; 3 March 1830–19 Feb. 1922; Oak Grove Bapt. Ch. Cem., Watauga Co.
Hodges, William J.; Pvt.; I; Watauga
Hodges, William Mastin; Capt.; I; Watauga; 2 June 1830–19 Jan. 1928; Piney Grove Cem., Watauga Co.
Hoffman, Levi; Pvt.; H; Caldwell; d. 20 Sept. 1863; Chickamauga, Ga.
Hogan, Alfred; Pvt.; F; McDowell; b. ca. 1823
Hogan, John C.; Pvt.; A
Hogler, John C.; ---; G
Holaway, John; Pvt.; G; Camp Holmes; d. 13 Feb. 1864; Rock Island, Ill.
Holcomb, John Lorenzo; Pvt.; C; Yancey; ca. 1842–17 June 1905; Oklahoma City, Okla.
Holcombe, Robert M.; Pvt.; C/D; Yancey; ca. 1818–11 Dec. 1887
Holder, David W.; Pvt.; I; Watauga; b. 1845
Holder, Elijah Thomas; Cpl.; I; Watauga; b. 1832
Holdsclaw, Marion F.; Pvt.[13]
Holeman, James; Pvt.; M/G; Watauga; 1 March 1841–8 May 1908; Howell Cem., Watauga Co.
Holeman, Smith; Pvt.; M/G; Watauga; 23 Nov. 1842–10 Aug. 1864; Forsyth, Ga.
Holeman, Thomas; ---; I; Watauga; 10 July 1838–25 June 1862; Richmond, Va.[14]
Holifield, Jasper; Pvt.; A/D; Mitchell; 30 Dec. 1839–29 March 1921; Snow Hill Cem., Mitchell Co.
Holifield, Joel A.; Pvt.; E; Caldwell; b. ca. 1842
Holifield, Joseph; Pvt.; A/D; Mitchell; b. ca. 1839
Holifield, Milas; Pvt.; A; Mitchell; d. 2 April 1863
Hollifield, Joseph H.; ---; G
Hollifield, Riley Perol; Pvt.; F; McDowell; 22 Jan. 1830–27 March 1914; Grassy Creek Cem., McDowell Co.
Hollers, William Thomas; Pvt.; D; Watauga; 12 July 1841–22 Feb. 1929
Holly, George; Pvt.; D; Mitchell
Holman, Thomas; ---; I
Holsclaw, Francis M.; Pvt.; D; Watauga
Holsclaw, Rufus L.; Pvt.; D; Watauga; 8 May 1831–12 Aug. 1909; Hodges Cem., Watauga Co.
Holsclaw, Wiley; ---; D; Watauga; 2 April 1828–25 Jan. 1893; Cove Creek Bapt. Ch. Cem., Watauga Co.
Holsclaw, William L.; Pvt.; D; Watauga; b. ca. 1812
Honeycutt, David D.; Pvt.; C; Yancey; ca. 1843–12 May 1863; Clinton, Tenn.
Honeycutt, George W.; Pvt.; G; Yancey; ca. 1841–ca. 1870
Honeycutt, Jacob S.; Pvt.; C; Yancey; 14 April 1846–12 March 1916; Marion Co., Ark.
Honeycutt, Lafayette Peter; Pvt.; G; Yancey; 1841–1932; Erwin, Tenn.
Honeycutt, Sampson; Pvt.; B; Haynesville, Tenn.; 1812–1887; Mt. Pleasant Cem., Yancey Co.
Honeycutt, Samuel C.; Pvt.; C; 1836–1 Aug. 1863
Hoover, Milas; Pvt.; F; McDowell; b. ca. 1830
Hopkins, George W.; 1st Lt.; M/G; Watauga; 16 Jan. 1830–20 March 1910; George W. Green Cem., Ashe Co.
Hopson, George; Pvt.; B; Mitchell; b. ca. 1809
Hopson, John; Pvt.; B/K; Mitchell; b. ca. 1837
Horn, Hilliard; Pvt.; B; Mitchell; ca. 1826–11 March 1863; Jacksboro, Tenn.
Horton, James Harrison; Adj.; I/F&S; Watauga; 27 May 1841–24 Dec. 1863; City Cemetery, Augusta, Ga.
Horton, Jonathan Philmore; Capt.; C; Yancey; 5 March 1836–1863; Watauga Co.
Horton, Lorenzo D.; Pvt.; C; 30 July 1836–25 Aug. 1862; Johnson's Depot, Tenn.
Horton, Phineas; Pvt.; C; Yancey; 20 Dec. 1833–2 Oct. 1862; Cumberland Gap, Tenn.
Horton, William Hamilton; Pvt.; I; Watauga; 28 Feb. 1834–13 April 1913; Shull Cem., Watauga Co.
Houck, Joseph F.; Pvt.; L; Ashe; b. Oct. 1826
Houston, John; Pvt.; D; Watauga
Howard, Alfred M.; Pvt.; H; Yadkin
Howell, Aaron; ---; K
Howell, Alvin Powell; Pvt.; L; Ashe; 2 Feb. 1844–4 Aug. 1912; Howell Hill Comm. Cem., Ashe Co.
Howell, Amos; Pvt.; I; Watauga; 9 April 1832–7 March 1875; Old Dugger Cem., Watauga Co.
Howell, George; Pvt.; L; Ashe
Howell, Henry; ---; G; 1847–1934; Peterson Hill Cem., Yancey Co.
Howell, Jackson H.; Pvt.; L; Ashe; b. ca. 1834
Howell, James H.; Pvt.; H; Caldwell; b. ca. 1847
Howell, James J.; Pvt.; Misc.; Ashe
Howell, Jeremiah W.; Pvt.; L; Ashe; b. ca. 1827; Old Howell/Powers Cem., Ashe Co.
Howell, John; Pvt.; H; Caldwell; ca. 1836–12 Dec. 1864; Camp Douglas, Ill.
Howell, Peter; Pvt.; G; Howell Cem., Yancey Co.
Howell, Robert V.; Cpl.; C/B; Yancey; b. ca. 1844
Howell, Solomon; Pvt.; L; Ashe; ca. 1825–12 Dec. 1864; North Carolina
Howell, Swinfield D.; Pvt.; C; Yancey; 1822–1900s
Howell, Thomas; Pvt.; G; Yancey
Howell, William; ---; D
Howington, Noel; Pvt.; D; Watauga; 1806–prior to 1900; Washington Co., Va.
Howington, William M.; 2nd Lt.; D; Watauga; May 1840–20 May 1904; Washington Co, Tenn.

Hoyl, Jeremiah F.; Pvt.; F; McDowell; 2 Feb. 1824–15 April 1891; Collins Cem., Caldwell Co.
Huffman, Able; Pvt.; H; Burke/Caldwell; b. ca. 1846
Huffman, George D.; Pvt.; D; Watauga
Huffman, John; Pvt.; A; Mitchell
Hughes, Charles; Pvt.; G; Camp Martin; ca. 1842–1921; Jerry's Creek, Avery Co.
Hughes, Iven; Pvt.; B; Mitchell; ca. 1842–27 June 1916; Blevins-Branch Cem., Mitchell Co.
Hughes, Jeremiah; ---; K; Yancey Co.; 1 Jan. 1846–30 Dec. 1929; Hughes-Jones Cem., Yancey Co.
Hughes, Jeremiah, Sr.; ---; H
Hughes, Jonathan; Pvt.; C; Yancey
Hughes, William J.; Pvt.; E/K; Caldwell; 10 June 1823–3 May 1889; Hughes-Jones Cem., Yancey Co.
Hughs, Amos; Pvt.; G; Yancey; b. ca. 1844
Hughs, David, Jr.; Pvt.; G; Yancey
Hughs, David, Sr.; Pvt.; G; Camp Huston
Hughs, James; Pvt.; G/C; b. ca. 1846
Hughs, Jason; Pvt.; G; 21 March 1820–21 July 1903; Hughes Cem., Avery Co.
Hughs, John; Sgt.; C; Yancey; b. ca. 1837
Hughs, Landon C.; Pvt.; B; Mitchell; b. ca. 1840
Hunter, James Wesley; Cpl.; F; McDowell; ca. 1828–ca. 1863
Hunter, John W.; Pvt.; C; Yancey; ca. 1844–4 Jan. 1863; Jacksboro, Tenn.
Hunter, Samuel M.; ---; C
Hurley, David D.; Pvt.; L; Ashe; ca. 1845–8 July 1864; Oxford, Ga.
Hurley, Elisha Howard; 3rd Lt.; L; Ashe; 25 July 1844–10 Dec. 1925; Scott-Blevins Cem., Ashe Co.
Hurley, Harvey; Pvt.; L/F; Ashe; b. ca. 1833
Hurley, James F.; Cpl.; L; Ashe; ca. 1827–31 Aug. 1864; Jonesboro, Ga.
Hurley, Jasper; Pvt.; L; Ashe; b. ca. 1825
Hurley, Leander; 1st Lt.; L/F; Ashe; 16 July 1837–23 Oct. 1898; Elihu Tucker Cem., Ashe Co.
Hurley, Thomas; Pvt.; L/F; Ashe; b. ca. 1834
Husier, Alexander; Pvt.; F; Camp Holmes; d. 4 April 1864; Atlanta, Ga.
Huskins, Horace; Pvt.; B
Huskins, Jacob; Pvt.; D; Surry
Huskins, John S.; ---; K
Huskins, Patterson; Pvt.; A; Anderson Co., Tenn.
Huskins, Samuel P.; Pvt.; A; Yancey; b. ca. 1844
Huskins, Samuel P.; Sgt.; K; 29 May 1842–18 Nov. 1913; Huskins Cem., Yancey Co.
Huskins, William M.; Pvt.; A; Mitchell; ca. 1837–ca. 1867
Hutchings, Wright; Pvt.; F; McDowell; ca. 1820–4 May 1864; Dalton, Ga.
Hutchins, Albert; Pvt.; B; Dalton, Ga.
Hutchins, James; Pvt.; B; Mitchell; ca. 1845–1862 or 1863
Hutchins, William B.; Pvt.; G; Mitchell/Camp Holmes
Ingle, John Jackson; Pvt.; K; 31 March 1823–20 Dec. 1895; Madison Co.
Inglis, James; Sgt. Maj.; H/F&S; Caldwell; ca. 1832–25 Feb. 1864; Confederate Cem., Dalton, Ga.
Isaacs, Harvey; Pvt.; D; Watauga; ca. 1845–5 April 1885; possibly Oklahoma
Isaacs, Hugh M.; Pvt.; I; Watauga; b. 13 May 1839
Isaacs, James; Pvt.; D
Isaacs, James, Sr.; Pvt.; I; Watauga; 14 Dec. 1835–11 May 1908; Old Wilson Cem., Watauga Co.
Isaacs, Noah; Pvt.; D/I; Watauga; 8 Feb. 1838–4 May 1918; Swift Cem., Watauga Co.
Isaacs, Reuben J.; Pvt.; D; Watauga; ca. 1847–1895 or 1896; Taney, Mo.
Isaacs, Richard Jr.; Pvt.; D; Watauga; b. ca. 1832
Isaacs, Solomon C.; Pvt.; I; Watauga; b. 2 June 1845
Jackson, Andrew; Pvt.; I; Watauga; b. ca. 1831
Jackson, Bill; Cook; Misc.; d. 25 Oct. 1862[15]
Jackson, Eli; 1st Lt.; H; Polk; b. ca. 1838
Jackson, James R.; Pvt.; D; Watauga; ca. 1842–prior to 1867
James, Eli; Pvt.; D; Watauga; ca. 1842–24 Sept. 1863; Cumberland Gap, Tenn.
James, Thomas Redden; Sgt.; H; Buncombe; 6 July 1839–24 Feb. 1906; Leicester, Buncombe Co.
Jamison, Newton A.; Pvt.; H; Buncombe; b. ca. 1831
Janes, Losen M.; Pvt.; F; Cumberland Gap; d. 27 Feb. 1863; Jacksboro, Tenn.
Jarrett, Daniel; Pvt.; F; McDowell; b. ca. 1841
Jarrett, Eli; Cpl.; B/D; Mitchell; 8 March 1828–13 Feb. 1925; Peebles Cem., Carter Co., Tenn.
Jarrett, George Y.; Sgt.; F; McDowell
Jarrett, Killian Mills; Pvt.; F; McDowell; 3 June 1843–17 Oct. 1899; Nebo Cem., McDowell Co.
Jarrett, Levi Franklin; Pvt.; B; Mitchell; 14 Nov. 1830–8 Nov. 1863; Atlanta, Ga.
Jarrett, Samuel Carson; Pvt.; F; Cumberland Gap; 28 May 1829–29 Jan. 1898; Nebo Cem., McDowell Co.
Jasper, William; Pvt.; E; d. 29 June 1864; Alton, Ill.
Jefferson, Adkins; Pvt.; L; Ashe; ca. 1830–2 Oct. 1864; Camp Douglas, Ill.
Jemerson, John; Pvt.; F; McDowell; ca. 1838–11 Feb. 1863; Jacksboro, Tenn.
Jenkins, William C.; Pvt.; E; Cocke Co., Tenn.
Jessups, Ira; Pvt.; G; Surry/Camp Holmes ca. 1829–prior to 1 Sept. 1864
Jester, William; Pvt.; E; Yadkin; ca. 1825–14 May 1864; La Grange, Ga.
Jimerson, James A.; Pvt.; C; Yancey; d. 20 Sept. 1863; Chickamauga, Ga.
Johnson, Bartlett; Pvt.; D; Watauga; b. ca. 1829
Johnson, Braxton; ---; I; Watauga; 16 Jan. 1823–20 July 1890; Forest Grove Cem., Watauga Co.

Johnson, Henderson; ---; K
Johnson, Isaac A.; Pvt.; A; 5 March 1847–12 May 1905; Johnson Cem., Avery Co.
Johnson, Jacob Sr.; Pvt.; D/I; Watauga; prior to 1843–prior to 11 March 1863; Big Gap Creek, Tenn.
Johnson, James; Pvt.; L; Ashe
Johnson, John T.; Pvt.; I; Watauga; b. ca. 1831
Johnson, Madison; Pvt.; D; Watauga; ca. 1818– prior to 2 March 1863; Big Gap Creek, Tenn.
Johnson, Samuel; Pvt.; A; Mitchell; b. ca. 1831
Johnson, William N.; Pvt.; I; Camp Holmes; b. ca. 1835
Jolly, Hile; Pvt.; L; Chattanooga, Tenn.; b. ca. 1818
Jones, Edmond R.; Pvt.; M/G; Watauga; 9 May 1828–1 Nov. 1886; Meat Camp Bapt. Ch. Cem., Watauga Co.
Jones, Jason; Pvt.; L; Ashe; b. ca. 1840
Jones, Jesse F.; Pvt.; L; Ashe; ca. 1838–5 Aug. 1864; Griffin, Ga.
Jones, John; Pvt.; L; Ashe/Clinton, Tenn.
Jones, John H.; Pvt.; H; Caldwell; b. ca. 1832
Jones, Johnson; Pvt.; F; McDowell; ca. 1843–20 Sept. 1863; Chickamauga, Ga.
Jones, L. B.; ---; K
Jones, Larkin G.; Pvt.; M; Watauga; ca. 1847–31 March 1863; Jacksboro, Tenn.
Jones, Larkin P.; Musc.; C; Yancey; 5 May 1841–11 April 1928; Hughes-Jones Cem., Yancey Co.
Jones, Memoch; Pvt.; L; Ashe; d. 20 Sept. 1863; Chickamauga, Ga.
Jones, Nelson; Pvt.; G; Yancey; 1846–1916; Oak Grove Cem., McDowell Co.
Jones, Posey W.; Pvt.; H; Buncombe Co.; b. ca. 1833
Jones, Robert; Pvt.; M/G; Ashe/Watauga
Jones, William J.; Musc.; C; Yancey; ca. 1830–14 Jan. 1863; Jacksboro, Tenn.
Joplin, J. Wesley; Pvt.; H; Caldwell; b. ca. 1847
Jopling, George Joshua; Pvt.; K/E; Caldwell; b. ca. 1836
Justice, Henry; Pvt.; E/K; Mitchell; ca. 1844– after May 1864[16]
Justice, William; Pvt.; E/K
Kanipe, Eli; Pvt.; F; McDowell; ca. 1844–7 March 1865; Camp Chase, Ohio
Kanipe, Zephaniah; Pvt.; F; Dalton, Ga.; 21 Sept. 1845–30 Oct. 1911; Corpus Christi, Texas
Kavanaugh, Pat; Pvt.; H; Mobile, Ala.
Kayler, George; Pvt.; F; McDowell; b. ca. 1836
Kaylor, John; ---; F
Keener, George; Pvt.; G; Camp Holmes; d. 15 Jan. 1864; Confederate Cemetery, Dalton, Ga.
Keener, Jesse; Pvt.; E; Buncombe; 1824–2 June 1864; Rock Island, Ill.
Keener, John C.; Lt. Col.; F&S; 11 July 1818–10 Oct. 1910; Pine Grove UMC, Avery Co.
Keller, Jesse Robert; Pvt.; M/G; Watauga; ca. 1842–28 Sept. 1918; Mt. Zion Cem., Watauga Co.
Keller, John W.; Pvt.; A; Burke; b. ca. 1840; Pineola Pres. Ch., Avery Co.
Keller, Joshua; Pvt.; A; McDowell; ca. 1842–20 Sept. 1863; Chickamauga, Ga.
Keller, Michael; Pvt.; A
Keller, Nicholas; Pvt.; M/G; Watauga; b. ca. 1840
Keller, William; Pvt.; M/G; Wilkes/Watauga; b. ca. 1835
Kemp, John; Pvt.; L; Ashe; d. 26 Jan. 1864; Cassville, Ga.
Kennedy, John H.; Pvt.; F; Forsyth
Kenner, Ulrich; Pvt.; F; Camp Holmes
Kenney, Simpson; Pvt.; E; Randolph; ca. 1821–20 April 1865; Hart's Island, N.Y.
Kilby, Abraham; ---; D
Kilby, Milton; Pvt.; L; Ashe; 31 Oct. 1831–3 Jan. 1918; Milton Kilby Cem., Ashe Co.
Kilby, Thomas; Pvt.; G; Wilkes/Camp Holmes; b. ca. 1827
Kilby, William E.; Musc.; D; Watauga; b. ca. 1844
Killan, M. A.; Pvt.; H; Caldwell; b. ca. 1846
Kilpatrick, Franklin; Pvt.; A; d. 23 Dec. 1864; Camp Douglas, Ill.
King, David; Pvt.; L; Ashe
King, George; Pvt.; C; Yancey; 18 Jan. 1831–20 April 1900; King Cem., Yancey Co.
King, Jacob; Pvt.; L; Ashe; b. ca. 1832
King, John; Pvt.; A; Washington Co., Tenn.
Kirby, Edmund; Lt. Col./Adj.; F&S; d. 20 Sept. 1863; Chickamauga, Ga.
Kirby, John Marion; Pvt.; H; Caldwell
Knight, John; Pvt.; A; Mitchell
Knight, William W.; Pvt.; L; Ashe; b. ca. 1837
Lackey, James; Pvt.; F; McDowell; b. ca. 1841
Lail, Alfred; Pvt.; A; Hamilton Co., Tenn.; ca. 1821–19 Oct. 1864; Macon, Ga.
Landreth, Wagner; Pvt.; L; Ashe; ca. 1835–ca. 1872
Lane, William; Pvt.; F; Camp Holmes; b. ca. 1833
Lanier, David Anderson; Pvt.; E; McDowell; 24 May 1842–12 Feb. 1928; Shiloh UMC, Catawba Co.
Laurance, James J.; Pvt.; D; Watauga; 16 Nov. 1836–1 Nov. 1912; Mt. Gilead Bapt. Ch., Watauga Co.
Lawrence, John W.; Pvt.; G; Yancey
Laws, Bannester; Pvt.; G; d. 2 June 1864; Rock Island, Ill.
Laws, Joseph; Pvt.; G; Yancey; b. ca. 1838
Laws, Meshack Finley; ---; K; ca. 1820–7 March 1900; Micaville Cem., Yancey Co.
Ledford, Curtis; Pvt.; K; Mitchell; b. ca. 1835; Yancey Co.
Ledford, Henry F.; Pvt.; L; Chattanooga, Tenn.; d. 14 Feb. 1864; Rock Island, Ill.
Ledford, James; Pvt.; K; Mitchell; b. ca. 1843
Ledford, Jasper; Pvt.; E/K; Mitchell; b. ca. 1846
Ledford, Peter; Pvt.; G; Buncombe; b. ca. 1820
Ledford, William; Pvt.; B; d. 26 May 1865; Hart's Island, N.Y.

Ledford, William B.; Pvt.; C; Yancey; b. ca. 1834
Lefevers, John A.; Pvt.; H; Caldwell; b. ca. 1837
Lenoir, Walter Waighstill; 1st Lt.; H; Caldwell; 13 March 1823–26 July 1900; Fort Defiance Cem., Caldwell Co.
Letterman, Joseph; Pvt.; C; Yancey; 1840–1860s[17]
Letterman, Milton Panter; ---; K; ---; 13 Sept. 1847–2 Dec. 1930; Letterman Cem., Yancey Co.
Lewis, Daniel J.; Pvt.; D; Watauga; b. ca. 1847
Lewis, George; Pvt.; F; McDowell; ca. 1832–4 July 1864; Barnesville, Ga.
Lewis, J.; Pvt.; I
Lewis, Jacob; Pvt.; C; Yancey; b. ca. 1843
Lewis, James Cicero; Pvt.; M/G; Watauga; 6 May 1844–24 Dec. 1911; Watauga Co.
Lewis, Oscar M.; As. Surg.; F&S
Lewis, William; Pvt.; L; Ashe
Lindsay, John H.; Pvt.; E; Caldwell; ca. 1828–18 April 1863
Lindsay, Joseph Archibald; Pvt.; E; Caldwell; 19 Dec. 1838–8 July 1927; Lindsay Cem., Caldwell Co.
Lindsay, William Reid; Pvt.; E; Caldwell; b. ca. 1841
Lingle, Adam D.; 2nd Lt.; H; Caldwell; 5 June 1847–5 Jan. 1902
Lingle, J. H.; Pvt.; H; Caldwell; ca. 1836–23 May 1862
Lingle, John Moore; Pvt.; H; Caldwell; 14 Dec. 1834–10 March 1915; Burke Co.
Linsey, George Washington; 2nd Lt.; E; Buncombe; 17 Jan. 1840–23 April 1920; Haw Creek UMC, Buncombe Co.
Little, J. F.; Pvt.; F; Mecklenburg
Livingston, Thomas; Pvt.; K; Caldwell; 28 April 1843–19 Nov. 1901
Loftin, David M.; Pvt.; E; Caldwell; ca. 1829–20 Sept. 1863; Chickamauga, Ga.
Logan, William G.; Pvt.; E; Yadkin
Long, Hamilton C.; Capt.; I/G
Lonon, Oliver Powell; Cpl.; F; McDowell; 29 Nov. 1832–1 June 1915; Baxter Co., Ark.
Lorance, George Washington; Pvt.; M/G; Watauga; 24 April 1842–22 April 1910; Union Cem., Watauga Co.
Lovelace, Andrew; Pvt.; L; Ashe; b. ca. 1835
Loven, Anderson; Pvt.; F
Lowery, James L.; Pvt.; B; Haynesville, Tenn.
Lowery, John; Pvt.; A; Dalton, Ga.; d. 2 March 1864; Atlanta, Ga.
Lowrie, Samuel; Pvt.; A; McDowell; b. ca. 1841; Hicks Chapel Bapt. Ch., McDowell Co.
Lowrie, Stewart; Pvt.; A; Burke; b. ca. 1813
Loyd, George; Pvt.; C; Yancey
Loyd, Thomas; Pvt.; C; Yancey; ca. 1837–20 June 1922; Flag Pond, Tenn.
Lusbyfield, James; Pvt.; D; Mitchell
Lusk, Elkana; Pvt.; D; Watauga; 19 Jan. 1835–26 Nov. 1912; Pitman Cem., Avery Co.
Luther, Hillery; Pvt.; E; Randolph
Luther, Robert J.; Pvt.; H; Buncombe; b. 1840
Lyons, John; Pvt.; G; Wilkes
Mace, Jesse M.; Sgt.; A; Mitchell; b. 15 June 1840; Hollifield-Mace Cem., McDowell Co.
Mace, Joseph P.; Pvt.; A; Yancey; 1844–1893; Broughton Hospital, McDowell Co.
Mackey, James; Pvt.; F; McDowell; b. ca. 1835; Old Ebenezer Cem., McDowell Co.
Main, Harrison; Pvt.; M/G; Watauga; b. ca. 1841
Maney, Robert M.; Pvt.; C; Yancey; b. ca. 1844
Mangum, George T.; Pvt.; F; McDowell; b. ca. 1837
Mangum, Richard G.; Pvt.; F; McDowell; 14 Aug. 1831–15 March 1923; Drucilla Pres. Ch., McDowell Co.
Marcus, John; Pvt.; E; Caldwell; b. ca. 1845
Marcus, Serug; Pvt.; D; Watauga; 6 May 1935–11 Feb. 1917; Piney Grove Cem., Watauga Co.
Marler, James Benton; Capt.; E; Mitchell; 26 Nov. 1830–13 July 1874; Missouri
Marlin, I. J.; Sgt.; F; McDowell; 13 April 1833–22 Jan. 1911; Montford Cove Cem., McDowell Co.
Marlow, Isaac; Pvt.; F; Big Gap Creek, Tenn.
Marlow, John W.; ---; I; Watauga; b. ca. 1846
Martin, Jason Carson; Pvt.; H; Caldwell
Martin, Jeremiah; Pvt.; A; Mitchell; d. 20 Sept. 1863; Chickamauga, Ga.
Martin, Warren; Pvt.; E; Randolph; d. 17 June 1864; Rock Island, Ill.
Mashburn, William M.; Pvt.; C; Yancey; 23 Nov. 1828–25 May 1899; Old Fort Cem., McDowell Co.
Mask, Dudley M.; Pvt.; H; Caldwell; b. ca. 1842
Mask, Horry; Pvt.; H; Caldwell; b. ca. 1839
Mason, Harrison; Pvt.; G; Iredell/Camp Holmes; b. 1845
Mason, Joseph P.; ACS; F&S; Yancey
Massey, J. H.; Pvt.; F; Cumberland Gap; d. 17 March 1863; Jacksboro, Tenn.
Massey, John; Pvt.; F; Camp Holmes
Mast, Finley Patterson; 1st Sgt.; D; Watauga; 30 March 1832–12 June 1924; Mast Cem., Watauga Co.
Mast, John Allen; Pvt.; D; Watauga; 9 Sept. 1829–6 Feb. 1892; Bingham-Mast Cem., Watauga Co.
Mast, S. J.; ---; D
Mast, William Penn; 1st Lt.; D; 6 June 1834–10 Dec. 1889; Coos Co., Ore.
Matheson, Elijah Logan; Pvt.; H; Caldwell; ca. 1833–15 Dec. 1914; Yellowstone Co., Mont.
Matheson, Wesley Green; Pvt.; H; Caldwell; ca. 1837–26 May 1914; Greenhill Cem., Sullivan, Ill.
Mathis, Elcanna; Pvt.; H; Caldwell; b. ca. 1828
Mathis, John; Pvt.; G; Yancey; b. ca. 1845
Mathis, John; Pvt.; I; Camp Holmes
Mathis, Martin; Pvt.; F; McDowell; 19 Aug. 1843–20 Feb. 1927; Barnes Cem., Mitchell Co.

Mauney, J. R.; ---; C
May, Abraham; Pvt.; L; Ashe; b. ca. 1839
May, James M.; Pvt.; E; Caldwell; b. ca. 1842
May, John; Pvt.; L; Ashe; ca. 1845–22 June 1864; Kolb's Farm, Ga.
McBee, William; Cpl.; A; Mitchell; ca. 1843–20 Sept. 1863; Chickamauga, Ga.
McCall, Jacob M.; Pvt.; H; Caldwell; 6 Feb. 1834–11 July 1902; Fleming Chapel Cem., Caldwell Co.
McCall, John; Cpl.; F; McDowell; ca. 1844–3 or 12 May 1863; Clinton, Tenn.
McCall, John Rufus; Cpl.; H; Caldwell; 20 April 1845–27 May 1899; Fleming Chapel Cem., Caldwell Co.
McCanless, George S.; Pvt.; C; Yancey; b. ca. 1834
McCanless, James E.; Pvt.; C; Yancey
McCarson, Samuel; Pvt.; E; Henderson; b. ca. 1839: Old McCarson Cem., Henderson Co.
McClelon, Wilson; Pvt.; A; Mitchell
McCoury, George Washington; Pvt.; G; Yancey; d. 7 Feb. 1863; Jack's Creek, Yancey Co.
McCowry, James Lynn; Cpl.; C; Yancey; b. ca. 1831; Texas
McCullom D.; Sgt; I; d. 2 May 1865; Richmond, VA
McCurry, Phineas; Pvt.; A; Yancey; b. ca. 1844; Texas
McCurry, Tillman H.; Pvt.; A; Yancey; 17 June 1841–24 Jan. 1931; McCurry's Rock Ch. Cem., Avery Co.
McCurry, Walter; Pvt.; A; Burke; ca. 1825–31 March 1864
McCurry, Zephaniah; Pvt.; K/G; Mitchell; b. ca. 1838
McDowell, Riley; Pvt.; H; Randolph; b. ca. 1838
McEwin, Max C.; Pvt.; I; Watauga
McFalls, Arthur; Pvt.; A/K; Mitchell; ca. 1828–20 Sept. 1863; Chickamauga, Ga.
McFalls, Daniel J.; Pvt.; A; Mitchell; d. 19 May 1863; Knoxville, Tenn.
McFalls, George W.; Pvt.; A/K; Mitchell; ca. 1840–4 May 1864; Dalton, Ga.
McGahey, James; Pvt.; F; Camp Stokes, Tenn.
McGalliard, Robert; Cpl.; F/G; McDowell; 14 March 1844–12 April 1916; Nebo Cem., McDowell Co.
McGee, John S.; Pvt.; A/K; Mitchell; b. ca. 1841
McGee, Jordan Coucill; 1st Lt.; I; Watauga; 11 Oct. 1835–17 Oct. 1916; Boone City Cem., Watauga Co.
McGee, Robert S.; Pvt.; A/K; Mitchell; b. ca. 1844
McGimsey, Theodore Cicero; 2nd Lt.; F/G; McDowell; 15 Nov. 1835–13 March 1929; Mountain Grove UMC, McDowell Co.
McGuire, George Washington; Pvt.; L; Ashe; Nov. 1824–July 1901; McGuire Cem., Watauga Co.
McHargue, Thomas Litton; Pvt.; D; Watauga; b. 8 July 1832

McHone, Taylor Zachariah; Pvt.; A; Mitchell; 1 July 1844–7 Nov. 1938; McHone Cem., Mitchell Co.
McIntosh, Sidney; Pvt.; G; Camp Palmer; ca. 1827–after 1900
McIntosh, William M.; Pvt.; C; Yancey; d. 5 Jan. 1863; Jacksboro, Tenn.
McKiney, Henry; Pvt.; K; Mitchell; b. ca. 1823; Yellow Mt. Cem., Avery Co.
McKiney, Julius; Pvt.; A; Mitchell; d. 18 April 1863; Knoxville, Tenn.
McKiney, William; Pvt.; G; Yancey; ca. 1843–25 Sept. 1863[18]
McKinney, James; Pvt.; A/K; Mitchell; b. ca. 1838 or 33
McKinney, James H.; ---; B
McKinney, Jason C.; Pvt.; A/D; Mitchell; b. ca. 1839; McKinney Cem., Mitchell Co.
McKinney, John P.; Pvt.; E/K; Mitchell; b. ca. 1842
McKinney, Johnson S.; Sgt.; E/K; Mitchell; Aug. 1837–5 Jan. 1915; Green-Young Cem., Mitchell Co.
McKinney, Reuben B.; Pvt.; K; Mitchell; 23 June 1842–9 Jan. 1917; Grassy Creek Cem., Mitchell Co.
McKinney, Reuben M.; Pvt.; B; Big Creek Gap; b. ca. 1840; McKinney Cem., Mitchell Co.
McKinney, Samuel B.; ---; B; ---; 3 March 1841–2 March 1923
McKinney, Thomas; Pvt.; A; Mitchell; ca. 1834–March 1863; Big Creek Gap, Tenn.[19]
McKissick, Robert R.; Pvt.; F; McDowell; ca. 1834–14 May, 1864; Resaca, Ga.
McLaird, James W.; Pvt.; D; Watauga; 3 Dec. 1824–Jan. 1888
McLane, Hugh Franklin; Pvt.; D; Watauga; 8 May 1843–27 April 1916; Caldwell Co.
McLeod, Samuel; Pvt.; H; Caldwell; b. ca. 1820
McLour, Henry S.; Pvt.; L; Ashe
McMahan, James; Pvt.; G; Yancey; b. ca. 1832
McMahan, Sanders; Pvt.; G; Yancey; ca. 1829–1860s; Tennessee
McMahan, Thomas; Pvt.; C; Yancey; b. ca. 1834
McMahan, William B.; Pvt.; C; Yancey; b. ca. 1841; Riddle Cem., Yancey Co.
McMillen, James; Pvt.; E; Caldwell
McPeters, Jonathan Harrison; Cpl.; G; Yancey; 2 Sept. 1838–12 June 1925; McIntosh Cem., Yancey Co.
McPeters, Samuel S.; Cpl.; G; Yancey; 2 March 1843–25 May 1921; Good Cem., McDowell Co.
McVay, William; Pvt.; B; Mitchell; ca. 1841–24 March 1863; Jacksboro, Tenn.
McVee, William; Pvt.; A; Mitchell; b. ca. 1843
Meadows, John P.; Pvt.; H; Madison; b. ca. 1835
Medaris, John Enzor; QSgt.; E/F&S; Caldwell; 1836–4 Jan. 1904; Broughton Hosp. Cem., Burke Co.

Medlock, Henry B.; Pvt.; E; Alexander; 1830–1863; Clinch Mt., Tenn.
Merrill, A. B.; Pvt.; L
Messicks, Finley G.; Pvt.; H; Yadkin; b. ca. 1845
Metcalf, Henry C.; Pvt.; C; Yancey; b. ca. 1846
Michael, John Thomas; Pvt.; I; Watauga; ca. 1844–31 March 1863; Jacksboro, Tenn.
Mikeal, Alexander; Pvt.; M/G; Ashe/Watauga; b. ca. 1841
Mikeal, Frederick; Pvt.; M/G; Watauga; 29 June 1838–1 Nov. 1920; Wilkes Co.
Mikeal, Isaac; Pvt.; M/G; Watauga; ca. 1842–3 Feb. 1865; Camp Chase, Ohio
Mikeal, Riley; Pvt.; G; Watauga; b. ca. 1824
Miller, Alfred Hamilton; Pvt.; I; Watauga; 2 Sept. 1841–2 March 1923
Miller, Andrew; Pvt.; B/E; Mitchell; b. ca. 1840
Miller, Curtis; Pvt.; C; Yancey; ca. 1844–10 March 1864; Atlanta, Ga.
Miller, Daniel D.; Pvt.; G; Yancey; 17 June 1833–31 Oct. 1914; Miller Freewill B C., Yancey Co.
Miller, David D.; Pvt.; I; Watauga; 20 May 1845–7 March 1863; Big Gap Creek, Tenn.
Miller, Ephraim N.; Pvt.; I; Watauga; b. ca. 1847
Miller, Franklin; Pvt.; I; Watauga; 8 April 1840–12 Oct. 1918; Hopewell Methodist Cem., Watauga Co.
Miller, George M.; Pvt.; D/I; Watauga; ca. 1835–8 Jan. 1863
Miller, Henry; Pvt.; H; Caldwell; d. prior to 30 April 1864
Miller, Hiram; Pvt.; B; Mitchell; ca. 1826–10 Aug. 1914; Mitchell Co.
Miller, John; Pvt.; G; Mitchell/Camp Huston
Miller, John H.; Pvt.; I; Watauga
Miller, John M.; Pvt.; D/I; Watauga; 13 Oct. 1843–27 April 1930; Morphew Cem., Watauga Co.
Miller, Jonathan Benjamin; 1st Lt.; I/G; Watauga; 11 May 1841–1 Dec. 1914; Hopewell UMC, Watauga Co.
Miller, Lorenzo Dow; Musc.; I; Watauga; 8 Nov. 1843–6 Nov. 1929; Hopewell UMC, Watauga Co.
Miller, Mack; Pvt.; A; Mitchell; b. ca. 1837
Miller, Moses; Pvt.; G; Camp Palmer; 12 Feb. 1835–20 Oct. 1912; Miller Cem., Mitchell Co.
Miller, Samuel; Pvt.; B/G; Mitchell; b. ca. 1843
Miller, Solomon; Pvt.; G; Yancey; b. ca. 1843; Jobe Cem., Unicoi Co., Tenn.
Miller, T. Calvin; Sgt.; D/I/G; Watauga; b. ca. 1844
Miller, Thomas; Pvt.; B; Mitchell; b. ca. 1834
Miller, Thomas; Pvt.; B; Mitchell; b. ca. 1827
Miller, William; Pvt.; B; Mitchell; b. ca. 1838
Miller, William; Capt.; I; Watauga; 4 Nov. 1814–1 March 1908; Red Boiling Springs, Tenn.
Mitchell, George; Pvt.; I; Watauga; 21 June 1832–31 Jan. 1918; Soldiers Home, Wake Co.
Mitchell, Michael; Pvt.; D/I; Watauga; 19 Feb. 1833–11 May 1902; Henson's Chapel UMC, Watauga Co.
Mitchell, Robert; Pvt.; I/G; Watauga; b. ca. 1846
Mitchell, Thomas; Pvt.; I; Watauga; b. ca. 1828
Mitchell, Thomas J.; As. Surg.; F&S
Mitchum, Nathaniel Aaron; Pvt.; H; Caldwell; 26 Sept. 1841–8 Feb. 1910; Sardis Cem., Caldwell Co.
Moffitt, John Whitaker Lawrence; Cpl.; F; McDowell; 7 Dec. 1836–9 Oct. 1894; Ebenezer Cem., McDowell Co.
Moffitt, Nelson; Pvt.; F; McDowell; ca. 1828–5 Aug. 1863
Molly, James; Pvt.; C
Moody, Benjamin, Jr.; Pvt.; M/G; Watauga; ca. 1837–9 April 1879; Tolbert Cem., Watauga Co.
Moody, George W.; Pvt.; I; Watauga; 22 July 1830–16 Oct. 1908; Cove Creek Cem., Watauga Co.
Moody, Henry H.; Pvt.; D; Watauga; b. ca. 1845
Moody, Robert; Pvt.; E; Caldwell; ca. 1842–1 March 1863
Moody, Robert L.; Pvt.; F; McDowell; b. ca. 1840
Moore, Andrew Jackson; Pvt.; H; Caldwell; b. ca. 1828
Moore, Charles M.; Pvt.; F; McDowell; ca. 1832–15 May 1864; Resaca, Ga.
Moore, Elijah L.; Pvt.; E; Caldwell; 22 Jan. 1839–1 March 1903
Moore, George Washington; Pvt.; E; Caldwell; 8 Aug. 1830–19 Feb. 1909; Moore Cem., Caldwell Co.
Moore, Hight C.; Musc.; E; Caldwell; ca. 1835–1864; Fort Valley, Ga.
Moore, Jacob C.; Pvt.; F; Camp Vance; 1826–24 March 1864; Drucilla Pres. Ch.
Moore, Jasper Elijah; Pvt.; E; Caldwell; 10 April 1841–20 July 1910; Moore Cem., Caldwell Co.
Moore, Jesse, Jr.; Pvt.; E; Caldwell; 3 Sept. 1827–22 June 1906; Moore Cem., Caldwell Co.
Moore, Judson; Pvt.; E; Caldwell; 13 June 1833–27 Jan. 1911; Globe, Caldwell Co.
Moore, Lewis; Pvt.; E
Moore, Martin Luther; Pvt.; E; Caldwell; d. 1 Dec. 1863
Moore, Newton; Pvt.; E; Caldwell; 11 Feb. 1839–10 May 1905; Moore Cem., Watauga Co.
More, John; ---; D
Moretz, John; Pvt.; I; Watauga; 29 Nov. 1830–5 Feb. 1912; Old Bethany Lutheran Cem., Watauga Co.
Moretz, William; Pvt.; I; Watauga; 23 Jan. 1835–1942; Old Bethany Lutheran Cem., Watauga Co.
Morgan, Elijah P.; Pvt.; F; McDowell; ca. 1828–25 Feb. 1864; Marietta, Ga.
Morgan, J. H.; Pvt.; F; Camp Stokes
Morgan, Jethro; Pvt.; F; McDowell; b. ca. 1834; Sugar Hill Bapt. Ch., McDowell Co.
Morgan, Jethro C. (Franklin); Pvt.; F; Dalton,

Ga.; 19 Sept. 1844–24 March 1925; Sugar Hill Bapt. Ch., McDowell Co.
Morgan, John B.; 2nd Lt.; F/H; McDowell; Sugar Hill Bapt. Ch., McDowell Co.
Morgan, John Simeon; Pvt.; F; McDowell; ca. 1843–7 July 1863; Clinton, Tenn.
Morgan, Jonathan; Pvt.; F
Morgan, Marion H.; Pvt.; H
Morgan, Nathan; Pvt.; K; Caldwell; b. ca. 1828
Morgan, Permenter; Pvt.; F; McDowell; ca. 1841–20 Sept. 1863; Chickamauga, Ga.
Morris, John H.; 2nd Lt.; F; McDowell; 1828–1875; Bethel Bapt. Ch. Cem., McDowell Co.
Morrison, Francis M.; Pvt.; F; McDowell; ca. 1834–; Pinnacle UMC, McDowell Co.
Morrison, James Dysart; 1st Lt.; F; McDowell; ca. 1827–20 Sept. 1863; Chickamauga, Ga.
Morrow, Daniel; Pvt.; H; Caldwell; ca. 1828–30 March 1863; Clinton, Tenn.
Morrow, Gordon; Pvt.; H; Caldwell; 25 Aug. 1812–29 Aug. 1918; Absher Cem., Caldwell Co.
Morrow, Higgins; Pvt.; F; McDowell; d. 25 Feb. 1864; Atlanta, Ga.
Morrow, John; Pvt.; F; McDowell; ca. 1823–4 Aug. 1864; Camp Douglas, Ill.
Morrow, Nathan; Pvt.; H; Caldwell; ca. 1840–3 Aug. 1862; Caldwell Co.
Mosely, Samuel E.; Pvt.; A; Mitchell; b. ca. 1845
Moss, Benjamin J.; 1st Lt.; C; Yancey; 6 June 1814–22 Nov. 1886
Mosteller, Daniel Lutz; Pvt.; F; McDowell; 9 Sept. 1827–14 April 1891; Bethel Bapt. Ch. Cem., McDowell Co.
Moxely, William; Pvt.; A; Hamilton Co., Tenn.
Mulkey, Robert; Pvt.; G
Mullis, George W.; Pvt.; G; Iredell/Camp Holmes
Mulwee, James O.; Pvt.; E; Caldwell; b. ca. 1824
Murdock, J. C.; Pvt.; F; d. 31 March 1865; Hart's Island, N.Y.
Murphy, Archibald D.; Pvt.; F; Camp Reynolds; b. ca. 1835
Murphy, John; ---; K
Murphy, Wesley; ---; K; Charles Robinson Cem., Yancey Co.
Myers, Milton; Pvt.; G; Iredell/Camp Holmes; ca. 1830–17 May 1864; Newnan, Ga.
Naney, Isaiah; Pvt.; G; Rutherford/Yancey; 13 Oct. 1839–24 Sept. 1880; Hill/Justice Cem., Rutherford Co.
Naney, Jordan; Pvt.; G; Rutherford/Yancey; 1844–3 Feb. 1863
Nanney, Martin Lee; Pvt.; F; McDowell; 2 Nov. 1834–1863
Nelson, George; Pvt.; E; Guilford
Nelson, James W.; Pvt.; I; Watauga
Nelson, William; Pvt.; L; Camp Holmes; d. 29 March 1864; Cassville, Ga.
Nelson, William R.; Sgt.; E; Caldwell; 20 July 1839–31 March 1901; Harper's Chapel Cem., Caldwell Co.
Newman, William; Pvt.; G; Chatham/Camp Holmes; b. ca. 1825
Nichols, James Walter; Pvt.; C/F; Yancey; ca. 1831–after 1880
Nichols, Jonathan A.; Pvt.; C/F; Yancey; 30 Aug. 1831–31 Dec. 1913; Monford Cove Bapt. Ch., Rutherford Co.
Nichols, William A.; Pvt.; F; Yancey; ca. 1833–15 March 1863; Jacksboro, Tenn.
Norris, Elijah Jonathan; Sgt.; D; Watauga; 4 Sept. 1843–18 May 1933; Jont. Brown Cem., Watauga Co.
Norris, Isaac; Pvt.; M/G; Watauga; 9 Feb. 1837–22 Nov. 1913; Norris Cem., Watauga Co.
Norris, Jacob; Pvt.; I; Watauga; 10 Nov. 1841–16 June 1921; Swift Cem., Watauga Co.
Norris, John; Pvt.; I; Watauga; ca. 1844–3 March 1863; Jacksboro, Tenn.
Norris, John N.; Pvt.; M; Watauga; ca. 1853–27 June 1930; Norris Cem., Watauga Co.
Norris, John Riley; 2nd Lt.; M/G; Watauga; 22 Oct. 1828–3 Nov. 1889; Norris Cem., Watauga Co.
Norris, Thomas; Pvt.; I; Watauga; b. ca. 1845
Norris, William W.; Sgt.; M/G; Watauga; 9 April 1834–30 April 1864; Norris Cem., Watauga Co.
Odeer, Albert M.; Pvt.; G; Yancey; d. 31 July 1863; Bethel Cem., Knoxville, Tenn.
Odom, Abraham; Pvt.; B; Mitchell; ca. 1834–1862 or 1863
Odom, John; Pvt.; B; Mitchell; ca. 1840–1862 or 1863
Oliver, John S.; Pvt.; I; Watauga
Ollis, George W.; Pvt.; A; Mitchell; b. ca. 1828
Ollis, James McB.; Pvt.; A; Burke; b. ca. 1834
Ollis, John; 1st Lt.; A; Mitchell; 27 Sept. 1819–18 Oct. 1891; Avery Co.
Ollis, Joseph Taylor; Pvt.; ---; 17 Sept. 1847–1 May 1936; Green Valley Bapt. Ch., Avery Co.
Ollis, Leonard; Cpl.; A; Mitchell; 22 Feb. 1845–8 May 1935; Mt. Vernon Christian Ch., Walton Co., Ga.
Orrant, James C.; Pvt.; D; Watauga; b. ca. 1842
Osborn, Alexander; Pvt.; L; Ashe
Osborn, Alfred; Pvt.; L; Ashe; 23 July 1838–28 Jan. 1874; Green Valley Cem., Ashe Co.
Osborn, Aris; Pvt.; L; Ashe; 13 July 1843–1920s; Green Valley Cem., Ashe Co.
Osborn, George; Pvt.; L; Ashe; b. ca. 1841
Osborn, John; Pvt.; L; Ashe
Osborn, William; Pvt.; L; Ashe; 22 April 1830–30 July 1873; Green Valley Cem., Ashe Co.
Osborne, David; Pvt.; B; Mitchell; b. ca. 1838
Osborne, George; Pvt.; E; Watauga; b. ca. 1835
Osborne, Jesse; Pvt.; L; Ashe; b. 1834
Owensby, Aaron Whitenton; Pvt.; F; McDowell; ca. 1836–6 Jan. 1863; Jacksboro, Tenn.
Oxford, James Henry; Pvt.; E; Alexander; 1834–1895; Cooke Co., Texas[20]
Oxford, John McLeod; Pvt.; E; Alexander; 15 July

1841–16 Sept. 1928; Three Forks Bapt. Ch. Cem., Alexander Co.
Oxford, William C.; Pvt.; E; Caldwell; 29 March 1829–27 Feb. 1903; Antioch Cem., Alexander Co.
Page, Lafayette A.; 3rd Lt.; H; Caldwell; ca. 1833–9 March 1864; Atlanta, Ga.
Palmer, Daniel M.; Pvt.; H; Caldwell; ca. 1829–20 Sept. 1863; Chickamauga, Ga.
Palmer, George C.; Pvt.; H/B; Caldwell; 12 Feb. 1832–16 Dec. 1925; Dudley Shoals Bapt. Ch., Caldwell Co.
Palmer, John Boyton; Col.; F&S; Mitchell; 13 Oct. 1826–10 Dec. 1893; Elmwood Cem., Columbia, SC
Pangle, Henry; Pvt.; F; Camp Vance; d. 1864
Paris, Josiah; ---; E
Parker, Alfred T.; Pvt.; A; Mitchell; b. ca. 1829
Parker, James; Pvt.; C; Yancey; b. ca. 1830
Parker, William H.; Pvt.; F; McDowell; b. ca. 1845
Parkes, Clinton Lafayette; Pvt.; E; Burke; 6 Aug. 1831–11 July 1885; Burke Co.
Parkes, Samuel M.; Pvt.; E; Caldwell; ca. 1843–3 Oct. 1864; Camp Douglas, Ill.
Parsons, George W.; Pvt.; L; Ashe; 5 Dec. 1835–20 Jan. 1905; Floyd W. Welch Cem., Ashe Co.
Parsons, William H.; Pvt.; L; Ashe; d. 4 Feb. 1865; Camp Morton, Ind.
Pate, George Washington; Pvt.; G; Yancey; 4 June 1824 or 1834–23 Dec. 1906
Patterson, John; ---; E
Patterson, Samuel F.; Pvt.; G; Yancey/Mitchell; ca. 1845–11 May1863; Clinton, Tenn.
Patton, Robert V.; Pvt.; F; McDowell; b. ca. 1830
Pearce, Alfred; Pvt.; E; Randolph
Pearce, Allen; Pvt.; I
Pearce, Redmond T.; Pvt.; H; Caldwell; b. ca. 1839
Pearey, Aaron; Pvt.; E; Mitchell; b. ca. 1837
Pearson, Robert Caldwell; As. Surg.; F&S; Burke; 27 May 1837–28 Jan 1908; Forest Hill Cem., Burke Co.
Peek, John Willis; Capt.; G; Yancey; 2 Oct. 1810–13 July 1890; Peake Cem., Yancey Co.
Pendley, William N.; Pvt.; E; Burke; ca. 1832–20 Sept. 1863; Chickamauga, Ga.
Penington, Dow; Pvt.; L; Ashe; b. ca. 1817
Penington, Samuel; Pvt.; L; Dalton, Ga.
Penington, Thornton; Pvt.; L; Ashe; ca. 1839–20 Sept. 1863; Chickamauga, Ga.
Penland, Charles M.; Pvt.; C; Yancey; 29 April 1845–13 Jan. 1924; Penland Cem., Yancey Co.
Penland, Milton F.; Pvt.; C; Yancey; 1840–1916; Swingle Cem., Unicoi Co., Tenn.
Penley, Ransom; ---; C; ca. 1847–3 May 1929; Buncombe Co.
Pennel, Joshua T.; Pvt.; E; Caldwell; b. ca. 1843
Pennel, Milton Columbus; Pvt.; E; Caldwell; b. 25 March 1828

Percy, Jesse; Pvt.; E; Caldwell; ca. 1843–25 Sept. 1863
Percy, Job; Pvt.; E; Caldwell; b. ca. 1830
Percy, John; Pvt.; E; Mitchell
Percy, Sidney S.; Pvt.; E; Burke; 8 April 1826–19 Jun 1912; Burke Co.
Perkins, Franklin; Pvt.; M/G; Ashe/Watauga
Perkins, John; Pvt.; M/G; Ashe/Watauga; b. ca. 1841
Perry, Benjamin L; Adj.; F&S
Perry, Richard M.; Sgt.; Misc.
Peterson, Allen; Pvt.; G; Yancey; b. ca. 1842
Peterson, Charles Jefferson; Pvt.; G; Yancey; b. ca. 1836
Peterson, John; Pvt.; G/E; Yadkin/Yancey; b. ca. 1828
Peterson, Lawson; Pvt.; G; Yancey; 4 June 1840–29 July 1923; Peterson Cem., Unicoi Co., Tenn.
Peterson, Moses; Pvt.; G; Yancey; 10 April 1846–17 June 1916
Peterson, Moses Jefferson; ---; H; ---; 15 Nov. 1848–26 Sep. 1941; Peterson Cem., Yancey Co.
Peterson, Reuben; Pvt.; G; Yancey; 25 April 1831–26 July 1916; Peterson Cem., Yancey Co.
Phifer, William L.; Pvt.; A; d. 20 Sept. 1863; Chickamauga, Ga.
Phillips, Alfred; Pvt.; G/D; Yancey; b. ca. 1834
Phillips, Crisenbery; Musc.; B; Camp Jackson; d. 25 Sept. 1863
Phillips, Daniel; Pvt.; E; Burke; ca. 1837–15 Nov. 1863; Myrtle Hill Cem., Rome, Ga.
Phillips, Elijah; Pvt.; M; 1829–9 May 1863; Knoxville, Tenn.
Phillips, Hamilton; Pvt.; M/G; Ashe/Watauga; b. ca. 1832
Phillips, Hugh M.; Pvt.; M/G; Ashe/Watauga; 27 Jan. 1833–30 Aug. 1915; Blue Ridge Bapt. Ch. Cem. Ashe Co.
Phillips, John W.; Pvt.; C; Yancey; ca. 1842–20 Feb. 1863; Jacksboro, Tenn.
Phillips, Jonathan Lenard; Capt.; M/G; 7 Sept. 1835–24 Jan. 1865; Howell Cem., Watauga Co.
Phillips, Joseph T.; Pvt.; A
Phillips, Nathan; Pvt.; M/G; Ashe/Watauga; ca. 1835–7 Aug. 1864; Camp Morton, Ill.
Phillips, Payton; Pvt.; M/G; Ashe/Watauga; b. Sept. 1831
Phillips, R. B.; ---; K
Phillips, Reuben Orlando; Pvt.; E; Caldwell; 22 June 1845–25 Feb. 1931; Belleview Cem., Caldwell Co.
Phillips, Samuel C.; Pvt.; A; Mitchell; b. ca. 1828
Phillips, Stephen; Pvt.; C; Yancey; b. ca. 1842
Phipps, Conarah D.; Pvt.; C; Yancey; ca. 1835–2 Jan. 1863; Jacksboro, Tenn.
Phipps, John W.; Pvt.; G; Yancey; b. ca. 1837
Pickett, Anderson Wiley; Pvt.; E; Randolph; 23 Sept. 1847–18 Jan. 1864; Atlanta, Ga.
Pierce, Joseph; Pvt.; I; Bristol, Tenn.; d. 8 Aug. 1864; Camp Morton, Ind.

Pipes, John Wiley; Pvt.; M/G/E; Watauga; 5 March 1828–13 Nov. 1863; Nashville, Tenn.
Portia, John; Pvt.; A/K; Mitchell; b. ca. 1827
Poteet, Samuel A.; Sgt.; A; Mitchell; ca. 1837–20 Sept. 1863; Chickamauga, Ga.
Potter, Levi; Pvt.; D; Watauga; d. 26 Jan. 1863; Jacksboro, Tenn.
Powell, A. D.; Pvt.; F; McDowell
Powell, Denny; Pvt.; F; McDowell; b. ca. 1822
Powell, Pinkney; Pvt.; E; Caldwell; ca. 1844–25 June 1864; Point Lookout, Md.
Prather, George Washington; Pvt.; E; Madison
Presnell, Benjamin L.; Cpl.; D; Watauga; ca. 1844–March 1865; Bentonville, N.C.
Presnell, David A.; Pvt.; C/G; ca. 1835–1 Dec. 1862; Cumberland Gap, Tenn.[21]
Presnell, Henry; Pvt.; C; Yancey; b. ca. 1835; Bailey Hill Cem., Yancey Co.
Presnell, James; Pvt.; D; Watauga; 7 July 1847–28 May 1923; Watauga Co.
Presnell, James Bartley; Pvt.; C; Yancey; b. ca. 1832; Cane River Bapt. Ch. Cem., Yancey Co.
Presnell, John C.; Pvt.; C; Yancey; b. ca. 1841
Presnell, Nathaniel; Pvt.; D; Watauga; 16 July 1838–29 Aug. 1887; Mast Cem., Watauga Co.
Presnell, Squire Adams; Pvt.; D; Watauga; b. 7 Aug. 1842
Presnell, Thomas S.; Pvt.; K; Caldwell; b. ca. 1843; Union Bapt. Ch. Cem., Caldwell Co.
Presnell, Wesley Wayne; Pvt.; D; Watauga; 22 July 1837–24 Aug. 1925; Greer Cem., Watauga Co.
Prestwood, Sydney E.; Pvt.; B; Mitchell; 1 Jan. 1832–3 June 1889; Phillips Cem., Mitchell Co.
Pritchard, Alexander; Pvt.; G/E; Yancey; d. 13 Feb. 1864; Rock Island, Ill.
Pritchard, Azor M. C.; 3rd Lt.; B
Pritchard, Campbell; Pvt.; E; Caldwell; ca. 1838–1910; McDowell Co.
Pritchard, J. C.; Pvt.; A; ca. 1813–16 Sept. 1892; Smith Co., Texas
Pritchard, Rufus; Pvt.; E; Caldwell; ca. 1832–13 Feb. 1864; Rock Island, Ill.
Prichard, William A.; Pvt.; E; Burke; b. ca. 1841
Prim, Isaac; Pvt.; E; Yadkin; b. ca. 1835
Proctor, Reuben; Pvt.; B
Proffitt, Jesse; Pvt.; I; Watauga; ca. 1843–29 March 1863; Big Gap Creek, Tenn.
Proffitt, John; Pvt.; I; ca. 1824–ca. 1895; Meat Camp Bapt. Ch. Cem., Watauga Co.
Proffitt, William Holeman; Pvt.; I; Watauga; 28 Jan. 1826–17 Oct. 1895; Meat Camp Bapt. Ch., Watauga Co.
Proffitt, William W.; Lt. Col.; F&S; Yancey; 25 Dec. 1827–13 Jan. 1901; Gibbs Cem., Yancey Co.
Puckett, John; Pvt.; E
Puett, Elisha; Cpl.; E; Caldwell; 28 Jan. 1843–25 Oct. 1871; Caldwell Co.
Puett, Joseph; Pvt.; E; Caldwell; Dec. 1840–4 Jan. 1905; Caldwell Co.

Putnam, James W.; 2nd Lt.; B; Mitchell; 7 June 1838–24 Sept. 1914; Mitchell Co.
Pyatt, Leander; Pvt.; A; Dalton, Ga.; 1823–10 Jan. 1864; Atlanta, Ga.
Queen, Cyrus; Pvt.; H; Wilkes; d. 8 June 1864; Alton, Ill.
Queen, Peter Waits; Pvt.; G; Yancey; 20 Dec. 1846–25 May 1932; Grassy Creek Cem., Mitchell Co.
Quinn, William B.; Pvt.; F; McDowell; b. ca. 1835
Rabey, George W.; Pvt.; E; Caldwell; b. ca. 1836
Rabey, James C.; Pvt.; H; Caldwell; b. ca. 1832
Rabey, John Wesley; Chaplain; F&S; Caldwell; 11 May 1838–18 Jan. 1930; Old Runnels Cem., Runnels Co., Texas
Raby, William Rufus; Pvt.; H; Caldwell; d. 22 Jun. 1864; Kolb's Farm, Ga.
Rainey, William H.; Pvt.; M; Johnson Co., Tenn./Watauga
Ramsey, Alexander; Pvt.; F; Camp Vance
Ramsey, Joseph R.; Pvt.; B; Mitchell; b. ca. 1843
Ramsey, Riley C.; Pvt.; B; Mitchell; b. ca. 1836
Randles, Joseph; Pvt.; I; Ashe; b. ca. 1840
Randolph, James Burton; Pvt.; G; Yancey; 1827–1922; Higgins Cem., Yancey Co.
Randolph, Morgan; Pvt.; G; Camp Palmer; b. ca. 1828
Randolph, Reuben; Pvt.; K; Mitchell; 1834–1894; Buchanan Cem., Mitchell Co.
Randolph, Thomas M.; Pvt.; G; Yancey; b. 1840
Randolph, William J.; Pvt.; G; Yancey; 2 July 1828–24 Feb. 1916; Whitson Cem., Yancey Co.
Rankin, James Eugene; QSgt.; F/F&S; Clinton, Tenn.; 27 April 1845–12 Feb. 1928; Riverside Cem., Buncombe Co.
Rash, Payton; Pvt.; M/G; Watauga; d. 10 Sept. 1863; Fort Delaware, Del.
Rash, Joseph Stephen; Pvt.; I; Watauga; 25 Aug. 1838–22 Oct. 1877; Stephen Bumgarner Cem., Wilkes Co.
Ray, Garrett DeWeese; Pvt.; C; Madison; 6 July 1833–14 May 1912; Academy Hill Cem., Yancey Co.
Ray, Leander T.; Pvt.; C; Yancey; b. ca. 1823; Riddle Cem., Yancey Co.
Ray, Leroy C.; Pvt.; C; Yancey; ca. 1827–15 March 1864; Rock Island, Ill.
Ray, Thomas; 2nd Lt.; M/G; Ashe; b. ca. 1833
Ray, William Henry; Pvt.; C/D; Yancey; b. ca. 1833
Reace, William; Pvt.; M/G; Watauga
Read, Samuel; Pvt.; F; McDowell; ca. 1830–20 Sept. 1863; Chickamauga, Ga.
Redding, William; Pvt.; E; Randolph; ca. 1822–23 June 1864; Alton, Ill.
Reece, Aaron B.; Pvt.; E; Caldwell; ca. 1831–13 or 14 May 1864; Resaca, Ga.
Reed, Andrew Homer; Pvt.; F; McDowell; b. ca. 1828; Hice Hill Cem., Buncombe Co.
Reed, John C.; Pvt.; A; Caldwell

Reedy, George Washington; Pvt.; L; Ashe; 9 Feb. 1835–26 March 1904; John Reedy Cem., Ashe Co.
Reel, William; Pvt.; F; McDowell/Camp Vance; b. ca. 1826
Reid, Burgess G.; Pvt.; H; Clinton, Tenn.
Reid, Malan; Pvt.; H; Caldwell; b. 1827
Renfro, David; Pvt.; C
Revis, Thomas H.; ---; I; 1843–28 April 1921; Madison Co.
Rhodes, Samuel D.; ---; F
Rhodes, William; Pvt.; F; Charleston, Tenn.
Rice, James L.; Pvt.; H; Caldwell; d. 26 Aug. 1864; Camp Morton, Ind.
Richards, Isaac M.; Pvt.; H; Caldwell; d. 1864; Vicksburg, Miss.
Richardson, James; Pvt.; L; Ashe; d. 22 Nov. 1862; Bethel Cem., Knoxville, Tenn.
Riddle, James Garrett; Pvt.; C/D; Yancey; 1828–1888
Riddle, James Marion; Hos. Ste.; F&S/A; Mitchell; b. ca. 1845
Riddle, John; Pvt.; B; Mitchell; b. ca. 1830
Riddle, John; Pvt.; G; Yancey; 1840–1889; Sams Cem., Unicoi Co., Tenn.
Riddle, Nathan; Pvt.; A; Mitchell; 1 March 1823–30 April 1889; Pisgah UMC, Avery Co.
Riddle, Robert T.; 1st Sgt.; G; Yancey; 1834–1892
Riddle, Samuel; Pvt.; C; 1838–1920; Riddle Cem., Yancey Co.
Riddle, William P.; Pvt.; G; Yancey; 1843–1924; Riddle Cem., Yancey Co.
Rimer, Eli; Pvt.; G; Camp Holmes; b. ca. 1825
Roark, Joshua Milton; Pvt.; L; Ashe; 1830–1892; Joshua Roark Cem., Ashe Co.
Roark, Solomon; Pvt.; L; Ashe; ca. 1832–ca. 1863
Roark, William; Pvt.; L; Camp Holmes
Robbins, Anderson; Pvt.; F; McDowell; b. ca. 1830
Robbins, James B.; Pvt.; E; Watauga; 1847–7 March 1929; Caldwell Co.
Robbins, James Larkin; Pvt.; E; Caldwell; 2 Feb. 1827–March 1910; Caldwell Co.
Robbins, Reuben Rufus; Pvt.; E; Caldwell; 32 March 1831–1899
Roberson, E. Edward; Pvt.; C; Yancey; b. ca. 1838; Edward Roberson Cem., Yancey Co.
Roberson, George; Pvt.; C; Yancey; b. ca. 1832; Roberson Cem., Yancey Co.
Roberson, James H.; Pvt.; C; Yancey; d. 3 Dec. 1863; Marietta, Ga.
Roberson, John; Pvt.; C; Yancey
Roberson, John C.; Pvt.; C; Yancey
Roberson, Julius; Cpl.; C; Yancey; b. ca. 1839; Austin-Roberson Cem., Yancey Co.
Roberson, Milton; Pvt.; F; Mitchell; b. ca. 1847
Roberson, Stephen Morgan; Pvt.; C; Yancey; b. ca. 1844
Roberson, Thomas; Pvt.; K
Roberson, William C.; Pvt.; C; Yancey; d. 10 May 1863; Knoxville, Tenn.
Roberts, Garrett Monroe; Pvt.; C; Yancey; b. ca. 1838; Ga.
Roberts, J. B.; Cpl.; A;
Roberts, James; Pvt.; A; Yancey; b. ca. 1843
Roberts, James; Pvt.; K
Robertson, E. M.; ---; K
Robertson, Merritt B.; ---; K; ---; W. Burnsville Bapt. Ch. Cem., Yancey Co.
Robinson, Benjamin F.; Pvt.; L; Ashe
Robinson, Ned; ---; K
Robinson, Thomas B.; ---; K; ---; Silver Chapel Bap. Cem., Mitchell Co.
Robison, Wilborn C.; Pvt.; L; Ashe
Rogers, Hiram David; Pvt.; G; Yancey; ca. 1830–5 May 1863; Knoxville, Tenn.
Rose, Joel; Pvt.; A; Yancey; ca. 1843–4 April 1863
Rose, Samuel; Pvt.; A/K; Mitchell; b. ca. 1846
Rose, Wyatt; Pvt.; L; Ashe
Roten, James; Pvt.; L; Ashe; b. ca. 1837
Rowe, Conradrado; Pvt.; K; Caldwell; b. ca. 1820
Rowland, Michael; Pvt.; D; Watauga; b. ca. 1837; Pine Grove UMC, Avery Co.
Rowland, Robert H.; Pvt.; C; Yancey; ca. 1832–16 May 1864; Resaca, Ga.
Rowland, Silas; Pvt.; C; Yancey; b. ca. 1836
Rowland, William Henry; Pvt.; G; Yancey; b. ca. 1841
Rush, Henry; Pvt.; E; Randolph; 17 March 1822–1 Oct. 1901; Farmer Cem., Randolph Co.
Sale, William J.; Pvt.; G; Camp Holmes; b. 3 Dec. 1826
Sales, John T.; 1st Lt.; C
Sales, Joseph B.; Pvt.; C
Sams, Jacob F.; ---; B; b. ca. 1851; Cane River Bapt. Ch. Cem., Yancey Co.
Sanders, Jessie Washington; Pvt.; E; Caldwell; 5 Jan. 1825–19 April 1907; Mt. Pleasant UMC, Burke Co.
Scoggins, John B.; Sgt.; B; Mitchell; b. ca. 1827
Scott, James A.; ---; B
Scott, Lorenzo D.; Pvt.; B; Mitchell; b. ca. 1829
Scotton, John; Pvt.; E; Randolph; 1837–1865 or 1866; Randolph Co.
Seagle, John A.; Pvt.; F; McDowell; Feb. 1835–ca. 1900; McDowell Co.
Seals, Alfred; ---; A; d. 2 Oct. 1864; Macon, Ga.
Seats, Robert E.; Pvt.; I; Ashe; ca. 1837–1862
Sellers, Joseph; Pvt.; A
Sellers, J. Pink; ---; K
Setser, Ephraim D.; Pvt.; E; Caldwell; ca. 1836–ca. 1876; Setzer Cem., Caldwell Co.
Setser, Joshua; Pvt.; E; Caldwell; ca. 1833–22 Feb. 1894; Littlejohns Cem., Caldwell Co.
Setser, William Azor; Pvt.; E; Caldwell; 21 April 1838–25 April 1927; Suddreth Cem., Caldwell Co.
Settlemire, Sidney; Pvt.; H; Caldwell; d. 1862
Shaver, William Lee; Pvt.; G; Iredell/Camp Holmes; d. 6 July 1864; Macon, Ga.
Shaw, Alfred; Pvt.; M/G; Ashe/Watauga; 30 April

1836–22 March 1911; McKinney Cem., Carter Co., Tenn.
Shaw, Doctor Newton; Pvt.; L; Ashe; 24 Aug. 1841–24 Nov. 1918; Carter Co., Tenn.
Shaw, John; Pvt.; M/G; Ashe/Watauga; b. ca. 1830
Shaw, Solomon; Pvt.; M/G; Ashe/Watauga; 1834–1911; Ellis County, Texas
Sheets, Linville William Douglas; Pvt.; L; Ashe; ca. 1821–5 March 1897; Elrod Cem., Ashe Co.
Shehan, Albert; Pvt.; F; Camp Reynolds; b. ca. 1838
Shehan, Andrew; Pvt.; F; McDowell; 11 April 1826–27 Feb. 1922; Pleasant Gardens Bapt. Ch., McDowell Co.
Shehan, James E.; Pvt.; C; Yancey; ca. 1843–21 Oct. 1925; Washington Co., Tenn.
Shehan, Pinkney; Pvt.; F; Rutherford/Camp Reynolds; b. ca. 1840
Shehan, Washington; Pvt.; F; McDowell/Camp Vance; b. ca. 1830
Shell, Franklin Dugger; Pvt.; D; Watauga; 3 July 1832–25 Dec. 1892; Harmon Cem., Watauga Co.
Shell, John Tipton; Pvt.; E; Caldwell; 28 Jan. 1828–22 Oct. 1910; Dudley Shoals Bapt. Ch., Caldwell Co.
Shelton, David; Pvt.; E; Madison; b. ca. 1823
Shepherd, David; Pvt.; F; McDowell; b. ca. 1828
Shepherd, Grandison; Pvt.; C; Yancey; 1826–20 Nov. 1862; Jacksboro, Tenn.
Shepherd, Thomas Erwin; Cpl.; C/D; b. 1847
Sherill, Abner Raynor; Pvt.; E; Caldwell
Sherlin, Henry H.; Pvt.; F; McDowell; 1 Sept. 1833–1909; Pinelog Methodist Ch. Cem., Clay Co.
Sherrell, James Milton; Pvt.; K; Caldwell; 13 July 1836–6 May 1900
Sherrill, Adam Carter; Pvt.; E; Caldwell; 15 July 1840–7 April 1928; Sherrills Cem., Caldwell Co.
Sherrill, Isaac Ira; Pvt.; E; Caldwell; 15 April 1838–1928; Caldwell Co.
Sherrill, William Wesley; Pvt.; E; Caldwell; 23 Jan. 1828–11 Jan. 1903
Sherwood, Theron; Pvt.; A; Mitchell; d. 20 Sept. 1863; Chickamauga, Ga.
Shewford, James S.; Pvt.; C/D; Yancey; b. ca. 1844
Shipman, William R., Jr.; Pvt.; E; Henderson; 25 Sept. 1843–27 Aug. 1925; Beulah Bapt. Ch. Cem., Henderson Co.
Shook, Jacob D.; Pvt.; D; Watauga; ca. 1845–31 Dec. 1863; Confederate Cem., Dalton, Ga.
Shook, Stephen S.; Pvt.; A; Mitchell; b. ca. 1832; Upper Laurel Bapt. Cem., Madison Co.
Shuffler, Jacob Cicero; Pvt.; A/E; Burke; 16 March 1834–11 May 1925; Big Springs Cem., Young Co., Texas
Shuffler, James; ---; A
Shuffler, Posey C.; Pvt.; A/E; Caldwell; 17 Sept. 1842–4 April 1913; Greenlawn Cem., Rowan Co.

Shull, John F.; Pvt.; D; Watauga; 30 April 1837–12 Oct. 1914
Shull, William R.; Pvt.; I; Watauga; ca. 1837–17 May 1938; Shulls Mill, Watauga Co.
Shumaker, James; Pvt.; L; Chattanooga, Tenn.; d. 23 May or 10 June 1864; Madison, Ga.
Sidden, John; Pvt.; H; Surry
Side, William; Pvt.; E; Wilkes
Sifford, George H.; Pvt.; D; Watauga; b. ca. 1829
Sifford, Joel; ---;
Sifford, John; Pvt.; D; Watauga; b. 1830s
Sigmon, Ambrose; Pvt.; A; Mitchell; ca. 1830–20 Sept. 1863; Chickamauga. Ga.
Silver, Alexander; Pvt.; K; Mitchell; b. ca. 1846; Higgins Freewill Bapt. Ch., Yancey Co.
Silver, David H.; 1st Sgt.; C; Yancey; b. ca. 1838; Micaville Cem., Yancey Co.
Silver, David Ralph; Capt.; K; Mitchell; 21 Feb. 1832–26 Aug. 1911; Kona, Mitchell Co.
Silver, Edmund Drury; 1st Sgt.; E/K; Mitchell; 14 Sept. 1838–28 March 1910; Blue Rock Ch. Cem., Yancey Co.
Silver, Levi Dewise; 2nd Lt.; E/K/F; Mitchell; b. 16 Sept. 1836; Kona Cem., Mitchell Co.
Silver, Samuel Marion; Lt. Col.; E/K/F&S Mitchell; 30 Dec. 1833–15 May 1922; Bartlet Cem., Wallowa Co., Ore.
Silver, Tilman Blalock; Cpl.; A/K/F; Mitchell; 26 Nov. 1839–Dec. 1906; Bailey Cem., Madison Co.
Silver, William R.; Pvt.; C; Yancey; 1833–20 March 1915
Simmons, Elliott; Pvt.; C; Yancey; 14 March 1846–26 Dec. 1926; Liberty Hill Bapt. Ch., Mitchell Co.
Simmons, James Marion; Pvt.; F; McDowell; 30 Aug. 1831–8 July 1910; Harmony Grove Bapt. Ch., McDowell Co.
Simons, Stewart; ---
Singleton, James C.; Pvt.; A; Yancey; 12 Nov. 1843–25 Sep. 1928; Highlands Cem., Elizabethton, Tenn.
Singleton, Samuel T.; Pvt.; A; Montgomery; ca. 1836–prior to 1 March 1863; Cumberland Gap, Tenn.
Sisemore, James; Pvt.; A; Mitchell; 4 Oct. 1846–24 May 1912; Buffalo Cem., Union Co., S.C.
Sisemore, John J.; Pvt.; A; Mitchell; 1822–24 Dec. 1905
Sisemore, Thomas; Cpl.; A; Mitchell; b. 1845
Sisk, Marion M.; Pvt.; F; McDowell; b. ca. 1842; Providence UMC, McDowell Co.
Sisk, Robert Harrison; 3rd Lt.; F; McDowell; b. ca. 1841
Slagle, A. D.; Pvt.; B; Dalton, Ga.
Slagle, Adolphus; Pvt.; B/E; Mitchell; b. ca. 1841
Slagle, John L. L.; Pvt.; E; Yancey; ca. 1829–1915; Newport, Tenn.
Slagle, Simeon; Pvt.; B/C/D; Mitchell; 30 March 1838–30 Aug. 1920

Sloan, Solomon; Pvt.; D; d. Jan. 1864; Nashville Tenn.
Sluder, David; Pvt.; L; Ashe; b. ca. 1829
Sluder, Felix; Pvt.; L; Ashe; b. ca. 1824
Smith, Andrew; Pvt.; I; Watauga; 17 March 1835–8 Aug. 1920; Maples Cem., Henderson Co.
Smith, Andrew J.; Pvt.; G/K; Camp Huston; d. 15 June 1863; Clinton, Tenn.
Smith, Austin; Pvt.; H; Caldwell; 1835–15 May 1864; Resaca, Ga.
Smith, G. W.; Pvt.; F; Camp Vance
Smith, George L.; Pvt.; I; Watauga; ca. 1840–20 Sept. 1863; Chickamauga, Ga.
Smith, James A.; Pvt.; I; Camp Holmes
Smith, James Henry; Pvt.; H; Caldwell; 5 May 1840–27 March 1914
Smith, Joab Elbert; Pvt.; H; Caldwell; 30 Aug. 1826–7 May 1900
Smith, John N.; 1st Sgt.; I; Watauga; 16 July 1833–15 April 1873; Watauga Co.
Smith, Julius; Cpl.; H; 12 Aug. 1840–11 July 1923
Smith, Julius Pinkney; Sgt.; H; Caldwell; 16 Sep. 1844–7 April 1925
Smith, Lafayette; ---; H
Smith, Maston D.; Pvt.; E; Caldwell; b. ca. 1834
Smith, Nelson; Pvt.; I
Smith, Richard Walter; Pvt.; H; Caldwell; 19 Jan. 1835–6 July 1900
Smith, Robert M.; Cpl.; H; Wilkes/Caldwell; ca. 1825–20 Sept. 1863; Chickamauga, Ga.
Smith, Rufus; Pvt.; H; Caldwell; b. ca. 1830
Smith, Samuel; ---; A
Smith, Solomon; Pvt.; I; Watauga; b. ca. 1846
Smith, Thomas; Pvt.; I; Watauga; 15 Sep. 1837–4 Jan. 1914; Heaton Cem., Watauga Co.
Smith, William J.; Pvt.; C; Yancey; 15 Feb. 1842–1 Jan. 1916; Pete Young Cem., Yancey Co.
Smith, William M.; Pvt.; I; Watauga; b. 18 Sept. 1842
Smith, William W.; Pvt.; H; Caldwell; b. ca. 1823
Snipes, Merrit; Sgt.; A; Mitchell; 5 April 1836–2 Nov. 1899; Spruce Pine Cem., Mitchell Co.
Snyder, Thomas; Pvt.; C; d. 9 Jan. 1864; Rock Island, Ill.
Sorrells, Joshua Maceborn; Pvt.; A; b. ca. 1842
South, Harrison; Pvt.; I; Watauga; ca. 1841–13 May 1863; Clinton, Tenn.
Sparks, Clingman; Pvt.; H; Caldwell; b. ca. 1844
Sparks, George; Pvt.; F; McDowell; b. ca. 1820
Sparks, Jackson C.; ---; K; 18 May 1848–5 Jan. 1934; Sparks Cem., Mitchell Co.
Sparks, Jeremiah P.; Cpl.; A/K; Mitchell; ca. 1844–ca. 1862
Sparks, John; Pvt.; F; McDowell; ca. 1833–prior to 25 April 1863
Sparks, Joseph M.; Cpl.; A/K; Mitchell; b. ca. 1844
Sparks, Matthew L.; Pvt.; A; 4 Feb. 1813–30 Sept. 1892; Bear Creek Cem., Mitchell Co.

Sparks, Samuel B.; Pvt.; A; Burke; 25 Jan. 1822–11 Feb. 1902; Sparks Cem., Mitchell Co.
Sparks, Samuel D.; Pvt.; A; 5 Feb. 1832–12 Jan 1897; Lily Branch Bapt. Cem., Mitchell Co.
Sparks, Thomas M.; Pvt.; A
Sparks, William M.; Sgt.; H; Caldwell; b. ca. 1840
Spencer, Isaac Thomas Avery; Cpl.; E; Caldwell; b. 23 Oct. 1829
Spivey, Jesse; Sgt.; L/F; Ashe; ca. 1840–after 19 March 1865; North Carolina
Sprinkle, Obadiah; Pvt.; G; Wilkes/Camp Holmes; 1823–4 July 1885; Wilkes Co.
Stafford, Joseph A.; Pvt.; H; Caldwell; 31 May 1845–31 Oct. 1890; Penland Cem., Mitchell Co.
Stafford, Julius Andrew; Sgt.; H; Caldwell; b. 1838; Stafford Cem., Gray, Tenn.
Stafford, William Henry; Pvt.; H/B; Caldwell; 20 Sept. 1862–26 Dec. 1925; Limestone, Tenn.
Stallings, Nelson; Pvt.; H; Caldwell; 17 Feb. 1821–22 Dec. 1904; Collins Cem., Caldwell Co.
Stamey, Elias Alexander; Pvt.; A; Mitchell; 12 July 1835–9 Jan. 1917; Stameytown Cem., Avery Co.
Stamey, George; Pvt.; A; Mitchell; 24 May 1838–21 April 1912; Stameytown Cem., Avery Co.
Stamey, Logan; Sgt.; A; Mitchell; 25 Jan. 1833–17 July 1898; Burke Co.
Stanberry, Jesse H.; Pvt.; G; Watauga; b. ca. 1826
Stanberry, Joshua S.; Pvt.; M/G; Watauga; b. ca. 1837
Stanberry, Nathan W.; Pvt.; M/G; Watauga; 20 Feb. 1834–13 Sept. 1914; Stanberry Cem., Watauga Co.
Starnes, Jonas C.; Pvt.; H; Caldwell; ca. 1835–ca. 1922; Caldwell Co.
Starnes, Valentine; Sgt.; H; Mecklenburg/Caldwell; 24 April 1830–19 Jan. 1908; Union Co.
Steele, John L.; Pvt.; E; Caldwell; b. ca. 1842
Stephens, Jackson; Pvt.; B; Mitchell; b. ca. 1841
Stephens, John; Cpl.; B/E; Mitchell; b. ca. 1841
Stephens, Joshua; Pvt.; B; Mitchell; ca. 1822–28 March 1870
Stephens, Sherred; Pvt.; B/E; Mitchell; b. ca. 1836
Stepp, Robert J.; Sgt.; C; Buncombe; 4 Dec. 1839–11 Nov. 1911; Newton Academy Cem., Buncombe Co.
Stevens, Merrit Foster; Pvt.; H; 9 Dec. 1834–30 Nov. 1911; Newton Academy Cem., Buncombe Co.
Stevens, Polk; Pvt.; F
Stevens, Wash; Pvt.; F; Gaston, Ga.; d. 25 Nov. 1863; Confederate Cem., Dalton, Ga.
Steward, Berry; Sgt.; B; Camp Jackson; b. ca. 1841
Steward, Jasper; Sgt.; E/B; d. 22 June 1864; Kolb's Farm, Ga.
Steward, William R.; Pvt.; B; Mitchell; b. ca. 1825; Burleson Cem., Mitchell Co.
Stewart, Alfred Theodore; Maj.; F&S; Caldwell Co.; ca. 1833–31 Aug. 1864; Jonesboro, Ga.
Stewart, Benjamin; ---; B

Stewart, Jackson; 2nd Lt.; B/E; Mitchell; b. ca. 1804–1865; Green Cem., Mitchell Co.
Stewart, James; Pvt.; A; Yancey; b. ca. 1844; Pineola Pres. Ch. Avery Co.
Stewart, James; Pvt.; B; Mitchell; b. 1844
Stewart, Joseph; Pvt.; A; Mitchell; d. 31 March 1863; Jacksboro, Tenn.
Stewart, William; Pvt.; C/D/E/K; b. ca. 1844
Stikes, Joseph W.; Pvt.; L; Ashe; b. 18 Feb. 1838
Storie, Jesse; Pvt.; M/G; Watauga; 22 June 1837–14 March 1926
Storie, Noah; Pvt.; M/G; Watauga; ca. 1838–Sept. 1864; Knoxville National Cem., Knoxville, Tenn.
Story, Thomas Walter; Pvt.; E; Watauga; ca. 1825–11 Jan. 1864; Rock Island, Ill.
Stradley, Thomas; Pvt.; C; Carter Co., Tenn.
Street, Samuel M.; Pvt.; B/E; Mitchell; b. ca. 1836
Strickland, Moore; Pvt.; D; Watauga; 15 Nov. 1843–9 March 1916; Fine Cem., Washington Co., Tenn.
Stricklin, Henry; Pvt.; G; Camp Holmes; d. 8 Sept. 1864; Rock Island, Ill.
Stuard, Simon; Pvt.; F; Macon Co.
Stuart, William H.; Pvt.; E/K; Mitchell; ca. 1844–5 Aug. 1864; Greensboro, Ga.
Styles, John Wesley; Pvt.; C; Yancey; 7 Feb. 1836–Oct. 1920; Styles Cem., Yancey Co.
Styles, Noah V.; Pvt.; C; Yancey; 6 Oct. 1842–2 Nov. 1919; Styles Cem., Yancey Co.
Sudderth, James Newton; Pvt.; E; Caldwell; ca. 1840–6 Oct. 1863; Atlanta, Ga.
Sudderth, John Marshall; Pvt.; E; Caldwell; 12 Sept. 1831–6 April 1920; Confidence Advt. Ch., Caldwell Co.
Sudderth, Newton N.; Pvt.; E; Caldwell
Sudderth, Toliver F.; Pvt.; E; Caldwell; ca. 1840–17 May 1918; Clarke Cem., Caldwell Co.
Suits, James; Pvt.; G; Wilkes/Camp Holmes
Sullins, Andrew Wilkerson; Pvt.; A; Mitchell; 26 Nov. 1825–28 Jan. 1908; Sullins Cem., Mitchell Co.
Sumit, Eli; ---; E
Sutherland, William Henry Harrison; Pvt.; D/I; Watauga; b. ca. 1841
Swann, James Molton; Cpl.; A; McDowell; 25 March 1843–12 June 1923; Swann Cem., Mitchell Co.
Swanson, Lawson Calvin; Pvt.; H; Caldwell; 6 July 1837–24 March 1922; Sardis Bapt. Ch. Cem., Caldwell Co.
Swift, Willborn; Pvt.; I; Watauga; b. ca. 1831
Tallent, Samuel; Pvt.; A; Mitchell; b. 13 Dec. 1831; Gilead Bapt. Ch. Cem., Burke Co.
Tate, Hugh Columbus; Pvt.; F; McDowell; 29 May 1829–25 May 1903
Taylor, Andrew J.; Pvt.; H; Caldwell; b. ca. 1815
Taylor, George W.; Pvt.; H; Caldwell; Dec. 1831–1910s; Old Clark Cem., Caldwell Co.
Taylor, Jacob; Pvt.; E; Burke/Caldwell; 10 April 1844–20 Dec. 1878; Taylor Fam. Cem., Burke Co.
Taylor, James E.; Pvt.; I/E; ca. 1839–7 May 1865; Camp Douglas, Ill.
Taylor, John; Pvt.; E; Burke; b. ca. 1831
Taylor, Weistell; Pvt.; E; Burke; d. 6 June 1864; Cassville, Ga.
Taylor, William; Pvt.; G; Yancey
Teague, James; Pvt.; E; Caldwell
Teague, James Iverson; Pvt.; E; Caldwell; b. 2 Nov. 1846
Teague, John Bloomington; Pvt.; E; Caldwell; 28 July 1848–30 July 1864; Louisville, Ky.
Teague, Logan; ---; E; Mitchell
Teague, Vandaver M.; Pvt.; I; Camp Holmes; b. ca. 1829
Team, Israel; Pvt.; E; Caldwell; b. Oct. 1837; Graveyard Hill Cem., Avery Co.
Teaster, Finley P.; Pvt.; D; Watauga; b. ca. 1844
Teaster, Ransom; Pvt.; D; Watauga; ca. 1818–10 June 1864
Testerman, Frank M.; Pvt.; B; Dalton, Ga.
Testerman, Hugh; Pvt.; L; Ashe; b. ca. 1845
Testerman, Morgan Bryant; Pvt.; L; Ashe/Dalton, Ga.; 1822–1871; Hamblen Co., Tenn.
Thomas, Aaron; Pvt.; C/D; Yancey; 1824–ca. 1909; Silver Chapel Bapt. Ch. Cem., Mitchell Co.
Thomas, Abijah; Pvt.; A/K; Mitchell; b. ca. 1830
Thomas, Hezekiah; Pvt.; D; Watauga; 17 Oct. 1846–5 Jan. 1926; Johnson Co., Tenn.
Thomas, James Henry; Pvt.; K
Thomas, Job; Pvt.; C/D; Yancey; b. ca. 1838
Thomas, S. F.; ---; K
Thomas, Thomas; Pvt.; A/K; Mitchell; 1829–24 July 1912; Thomas Cem., Yancey Co.
Thomason, John H.; Pvt.; D/A
Thomason, Pleasant A.; Pvt.; A/K; Mitchell; b. ca. 1827
Thomason, William J.; Pvt./Hos. Swd.; K/F/F&S
Thompson, John M.; Pvt.; Misc.; 1836–1911; Avery Co.
Thompson, John W.; Pvt.; E; Caldwell; b. ca. 1830
Thompson, Joseph Lafayette; Pvt.; E/A; Caldwell; 21 May 1838–16 Sept. 1920
Thompson, Matthew C.; Pvt.; E; Caldwell; b. ca. 1831
Thompson, Moses Elkanah; Sgt.; E; Caldwell; 30 July 1835–1 July 1912; Thompson Cem., Caldwell Co.
Thompson, William J.; Pvt.; E/K; Mitchell/Caldwell; b. ca. 1828
Tipton, David Mc.; Pvt.; B; Mitchell; b. ca. 1840
Tipton, Jacob; Pvt.; G; Yancey; b. ca. 1836; Jobe Cem., Unicoi Co.
Tipton, John; 1st Lt.; G; Yancey; 12 March 1821–13 Aug. 1907; Tipton Hill Cem., Mitchell Co.
Tipton, John D.; Pvt.; G; Yancey; ca. 1836–14 May 1920
Tipton, Jonathan; Pvt.; G; Camp Palmer; 12 March 1842–10 March 1924

Tipton, Thomas G.; Pvt.; G/B; Camp Iredell; d. 20 Sept. 1863; Chickamauga, Ga.
Tipton, William; Pvt.; B; Camp Jackson; d. 21 Sept. 1912; Huntdale, N.C.
Tiptus, John; ---; D
Tise, Charles; Pvt.; F; Forsyth
Tobey, Frederick Albert; Capt.; A; Mitchell; 6 Sept. 1842–24 Nov. 1924; Hollybrook Cem., Lincoln Co.
Tolley, Joseph R.; Pvt.; A; Mitchell; b. ca. 1824
Tolley, Sanders; ---; A; ---; b. ca. 1839
Tolley, Swinfild; Pvt.; A; Mitchell; 7 May 1838–1940; Carter Co., Tenn.
Tolley, William; Pvt.; A; 1837–1 March 1864; Atlanta, Ga.
Tooms, William F.; Pvt.; E; Guilford
Towery, Edwards; Pvt.; F; McDowell; ca. 1830–15 Nov. 1862; Tenn.
Townsend, Jacob; Pvt.; D; Watauga; ca. 1836–20 July 1938; Old Townsend/Clark Cem., Watauga Co.
Townsend, Joel; Pvt.; D; Watauga; 1841–10 May 1865; Mecklenburg Co.
Townsend, Larkin; Pvt.; D; Watauga; 15 April 1832–21 June 1922; Avery Co.
Townsend, Levi D.; Pvt.; D; Watauga; 20 Nov. 1833–18 Feb. 1907; Holy Comm. Lutheran Cem., Watauga Co.
Townsend, Miles; Pvt.; D; Watauga; 1836–8 July 1864; Atlanta, Ga.
Toxey, William; Surg.; F&S
Treadway, Henry; Pvt.; L; Ashe; ca. 1841–18 Nov. 1864; Camp Douglas, Ill.
Tredway, William; Pvt.; L; Ashe; d. 19 March 1863; Big Gap Creek, Tenn.
Triplett, Abner; Pvt.; H; Caldwell; b. ca. 1806
Triplett, Jesse O.; Cpl.; M; Watauga; ca. 1828–15 April 1863; Clinton, Tenn.
Triplett, Thomas H.; Pvt.; K/M; Watauga; 8 March 1831–20 March 1909; Friendship Meth. Cem., Watauga Co.
Triplett, William; Pvt.; D; Watauga; b. ca. 1832
Tritt, Henry T.; Pvt.; E; Caldwell; ca. 1848–1 Sept. 1923; Caldwell Co.
Tritt, J. H.; ---; E
Trivett, Elisha; Pvt.; D; Watauga; b. ca. 1835
Trivett, Jesse; Pvt.; I; Watauga; d. Feb. 1863
Trivett, Joel; Pvt.; D; Watauga; 16 Nov. 1840–21 Dec. 1923; Avery Co.
Trivett, Lazarus; Pvt.; I/D; Watauga; 10 Nov. 1835–6 July 1920; Norris Cem., Watauga Co.
Trivett, Lewis W.; Pvt.; M/G; Ashe/Watauga; ca. 1833–28 Sept. 1864; Alton, Ill.
Trivett, Riley; Pvt.; D; Watauga; 14 June 1829–14 March 1906; Trivette Cem., Watauga Co.
Troutman, George W.; Pvt.; B; Camp Stokes; ca. 1815 to 1824–4 Nov. 1888; Hill Cem., Mitchell Co.
Tucker, Beacum; ---; E
Tucker, James; Pvt.; M/G; Watauga; b. ca. 1833
Tucker, Zephaniah; Pvt.; C/D; Yancey; b. ca. 1842
Tugman, Benjamin Franklin; Pvt.; I/G; Watauga; 10 Dec. 1845–5 Jan. 1900; Hopewell UMC Cem., Watauga Co.
Tugman, James; ---; I; Watauga; b. ca. 1844
Turbyfield, James Pickney; Pvt.; B; Camp Jackson; 26 July 1835–14 Feb. 1924; Avery Co.
Turner, A. J.; Pvt.; M/G; Watauga
Turner, John; Cpl.; F; McDowell; ca. 1844–22 Nov. 1863; Cassville, Ga.
Turnmire, John N.; Pvt.; H; Caldwell; b. ca. 1840
Turnmire, Joseph A.; Pvt.; H; Caldwell; 23 May 1843–27 Jan. 1920; Caldwell Co.
Tweed, James Hamilton; Sgt.; H; Buncombe; 2 May 1841–11 Dec. 1922; Tweed Chapel Cem., Henderson Co.
Tweed, Thomas Wilson; Pvt.; H; Murfreesboro, Tenn.; 25 Jan. 1845–22 March 1927; Buncombe Co.
Upchurch, Ansel M.; Pvt.; H; Caldwell; ca. 1840–1927; Green, Co. Tenn.
Upchurch, William S.; Pvt.; H; Caldwell; b. ca. 1833; Tenn.
Vance, Fleming; Pvt.; A; Mitchell; 12 Aug. 1837–2 Aug. 1918; Daniels Comm. Cem., Avery Co.[22]
Vance, John; Pvt.; A; Mitchell; 5 Dec. 1841–11 May 1917; Daniels Comm. Cem., Avery Co.
Vance, John J.; ---; E; Mitchell
Vance, John W.; Pvt.; A; Yancey; b. ca. 1841; Daniels Cem., Avery Co.
Vance, Lewis; Pvt.; A; Mitchell; b. ca. 1802
Vance, Thomas DeKalb; Pvt.; A; Yancey; 29 Jan. 1834–10 May 1922; Yellow Mountain Cem., Avery Co.
Vance, William; Pvt.; A; Mitchell; 1827–1910
Vance, William A.; 3rd Lt.; A; 1841–25 May 1875; Johnson Cem., Avery Co.
Vandike, Emanuel; Pvt.; M/G; Watauga; b. 1837
Vandike, George Elcana; Sgt.; I; Watauga; 17 Jan. 1843–2 March 1922; Critcher Cem., Watauga Co.
Vanhorn, David; ---; A; Mitchell; b. May 1827
Vannoy, William; Pvt.; G; Wilkes/Camp Holmes; ca. 1820–2 Jan. 1864; Atlanta, Ga.
Vannoy, William H.; Pvt.; G; Alleghany/Camp Holmes
Vanover, Charles; Pvt.; D/I; Watauga; b. ca. 1839
Wacaster, Elijah; Pvt.; G; Camp Huston; b. 1832; Carter Co., Tenn.
Wacaster, Jacob Hassel; Pvt.; G/A; Camp Huston; 19 April 1829–11 Jan. 1917; Collis Cem., Mitchell Co.
Waddle, William; 1st Sgt.; L/F; Ashe; 7 Jan. 1832–5 Nov. 1912; William Waddle Cem., Ashe Co.
Wakefield, Richard A.; Pvt.; H; Caldwell
Waldrope, Eli; Pvt.; A; Mitchell; b. 1828; Hensley Cem., Yancey Co.
Waldrope, Joseph; Pvt.; A; Mitchell; b. 1826
Walker, David; Pvt.; F; McDowell; 7 Sept. 1837–

17 Dec. 1910; Dysartville Bapt. Ch., McDowell Co., NC
Walker, Jeremiah C.; Pvt.; F; Forsyth
Walker, Jesse F.; Pvt.; G; d. 21 Feb. 1864; Rock Island, Ill.
Walker, Joseph; Pvt.; A/K; Mitchell; b. ca. 1839
Walker, Zephaniah; Cpl.; G; Camp Holmes; ca. 1821–22 June 1864; Kolb's Farm, Ga.
Wallace, Cornelius R.; ---; K; Peterson Hill Cem., Yancey Co.
Wallis, William S.; Pvt.; L; Ashe; b. ca. 1837
Walls, Madison; Pvt.; F; McDowell; ca. 1844–21 Sept. 1862
Ward, Duke B.; Pvt.; D; Watauga; ca. 1843–15 Jan. 1926; Ward Branch Cem., Watauga Co.
Ward, Jethro; ---; A; 15 Sept. 1835–29 June 1918; Bethel Bapt. Ch., McDowell Co.
Ward, Joseph; Pvt.; G; Mitchell; b. ca. 1843; Greenlee Cem., Mitchell Co.
Ward, Michael; Pvt.; D; Watauga; b. ca. 1837–4 May 1864; Dalton, Ga.
Washburn, Daniel M.; Sgt.; A/D; Mitchell; b. ca. 1833; Grassy Creek Cem., Mitchell Co.
Washburn, Joseph; ---; I
Watson, Alfred; Pvt.; M; Watauga; ca. 1832–19 Feb. 1863; Big Creek Gap, Tenn.
Watson, Ambrose Lee Parks; Pvt.; M/G; Watauga; ca. 1834–13 Jan. 1899; Watauga Co.
Watson, Calaway; Pvt.; M; Watauga
Watson, Henry Eli; Pvt.; H; Caldwell; b. ca. 1839
Watson, John M.; Pvt; I; Watauga; ca. 1824–28 March 1863; Jacksboro, Tenn.
Watson, Noah Odell; Pvt.; H; Caldwell; ca. 1835–7 July 1887; Corpening Town Cem., Caldwell Co.
Watts, James W.; Pvt.; G; Yancey; b. ca. 1828
Watts, Riley; Pvt.; E; Burke; b. ca. 1825
Watts, Thomas G.; Cpl.; K; Wilkes/Caldwell
Weatherman, Samuel; Pvt.; A; Mitchell; 28 June 1828–2 April 1900; Green Valley Cem., Avery Co.
Webb, Franklin; Pvt.; B; Mitchell; ca. 1845–21 Dec. 1863; Marietta, Ga.
Webb, James; Pvt.; A; Mitchell; ca. 1832–19 April 1862; Richmond, VA
Webb, Joseph Milton; Pvt.; A; 1838–1913; Webb/Hollander Cem., Avery Co.
Webb, Noah; Pvt.; A; Mitchell; 1839–1904; Webb Cem., Avery Co.
Webster, Noah L.; Pvt.; H; Caldwell; b. ca. 1839
Weisenfeld, Moretz; Pvt.; I; Watauga
Wells, W. Henry; Pvt.; E; Tullahoma, Tenn.
Wesley, Ryentt; Sgt.; D; Mitchell
West, Alexander Steven Commodore Decatur; Pvt.; E/K; Caldwell; 30 Oct. 1836–8 Dec. 1929; Union Bapt. Ch. Cem., Caldwell Co.
Wheeler, Daniel; Pvt.; D; Watauga; ca. 1829–11 Nov. 1902; Rymer Cem., Watauga Co.
Wheeling, Carson E. C.; ---; K
Whisenhunt, Elias; Pvt.; F; McDowell; ca. 1835–October 1862; Cumberland Gap, Tenn.
White, A. J.; Pvt.; F; Mecklenburg
White, Ambrose; Pvt.; M/G; Watauga; 13 March 1837–20 Oct. 1929; Long Point Graveyard, Floyd Co., Ky.
White, Harrison T.; Pvt.; F; McDowell; b. ca. 1829; Bethlehem Cem., McDowell Co.
White, I. F.; Pvt.; G; b. ca. 1835
White, Isaac; Pvt.; E; Randolph; b. ca. 1816
White, James; Pvt.; F; McDowell; ca. 1837–5 March 1865; Camp Douglas, Ill.
White, James Alfred; Pvt.; E; Caldwell; 25 Oct. 1836–24 April 1912; Estes Cem., Caldwell Co.
White, James T.; Pvt.; F; Camp Holmes
White, Joseph; ---; A; Mitchell
White, Joseph H.; ---; E; Caldwell; 1823–after 1880; Glen Alpine Cem., Burke Co.
White, Lorenzo W.; As. Surg.; F&S
White, P. Henderson; Pvt.; H; Caldwell; ca. 1839–26 June 1862
White, Robert W.; Capt.; H; Buncombe; b. ca. 1831
White, William; Pvt.; F; McDowell; ca. 1828–ca. 1862; Tenn.
Whitener, Sidney M.; Pvt.; E; Caldwell; 20 April 1835–20 Aug. 1908; Cedar Valley UMC, Caldwell Co.
Whitson, Clayton; Pvt.; G; Yancey; ca. 1836–3 Feb. 1863; Camp Palmer
Whitson, William W.; Pvt.; B; Camp Jackson; ca. 1836–19 Nov. 1864; Rowan Co.
Wilcox, Alvin; ---; D
Wilcox, Francis Marion; Pvt.; M; Watauga; b. 13 Nov. 1843
Wilcox, Isaiah; ---; D
Williams, Hezekiah R.; Pvt.; F; Yadkin
Williams, Hugh L.; Pvt.; L; Ashe
Williams, Isaker R.; Pvt.; E; Yadkin
Williams, Jesse Franklin; Pvt.; E; Guilford
Williams, John W.; Pvt.; A; Dalton, Ga.
Williams, Mac; Pvt.; Misc.; Yancey
Williams, Ransom H.; Pvt.; G; Lincoln/Yancey; b. ca. 1834
Williams, W. A.; ---; F; 28 June 1836–12 Feb. 1911
Williams, Yancey; Pvt.; E; Randolph; b. ca. 1830
Willis, Benjamin; Pvt.; E/K; Mitchell; ca. 1843–20 Sept. 1863; Chickamauga, Ga.
Willson, William A.; Pvt.; G; Yancey; b. ca. 1839
Wilson, Alexander; Pvt.; C; Yancey; 22 April 1823–18 Jan. 1906
Wilson, Bartlett; Sgt.; E/K; Mitchell; 6 June 1832–ca. 1862; Virginia
Wilson, Calloway; Pvt.; G; Watauga
Wilson, David R.; Cpl.; C; d. 25 Sept. 1862; Big Springs, Tenn.
Wilson, Edward; Pvt.; G/C; Yancey; b. 1832; Hughes Cem., Yancey Co.
Wilson, Edward M.; Pvt.; C; Yancey; d. 7 Feb. 1863; Wilson Cem., Yancey Co.
Wilson, H. W.; Pvt.; H; McDowell
Wilson, Henry; Pvt.; F; McDowell; ca. 1833–20 Sept. 1863; Chickamauga, Ga.

Wilson, Hiram; Pvt.; F
Wilson, John H.; Pvt.; M/G; Watauga; b. ca. 1844
Wilson, John H.; Pvt.; I; Watauga; ca. 1838–20 Sept. 1863; Chickamauga, Ga.
Wilson, John L.; Pvt.; L; Ashe
Wilson, John W.; Pvt.; C; Yancey; 1834–1922; Wilson Cem., Yancey Co.
Wilson, Jonathan J.; Pvt.; M/G; Watauga; 16 April 1840–5 June 1916; J. J. Wilson, Watauga Co.
Wilson, Joseph; Pvt.; I;
Wilson, Joseph C.; Pvt.; E; Caldwell; b. ca. 1836
Wilson, L. E.; 1st Sgt.; H; Buncombe; b. ca. 1842
Wilson, Lemuel Alexander; Pvt.; F/I; Watauga/McDowell; ca. 1834–18 March 1864; Atlanta, Ga.
Wilson, Levi; Pvt.; G; Yancey
Wilson, Nathaniel; Pvt.; C; Yancey
Wilson, P. A.; ---; K
Wilson, Samuel N., Sr.; Pvt.; F; McDowell
Wilson, Sidney L.; Pvt.; E/K; Mitchell; 28 Dec. 1844–15 June 1925
Wilson, Thomas F; Pvt.; C
Wilson, William; Pvt.; I/D; Watauga; ca. 1844–16 Feb. 1863
Wilson, William H.; Pvt.; C; Yancey; d. 18 Dec. 1863; La Grange, Ga.
Wilson, William J.; Pvt.; K; Mitchell; 30 Sept. 1835–17 July 1930
Winebarger, Abel; Pvt.; I; Watauga; 1836–15 Oct. 1923; Winebarger Cem., Watauga Co.
Winebarger, Hiram; Pvt.; I; Watauga; 15 Jan. 1830–16 April 1905; Peak View Meth. Ch., Ashe Co.
Winebarger, Levi; Cpl.; M/G/I; Watauga; Sept. 1832–2 Sept. 1914; Winebarger Cem., Ashe Co.
Winters, Stephen M.; Pvt.; E/K; Mitchell; ca. 1827–29 March 1896; Carter Co., Tenn.
Wise, James N.; ---; A; Mitchell; ca. 1842–24 March 1863
Wise, Jasper J.; 2nd Lt.; A; Mitchell; 28 Jan. 1842–19 Jan. 1928; Oak Grove Bapt. Ch., Burke Co.
Wiseman, Alexander; Pvt.; A/D; 22 April 1822–28 Feb. 1897; Pine Grove UMC, Avery Co.
Wiseman, Berry G.; Pvt.; A
Wiseman, Ensor C.; Sgt.; A; 1 Jan. 1838–1880s; Wiseman Cem., Mitchell Co.
Wiseman, James Henry; Pvt.; A; Mitchell; 19 Dec. 1823–22 Oct. 1907; Wiseman Cem., Mitchell Co.
Wiseman, John Wess; 3rd Lt; A; Mitchell; ca. 1841–20 Sept. 1863; Chickamauga, Ga.
Wiseman, Josiah Lafayette; Pvt.; A; Mitchell; 13 Aug. 1842–15 Aug. 1932; Pine Grove UMC, Avery Co.
Wiseman, Martin Davenport; Capt.; A; Mitchell; 13 Aug. 1818–27 Jan. 1909; Grassy Creek Meth. Cem., Mitchell Co.
Wiseman, Thomas J.; Pvt.; A; Mitchell; b. ca. 1835; Gurley Cem., Yancey Co.
Wiseman, William Henry; 1st Lt.; A; 3 Feb. 1840–15 May 1909; Pisgah UMC, Avery Co.
Wiseman, Wilson; Pvt.; A; Mitchell; b. ca. 1835
Wolf, James P.; Pvt.; H; Buncombe; b. 10 June 1832
Wood, Rufus; Pvt.; L/F; Ashe; b. ca. 1843
Wood, Spencer; Pvt.; E; Randolph; 29 Oct. 1821–12 Dec. 1886; New Hope UMC, Randolph Co.
Wood, William; Pvt.; E; Randolph; 11 Sept. 1821–13 Feb. 1896; Concord UMC, Randolph Co.
Wood, William; Pvt.; L; Ashe; b. ca. 1838
Woodring, Marcus L.; Pvt.; I; Watauga; 29 Sept. 1834–11 June 1916; Hopewell UMC., Watauga Co.
Woodring, Rufus; Pvt.; I; Watauga; b. ca. 1837
Woods, Gaston; Pvt.; E; Caldwell; d. 20 Sept. 1863; Chickamauga, Ga.
Woodside, Benjamin F.; Pvt.; F; McDowell; b. ca. 1839
Woody, David; Pvt.; C; Yancey; b. ca. 1840
Woody, Green Berry; Ensign; F&S; Yancey; 28 July 1829–23 Oct. 1903; Woody Cem., Yancey Co.
Woody, Posey; Pvt.; C; Dalton, Ga.
Woody, Wyatt; Pvt.; C; Yancey; ca. 1838–20 Sept. 1863; Chickamauga, Ga.
Word, Joseph; Pvt.; G; Camp Huston
Worley, Samuel; Pvt.; M/G; Watauga; ca. 1841–ca. 1919; Giles Graham Cem., Ashe Co.
Wright, Solomon H.; Pvt.; B; Mitchell; ca. 1807–1880s
Yates, Thomas P.; Pvt.; G; Camp Palmer
Yelton, Barnett C.; Pvt.; D/I; Watauga; 18 Jan. 1844–26 Dec. 1914; Mill Creek Cem., Phelps County, Mo.
Yelton, John L.; Pvt.; B/I; Mitchell; 29 Sept. 1834–5 May 1915
Younce, Andrew J.; Pvt.; M/G; Watauga; ca. 1831–3 March 1864; Atlanta, Ga.
Younce, William H.; Pvt.; L; Ashe; 26 July 1842–27 May 1922; Greenlawn Cem., Franklin, Ind.
Young, John Wesley; Pvt.; B; Camp Jackson; 1846–17 March 1918; Young-Hyatt Cem., Yancey Co.
Young, Joseph P.; ---; A; Mitchell; b. ca. 1840
Young, Melvin H.; Pvt.; C; Yancey; 25 Oct. 1842–6 May 1906; Young-Hyatt Cem., Yancey Co.
Young, Merritt; Pvt.; B/K; Mitchell; b. ca. 1830
Young, Moses; Cpl.; E/K; Mitchell; 23 Dec. 1824–16 Jan. 1906; Roan Mtn. Bapt. Ch., Mitchell Co.
Young, Reuben M., Jr.; Pvt.; B; Mitchell; 23 Sept. 1843–19 Aug. 1917; Burleson Cem., Mitchell Co.
Young, Samuel P.; Sgt.; C
Young, Thomas; Pvt.; B; Mitchell; 1834–1909
Young, Thomas S.; Pvt.; C/B; Yancey; 28 Sept. 1830–28 Nov. 1891; Thomas Young Cem., Yancey Co.
Young, Thomas S.; Hos. Ste.; F&S
Youngblood, Hiram; Pvt.; F; Rutherford; d. 4 May 1864; Dalton, Ga.
Younts, E. F.; Pvt.; H; Athens, Ga.; d. 4 May 1864; Dalton, Ga.

Appendix B:
Fifty-Eighth North Carolina Parolees

Name	Rank
F&S	
Blair, John Caldwell	Drum Maj.
Coleman, Thaddeus C.	Lt. Col.
Hensley, John A.	Or. Sgt.
Medaris, John Enzor	Qsgt.
White, Lorenzo W.	As. Surg.
Company A	
Baird, Benjamin Franklin	Capt.
Coffey, William Columbus	1st. Lt.
Davis, Albert F.	2nd Lt.
Hodges, Gilbert W.	Cpl.
Hodges, Larkin Gilbert	Sgt.
Reed, John C.	Pvt.
Sorrells, Joshua M.	Pvt.
Thomason, John H.	Pvt.
Thompson, Joseph Lafayette	Pvt.
Company B	
*Briggs, Suel B.	Capt.
*Duncan, Jonathan A. W.	2nd Lt.
*Gilbert, Larkin	1st Lt.
*Anglin, Raborn B.	Pvt.
*Gilliland, Joseph J.	Pvt.
*Gilliland, Robert	Pvt.
*Howell, Robert V.	Cpl.
*Palmer, George C.	Pvt.
*Stafford, Simeon	Pvt.
*Young, Thomas S.	Pvt.
Company C	
Clayton, Edwin M.	Capt.
Brooks, Stephen	2nd Lt.
Sales, John T.	1st Lt.

Name	Rank
Giles, James B.	Pvt.
Stepp, Robert J.	Sgt.
Wilson, Thomas F.	Pvt.
Young, Samuel P.	Sgt.
Company D	
*Tobey, Frederick Albert	Capt.
*Conley, James C.	1st Lt.
*Abee, James E.	Pvt.
*Brooks, Alfred	Pvt.
*Gardner, Elisha M.	Pvt.
*Hileman, Jacob	Pvt.
*Holifield, Jasper	Pvt.
*Hollers, Joseph	Pvt.
*Holly, George	Pvt.
Huskins, Jacob	Pvt.
*Jarrett, Eli	Cpl.
*Lusbyfield, James	Pvt.
*McKinney, Jason C.	Pvt.
*Phillips, Alfred	Pvt.
*Washburn, Daniel M.	1st Sgt.
*Wesly, Ryentt	Sgt.
*Wiseman, Alexander	Pvt.
Company E	
Alexander, William R.	Capt.
Clayton, Robert M.	1st Lt.
Lindsey, George W.	2nd Lt.
Alexander, Benjamin J.	Pvt.
Blanchard, T. C.	Pvt.
Buckner, Nimrod	Pvt.
Coche, Thomas A.	Pvt.
Cogdill, Fidella P.	Pvt.
Cook, A.	Pvt.
*Cook, William	Pvt.

*Denotes a member of the Fifty-Eighth North Carolina. Others were members of the Sixtieth North Carolina which was consolidated with the Fifty-Eighth.

Name	Rank
Davidson, William F.	Pvt.
Ensley, Alfred	Pvt.
Flemming, William J. B.	Pvt.
Gorenflo, J. F.	1st Sgt.
McCarson, Samuel	Pvt.
Moore, Lewis	Pvt.
Nelson, George	Pvt.
Prather, George W.	Pvt.
Shipman, William R., Jr.	Pvt.
Slagle, John L. L.	Pvt.
Wells, W. Henry	Pvt.
*White, Isaac	Pvt.

Company F

Name	Rank
*Blevins, Poindexter	Capt.
*Hurley, Leander	1st Lt.
*Silver, Levi D.	2nd Lt.
*Baker, John	Pvt.
*Berry, Pinkney	Pvt.
*Calloway, Jacob A.	Cpl.
*Dickson, James D.	Pvt.
*English, Aden	Pvt.
*Handy, F. Marion	Cpl.
*Hurley, Thomas	Pvt.
*Mangum, George T.	Pvt.
*Silver, Tilman B.	Sgt.
*Thomason, William J.	Pvt.
*Waddle, William	1st Sgt.
*Wood, Rufus	Pvt.

Company G

Name	Rank
Long, Hamilton C.	Capt.
*McGimsey, Theodore C.	2nd Lt.
*Miller, Jonathan B.	1st Lt.
*McGalliard, Robert	Cpl.
*Miller, T. Calvin	Sgt.
*Mitchell, Robert	Pvt.
*Tugman, Benjamin F.	Pvt. (In hospital)
White, I. F.	Pvt.

Company H

Name	Rank
White, Robert W.	Capt.
Fagg, Henry C.	2nd Lt.
Jackson, Eli	1st Lt.
Bishop, William P.	Pvt.
Brookshire, Thomas P.	Cpl.
Davis, Isaiah I.	Pvt.
*Edwards, Alex	Pvt.
Frisbee, Daniel H.	Pvt.
Giles, James B.	Pvt.
Green, Stewart	Pvt.
Hipps, Marcus B.	Sgt
James, Thomas R.	Sgt.
Jamison, Newton A.	Pvt.

Name	Rank
Jones, Posey W.	Pvt.
Luther, Robert J.	Pvt.
Meadows, John P.	Pvt.
Morgan, Marion H.	Pvt.
Stevens, Merrit F.	Pvt.
Tweed, James H.	Sgt.
Tweed, Thomas W.	Pvt.
Wilson, L. E.	1st Sgt.
Wolf, James P.	Pvt.

Company K

Name	Rank
*Silver, Alexander	Pvt. (Hospital)

58th NCT Paroled Morganton, N.C.

Company A

Pritchard, J. C. May 15, 1865
Shuffler, Jacob C. May 15, 1865
Shuffler, Posey C. May 15, 1865

Company C

Holcomb, John L. June 12, 1865

Company F

Benfield, John J. May 29, 1865
Benfield, W. A. May 16, 1865
Benfield, W. John May 29, 1865
Benfield, William H. May 16, 1865
Parker, William H. May 27, 1865
Powell, A. D. May 13, 1865
Rhodes, William May 29, 1865

Company H

Brown, Julius A. May 15, 1865

58th NCT Paroled Charlotte, N.C.

Company A

Snipes, Merritt 12 May 1865

Company B

Huskins, Horace May 6, 1865

Company D

Strickland, Moore May 4, 1865

Company E

Barrier, Samuel May 12, 1865

Company F

Alexander, Thomas M. May 11, 1865
Little, J. F. May 6, 1865

Company H

Coleman, Richard A. May 4, 1865

58th NCT Paroled Salisbury, N.C.

Company A
Faircloth, M. L. May 2, 1865

Company C
Holcombe, Robert M. June 12, 1865

Company H
Wakefield, Richard A. April 1865
Wilson, H. W. May 2, 1865

Paroled Selma, Ala.

Company E
Belton, Pleasant H. May 4, 1865

Paroled Statesville, N.C.

Company F
Conley, John F. May 27, 1865

Company G
Mason, Harrison May 28, 1865

Paroled Macon, Ga.

Company G
Goforth, William April 30, 1865

Paroled Newton, N.C.

Company H
Morgan, John B. April 19, 1865

Paroled Thomasville, N.C.

Company I
Green, Amos Jr. May 1, 1865

Appendix C: Members of the Fifty-Eighth Who Deserted and Joined the Union Army

Name	Rank	Co.	Desertion Date	Federal Regiment
Bailey, Jefferson	Pvt.	B		Co. F, 3rd N.C. Mount. Inf.
Barnett, Simon	Pvt.	B	5 Oct. 1863	Co. B, 13th Tennessee Cavalry
Bean, Thomas	Pvt.	H		Co. E, D, 2nd N.C. Mount. Inf.
Bennett, Archibald	Pvt.	B	5 Oct. 1863	Co. A/F 3rd N.C. Mount. Inf.
Bennett, John	Pvt.	G	March–June 1863	Co. A, 3rd N.C. Mount. Inf.
Bennett, Uriah	Pvt.	G	March–April 1863	Co. A and F, 3rd N.C. Mount. Inf.
Bennett, William J.	Pvt.	G	March–April 1863	Co. A and F, 3rd N.C. Mount. Inf.
Bishop, Elbert	Pvt.	D	25 Aug. 1862	Co. I, 13th Tennessee Cavalry
Brooks, John	Pvt.	B	5 Oct. 1863	Co. B, 13th Tennessee Cavalry
Bryant, Thomas	Pvt.	D		Co. A, 3rd N.C. Mount. Inf.
Buchanan, Greenbury Y.	Sgt.	B		Co. E, 3rd N.C. Mount. Inf.
Buchanan, William A.	Pvt.	B	10 Sept. 1864	Co. E, 3rd N.C. Mount. Inf.
Buchanan, William W.	Pvt.	K	11 Jan. 1863	13th Tennessee Cavalry
Buchanan, William W.	Pvt.	K	6 Aug. 1862	13th Tennessee Cavalry
Bumgarner, George W.	Pvt.	L		U.S. Navy
Burchfield, John	Pvt.	K	3 July 1863	Co. B, 13th Tennessee Cavalry
Burlison, Joseph M.	Pvt.	A	6 June 1863	Co. C, 13th Tennessee Cavalry
Butler, Allen	Pvt.	B		U.S. Navy (Captured)
Byrd, Carson	Pvt.	A	24 July 1863	Co. B, 13th Tennessee Cavalry
Calaway, William H.	Pvt.	D	5 June 1863	Co. F, 3rd N.C. Mount. Inf.
Cannon, Stephen	Pvt.	G		Co. A, 3rd N.C. Mount. Inf.
Caraway, William H.	Pvt.	G		Co. C, 13th Tenn. Cavalry
Church, Jordan	Pvt.	G		Co. H, 3rd N.C. Mount. Inf.
Clark, Robert P.	Pvt.	D		Co. C, 13th Tennessee Cavalry
Cloud, Terrell C.	Pvt.	A	27 Aug. 1863	Co. C, 13th Tennessee Cavalry
Cobb, Newton	Pvt.	H	23 Sep. 1863	Co. L, 11th Tennessee Cavalry/ Co. L, 9th Tennessee Cavalry
Coffee, Thomas	Pvt.	K		Co. B, 4th Tennessee Cavalry
Cornett, Isaac	Pvt.	I	29 Aug. 1863	Co. F, 13th Tennessee Cavalry
Davis, Josiah	Pvt.	K		Co. E, 3rd N.C. Mount. Inf.
Done, Morgan	Pvt.	C		Co. K, 3rd N.C. Mount. Inf.
Eastridge, Barnabas	Pvt.	L		Co. G, 6th U.S. Vol.
Eastridge, Henry	Pvt.	L	8 July 1864	Co. E, 13th Tennessee Cavalry

Members of the Fifty-Eighth Who Deserted and Joined the Union Army

Name	Rank	Co.	Desertion Date	Federal Regiment
Edwards, John W.	Pvt.	G	5 April 1863	Co. F, D, 8th Tenn. Cavalry/ Co. A, 3rd N.C. Mount. Inf.
Elkins, Joseph	Pvt.	B	15 May 1863	Co. B, 13th Tennessee Cavalry
Elliott, Stephen	Pvt.	L		Co. H, 3rd U.S. Vol. Inf.
Estepp, Samuel	Pvt.	G		Co. K, 3rd N.C. Mount. Inf.
Fender, William	Pvt.	G	10 May 1864	Co. G, 3rd N.C. Mount. Inf.
Fletcher, Spencer	Pvt.	I		Co. A, 3rd Tenn. Mount. Inf.
Fletcher, Thomas B.	Pvt.	I		Co. C, 6th U.S. Volunteers
Franklin, Levi A.	Pvt.	A	24 Sept. 1863	Co. C, 13th Tennessee Cavalry
Frasier, John W.	Pvt.	B	5 Sept. 1863	Co. B, 13th Tennessee Cavalry
Fullwood, James M.	Pvt.	F		U.S. Navy
Garland, Elisha M.	——	E		Co. B, 13th Tennessee Cavalry
Garland, Ezekiel	Pvt.	B	16 Nov. 1862	Co. E, 3rd N.C. Mount. Inf.
Garland, John	Pvt.	B	10 Jan. 1863	Co. E, 3rd N.C. Mount. Inf.
Gilly, Alfred	Pvt.	L	26 Jan. 1863	Co. I, 13th Tennessee Cavalry
Green, Levy	——	D		Co. D/E, 2nd N.C. Mount. Inf.
Green, Paterson	Pvt.	A	6 June 1863	Co. C, 13th Tennessee Cavalry
Greer, Elijah	Pvt.	G		Co. I, 13th Tenn. Cav.
Greer, Jordan	Pvt.	G		Co. G., 4th Tenn. Inf.
Guy, John C.	Pvt.	D	25 May 1863	Co. G, 8th Tenn. Inf.
Hamlett, Oliver M.	Pvt.	G		Co. G, 4th Tennessee Infantry
Hampton, William F.	Pvt.	G		U.S. Navy
Harmon, Andrew J.	Pvt.	D	20 Sept. 1863	Co. E, 13th Tennessee Cavalry
Harmon, Andrew J.	Pvt.	I		Co. E, 13th Tennessee Cavalry
Harrison, Joseph W.	Pvt.	M/G		Co. E, 13th Tennessee Cavalry
Hatley, John F.	Pvt.	D	31 Aug. 1863	Co. E, 13th Tennessee Cavalry
Hatley, Riley B.	Pvt.	D		Co. E, 13th Tennessee Cavalry
Hatley, Wiley S.	Pvt.	D		Co. E, 13th Tennessee Cavalry
Hatton, Warren A.	Pvt.	M/G		Co. E, 13th Tennessee Cavalry
Hensley, John	Pvt.	G		Co. G, 3rd N.C. Mount. Inf.
Higgins, James Erwin	Pvt.	G		Co. I, 2nd U.S. Vol. Inf.
Hileman, John	Pvt.	B	10 Oct. 1863	Co. E, 3rd N.C. Mount. Inf.
Hilton, John W.	Pvt.	L		U.S. Navy
Holifield, Joel A.	Pvt.	E	25 Sept. 1863	Co. A, 3rd N.C. Mount. Inf.
Honeycutt, Lafayette P.	Pvt.	G	8 Sept. 1863	13th Tennessee Cavalry
Howell, Alvin P.	Pvt.	L		U.S. Army
Howell, James H.	Pvt.	H		Co. F, 5th U.S. Volunteers
Hughes, Charles	Pvt.	G	1 July 1863	Co. C, 13th Tennessee Cavalry
Hughes, William J.	Pvt.	K		Co. H, 6th U.S. Vol. Inf.
Hughs, Landon C.	Pvt.	B	15 Oct. 1863	Co. M, 8th Tennessee Cavalry
Isaacs, Noah	Pvt.	I	29 Aug. 1863	Co. A, 3rd Tenn. Mount. Inf.
Isaacs, Solomon C.	Pvt.	I		U.S. Navy
Jackson, James R.	Pvt.	D	Jan.–Feb. 1863	Co. F, 13th Tennessee Cavalry
Johnson, Isaac A.	Pvt.	A	1 March 1863	Co. F, 3rd N.C. Mounted Infantry
Keller, Jesse R.	Pvt.	G	1 July 1863	Co. F, 3rd N.C. Mount. Inf.
Keller, Nicholas	Pvt.	G	prior to 1 July 1863	Co. F, 3rd N.C. Mount. Inf.
Kilby, William E.	Musc.	D	17 April 1864	Co. I, 13th Tennessee Cavalry
Ledford, Jasper	Pvt.	K		U.S. Navy
Lewis, James	Pvt.	M/G		Co. G, 3rd N.C. Mount. Inf.
Lonon, Oliver P.	Cpl.	F		U.S. Navy
Loyd, Thomas	Pvt.	C	17 Sept. 1863	Co. B, 3rd N.C. Mount. Inf.
Main, Harrison	Pvt.	M/G		Co. C, 4th Tennessee Cavalry
McCurry, Zephaniah	Pvt.	G	prior to 1 July 1863	Co. K, 3rd N.C. Mount. Inf.
McKinney, Samuel B.	Pvt.	B		Co. I, 3rd N.C. Mount. Inf.
McMahan, James	Pvt.	G	23 Sept. 1863	Co. K, 3rd N.C. Mount. Inf.

Name	Rank	Co.	Desertion Date	Federal Regiment
McMahan, William B.	Pvt.	C		Co. A, 3rd N.C. Mount. Inf.
Merrill, A. B.	Pvt.	L		U.S. Navy
Mikeal, Isaac	Pvt.	M/G	prior to 1 July 1863	Co. A, 3rd N.C. Mount. Inf.
Miller, Hiram	Pvt.	B		Co. A, 3rd N.C. Mount. Inf.
Miller, John H.	Pvt.	I		U.S. Navy
Miller, Samuel	Pvt.	B/G	20 May 1864	U.S. Navy
Moody, Benjamin Jr.	Pvt.	G		Co. A, 13th Tennessee Cavalry
Mosely, Samuel E.	Pvt.	A	10 June 1864	U.S. Navy (capt.)
Osborn, Alfred	Pvt.	L	6 Jan. 1863	Co. E, 13th Tennessee Cavalry
Osborn, Aris	Pvt.	L	26 Jan. 1863	Co. G, 13th Tennessee Cavalry
Osborn, George	Pvt.	L	26 Jan. 1863	Co. I, 13th Tennessee Cavalry
Osborn, William	Pvt.	L	22 Aug. 1863	Co. G, 13th Tennessee Cavalry
Osborne, David	Pvt.	B	31 Jan. 1864	Co. D, 3rd N.C. Mount. Inf.
Osborne, George	Pvt.	E	6 Oct. 1863	Co. I, 13th Tennessee Cavalry
Pate, George W.	Pvt.	G	30 June 1863	Co. F, 3rd N.C. Mount. Inf.
Pearce, Redmond T.	Pvt.	H		Co. G, 3rd U.S. Volunteers
Peterson, Lawson	Pvt.	G		Co. A, 3rd N.C. Mount. Inf.
Peterson, Moses	Pvt.	G		Co. F, 3rd N.C. Mount. Inf.
Peterson, Reuben	Pvt.	G		Co. A, 3rd N.C. Mount. Inf.
Phillips, Hugh	Pvt.	G	30 June 1863	Co. H, 3rd N.C. Mount. Inf.
Presnell, James B.	Pvt.	C	5 June 1863	Co. C, 13th Tennessee Cavalry
Proctor, Reuben	Pvt.	B	5 Aug. 1864	Co. G/K, 8th Tennessee Cavalry
Ramsey, Joseph	Pvt.	B	15 Oct. 1862	Co. A, 3rd N.C. Mount. Inf.
Randolph, Reuben	Pvt.	K	7 Sept. 1863	Co. C, 13th Tennessee Cavalry
Ray, William H.	Pvt.	C		Co. K, 3rd N.C. Mount. Inf.
Riddle, John	Pvt.	B	10 Sept. 1864	Co. K, 3rd N.C. Mount. Inf.
Riddle, John	Pvt.	G	May–June 1863	Co. K, 3rd N.C. Mount. Inf.
Rose, Wyatt	Pvt.	L		U.S. Navy
Scott, Lorenzo D.	Pvt.	B		Co. H, 13th Tennessee Cavalry
Shehan, James E.	Pvt.	C	1 Feb. 1864	Co. A, 3rd N.C. Mount. Inf.
Shelton, David	Pvt.	E	10 Jan. 1864	Co. G, 3rd N.C. Mount. Inf.
Shepherd, Thomas E.	Cpl.	C		Co. K, 3rd N.C. Mount. Inf.
Sluder, Felix	Pvt.			U.S. Navy
Sprinkle, Obadiah	Pvt.	G		U.S. Navy
Storie, Jesse	Pvt.	M/G		Co. E, 13th Tennessee Cavalry
Storie, Noah	Pvt.	M/G		Co. E, 13th Tennessee Cavalry
Thomas, Hezekiah	Pvt.	D		Co. C, 6th U.S. Vol. Inf.
Thompson, Matthew C.	Pvt.	E		U.S. Navy
Tipton, David Mc.	Pvt.	B	10 Jan. 1863	Co. D, 3rd N.C. Mount. Inf.
Tipton, John D.	Pvt.	G		Co. A, F, 3rd N.C. Mount. Inf.
Tipton, William	Pvt.	B	15 Oct. 1863	Co. F, 3rd N.C. Mount. Inf.
Triplett, Thomas	Pvt.	M		Co. D, E 3rd N.C. Mount. Inf. Co. E, 13th Tennessee Cavalry
Wallis, William S.	Pvt.	L	10 Feb. 1863	Co. I, 13th Tennessee Cavalry
Ward, Joseph	Pvt.	G		Co. C, 13th Tennessee Cavalry
Watson, Noah	Pvt.	H		Co. G, 6th U.S. Volunteers
White, Ambrose	Pvt.	M/G	29 Feb. 1864	Co. I, 3rd N.C. Mount. Inf.
Wilcox, Francis M.	Pvt.	M		Co. D, 40th Kentucky Inf.
Williams, Isaker R.	Pvt.	E		Co. C, 3rd N.C. Mount. Inf.
Young, Merritt	Pvt.	B	8 June 1863	Co. C, 13th Tennessee Cavalry

Chapter Notes

Chapter 1
1. Bailey, *Toe River Valley Heritage*, 1: 353; Hardy, *Avery County Heritage*, 9: 5.
2. Cutler, *Genealogical and Family History of New York*, 1036–36; Palmer, *Early Days in Detroit*, 786; Farmer, *History of Detroit and Wayne County*, 869.
3. Cooper, *History of Avery County*, 35; 1860 United States Census, Watauga County.
4. McGough, *Childsville*, 115–116; Arthur, *Western North Carolina*, 200.
5. Ashe, *History of North Carolina*, 2: 661.
6. Arthur, *A History of Watauga County*, 54–55; Deyton, "The Toe River Valley to 1865," 434.
7. Fisher, *War at Every Door*, 52–56; Temple, *East Tennessee and the Civil War*, 371, 377.
8. Jordan, *North Carolina Troops*, 14: 275, 277, 280, 281, 285, 288; *Avery County Heritage*, 1: 206.
9. *Avery County Heritage*, 3: 152; Jordan, *North Carolina Troops*, 14: 275, 276.
10. Adjutant General Letter Book, 10 Dec. 1861 to 23 April 1862; 14 Jan. 1862 to Capt. Palmer, Morganton, N.C., from Martin; *McDowell County Heritage*, 8.
11. Anthony Pollygus, e-mail, 14 May 2007; Bailey, *Toe River Valley Heritage*, 2: 212. Local tradition has it that Palmer "trained the troops at Grassland Farms," see Wise, *A History of William Cuthbertson*, 12.
12. Henry T. Clark to John B. Palmer, 11 Jan. 1862, Letter Book, Henry T. Clark, 2: 232
13. Jordan, *North Carolina Troops*, 14: 282.

Chapter 2
1. Eaton, *A History of the Old South*, 487–490; Inscoe and McKinney, *The Heart of Confederate Appalachia*, 35–38
2. Vance to William Dickson, 7 Dec. 1860, found in Johnson, *Vance Papers*, 72; *North Carolina Standard*, 2 Jan. 1861.
3. Vance to W. W. Lenoir, 26 Dec. 1860, Johnston, *Vance Letters*, 74–78; W. W. Lenoir to Vance, 7 Jan. 1861; *Ibid.*, 79–81.
4. Bailey, *The Bailey Family of Yancey County*, 3: 1122; J. P. Eller to Vance, 28 Jan. 1861; Johnston, *Vance Letters*, 93; *North Carolina Standard*, 9 Jan. 1861.
5. *Raleigh Register*, 6 Nov. 1860; *North Carolina Standard*, 7 Feb. 1861. For more detailed accounts see Crawford, *Ashe County's Civil War*, 68–71.
6. See Sitterson, *Secession in North Carolina*, 239.
7. McElroy's company became Company C, Sixth North Carolina Volunteers, on June 1, 1861. While at Manassas Junction in late 1861, the company was re-designated the Sixteenth North Carolina Troops. Jordan, *North Carolina Troops*, 6: 1, 29; Inscoe and McKinney, *Heart of Confederate Appalachia*, 64.
8. *Highland Messenger*, 12 June 1846; Whitener, *History of Watauga County*, 43–44.
9. Sitterson, *The Secession Movement in North Carolina*, 243–245.
10. *Ibid.*, 247–248; Barrett, *The Civil War in North Carolina*, 15–16.
11. The Hornet's Nest Rifles became Company B, First North Carolina Volunteers; the Confederate Guards became Company K, Seventeenth North Carolina Troops (1st Organization); the Guilford Dixie Boys became Company M, Twenty-First North Carolina Troops; the Dixie Invincibles became Company F, Thirty-Third North Carolina; and the Shady Grove Rangers became Company E, Thirty-Fourth North Carolina Troops.

Chapter 3
1. Johnston, *Vance Letters*, 119–120.
2. *Ibid.*, 132–133.
3. *Ibid.*, 134.
4. Hickerson, *Echoes of Happy Valley*, 81.
5. Johnston, *Vance Letters*, 137.
6. *Raleigh Weekly Standard*, 6 March 1861.
7. Harper, diary, 1: 1; Raiford, *The 4th North Carolina Cavalry*, 6; Lenoir, diary, 8.
8. Johnston, *Vance Letters*, 138 n. 548.
9. *Ibid.*, 139, 142–144; Jordan, *North Carolina Troops*, 14: 382. The last name is also spelled Settlemire and Settlemoir.
10. *Official Records*, Ser. 1, Vol. 51, Pt. 2: 571–672. All entries are from Series 1 unless noted. Lenoir diary, 9.

Chapter 4
1. Adjutant General to Palmer, 14 Jan. 1862, Adjutant General Letter Book 10 Dec. 1861 to 23 April 1862; AG to Palmer, 17 Feb. 1862; *Ibid.*, 337; *Ibid.*, 518.
2. *Asheville News*, as reported in the *Hillsborough Recorder*, 7 May 1862.
3. Weitz, *More Damning Than Slaughter*, 40–41, 78; Hilderman, *They Went Into the Fight Cheering*, 37–38; Wert, "Confederate Conscription Woes," 9; Yearns, *The Confederate Congress*, 64–66.
4. Jordan, *North Carolina Troops*, 14: 214; Weaver, *The 5th and 7th Battalions North Carolina Cavalry*, 7–8.
5. Jordan, *North Carolina Troops*, 14: 213; for an

example of the use of Fifth Battalion Partisan Rangers, see Adkins Jefferson, Compiled Military Service Records (hereafter, CMSR), M-270, Roll #536, National Archives and Records Administration (hereafter, NARA); *Asheville News*, 31 July 1862.

6. Bailey, *Toe River Valley Heritage*, 1: 160; Jordan, *North Carolina Troops*, 14: 290; Hewett, *Supplement to the Official Records*, 49: 432.

7. Jordan, *North Carolina Troops*, 14: 290–300.

8. Ibid., 293, 300.

9. Ibid., 300–311; Hewett, *Supplement to the Official Records*, 49: 433.

10. Bailey, *Toe River Valley Heritage*, 8: 29.

11. Jordan, *North Carolina Troops*, 14: 311–323; Hardy, "Watauga County and the Civil War"; Hewett, *Supplement to the Official Records*, 49: 434.

12. *Avery County Heritage*, 2: 168–169; Hewett, *Supplement to the Official Records*, 49: 436; Jordan, *North Carolina Troops*, 7: 533, 539; 14: 323–343.

13. Ibid., 343–358; Hewett, *Supplement to the Official Records*, 49: 437–438; e-mail, Cliff Mosteller, 3 Jan. 2008.

14. Jordan, *North Carolina Troops*, 14: 358–374; Bailey, *Toe River Valley Heritage*, 8: 148; Pension record of John W. Edwards, sent to the author by Tina Cole, 27 Jan. 2008.

15. Lenoir, diary, 6; Harper, diary, 1: 4; Jordan, *North Carolina Troops*, 14: 374–386. For details of Lenoir's service in the Thirty-Seventh, see Hardy, *The Thirty-seventh North Carolina Troops*, 82–104.

16. Hardy, "Watauga County and the Civil War"; Jordan, *North Carolina Troops*, 14: 386–396.

17. Jordan, *North Carolina Troops*, 14: 396–404.

18. Jordan, *North Carolina Troops*, 14: 405–416; Younce, *Adventures of a Conscript*, 13–14.

19. Kautz, *Customs of Service for Non-Commissioned Officers and Soldiers*, 131–149.

20. Miller, *The Watauga Boys in the Great Civil War*, 1; Harper, "Fifty-Eighth Regiment," 26; Jordan, *North Carolina Troops*, 14: 272, 275, 290, 301, 311, 324, 343, 358, 374, 387, 396, 404.

21. Coffey, daybook, 2; Younce, *Adventures of a Conscript*, 7–8.

22. *Watauga Democrat*, 15 Sept. 1901.

Chapter 5

1. For further information on Unionists and exposed gaps, see McKnight, *Contested Borderland*, 32–35, 69; on guarding railroad bridges, see *Official Reports*, Vol. 16, Pt. 2: 773; on Halleck's army, see Horn, *The Army of Tennessee*, 147.

2. Jordan, *North Carolina Troops*, 14: 272–275; Wise, *The Military History of the Virginia Military Institute from 1839 to 1865*, 444.

3. Coffey, Daybook, 2.

4. L. L. Estes to sister, 29 July 1862, Estes letters.

5. Hardee, *Rifle and Light Infantry Tactics*, 6, 9; McKee and Harris, *The Civil War Letters of the Gouge Family*, 19 (hereafter *Gouge Letters*).

6. L. L. Estes to father and mother, 23 July 1862, Estes letters; Hardee, *Rifle and Light Infantry Tactics*, 16–64.

7. L. L. Estes to father and mother, 23 July 1862, Estes letters; no Moore in the Fifty-Eighth North Carolina had a first name that started with P; Arthur McFalls to Dear Companion, 1 Aug. 1862, McFalls letters.

8. William Bailey to Rebecca Bailey, 16 Aug. 1862, Bailey, *Bailey Family*, 1: 386; William Gouge to father, mother and sister, 24 August 1862, *Gouge Letters*, 19. The records state that J.H. Lingle and William C. Baird, both of Caldwell County, died on May 23, 1862. P. Henderson White of Caldwell County died on June 26, 1862. These were all prior to the formation of the Fifty-Eighth North Carolina. Jordan, *North Carolina Troops*, 14: 305, 376, 381, 386.

9. Jonathan Green to sister, July 7, 1862; William Gouge to parents, 24 Aug. 1862, *Gouge Letters*; William Bailey to wife, 16 Aug. 1862, *Bailey Family*, 1: 388; *Silver Letters*, Vol. 3, Issue 8, (July-August 2005): 6.

10. Jordan, *North Carolina Troops*, 14: 281, 336; *Avery County Heritage*, 2: 85; Robert McNeely, e-mail, 5 Oct. 2007. John's recovery took several weeks. He later served in the Second North Carolina Cavalry.

11. Harper, diary, 1: 5; *Official Records*, Vol. 16, Pt. 2: 773.

12. Warner, *Generals in Gray*, 292–293.

13. Ibid., 279–280; Eicher and Eicher, *Civil War High Commands*, 493–4.

14. *Official Records*, Vol. 16, Pt. 2: 766.

15. Ibid., 779.

16. Harper, diary, 1: 5–7.

17. Kincaid, *The Wilderness Road*, 247–250; Davis, "Cumberland Gap, 1862," 25–29.

18. *Gouge Letters*, 22. The letter is dated September 21, 1862. The editor made this note: This letter was unsigned. But it is probably from Tilman B. Silver to his father Alfred Silver; Harper, diary, 1: 8; Arthur McFalls to dear companion, 27 Sept. 1862, McFalls letters.

19. Bishop, in his 1987 history of the regiment for the Watauga County Historical Society, estimates that there were 300 prisoners, a number that could not be documented. He also writes that the prisoners who were not exchanged were to be sent to Richmond, Virginia. Bishop, "The 58th North Carolina Infantry," 3; *Official Records*, Series II, Vol. 4: 897. Volume 4 of Series II contains many letters regarding prisoners of war exchanges at Cumberland Gap.

20. Jordan, *North Carolina Troops*, 14: 317, 318, 332; Gaffney, *The Heritage of Watauga County*, 1: 244.

21. *Official Records*, Vol. 16, Pt. 2: 847; Hilliard's Legion was commanded by Col. Henry Hilliard and contained three infantry battalions, a cavalry battalion, and an artillery battalion. While Hilliard's command was larger than Palmer's, Palmer outranked Hilliard.

22. Edmund Kirby to brother, 22 Oct. 1862, Kirby letters; unknown Asheville newspaper, 24 March 1937.

23. *Official Records*, Vol. 16, Pt. 2: 887, 896; Harper, diary, 1: 10–11; John Blair to M. Blair, 7 Oct. 1862, Blair letters.

24. Harper, diary, 1: 11; W. H. Horton to sister, 23 Oct. 1862, Mary Council Papers, Duke University.

25. *Official Records*, Vol. 16, Pt. 2: 985; Warner, *Generals in Gray*, 113–114.

26. Jordan, *North Carolina Troops*, 14: 346, 347, 357.

Chapter 6

1. *Official Records*, Vol. 20, Pt. 2: 384; Parks, *General Edmund Kirby Smith, CSA*, 246–247; Conley, *Autumn of Glory*, 18–19.

2. *Official Records*, Vol. 16, Pt. 2: 981.

3. Edmund Kirby Smith to Carrie S. Smith, 13 March 1862, Kirby Smith Papers; *Official Records*, Vol. 10, Pt. 2: 397–402.

4. *Silver Threads*, Vol. 2, Issue 8 (July-August 2005) 7; Dugger and Hodges, diary, *The Watauga Democrat*, 14 May 1891; Harper, diary, 1: 12.

5. *Official Records*, Vol. 20, Pt. 2: 466; Harper, diary, 1: 12; Edmund Kirby to brother, 12 Dec. 1862, Kirby letters.
6. McDonald, *Campbell County, Tennessee*, 1: 31; "The Ten Springs of Jacksboro in 1808 and Today," 4–6.
7. Ridenour, *The Land of the Lake*, 69; Estes to mother, 29 Nov. 1862, Estes papers.
8. Miller, *Watauga Boys*, 3.
9. Estes to mother, 16 Nov. 1862; Fisher, *War at Every Door*, 76–77; *Gouge Letters*, 38.
10. Hewett, *Supplement to the Official Records*, Vol. 2, Pt. 7: 89; Harper, diary, 1: 29–31; Dugger and Hodges, diary, 1–2, *Watauga Democrat*, 14 May 1891.
11. Bailey, *Toe River Valley Heritage*, 8: 29.
12. *Gouge Letters*, 24, 26, 32; Harper, diary, 1: 12, 27.
13. Jordan, *North Carolina Troops*, 7: 495; 14: 416–17; Jonathan Phillips, CMSR, M-270, Roll # 537, NARA; Journal of Francis Marion Wilcox, n.p.
14. Harper, diary, 1: 16, 17, 18, 28.
15. Gaffney, *The Heritage of Watauga County*, 1: 16; Jesse Hawkins to mother and wife, 27 March 1863, Hawkins letters; George Harper to wife, 20 April 1863, Harper Letters.
16. *Gouge Letters*, 26; Jesse Hawkins to wife and mother, 27 March 1863, Hawkins letters; Langston Estes to unknown 1 Feb. 1863, Estes letters; J. B. Buchanan to "Dearest companion," Buchanan letters.
17. Langston Estes to family, 1 Feb. 1863, Estes letters; *Gouge Letters*, 33; Jesse Hawkins to wife and mother, 21 May 1863, Hawkins letters; *Watauga County Heritage* 1: 16; Jordan, *North Carolina Troops*, 14: 422.
18. Harper, diary, 1: 13, 28.
19. James Anglin, CMSR, M-270, Roll # 534, NARA; *Regulations for the Army of the Confederate States*, 175–177.
20. Jonathan Phillips, CMSR, M-270, roll # 537, NARA; Jacob Bowman, CMSR, M-270, roll # 534, NARA.
21. Kautz, *Customs of Service*, 134–135; *Regulations for the Army of the Confederate States*, 236–7.
22. Moore, qtd. in H. H. Cunningham, *Doctors in Gray*, 165; Jordan, *North Carolina Troops*, 14: 297, 309, 356.
23. Cunningham, *Doctors in Gray*, 194–195, 202; Jordan, *North Carolina Troops*, 14: 284, 287, 306, 314, 421.
24. *Gouge Letters*, 24, 33; Langston Estes to family, 27 March 1863, Estes Letters. Finley Coffee is probably Jesse F. Coffey, who died March 7, 1863. Jordan, *North Carolina Troops*, 14: 273, 291, 343, 397.
25. Bailey, *The Bailey Family History*, 3: 1124a.
26. Jordan, *North Carolina Troops*, 14: 272, 291, 343, 397; *Avery County Heritage*, 2: 168.
27. Jordan, *North Carolina Troops*, 14: 275; 276; 291, 358, 387.
28. Ibid., 290, 359; Haughton, *Training, Tactics, and Leadership*, 86–88.
29. Jordan, *North Carolina Troops*, 14: 272, 291, 301, 344.
30. Ibid., 274, 311, 358, 359.
31. Bailey, *The Bailey Family History*, 3: 1145a–45b; Jordan, *North Carolina Troops*, 14: 290, 301, 405.
32. T.J. Dula to Gov. Vance, 15 Jan. 1863, Vance Letters; Jordan, *North Carolina Troops*, 14: 593, 651.
33. Langston Estes to father and mother, 26 Sept. 1862, Estes letters.
34. Jordan, *North Carolina Troops*, 14: 359–374, 418, 419.
35. Miller, *Watauga Boys*, 4; Younce, *Adventures of a Conscript*, 4.
36. Younce, *Adventures of a Conscript*, 19–36.
37. *Regulations for the Army of the Confederate States*, 410; Harper diary: 22; Jordan, *North Carolina Troops*, 14: 315, 355; Arthur McFalls to Dear Companion, 4 Aug. 1863, McFalls letters; e-mail, Kay Bodeen, 18 Aug. 2008.
38. Lewis, *History of Cove Creek Baptist Church*, 10; Jordan, *North Carolina Troops*, 14: 315.
39. Wilcox, *A Journal Written by Francis Marion Wilcox*, n.p.
40. *Regulations for the Army of the Confederate States*, 410; Younce, *Adventures of a Conscript*, 15.
41. Younce, *Adventures of a Conscript*, 15; Deyton, "Toe River Valley," 362; Ella Harper to husband, George, 18 Nov. 1862, Harper Papers; Joseph C. Norwood to Walter Lenoir, 17 Nov. 1863, Lenoir Papers.
42. Younce, *Adventures of a Conscript*, 16.
43. Jordan, *North Carolina Troops*, 14: 412.
44. Donna Rominger-Barber, telephone interview, 11 June 2007.
45. Jordan, *North Carolina Troops*, 14: 324; 358, 375, 384, 396, 405; *Regulations for the Army of the Confederate States*, 16; *Mountain Mercury*, 7 Jan. 1863; Elisha Trivett papers.
46. Weitz, *More Damning than Slaughter*, 152–3.
47. *Official Records*, Vol. 18, 860–861.
48. *Official Records*, Series 4, Vol. 2, 687–688.
49. Bearman, "Desertion as Localism," 324; Eicher and Eicher, *Civil War High Commands*, 869; *Official Records*, Vol. 23, Pt. 2: 964–65, 950.
50. McKenzie, *Lincolnites and Rebels*, 137–138; Jordan, *North Carolina Troops*, 14: 298, 328, 349, 354, 355, 357, 364, 374, 376, 381, 383, 393, 395, 397, 407, 409, 412, 419.
51. Harper, diary, 1: 25, 26; Dugger and Thomas, diary, 1; Coffey, diary, 4; Langston Estes to brothers and sisters, 5 April 1863, Estes letters; *Gouge Letters*, 33.
52. Harper, diary, 1: 26–27; *Official Records*, Vol. 26, Pt. 2: 265.
53. *Official Records*, Vol. 23, Pt. 2: 792, 806; Jordan, *North Carolina Troops*, 14: 272.
54. Harper, diary, 1: 29, 32.
55. *Official Records*, Vol. 23, Pt. 2: 865, 946; *Gouge Letters*, 42.
56. Warner, *Generals in Gray*, 93; Eicher and Eicher, *High Commands*, 597. Frazier's appointment was later rejected by the Confederate Senate.
57. Harper, diary, 1: 33 George Harper to Ella Harper, 15 June 1863, Harper letters.
58. *Official Records*, Vol. 23, Pt. 2: 878; John C. Blair to Mr. Blair, 15 July 1863, Blair letters.
59. McKenzie, *Lincolnites and Rebels*, 146; Harper, diary, 1: 34–35; Dugger and Hodges, diary, 2; *Gouge Letters*, 44.
60. Gouge letters, 43.
61. Harper, diary, 1: 35; Hewett, *Supplement to Official Records*, 4: 184.
62. Dugger and Hodges, diary, 2–3; John B. Palmer, CMSR, M-270, Roll # 537, NARA; *Official Records*, Vol. 23, Pt. 2: 948; J. J. Hawkins to mother and wife, 12 Aug. 1863, Hawkins letters; Harper, diary, 2: 6; Sherry Reeter, e-mail, 25 Sept. 2008; Bob Isaacs, e-mail, 25 Sept. 2008; Jordan, *North Carolina Troops*, 14: 391.

Chapter 7

1. Woodworth, *Six Armies in Tennessee*, 53–57; McKenzie, *Lincolnites and Rebels*, 147.
2. Warner, *Generals in Gray*, 168–9; John H. Kelly file, Chickamauga and Chattanooga National Military Park.

3. Robertson, "The Chickamauga Campaign: The Fall of Chattanooga," 12–25, 44; Dugger and Hodges, diary, 3.
4. For conflict regarding Bragg, see Woodworth, *Jefferson Davis and His Generals*, 159–62, 166–68, 238–42; Woodworth, *Leadership and Command*, 29–65.
5. Dugger and Hodges, diary, 3.
6. See Robertson, "The Chickamauga Campaign," and Susan K. Kegon, "Near Miss at Davis Cross Roads" for more information about the activities in McLemore's Cove.
7. Dugger and Hodges, diary, 3; Conley, *Autumn of Glory*, 178; *Official Records*, Vol. 30, Pt. 2: 294, 301; Woodworth, *Six Armies in Tennessee*, 70.
8. Ibid., 72–73; Robertson, "The Chickamauga Campaign," 42–45.
9. *Official Records*, Vol. 30, Pt. 2: 308; Dugger and Hodges, diary, 3.
10. Ibid.
11. Warner, *Generals in Gray*, 246; Eicher and Eicher, *Civil War High Commands*, 439.
12. Dugger and Hodges, diary, 3.
13. Ibid., 4; Palmer, "The 58th North Carolina at the Battle of Chickamauga," 454.
14. Dugger and Hodges, diary, 4; Cozzens, *This Terrible Sound*, 119; Bailey, "Additional Sketches of the Fifty-Eighth," 3: 449.
15. Ibid.; *Official Records*, Vol. 30, Pt. 2: 413–414, 440; Jordan, *North Carolina Troops*, 14: 355.
16. Ibid., 306, 316, 319, 416.
17. Cozzens, *This Terrible Sound*, 316.
18. Bailey, "Additional Sketches," 3: 450; *Official Records*, Vol. 30, Pt. 2: 440.
19. *Official Records*, Vol. 30, Pt. 2: 289, 415; Jordan, *North Carolina Troops*, 14: 274, 296, 299, 384.
20. *Official Records*, Vol. 30, Pt. 2: 415.
21. Palmer, "The 58th North Carolina," 454; Jordan, *North Carolina Troops*, 14: 275, 277, 283, 284, 285, 286; *Official Records*, Vol. 30, Pt. 2: 445.
22. Bailey, "Additional Sketches," 3: 452; Palmer, "The 58th North Carolina," 455.
23. Anderson and Hawkins, *The Heritage of Caldwell County*, 433–434; Thomas G. Garrett to F.A. Tobey, 3 June 1908, found in McGough, *Childsville*, 457–58; newspaper clipping from Morganton, N.C., in the files of the Chickamauga-Chattanooga National Military Park; Friel, *The Phillips Family*, 295; *The Lenoir News*, 31 Dec. 1909.
24. *Official Records*, Vol. 30 Pt. 2: 445–6.
25. *Official Records*, Vol. 30, Pt. 2: 446; Jordan, *North Carolina Troops*, 14: 224; Raleigh *Daily Progress*, 8 Oct. 1863.
26. Bailey, "Additional Sketches," 3: 452–3; Jordan, *North Carolina Troops*, 14: 299, 301, 354.
27. Ibid., 273–4; It is not clear if Dr. Harriss had reported for duty yet; Palmer wrote to Colonel Childs that a deserted house "was a temporary hospital by Genl. Preston's Division & some others—It was about three miles from Lee's Mill," McGough, *Childsville* 398.
28. Deering J. Roberts, quoted in Cunningham, *Doctors in Gray*, 220; Schroeder-Lein, *Confederate Hospitals on the Move*, 125–129; information on Lanier from family files submitted by Amy Edwards Towery.
29. *Gouge Letters*, 56; *Official Records*, Vol. 30, Pt. 2: 417; McGough, *Childsville*, 397–8.
30. Ibid., 399; Richmond *Daily Dispatch*, 30 Oct. 1863; Ibid. 31 Oct. 1863.

Chapter 8

1. These numbers compiled from the roster in Jordan, *North Carolina Troops*, Vol. 14. In comparison, when the Thirty-Seventh North Carolina Troops mustered into service on November 20, 1861, 939 men were present. See Hardy, *The Thirty-seventh North Carolina Troops*, 24.
2. Dugger and Hodges, diary, 4; Harper, diary 2: 9; DiNardo and Furqueron, "The Day After: Braxton Bragg and the Aftermath of Chickamauga," 31–37.
3. Jordan, *North Carolina Troops*, 14: 272, 301, 358, 374.
4. Simon Buckner to unknown, 2 Oct. 1863; William Preston to "sir," 4 Oct. 1863; Carter Stevenson to James A. Seddon, 7 Oct. 1863. John B. Palmer, CMSR, M-270, Roll # 537, NARA.
5. Conley, *Autumn of Glory*, 235–247.
6. Stickley, *Simon Boliver Buckner*, 232–241.
7. Dugger and Hodges, diary, 5; Harper, diary, 2: 9–11.
8. *Official Records*, Vol. 11, Pt. 2: 992; Jordan, *North Carolina Troops*, 14: 275, 292, 306, 313, 337, 350, 363, 377, 389, 399, 411.
9. Clark, *Histories of the Several Regiments*, 3: 425; Charlotte *Bulletin*, 5 Oct. 1863; Jordan, *North Carolina Troops*, 14: 311.
10. Harper, diary, 2: 5; Glenn Tucker, in his book on Chickamauga, stated that the soldiers performed this gesture on going into battle at Chickamauga. Jeffrey Weaver, in his unpublished manuscript on the regiment, stated that this gesture occurred during a visit by Governor Vance. Neither story is credited. However, Bailey, in his "Additional Sketch of the Fifty-Eighth" in Clark, writes that they were not permitted to cheer Bragg prior to the battle of Chickamauga, and took off and waved their hats. Tucker, *Chickamauga*, 356; Weaver, "58th North Carolina Regiment," n.p.; Bailey, "Additional Sketches," 3: 448–49; G.W.F. Harper to Ella, 6 Nov. 1863, Harper letters.
11. Harper, diary, 2: 5; Jordan, *North Carolina Troops*, 14: 353.
12. Harper, diary, 2: 14; Jordan, *North Carolina Troops*, 14: 285, 317, 348, 349, 350, 376, 377, 412; G.W.F. Harper to Ella, 9 Nov. 1863, Harper Letters.
13. Keever, *Iredell*, 230.
14. Jordan, *North Carolina Troops*, 14: 371, 411, 415; John W. Hilton, Navy Widow Certificates, M1279, NARA; Felix Sluder, Navy Widow Certificates, M1279, NARA; Obadiah Sprinkle, Navy Widow Certificates, M1279.
15. Harper, diary 2: 14; *Official Records*, Vol. 31, Pt. 2: 686.
16. Eicher and Eicher, *Civil War High Commands*, 450; Warner, *Generals in Gray*, 254–55; Jordan and Chapla, "O What a Turbill Affair," 315–316.
17. Barrett, *The Civil War in North Carolina*, 200–201; *Official Records*, Vol. 31, Pt. 3: 711.
18. Jordan, *North Carolina Troops*, 14: 272, 273, 274.
19. Harper, diary, 2: 15, G.W.F. Harper to Ella, 18 Nov. 1863, Harper letters.
20. Jordan, *North Carolina Troops*, 3: 25; 14: 502, 503–4; Taylor, "The 60th North Carolina Regiment," 11–12, 19.
21. Harper, diary, 2: 15.
22. *Official Records*, Vol. 31, Pt. 3: 732–33; Harper, diary, 2: 16.
23. "Caldwell," "The Battle of Missionary Ridge," in the files of the Caldwell Historical Museum, undoubtedly

written by George W. F. Harper. *Official Records*, Vol. 31, Pt. 2: 745–5; Cozzens, *The Shipwreck of Their Hopes*, 137–140; Conley, *Autumn of Glory*, 272.

24. Jordan and Chapla state in their article on the brigade at Missionary Ridge that the brigade was positioned this way. Whether the Fifty-Eighth and Sixtieth functioned as separate commands or fought consolidated is an unanswered question; Patton and Chapla, "O What a Turbill Affair," 327; Hoffman, *The Confederate Collapse at Missionary Ridge:* 23, 73; *Official Records*, Vol. 31, 2: 745–6; Harper, "Fifty-Eighth Regiment," 3: 436–37; "Caldwell," "The Battle of Missionary Ridge"; Captain Silver wrote after the war that he returned from sick furlough the day before the battle and assumed command of the regiment. See *Lenoir News*, 22 March 1910; Ella Harper to Mollie, 13 Dec. 1863; Harper-Beall Papers.

25. "Caldwell," "The Battle of Missionary Ridge"; Harper, "Fifty-Eighth," 436; Hoffman, *The Confederate Collapse at Missionary Ridge*, 73, 74.

26. *Lenoir News*, 22 March 1910.

27. Cozzens, *The Shipwreck of Their Hope*, 268; "Caldwell," "The Battle of Missionary Ridge."

28. Hoffman, *The Confederate Collapse at Missionary Ridge*, 75.

29. Cozzens, *The Shipwreck of Their Hopes*, 286; Hoffman, *The Confederate Collapse at Missionary Ridge*, 75; Miller, *The Watauga Boys*, 6.

30. Hoffman, *The Confederate Collapse at Missionary Ridge*, 75.

31. Cozzens, *The Shipwreck of Their Hopes*, 296; Hoffman, *The Confederate Collapse at Missionary Ridge*, 75; E.J. Norris, "Biographical Sketch of Confederate Veteran," *Watauga Democrat*, undated.

32. "Caldwell," "The Battle of Missionary Ridge"; Hoffman, *The Confederate Collapse at Missionary Ridge*, 77.

33. Jordan, *North Carolina Troops*, 14: 232, 276, 319, 328, 362, 399; 414; Norris, "Biographical Sketch of Confederate Veteran"; *Lenoir News*, 22 March 1910; Ella Harper to Mollie, 13 Dec. 1863; Harper-Beall Papers.

34. Hoffman, *The Confederate Collapse at Missionary Ridge*, 77; Harper, "Fifty-Eighth Regiment," 3: 437.

35. *Official Records*, Vol. 31, Pt. 2: 665, 741–742; Braxton Bragg to Edward Turner Skyles, 8 Feb. 1873, in Polk, *Leonidas Polk*, 2: 310.

36. Harper, diary, 2: 16; Ella Harper to Mollie, 13 Dec. 1863; Harper-Beall Papers.

Chapter 9

1. Weaver and Sherwood, *The 54th Virginia Infantry*, 93; Jordan, *North Carolina Troops*, 14: 294.
2. *Ibid.*, 337, 392.
3. Speer, *Portals to Hell*, 154–155; Chapman, *A Wiseman's Family*, 386.
4. Jordan, *North Carolina Troops*, 14: 310, 337, 340, 363, 364, 373, 407, 413; Speer, *Portals to Hell*, 155, 321–22.
5. E-mail, Dan Styles, 27 Sept. 2009.
6. Jordan, *North Carolina Troops*, 14: 364, 365, 392, 409, 411, 413, 415.
7. *Ibid.*, 399, 414.
8. Bearman, "Desertion as Localism," 329; Jordan, *North Carolina Troops*, 14: 307, 319, 373.
9. Harper, diary, 2: 17, 18, 19; Ella Harper to Mollie, 13 Dec. 1863; Harper-Beall Papers.
10. Conley, *Autumn of Glory*, 277; Hallock, *Braxton Bragg and Confederate Defeat*, 149, 150.
11. Conley, *Autumn of Glory*, 282; Warner, *Generals in Gray*, 161–162.
12. Symonds, *Joseph E. Johnston*, 249; Harper, diary, 2: 20; *Official Records*, Vol. 31, Pt. 3: 860.
13. Symonds, *Joseph E. Johnston*, 250; *Watauga County Heritage*, 1: 387; Harper, diary, 2: 20.
14. Harper, G.W.F. "A War-time Furlough," *The Lenoir News*, 4 Feb. 1910.
15. *Official Records*, Vol. 31, Pt. 2: 530–532.
16. *Ibid.*; Harper to wife, 25 Jan. 1864, Harper papers.
17. Dugger and Hodges, diary, 6; Radley, *Rebel Watchdog*, 33, 50; Harper, diary, 2: 23, 24–28; John Barnes (Company I) writes that the regiment stayed in Dalton for eight days. John G. Barnes to wife, 12 Jan. 1864, Barnes letters.
18. Harper, diary, 2: 24–28; Bunch, *Military Justice*, 2–4; Adkins Jefferson, CMSR, M270, Roll #534, NARA; Andrew Lovelace, CMSR, M-270, Roll # 536, NARA; James Shehan CMSR, M-270, Roll # 537, NARA. John G. Barnes to wife, 12 Feb. 1864, Barnes letters.
19. G.W.F. Harper to Ella, date unreadable; *Ibid.*, 14 Feb. 1864.
20. Castel, *Decision in the West*, 39–52.
21. Dugger and Thomas, diary, 6; *Official Records*, Vol. 32, Pt. 1: 478–481.
22. Dugger and Thomas, diary, 7, *Official Records*, Vol. 36, Pt. 1: 483; Jordan, *North Carolina Troops*, Vol. 14: 288, 320–321, 375, 395; Harper, diary, 2: 28; Alexander, *The History of the First Presbyterian Church of Lenoir*, n.p.; *Watauga County Heritage*, 387.
23. John G. Barnes to wife, 4 March 1864, Barnes letters.
24. *Official Records*, Vol. 52, Pt. 2: 578.
25. *Official Records*, Vol. 32, Pt. 2: 617, 651; John B. Palmer to Harper, 4 March 1864, Harper papers.
26. Harper, diary, 2: 31; Weaver and Sherwood, *The 54th Virginia*, 104.
27. Hewett, *Supplement to the Official Records*, Vol. 32, 210.
28. Harper, diary, 2: 31; Weaver and Sherwood, *The 54th Virginia*, 101; Hewett, *Supplement to the Official Records*, Vol. 32, 211.
29. Caleb Conley, CMSR, M-270, Roll #535, NARA; Harper, diary, 2: 33–34.
30. John G. Barnes to wife, 4 March 1863, Barnes letters; Jordan, *North Carolina Troops*, 14: 334, 416; *Official Records*, Vol. 32, Pt. 3: 100–101.
31. Auman, "Peace Movement," 871–72; John Barnes to wife, 12 Jan. 1864, Barnes letters.
32. Officers and the 58th and 60th to Governor Vance, 24 March 1864, Vance letters.
33. Jordan, *North Carolina Troops*, 7: 584, 14: 273, Drury C. Harmon, CMSR, M-270, Roll #535, NARA; Prim, "Born Again in the Trenches," 259; *Bethel Baptist Church Minutes, 1831–1885*, n.p.; W. H. Horton to M. A. Council, 23 Oct. 1862, Mary Council Papers; Poindexter Blevins to family, 27 March 1864, Ashe County Public Library.
34. Jordan, *North Carolina Troops*, 7: 583; 14: 280, 282, 284, 304, 323, 325, 347, 350, 358, 360, 361, 383, 386, 401, 417.
35. Bailey, *Toe River Valley Heritage 3*: 53–54; Jordan, *North Carolina Troops*, 14: 304; Dellinger family notes, courtesy of Tense Banks; Hunt, *David Dellinger*, 8.
36. *Daily Constitutionalist*, 5 May 1864; Daniel, *Soldering in the Army of Tennessee*, 113; Jordan, *North Carolina Troops*, 14: 382–3.
37. Taylor, "The 60th North Carolina Regiment," 32–33; Ridley, *Battles and Sketches of the Army of Tennessee*,

283–286; Daniel, *Soldiering in the Army of Tennessee*, 113; Hewitt, *Supplement to the Official Records*, Vol. 32, 116.
    38. Bailey, *Toe River Valley Heritage*, 3: 54.

Chapter 10

1. W. L. McConnico, The Compiled Service Records of Confederate Generals and Staff Officers, and Non-regimental Enlisted Men, M331, Roll # 65, NARA; *Official Records*, Vol. 32, Pt. 3: 801; Madaus, *The Battle Flags of the Confederate Army of Tennessee*, 63–64. The "58" and the "N.C." of the Fifty-Eighth's 1864 flag are in the Collections of the North Carolina Museum of History.
2. *Official Records*, Vol. 38, Pt. 1: 292, Pt. 3: 811; Dugger and Hodges, diary, 8; Harper, diary, 2: 35.
3. Jordan, *North Carolina Troops*, 14: 378, 393, 414.
4. Secrist, *The Battle of Resaca*, 14–15; McMurry, "Atlanta Campaign: Rocky Face to the Dallas Line, the Battles of May 1864," 20, 23.
5. *Ibid.*; Harper, diary, 2: 36; Dugger and Hodges, diary 8; Jordan, *North Carolina Troops*, 14: 370, 372.
6. Scaife, *The Campaign for Atlanta*, 27–28; *Official Records*, Vol. 38, Pt. 3: 812.
7. Harper, diary, 2: 36; Maj. Gen. David S. Stanley, quoted in Dolzall, "Opportunity Lost," 28; *Official Records*, Vol. 38, Pt. 1: 221, 488–9; Pt. 3: 812; anonymous Federal soldier, quoted in Castel, *Decision in the West*, 164; *The Lenoir Topic*, 23 March 1892.
8. *Official Records*, Vol. 38, 3: 812.
9. *Intelligencer* (Atlanta), unknown date, reprinted in *North Carolina Standard* (Raleigh), 22 June 1864.
10. *Ibid.*, 813; Harper, diary, 2: 36; Castel, *Decision in the West*, 188.
11. Jordan, *North Carolina Troops*, 14: 280, 307, 309, 338, 352, 353, 359, 376, 384, 398, 410; *Gouge Letters*, 59; James F. Hurley to wife and children, 30 May 1864, Hurley letters.
12. Harper, diary, 2: 36–39.
13. Symonds, *Joseph E. Johnston*, 383; Dugger and Hodges, diary, 9.
14. Dugger and Hodges, diary, 9; Castel, *Decision in the West*, 193; Symonds, *Joseph E. Johnston*, 287–288.
15. Dugger and Hodges, diary, 9; *Official Records*, Vol. 38, Pt. 4: 728.
16. *Official Records*, Vol. 38, Pt. 3: 983–84; Symonds, *Joseph E. Johnston*, 292.
17. Dugger and Hodges, diary, 9; Weiss, "'I Lead You to Battle': Joseph E. Johnston and the Controversy at Cassville," 424–452; Jordan, *North Carolina Troops*, 14: 331, 334, 335, 337, 338, 391, 392.
18. Dugger and Hodges, diary, 9.
19. McMurry, "'The Hell Hole': New Hope Church," 32–43; Jordan, *North Carolina Troops*, 301, 313, 320, 313–4, 336, 341, 351, 376, 380; *Official Records*, Vol. 38, Pt. 4: 318.
20. "Col. Robert C. Trigg, of Virginia," 65.
21. Dugger and Hodges, diary, 10.
22. *Ibid.*, 10; Miller, *Watauga Boys*, 7.
23. Dugger and Hodges, diary, 11; Conley, *Autumn of Glory*, 357.
24. Dugger and Hodges, diary, 12. General Polk was killed on June 14, 1864, at Pine Mountain. Dugger writes that Polk had climbed onto the breastworks of the Fifty-Eighth to observe the enemy when he was killed by a shell. This is not true. Polk was to the rear of Bate's division.
25. McMurry writes, "In the middle of the afternoon, advanced detachments of the Federals captured several men of the 58th and 60th North Carolina regiments." No source could be found. Richard M. McMurry, "The Battle of Kolb's Farm," 21; Dugger and Hodges, diary, 13. Dugger's entries for mid–June are off by one day.
26. Jordan, *North Carolina Troops*, 14: 336, 338, 340, 341; Castel, *Decision in the West*, 294.
27. *Official Records*, Vol. 38, Pt. 3: 814–5.
28. Jordan, *North Carolina Troops*, 14: 296, 299, 311, 343; Dugger and Hodges, diary, 13; *Official Records*, Vol. 38, Pt. 3: 415 McMurry, "The Battle of Kolb's Farm," 22–23; the typescript of this letter is signed "er Lawshe." See McGough, *Childsville*, 461.
29. Jordan, *North Carolina Troops*, 14: 272; *Official Records*, Vol. 38, Pt. 3: 815; Friel, *The Phillips Family*, 271.
30. Dugger and Hodges, diary, 13.
31. Jordan, *North Carolina Troops*, 14: 362, 387.
32. Johnston, quoted in Castel, *Decision in the West*, 329; Dugger and Hodges, diary, 13; Weaver and Sherwood, *54th Virginia Infantry*, 118; Weaver, *63rd Virginia Infantry*, 61.
33. *Supplement to the Official Records*, Vol. 49: 442; Jordan, *North Carolina Troops*, 7: 579; 14: 375, 377, 384, 385.
34. Castel, *Decision in the West*, 331–2; Scaife, *The Campaign for Atlanta*, 68; Dugger and Hodges, diary, 13; McMurry, *The Atlanta Campaign*, 114; Jordan, *North Carolina Troops*, 14: 348–9, 377, 378–9, 381, 383. Some believe that Stevenson's division was positioned in two lines of regular entrenchments, and that the first line was captured. The author believes that the line of detached rifle pits was captured, but that the main Confederate line held.
35. Sherman, *Memoirs of General William T. Sherman*, 2: 65; *Official Records*, Vol. 38, Pt. 1: 69; Scaife, *The Campaign for Atlanta*, 69–70.
36. Dugger and Hodges, diary, 14; *Supplement to the Official Records*, 49: 437; Jordan, *North Carolina Troops*, 14: 346, 353, 356.
37. Dugger and Hodges, diary, 14.
38. *Ibid.*
39. *Official Records*, Vol. 38, 5:885.
40. Miller, *Watauga Boys*, 11.

Chapter 11

1. *Official Records*, Vol. 38, Pt. 5: 876.
2. Warner, *Generals in Gray*, 142–3; Eicher and Eicher, *High Commands*, 302–3.
3. *Official Records*, Vol. 38, Pt. 5: 879–80; *Ibid.*, Vol. 39, Pt. 2: 712–14.
4. James Wysor to his father, July 19, 1864, quoted in Jordan, *North Carolina Troops*, 14: 252, n. 117; Capt. James Clark, qtd. in Weaver, *63rd Virginia*, 120.
5. *Official Records*, Vol. 38, Pt. 3: 679; Conley, *Autumn of Glory*, 437; numbers compiled from Jordan, *North Carolina Troops*, Vol. 14.
6. Dugger and Hodges, diary, 15; Hood, *Advance and Retreat*, 186.
7. Coffey, *John Bell Hood and the Struggle for Atlanta*, 147–50; McMurry, *John Bell Hood*, 126–28; Castel, *Decision in the West*, 368–78; Dugger and Hodges, diary, 15; *Official Records*, Vol. 38, Pt. 5: 896–97; Jordan, *North Carolina Troops*, 14: 348, 409.
8. Hood, *Advance and Retreat*, 174; Dugger and Hodges, diary, 15.
9. Castel, *Decision in the West*, 405; Conley, *Autumn of Glory*, 449–50; Coffey, *John Bell Hood*, 80; Dugger and Hodges, diary, 15; Jordan, *North Carolina Troops*, survey.
10. Jordan, *North Carolina Troops*, 14: 284, 336; Dug-

ger and Hodges, diary, 15; Davis "Atlanta Campaign," 9–10.
11. *Official Records*, Vol. 38, Pt. 5: 910; Eicher and Eicher, *High Commanders*, 345; Warner, *Generals in Gray*, 183.
12. Hattaway, *General Stephen D. Lee*, 127.
13. McMurry, *Atlanta 1864*, 157; Coffey, *John Bell Hood*, 90–92; *Official Records*, Vol. 38, Pt. 3: 762–63.
14. Dugger and Hodges, diary, 15; Scaife, *The Campaign for Atlanta*, 116; Jordan, *North Carolina Troops*, 14: 363, 388, 390, 413, 416.
15. *Official Records*, Vol. 38, Pt. 3: 763; Dugger and Hodges, diary, 16; Jordan, *North Carolina Troops*, 14: 314.
16. *Ibid.*, 304, 318, 321, 339, 344, 360, 361; Conley, *Autumn of Glory*, 456; G. D. Gouge to Rosannah Gouge, 25 Aug. 1864, *Gouge Letters*, 61.
17. Jordan, *North Carolina Troops*, 14: 256, 481; Warner, *Generals in Gray*, 227–28; Miller, *Watauga Boys*, 10. In Jordan there is no compelling reason why Palmer assumed command on August 23, even though Hardy is listed in command on a return in the Official Records on August 31 (Vol. 38, Pt. 3: 672). The November date comes from Palmer's biography. See Neff, *Tennessee's Battered Brigadier*, 117.
18. Weaver and Sherwood, *The 54th Virginia*, 126–127.
19. Dugger and Hodges, diary, 16.
20. Miller, *Watauga Boys*, 9; Dugger and Hodges, diary, 16; Hood, *Advance and Retreat*, 203.
21. Horn, *Army of Tennessee*, 364; Dugger and Hodges, diary, 16; Hood, *Advance and Retreat*, 205; *Official Records*, Vol. 38, Pt. 3: 764, 5: 997.
22. Clauss, "The Battle of Jonesboro," 17; Furqueron, "The Finest Opportunity Lost: The Battle of Jonesboro, August 31–September 1, 1864," 53; *Official Records*, Vol. 38, Pt. 3: 764; Dugger and Hodges, diary, 16.
23. Bailey, *Toe River Valley Heritage*, 8: 160; Jordan, *North Carolina Troops*, 14: 272.
24. Furqueron, "The Finest Opportunity Lost," 53; John C. Blair to mother, 5 Sept. 1864, Blair letters.
25. *Watauga Democrat*, undated; Jordan, *North Carolina Troops*, 14: 272, 286, 289, 302, 346, 349, 412; the information regarding the death of Lieutenant Estes comes from John C. Blair to mother, 5 Sept. 1864.
26. Hood, *Advance and Retreat*, 205, 207; *Official Records*, Vol. 38, Pt. 3: 765; Dugger and Hodges, diary, 17.
27. *Official Records*, Vol. 38, Pt. 3: 765; Castel, *Decision in the West*, 534.
28. *Official Records*, Vol. 38, Pt. 5: 1014; Jordan, *North Carolina Troops*, 14: 300, 312, 359, 378, 380, 393.
29. *Watauga Democrat*, no date; Jordan, *North Carolina Troops*, 14: 274.
30. George Mullis, CMSR, M-270, Roll # 537, NARA; Jordan, *North Carolina Troops*, 14: 366–67.
31. Hood, *Advance and Retreat*, 253; Blair, to Mother, 5 Sept. 1864, Blair letters; Dugger and Hodges, diary, 17; *Gouge Letters*, 62.
32. Harper, diary, 2: 51; *Official Records*, Vol. 38, Pt. 5: 1027; Hood, *Advance and Retreat*, 253; *Gouge Letters*, 63.
33. Conley, *Army of Tennessee*, 480; Hood, *Advance and Retreat*, 256–262; *Official Records*, Vol. 39, Pt. 1: 810; 3: 779, 790, 791, 805; Dugger and Hodges, diary, 17.
34. Hood, *Advance and Retreat*, 262; Dugger and Hodges, diary, 17–18; *Official Records*, Vol. 39, Pt. 1: 810–811; 3: 814.
35. McMurry, *John Bell Hood*, 161–162.
36. Hood, *Advance and Retreat*, 266; Miller, *Watauga Boys*, 10; *Official Records*, Vol. 39, Pt. 3: 818.
37. Dugger and Hodges, diary, 18; Harper, diary 2: 56; John C. Blair to father, 27 Oct. 1864. The date on Blair's letter must be wrong. The Fifty-Eighth was well past Gadsden on October 27.
38. Dugger and Hodges, diary, 18; Harper, diary, 2: 56–57; Harper to Ella, 26 Oct. 1864, Harper letters.
39. Hood, *Advance and Retreat*, 380. For an explanation of Forrest's movements, see Conley, *Autumn of Glory*, 487–88.
40. Harper, diary, 2: 57; Jordan, *North Carolina Troops*, 14: 272; G.W.F. Harper to Ella, 26 Oct. 1864, Harper letters; Chapman, *A Wiseman's Family*, 237.
41. *Official Records*, Vol. 39, Pt. 1: 811; Harper, diary, 2: 57–59; Dugger and Hodges, diary, 18; G.W.F. Harper to Ella, 26 Oct. 1864, Harper letters; Coffey diary.
42. Harper, diary, 2: 59
43. Dugger and Hodges, diary, 18–19; Harper, diary, 2: 60–61; McMurry, *Hood*, 169; *Official Records*, Vol. 45, Pt.1: 687.
44. Harper, diary, 2: 61.
45. *Ibid.*; *Official Records*, Vol. 45, Pt. 1: 693.
46. Harper, diary, 2: 61; *Official Records*, Vol. 45, Pt. 1: 693.
47. Harper, diary, 2: 63–64; G.W.F. Harper to Ella, 11 December 1864, Harper letters; *Ibid.*, 23 December 1864; *Official Records*, Vol. 45, Pt. 2: 651.
48. G.W.F. Harper to Ella, 29 Dec. 1864, Harper letters; Harper, diary, 2: 65; Coffey daybook.
49. Harper, diary, 2: 67.

Chapter 12

1. Kennett, "'Hell' or 'High Old Times,'" 46–52; McMurry, "On the Road to the Sea," 8–25.
2. Harper, diary, 2: 67; *Official Records*, Vol. 45, Pt. 1: 664; 2: 799.
3. *Ibid.*, Pt. 2: 781, 785, 805.
4. Harper, diary, 2: 68–70; *Official Records*, Vol. 45, Pt. 2: 793; Vol. 47, Pt. 2: 1078; Bradley, *Last Stand in the Carolinas*, 28–29.
5. Harper, "Fifty-Eighth Regiment," 440.
6. *Official Records*, Vol. 47, Pt. 2: 1101; Harper, diary, 2: 70–71; Neff, *Tennessee's Battered Brigadier*, 146; Jordan, *North Carolina Troops*, 14: 295, 378.
7. Harper, diary, 2: 71; *Official Records*, Vol. 47, Pt. 1: 406; 2: 1176; Miller, *Watauga Boys*, 12.
8. Harper, diary, 2: 71; Elmore, "The Burning of Columbia," 10, 12.
9. Harper, diary, 2: 72; Miller, *Watauga Boys*, 12; Lindsley, *The Military Annals of Tennessee*, 366; Jordan, *North Carolina Troops*, 14: 353.
10. See Elmore, "The Burning of Columbia"; Miller, *Watauga Boys*, 12.
11. Harper, diary, 2: 72–3; *Official Records*, Vol. 47, Pt. 2: 1262.
12. *Ibid.*, Pt. 2: 1248, 1274; Miller, *Watauga Boys*, 12.
13. Barrett, *Sherman's March*, 98–107.
14. *Official Records*, Vol. 47, Pt. 2: 1285; Harper, diary, 2: 73; Bradley, *Last Stand*, 27–28.
15. Harper, diary 2: 74; *Official Records*, Vol. 47, Pt. 2: 1317, 1321; Warner, *Generals in Gray*, 136–37.
16. Harper, diary, 2: 75; Samuel Silver, CMSR, M-270, Roll #537, NARA; Jordan, *North Carolina Troops*, 272.
17. G.W.F. Harper to Ella, 17 March 1865, Harper letters; Miller, *Watauga Boys*, 12.
18. Bradley, *Last Stand*, 148, 166, 177, 184; *Official*

Records, Vol. 47, Pt. 1: 1093, 1096, 1099.
19. Bradley, *Last Stand*, 156; *Official Report*, Vol. 47, Pt. 1: 1099.
20. Bradley, *Last Stand*, 198; *Official Reports*, Vol. 47, Pt. 1: 1094.
21. Harper places the time for the advance at 3 P.M. See Harper, diary, 2: 76; Brig. Gen. Palmer stated that the advance started at 3:15. See *Official Records*, Vol. 47, Pt. 1: 1099. Bradley places the time at 2:45. Bradley, *Last Stand*, 203.
22. *Official Records*, Vol. 47, Pt. 1: 1094, 1099; Harper, "Fifty-Eighth Regiment," 440; Hughes, *Bentonville*, 85; G.W.F. Harper, "Palmer's Brigade," *News and Observer*, 20 Dec. 1887.
23. Jordan, *North Carolina Troops*, 14: 311, 320, 329, 331, 379, 402; Harper, "Fifty-Eighth," 443.
24. Harper, "Palmer's Brigade"; *Official Records*, Vol. 47, Pt. 1: 1100; Bradley, *Last Stand*, 223, 225–254.
25. Harper, "Fifty-Eighth Regiment," 441; Jordan, *North Carolina Troops*, 14: 324.
26. Harper, "Fifty-Eighth," 441–42; Maj. Gen. Henry Clayton wrote that after asking for help, "A portion of Palmer[']s brigade of Stevenson[']s Division was sent[,] but moved too far to the right." Bradley, "Two Confederate Views of Bentonville," 97.
27. Harper, diary, 2: 76.
28. Bradley, *Last Stand*, 343; *Official Records*, Vol. 47, Pt. 1: 1056.
29. Bradley, *Last Stand*, 375, 395. Harper never mentions the regiment moving. Harper, diary, 2: 76.
30. Harper, "Fifty-Eighth," 444; *Official Records*, Vol. 47, Pt. 1: 1101.
31. Harper, diary, 2: 76; *Official Records*, Vol. 47, Pt. 1: 1096, 1100.
32. Harper, diary, 2: 76–77; *Official Records*, Vol. 47, Pt. 2: 1453–54.
33. *Official Records*, Vol. 47, Pt. 3: 715, 716; Bradley, *This Astounding Close*, 63.
34. Harper, diary, 2: 78–79.
35. Bradley, *This Astounding Close*, 67, 73, 79; Harper, diary, 2: 78, 79.
36. *Official Records*, Vol. 47, Pt. 3: 771; Neff, *Tennessee's Battered Brigadier*, 162–163.
37. Jordan, *North Carolina Troops*, 14: 272–275.
38. Jordan, *North Carolina Troops*, 14: 276, 290, 301, 312, 325, 334, 358, 359, 375, 387.
39. Warner, *Generals in Gray*, 32–33; Eicher and Eicher, *High Commands*, 142.
40. Harper, diary, 2: 79.
41. Bradley, *This Astounding Close*, 143; Harper, diary, 80.
42. Harper, diary, 2: 80, 81.
43. Foley and Whicker, *The Civil War Ends*, 33; Harper, diary, 2: 80.
44. Harper, diary, 2: 80.
45. Harper, diary, 2: 81.
46. Bradley, *This Astounding Close*, 171–72, 208; Symonds, *Johnston*, 357.
47. *Official Records*, Vol. 47, Pt. 3: 313, 321, 482.
48. Harper, diary, 2: 82; *Official Records*, Vol. 47, Pt. 3: 843–44; Foley and Whicker, *The Civil War Ends*, 56.
49. Bradley, *This Astounding Close*, 225–26; Weaver and Sherwood write, "Every man received one silver dollar and every seventh man received an extra [dollar]." *54th Virginia*, 156; Harper, "Fifty-Eighth Regiment," 444; The Greene family recalled the payment was "one Mexican silver dollar and fourteen cents." Bailey, *Toe River Heritage*, 1: 244.
50. Harper, diary, 2: 82; *Official Records*, Vol. 47, Pt. 1: 1061.
51. Harper, diary, 2: 83; Miller, *Watauga Boys*, 13; Harper, "Fifty-Eighth Regiment," 445.
52. Bailey, "Fifty-Eighth Regiment," 454.

Chapter 13

1. Hughes, *Valle Crucis*, 67.
2. Jordan, *North Carolina Troops*, 14: 318, 319, 391.
3. *Avery County Heritage*, 2: 221–22; Jordan, *North Carolina Troops*, 14: 285; Bailey, *Toe River Heritage*, 3: 132.
4. Bailey, *Toe River Heritage*, 1: 348; *The Lenoir Topic*, March 1926; McGough, *Childsville*, 114.
5. Bowers, *The Tragic Era*, 7; Morrill, "North Carolina and the Administration of Brevet Major General Sickles," 291–305; Powell, *North Carolina*, 380–403.
6. Tammy Logston, e-mail, 9 July 2007; Jordan, *N.C. Troops*, 14: 304; *Watauga County Heritage*, 152; Shelia Barnes, e-mail, 28 Oct. 1999.
7. Friel, *The Phillips Family*, 272, 295; Bailey, *Toe River Heritage*, 1: 115, 389; York, *Fort Defiance*, 159, 174–76; Wegner, *Phantom Pain*, 212–46; Jordan, *North Carolina Troops*, 14: 422.
8. Jordan, *North Carolina Troops*, 14: 380; *Heritage of Caldwell County*, 358; Bailey, *Toe River Heritage*, 1: 202; 2: 391.
9. *Ibid.*, 1: 131; 3: 222.
10. Talbott, "Combat Trauma," 41–47.
11. *Avery County Heritage*, 2: 169; *Watauga County Heritage*, 124; *McDowell County Heritage*, 136, 256; Lyle, "Green Berry Woody."
12. Bailey, *Toe River Heritage*, 1: 144, 2: 212.
13. Caldwell County, N.C., family newspaper articles; Bailey, *Toe River Heritage*, 1: 244, 407, 410; 2: 336; Darcy Marler, e-mail, 8 Dec. 2008; Tammy Logston, e-mail, 9 July 2007; Haney, *Stumbling Towards Jim*, 377; Kenneth J. Stasch, e-mail, 5 Oct. 2007; Nancy Stonebraker, e-mail, 24 Oct. 2007; *The Enterprise Record Chieftain*, 22 June 1922.
14. Tammy Logston, e-mail, 9 July 2007.
15. Bailey, *Toe River Heritage*, 2: 212; *Watauga County Heritage*, 124.
16. Coffey Family File, Caldwell Heritage Museum.
17. Bailey, *Toe River Heritage*, 1: 112, 160; McGough, *Childsville*, 466–69.
18. Bailey, *Toe River Heritage*, 1: 112; 8: 18, 26; Darcy Marler, e-mail, 8 Dec. 2008; McGough, *Childsville*, 124; Coffey Family File, Caldwell Heritage Museum; *Wilkes County Heritage*, 178; Nancy Stonebraker, e-mail, 24 Oct. 2007.
19. Tammy Logston, e-mail, 9 July 2007; Bailey, *Toe River Heritage*, 1: 173, 340, 407; 3: 269; 8: 156.
20. Jordan, *North Carolina Troops*, 14: 272; Case Files of Applications from Former Confederates for Presidential Pardons, 1865–67, NARA M1003; *The State*, 12 Dec. 1893.
21. Harper, diary, 2: 83; undated article in the *Lenoir Topic*; undated newspaper clippings, Harper Papers.
22. *Confederate Veteran* (1901); *Highland Messenger*, 11 June 1897.
23. *Watauga Democrat*, 31 Aug. 1891; 5 Oct. 1899; 21 Nov. 1889.
24. *Ibid.*, 17 May 1900.
25. *Ibid.*, 2 Nov. 1893; *Confederate Veteran*, Vol. 8, No. 3 (1905): 132–33; *Charlotte Observer*, 24 Sept. 1895, 11 Nov. 1905.
26. Lawton, *The History of the United Daughters of the Confederacy*, 1–4.
27. *Watauga Democrat*, 8 June 1905, 15 June 1905, 5

Oct. 1905; *The Lenoir News*, 7 June 1910.
   28. N.C. Confederate Pension Application; Bailey, *Toe River Heritage*, 2: 181–182. 8: 18–25. Dynamite was also not invented until after the war.
   29. *Watauga Democrat*, 6 Sept. 1917.

Chapter 14

1. Jones, *The 25th North Carolina Troops*, 169, 181; Taylor, "The 60th North Carolina Regiment," 110.
2. Jordan, *North Carolina Troops*, 14: 299–300; e-mail, Richard Howland, 15 July, 2009; all numbers compiled from Jordan, *North Carolina Troops*, Vol. 14, and CMSR, M-270, rolls 534–538, NARA.
3. Younce, *Adventures of a Conscript*, 9; Giuffre, "First in Flight," 260.
4. Scott and Angel, *Thirteenth Tennessee*, 451–499; Bumgarner, *Kirk's Raiders*, 147, 148, 155.
5. Jordan, *North Carolina Troops*, 14: 322.

Appendix A

1. It is possible that Beaver died at the Soldier's Home in Raleigh, N.C.
2. The author believes that Harrison Benfield and William Harrison Benfield (Company F) are the same person.
3. The author believes that W.A. Benfield and Weighstill Alexander Benfield (Company F) are the same person.
4. Edmond Blackburn is listed in Jordan, 14: 360, as having died on May 1, 1864.
5. Bolick's grave lies unmarked in the Globe section of Caldwell County.
6. The family believes that Burgin joined the Union Army and died of a fever in 1864.
7. According to one local historian, Byrd's body was brought back to Yancey County.
8. Childs was buried on the field at Chickamauga, but later re-interred in South Carolina.
9. Blair states that Estes died on this date, 5 Sept. 1864, Blair Letters.
10. In Ford's obituary, his name is listed as John Squire Ford. *Watauga Democrat*, 11 April 1910.
11. There is conflicting information on Freeman's place of burial. It could be in Virginia, or in the Penley Cemetery in Mitchell County.
12. E-mail. Jim Middleton, 10 Dec. 2007. Family records state that Samuel B. Fullwood was wounded on September 20, 1863, and died on 24 Sept. 1863.
13. The author believes that this soldier and Francis M. Holsclaw are the same person.
14. According to family notes, Holeman's horse fell on him. He developed a fever and died in Richmond, Virginia.
15. Jordan writes that Jackson possibly died at or near Big Creek Gap. Since the regiment was at Cumberland Gap at this time, it is more likely that Jackson died there.
16. Garrett Gouge wrote on May 22, 1864, that Henry Justice was "wounded in the right breast mortally." Gouge letters, 59.
17. According to the family, Joseph Letterman did not come home from the war.
18. According to Jordan, 14: 367, McKinney died during the war. The family claims that he returned.
19. According to Jordan, 14: 284, McKinney died in March 1863 in Tennessee. The family claims he survived the war.
20. The family states that his middle name was Harvey, not Henry.
21. The family has a letter stating that Presnell died at Cumberland Gap in 1862.
22. Avery County death certificates give dates as 12 Oct. 1838 and 2 April 1918.

Bibliography

Manuscript Sources

Appalachian State University. W.L. Eury Appalachian Collection. Boone, North Carolina.
    Harper-Beall Papers.
Ashe County Public Library. Jefferson, North Carolina.
    Poindexter Blevins Papers.
Caldwell Historical Museum. Lenoir, North Carolina.
    Coffey Family File.
    Langston L. Estes Letters.
Chickamauga-Chattanooga National Battlefield Park, Fort Oglethorpe, Georgia.
    John H. Kelly File.
Duke University. William R. Perkins Library, Manuscript Department. Durham, North Carolina.
    Mary Councill Papers.
National Archives, Washington, D.C.
    Case Files of Applications from Former Confederates for Presidential Pardons, 1865–1867.
    Compiled Service Records of Confederate Soldiers Who Served in Organizations from the State of North Carolina, National Archives Microfilm Series M270, rolls 534–538.
    Navy Widow Certificates, National Archives Microfilm Series, M1249.
North Carolina Department of Archives and History. Raleigh, North Carolina.
    Adjutant Generals Records.
    Henry T. Clark Letter Book.
    Zebulon Baird Vance Letters.
United States Army Military History Institute. Carlisle Barracks, Pennsylvania.
    Edmund Kirby Letters.
University of North Carolina. Southern Historical Collection. Chapel Hill, North Carolina.
    George W.F. Harper Collection.
    Lenoir Family Papers.
    Kirby Smith Collection.

Private Collections

John G. Barnes Letters. Courtesy of Helen Keever.
John C. Blair Letters. Courtesy of Robert Marshall.
J.B. Buchanan Letter. Courtesy of Mellanie Hensley Knight.
Elbert and Elijah Coffey Daybook. Courtesy of John W. Coffey.
Jonathan Green Letter. Courtesy of Diane Barefoot.
Jesse Hawkins Letters. Courtesy of Pat McNeil.
James F. Hurley Letter. Courtesy of Bonnie Hurley.
Walter W. Lenoir Diary. Courtesy of Ike Forrester.
Arthur McFalls Letters. Courtesy of Beth Stoney.
Elisha Trivett Papers. Courtesy of Vanessa Clark.

Newspapers

Charlotte Bulletin
Charlotte Observer
Daily Constitutionalist (Augusta, Georgia)
The Enterprise Record Chieftain (Oregon)
Highland Messenger (Asheville, North Carolina)
Hillsborough Recorder (North Carolina)
Lenoir News (North Carolina)
Mountain Mercury (Marion, North Carolina)
The State (Columbia, South Carolina)
Watauga Democrat (Boone, North Carolina)
Weekly Standard (Raleigh, North Carolina)
The Western Enterprise (Marion, North Carolina)

Books

Absher, W. O., ed. *The Heritage of Wilkes County, Vols. 1 and 2.* Winston-Salem, N.C.: Hunter, 1982–1990.
Alexander, Nancy T. *The History of the First Presbyterian Church of Lenoir.* Printing House, 1976.
Anderson, E. Carl, Jr., and John O. Hawkins, eds. *The Heritage of Caldwell County, North Carolina.* Winston-Salem, N.C.: Hunter, 1983.
Arthur, John Preston. *A History of Watauga County.* Johnson City, Tenn.: Overmountain Press, 1915, 1992.
Ashe, Samuel A'Court. *History of North Carolina.* 2 Vols. Raleigh: Edwards and Broughton, 1925.
Auman, William T. "Peace Movement," *Encyclope-*

dia of North Carolina. Chapel Hill: University of North Carolina Press, 2006: 871–72.

Avery County Heritage. Vol. 1. Banner Elk, N.C.: Puddingstone Press, 1976.

_____. Vol. 2. Banner Elk, N.C.: Puddingstone Press, 1979.

Bailey, Anne J. *The Chessboard of War: Sherman and Hood in the Autumn Campaigns of 1864*. Lincoln: University of Nebraska Press, 2000.

Bailey, Isaac. "Additional Sketches of the Fifty-Eighth Regiment," in Walter Clark, ed., *Histories of the Several Regiments and Battalions from North Carolina in the Great War, 1861 to 1865*. Raleigh, N.C.: E.M. Uzzell, 1901.

Bailey, Lloyd R., Sr. *The Bailey Family of Yancey County, North Carolina*. Vols. 1–4. Durham, N.C.: L.R. Bailey, 1983.

_____. *The Heritage of the Toe River Valley, Vol. 1*. Durham, N.C.: L.R. Bailey, 1994.

_____. *The Heritage of the Toe River Valley, Vol. 2*. Marceline, Mo.: Walsworth, 1997.

_____. *The Heritage of the Toe River Valley, Vol. 3*. Marceline, Mo.: Walsworth, 2001.

_____. *The Heritage of the Toe River Valley, Vol. 8*. Marceline, Mo.: Walsworth, 2009.

Barrett, John G. *The Civil War in North Carolina*. Chapel Hill: University of North Carolina Press, 1963.

_____. *Sherman's March Through the Carolinas*. Chapel Hill: University of North Carolina Press, 1956.

Bearman, Peter S. "Desertion as Localism: Army Unit Solidarity and Group Norms in the U.S. Civil War." *Social Forces* 70 (1991): 321–342.

Bethel Baptist Church Minutes, 1831–1885 [n.p.].

Bishop, Lyle D., III. "The 58th Regiment of North Carolina Infantry: A History of Its Travels." *Watauga County Times ... Past* 22–23 (1987): 1–56.

Bowers, Claude G. *The Tragic Era: The Revolution After Lincoln*. Columbia: State Company, 1931.

Bradley, Mark L. *Last Stand in the Carolinas: The Battle of Bentonville*. Campbell, Calif.: Savas, 1996.

_____. *This Astounding Close: The Road to Bennett Place*. Chapel Hill: University of North Carolina Press, 2000.

_____. "Two Confederate Views of Bentonville: The Official Report of Maj. Gen. Henry D. Clayton and Reminiscences of Col. Henry D. Bunn." *Civil War Regiments* 6 (1998): 93–106.

Bryan, Charles F., Jr. "Tories Amidst Rebels: Confederate Occupation of East Tennessee, 1861–1863." *East Tennessee Historical Society Publications* 60 (1988): 3–22.

Bumgarner, Matthew. *Kirk's Raiders: A Notorious Band of Scoundrels and Thieves*. Hickory, N.C.: Tar Heel Press, 2000.

Bunch, Jack. *Military Justice in the Confederate States Army*. Shippensburg, Pa.: White Mane, 2000.

Castel, Albert. *Decision in the West: The Atlanta Campaign of 1864*. Lawrence: University of Kansas, 1992.

Chapman, Thomas C. *A Wiseman's Family*. Occidental, Calif.: [n.p.], 1992.

Clark, Walter, ed. *Histories of the Several Regiments and Battalions from North Carolina in the Great War, 1861 to 1865*. Raleigh, N.C.: E.M. Uzzell, 1901.

Clauss, Errol. "The Battle of Jonesboro." *Civil War Times Illustrated* 7 (1969): 12–23.

Coffey, David. *John Bell Hood and the Struggle for Atlanta*. Abilene, Tx.: McWhiney Foundation Press, 1998.

"Col. Robert C. Trigg, of Virginia." *Confederate Veteran* 17 (1909): 65.

Conley, Thomas L. *Army of the Heartland: The Army of Tennessee, 1861–1862*. Baton Rouge: Louisiana State University Press, 1967.

_____. *Autumn of Glory: The Army of Tennessee 1862–1865*. Baton Rouge: Louisiana State University Press, 1971.

Cooper, Horton. *History of Avery County*, n.p., 1964.

Cozzens, Peter. *The Shipwreck of Their Hopes: The Battles for Chattanooga*. Urbana: University of Illinois Press, 1994.

_____. *This Terrible Sound: The Battle of Chickamauga*. Urbana: University of Illinois Press, 1992.

Crawford, Martin. *Ashe County's Civil War: Community and Society in the Appalachian South*. Charlottesville: University Press of Virginia, 2001.

Cunningham, H.H. *Doctors in Gray: The Confederate Medical Service*. Baton Rouge: Louisiana State University Press, 1958.

Cutter, William. *Genealogical and Family History of Central New York*. New York: Lewis Historical Pub., 1912.

Daniel, Larry J. *Soldering in the Army of Tennessee*. Chapel Hill: University of North Carolina Press, 1991.

Davis, Stephen. "Atlanta Campaign: Hood Fights Desperately; The Battles for Atlanta, July 10–September 2, 1864." *Blue and Gray Magazine* 6 (1989): 8–62.

Davis, William C. "Cumberland Gap, 1862." *Civil War Times Illustrated* 10 (1971): 25–29.

Deyton, John Basil. "The Toe River Valley to 1865." *North Carolina Historical Review* 24 (1947): 423–66.

DiNardo, Richard L., and James R. Furqueron. "The Day After: Braxton Bragg and the Aftermath of Chickamauga." *North and South* 3 (1998): 31–39.

Dolzall, Gary W. "Opportunity Lost." *America's Civil War*. Vol. 17, Is. 2 (May 2004): 24–30.

Eaton, Clement. *A History of the Old South; the Emergence of a Reluctant Nation*. New York: Macmillan, 1975.

Eicher, John H., and David J. Eicher. *Civil War High Commands.* Stanford: Stanford University Press, 2001.

Elmore, Tom. "The Burning of Columbia." *Blue and Gray Magazine* 21 (2004): 6–27.

Farmer, Silas. *History of Detroit and Wayne County and Early Michigan.* Detroit: S. Farmer, 1884.

Fisher, Noel C. *War at Every Door: Partisan Politics and Guerrilla Violence in East Tennessee, 1860–1869.* Chapel Hill: University of North Carolina Press, 1997.

Foley, Bradley R., and Adrian L. Whicker. *The Civil War Ends: Greensboro, April 1865.* Greensboro, N.C.: Guilford County Genealogical Society, 2008.

Friel, Shirley. *The Phillips Family: Our Heritage.* [n.p.], S.P. Friel, 1988.

Furqueron, James R. "The Finest Opportunity Lost: The Battle of Jonesboro, August 31–September 1, 1864." *North and South* 6 (2003): 48–63.

Gaffney, Sanna, ed. *The Heritage of Watauga County, North Carolina.* Vol. 1. Winston-Salem, N.C.: Hunter, 1984.

Garren, Terrell T. *Mountain Myth: Unionism in Western North Carolina.* Spartanburg, S.C.: Reprint, 2006.

Giuffre, Katherine A. "First in Flight: Desertion as Politics in the North Carolina Confederate Army." *Social Science History* 21 (1997): 245–263.

Hallock, Judith Lee. *Braxton Bragg and Confederate Defeat.* Vol. 2. Tuscaloosa: University of Alabama Press, 1991.

Haney, James L., Jr. *Stumbling Towards Jim: A Mosteller Chronicle.* Moorhead, Minn.: Sorbic Tower Press, 1991.

Hardee, W.J. *Rifle and Light Infantry Tactics.* Philadelphia: J.B. Lippincott, 1861.

Hardy, Michael C., ed. *Avery County Heritage Volume IX: Avery County Obituaries to 1950.* Raleigh, N.C.: Lulu, 2009.

_____. *A Short History of Old Watauga County.* Boone, N.C.: Parkway, 2006.

_____. *The Thirty-seventh North Carolina Troops: Tar Heels in the Army of Northern Virginia.* Jefferson, N.C.: McFarland, 2003.

_____. "Watauga County and the Civil War." Unpublished manuscript.

Harper, G.W.F. "Fifty-Eighth Regiment," in Walter Clark, ed., *Histories of the Several Regiments and Battalions from North Carolina in the Great War, 1861 to 1865.* Raleigh, N.C.: E.M. Uzzell, 1901.

_____. "Palmer's Brigade." *News and Observer,* 20 Dec. 1887.

Hattaway, Herman. *General Stephen D. Lee.* Jackson: University Press of Mississippi, 1976.

Haughton, Andrew. *Training, Tactics, and Leadership in the Confederate Army of Tennessee.* London: Frank Cass, 2000.

The Heritage of Iredell County, North Carolina. Winston-Salem, N.C.: Walsworth, 1980.

Hewett, Janet B., Noah Andre Trudeau, and Bryce A. Suderow, eds. *Supplement to the Official Records of the Union and Confederate Armies.* Wilmington, N.C.: Broadfoot, 1994–2001.

Hickerson, Thomas F. *Echoes of Happy Valley.* Chapel Hill: [n.p.], 1962.

Hilderman, Walter C. *They Went Into the Fight Cheering: Confederate Conscription in North Carolina.* Boone, N.C.: Parkway, 2006.

Hoffman, John. *The Confederate Collapse at Missionary Ridge: The Reports of James Patton Anderson and His Brigade Commanders.* Dayton, Ohio: Morningside, 1985.

Hood, John Bell. *Advance and Retreat.* Lincoln: University of Nebraska Press, 1996.

Horn, Stanley F. *The Army of Tennessee.* Norman: University of Oklahoma Press, 1953.

Hughes, I. Harding, Jr. *Valle Crucis: A History of an Uncommon Place.* Bookcrafters, 1951.

Hughes, Nathaniel C., Jr. *Bentonville: The Final Battle of Sherman and Johnston.* Chapel Hill: University of North Carolina Press, 1996.

Hunt, Andrew E. *David Dellinger: The Life and Times of a Nonviolent Revolutionary.* New York: New York University Press, 2006.

Inscoe, John C., and Gordon McKinney. *The Heart of Confederate Appalachia: Western North Carolina in the Civil War.* Chapel Hill: University of North Carolina Press, 2000.

Johnson, Robert Y., and Clarence C. Buel, eds. *Battles and Leaders of the Civil War,* 4 Vols. New York: Thomas Yoseloff, 1956.

Johnston, Frontis W., ed. *Zebulon B. Vance Letters.* Raleigh, N.C.: State Department of Archives and History, 1963.

Johnston, Joanne S. *McDowell County Heritage.* Waynesville, N.C.: [n.p.], 1992.

Jones, Carroll C. *The 25th North Carolina Troops in the Civil War.* Jefferson, N.C.: McFarland, 2009.

Jordan, Weymouth T., Jr., and John D. Chapla. "O What a Turbill Affair: Alexander W. Reynolds and His North Carolina-Virginia Brigade at Missionary Ridge, Tennessee, November 25, 1863." *The North Carolina Historical Review* 77 (2000): 312–336.

_____, and Louis H. Manarin, eds. *North Carolina Troops, 1861–1865.* 15 Vols. Raleigh: North Carolina Department of Archives and History, 1961 to present.

Kautz, August V. *Customs of Service for Non-Commissioned Officers and Soldiers.* Philadelphia: J.B. Lippincott, 1864.

Keever, Homer. *Iredell: Piedmont County.* [n.p.]: Brady Printing, 1976.

Kegon, Susan K. "Near Miss at Davis Cross Roads." *America's Civil War* 11 (1998): 33–36.

Kelly, Dennis. "The Battle of Kennesaw Mountain."

Blue and Gray Magazine 6 (1989): 8–30, 46–58.
Kennett, Lee B. "'Hell' or 'High Old Times,'" *America's Civil War* 17 (2005): 46–52.
Kincaid, Robert. *The Wilderness Road.* Kingsport, Tenn.: Arcata Graphics, 1992.
Lawton, Ruth Jennings, et al., *The History of the United Daughters of the Confederacy, 1894–1955.* Raleigh, N.C: Edwards and Broughton, 1956.
Lewis, Hattie, et al. *History of Cove Creek Baptist Church, 1799–1999.* Sugar Grove, N.C.: Cove Creek Baptist Church, 1999.
Lindsley, John. *The Military Annals of Tennessee.* Nashville, Tenn.: J.M. Lindsley, 1886.
Luvaas, Jay, and Harold W. Nelson, eds. *Guide to the Atlanta Campaign: Rocky Face Ridge to Kennesaw Mountain.* Lawrence: University Press of Kansas, 2008.
Lyle, Lucille Woody. "Green Berry Woody." Unpublished biography, copy in the author's possession.
Madaus, Howard M. *The Battle Flags of the Confederate Army of Tennessee.* Milwaukee, Wis.: Milwaukee Public Museum, 1976.
McCarley, J. Britt. *The Atlanta Campaign: A Civil War Driving Tour of Atlanta Area Battlefields.* Marietta, Ga.: Cherokee, 1984.
McDonald, Miller. *Campbell County, Tennessee.* Vol. 1. Lafollette, Tenn.: County Services Syndicate, 1993.
McGough, Claudia. *Childsville: Old Times There Are Not Forgotten.* Gettysburg, Pa.: [n.p.], 2003.
McKee, Sarah Gouge, and John Silver Harris, eds. *The Civil War Letters of the Gouge Family.* [n.p.], 2000.
McKenzie, Robert. *Lincolnites and Rebels: A Divided Town in the American Civil War.* Oxford: Oxford University Press, 2006.
McKinney, Gordon B. *Zeb Vance: North Carolina's Civil War Governor and Gilded Age Political Leader.* Chapel Hill: University of North Carolina Press, 2004.
McKnight, Brian D. *Contested Borderland: The Civil War in Appalachian Kentucky and Virginia.* Lexington: University Press of Kentucky, 2006.
McMurry, Richard M. *Atlanta 1864: Last Chance for the Confederacy.* Lincoln: University of Nebraska Press, 2000.
_____. "Atlanta Campaign: Rocky Face to the Dallas Line, the Battles of May 1864." *Blue and Gray Magazine* 4 (1989): 10–23, 46–49.
_____. "The Battle of Kolb's Farm." *Civil War Times Illustrated* 7 (1968): 20–27.
_____. "'The Hell Hole': New Hope Church." *Civil War Times Illustrated* 11 (1973): 32–43.
_____. "On the Road to the Sea: Sherman's Savannah Campaign." *Civil War Times Illustrated* 21 (1983): 8–25.
_____. *The Road Past Kennesaw: The Atlanta Campaign of 1864.* Washington, D.C.: National Park Service, 1972.
McPherson, James. *Battle Cry of Freedom: The Civil War Era.* New York: Oxford University Press, 1988.
McWhiney, Grady. *Braxton Bragg and Confederate Defeat.* Tuscaloosa: University of Alabama Press, 1969.
Miller, J.B. *The Watauga Boys in the Great Civil War.* [N.p., n.d.].
Moore, Mark A. *Moore's Historical Guide to the Battle of Bentonville.* Campbell, Calif.: Savis Publishing, 1997.
Morrill, James R. "North Carolina and the Administration of Brevet Major General Sickles." *North Carolina Historical Review* 42 (1965): 295–305.
Neff, Robert O. *Tennessee's Battered Brigadier: The Life of General Joseph B. Palmer.* Franklin, Tenn.: Hillsboro Press, 2000.
Norris, E.J. "Biographical Sketch of Confederate Veteran." *Watauga Democrat*, undated.
Palmer, Friend. *Early Days in Detroit Papers.* Detroit: Hunt and June, 1906.
Palmer, John B. "The 58th North Carolina at the Battle of Chickamauga." *Our Living and Our Dead* 3 (1875): 454–55.
Parks, Joseph H. *General Edmund Kirby Smith, C.S.A.* Baton Rouge: Louisiana State University, 1954, 1982.
Polk, William M. *Leonidas Polk: Bishop and General*, 2 Vols. New York: Longmans, Green, 1915.
Powell, William S. *North Carolina Through Four Centuries.* Chapel Hill: University of North Carolina Press, 1989.
Prim, G. Clinton, Jr. "Born Again in the Trenches: Revivals in the Army of Tennessee." *Tennessee Historical Quarterly* 43 (1984): 250–272.
Radley, Kenneth. *Rebel Watchdog: The Confederate State Army Provost Guard.* Baton Rouge: Louisiana State University Press, 1989.
Raiford, Neil. *The 4th North Carolina Cavalry in the Civil War.* Jefferson, N.C.: McFarland, 2003.
Randolph, Richard. "Inconstant Rebels: Desertion of North Carolina Soldiers in the Civil War." *North Carolina Historical Review* 41 (1964): 163–189.
Regulations for the Army of the Confederate States, 1863. Richmond, Va.: J.W. Randolph, 1863.
Ridenour, G.L. *The Land of the Lake: A History of Campbell County, Tenn.* Jacksboro, Tenn.: Action Printing, 1985.
Ridley, Bromfield L. *Battles and Sketches of the Army of Tennessee.* Mexico, Mo.: Missouri Print and Publishing, 1906.
Robertson, William G. "The Chickamauga Campaign: The Armies Collide." *Blue and Gray Magazine* 24 (2007): 6–28, 40–65.
_____. "The Chickamauga Campaign: The Fall of

Chattanooga." *Blue and Gray Magazine* 23 (2006): 6–28, 43–65.

———. "The Chickamauga Campaign: McLemores Cove." *Blue and Gray Magazine* 23 (2007): 6–26, 42–65.

Scaife, William R. *The Campaign for Atlanta*. Cartersville, Ga.: Scaife Publications, 1993.

Schroeder-Lein, Glenna R. *Confederate Hospitals on the Move: Samuel H. Stout and the Army of Tennessee*. Columbia: University of South Carolina, 1994.

Scott, Samuel W., and Samuel P. Angel. *History of the Thirteen Regiment Tennessee Volunteer Cavalry*. Philadelphia: P.W. Ziegler, 1903.

Secrist, Philip L. *The Battle of Resaca*. Macon, Ga.: Mercer University Press, 1998.

Sherman, William T. *Memoirs of General William T. Sherman*. 2 vols. Westport, Conn.: Greenwood Press, 1957.

Sitterson, Joseph C. *The Secession Movement in North Carolina*. Chapel Hill: University of North Carolina Press, 1939.

Speer, Lonnie R. *Portals to Hell: Military Prisons of the Civil War*. Mechanicsburg, Pa.: Stackpole Books, 1997.

Spruill, Matt. *Guide to the Battle of Chickamauga*. Lawrence: University Press of Kansas, 1991.

Stickley, Arndt M. *Simon Bolivar Buckner: Borderland Knight*. Chapel Hill: University of North Carolina Press, 1940.

Symonds, Craig L. *Joseph E. Johnston: A Civil War Biography*. New York: W.W. Norton, 1992.

Talbott, John. "Combat Trauma in the American Civil War." *History Today* 46 (1996): 41–47.

Temple, Oliver P. *East Tennessee and the Civil War*. Johnson City, Tenn.: Overmountain Press, 1899, 1995.

"The Ten Springs of Jacksboro in 1808 and Today." *The Campbell Countian* 9 (1998): 4–6.

Tucker, Glenn. *Chickamauga: Bloody Battle in the West*. Indianapolis: Bobbs-Merrill, 1957.

U.S. War Department. *War of the Rebellion: A Compilation of the Official Records of the Union and Confederate Armies*. 128 vols. Washington, D.C., 1880–1901.

Warner, Ezra J. *Generals in Gray: Lives of the Confederate Commanders*. Baton Rouge: Louisiana State University Press, 1959.

Weaver, Jeffrey C. *The 5th and 7th Battalions North Carolina Cavalry and the 6th North Carolina Cavalry*. Lynchburg, Va.: H.E. Howard, 1995.

———. *63rd Virginia Infantry*. Lynchburg, Va.: H.E. Howard, 1991.

———, and George L. Sherwood. *The 54th Virginia Infantry*. Lynchburg, Va.: H.E. Howard, 1993.

Wegner, Ansley Herring. *Phantom Pain: North Carolina's Artificial-Limbs Program for Confederate Veterans*. Raleigh: North Carolina Department of Cultural Resources, 2004.

Weiss, Timothy F. "'I Lead You to Battle': Joseph E. Johnston and the Controversy at Cassville." *Georgia Historical Quarterly* 91 (2007): 424–452.

Weitz, Mark A. *More Damning than Slaughter: Desertion in the Confederate Army*. Lincoln: University of Nebraska Press, 2005.

Wert, Jeffery. "Confederate Conscription Woes." *Civil War Times Illustrated* 45 (2006): 9–10.

Whitener, Daniel J. *History of Watauga County* [n.p.], 1949.

Wilcox, Francis Marion. *A Journal Written by Francis Marion Wilcox, 1897*. Johnson City, Tenn.: [n.p.], 1998.

Wise, Frank E. *A History of William Cuthbertson, Benjamin Wise, and Adjoining Families* [n.p.], 1990.

Wise, Jennings C. *The Military History of the Virginia Military Institute from 1839 to 1865*. Lynchburg, Va.: J.P. Bell, 1915.

Woodworth, Steven. *Jefferson Davis and His Generals*. Lawrence: University Press of Kansas, 1990.

———. *Nothing but Victory*. New York: Alfred A. Knopf, 2005.

———, ed. *Leadership and Command in the American Civil War*. Campbell, Va.: Savas Woodbury, 1995.

———. *Six Armies in Tennessee: The Chickamauga and Chattanooga Campaigns*. Lincoln: University of Nebraska Press, 1998.

Yearns, W. Buck. *The Confederate Congress*. Athens: University of Georgia Press, 1960.

York, Maurice C. *The Many Faces of Fort Defiance: A Report Submitted to Fort Defiance, Inc.* Chapel Hill, 1979.

Younce, William H. *Adventures of a Conscript*. Cincinnati: Editor Publishing, 1901.

Theses and Dissertations

Heath, Raymond A., Jr. "The North Carolina Militia on the Eve of the Civil War." Master's thesis, University of North Carolina, Chapel Hill, 1974.

Taylor, James C. "The 60th North Carolina Regiment: A Case Study of Enlistment and Desertion in Western North Carolina During the Civil War." Master's thesis, Western Carolina University, 1996.

Letters and E-mails

Ailenofe, Elke, 17 Oct. 2008.
Allen, Robert, 11 Feb. 2008; 18 April 2008.
Anglin, Sue, 14 Oct. 2007.
Ariciu, Janet, 26 Sept. 2007.
Atkins, Melanie, 8 Jan. 2008.
Austin, Tracy, 24 July 2007.
Autrey, Bill, 11 Feb. 2008.
Baker, Jerry, 31 July 2007.

Balche, Ken, 17 June 2007; 19 June 2007.
Ball, Matt, 24 July 2009.
Barnes, David, 4 Aug. 2007.
Barnes, Shelia, 28 Oct. 1999.
Bastounes, Dawn, 17 July 2007.
Beane, Robert, 23 July 2008.
Beaver, Tamara, 3 Feb. 2008.
Benfield, Melania, 23 June 2007.
Bledsoe, Barbara, 3 June 2009; 5 June 2009; 17 June 2009.
Blevins, Lance, 2 Jan. 2008.
Bodeen, Kay, 18 Aug. 2008.
Bowers, Craig, 7 July 2008.
Boyd, Lina, 20 July 2007.
Bristow, Ronda Sue, 30 Sept. 2008.
Brooks, W.W., 22 June 2007.
Brown, William, 12 July 2007.
Chamberlain, Jane, 28 April 2008.
Chesser, Diana, 4 Aug. 2007.
Clark, Donald, 21 Oct. 2007.
Coffey, Jack, 17 June 2007.
Cooper, Bernie, 3 Aug. 2007.
Cornett, James, 8 Aug. 2007.
Crawley, Robert, 5 Oct. 2000.
Cusce, Lena, 17 July 2007.
Elliott, Bill, 29 Oct. 2007.
Elliott, John, 24 Sept. 2008.
English, Candace, 5 Sept. 2007.
Estes, Sandra, 11 Oct. 2007.
Field, Alfred, 14 Dec. 2007.
Finney, Rose Eastridge, 8 Oct. 2007.
Fore, Millie, 16 Oct. 2007.
Forbey, Elizabeth, 20 March 2008.
Freeman, Bob, 16 Dec. 2007.
Galloway, David C., 13 July 2009.
Gandy, Betty, 11 July 2009.
Giles, Jenny, 7 June 2008.
Gladfellow, Terry, 15 July 2007.
Gordon, David Lee, 23 Sept. 2007.
Gouge, Calvin, 30 Sept. 2007.
Greene, David, 20 Dec. 2007.
Greer, Sharon, 6 Aug. 2007.
Grindstaff, Vanessa, 7 Aug. 2009.
Harrison, Melissa, 23 Aug. 2009.
Harvel, Charlie, 7 Feb. 2008.
Hayes, Benny, 30 April 2008.
Heinek, Margaret, 21 June 2007.
Hendrix, Philip, 18 Jan. 2008.
Hensley, Gregg, 30 Aug. 2009.
Higgins, Jack, 20 July 2007.
Hinson, Lauren, 19 Nov. 2007.
Hipps, Horace, 09 Aug. 2007.
Holley, Ron, 10 Dec. 2007.
Hollifield, Jim, 6 Jan. 2008.
Horton, David, 09 July 2007.
Horton, E. Anne, 10 Oct. 2000.
Howington, Richard, 20 March 2008; 15 July 2009.
Hunt, Cameron, 29 Nov. 2007.
Huggett, Cynthia, 2 June 2008.

Ingle, Pam, 25 Aug. 2008.
Isaacs, Bob, 25 Sept. 2008.
Jarrett, Jeanette, 14 Aug. 2007.
Johnson, Carmen, 16 May 2009.
Jones, David, 8 Feb. 2008.
Kidd, Sandra, 20 June 2007.
Kincaid, Larry, 3 April 2009.
Kirkwood, Betty, 21 Nov. 2007.
LaMel, Debra, 20 Sept. 2007.
Lane, David, 7 July 2008.
Lawson, Tresa, 23 June 2007.
Logston, Tammy, 9 July 2007.
Lynn, Shirley, 23 Feb. 2009.
Mahlberg, Karla, 11 July 2007.
Marler, Darcy, 8 Dec. 2008.
Marler, Don, 16 July 2007.
Marshall, Robert, 28 Oct. 2008.
Mashburn, Cliff, 21 Jan. 2008.
McCalmon, Leah, 16 June 2009.
McCarson, James, 12 Aug. 2007.
McCormack, Elizabeth, 30 Dec. 2007.
McDaniels, C., 23 June 2007.
McNelly, Robert, 5 Oct. 2007.
Medford, Jonathan, 12 July 2008.
Middleton, Jim, 14 Dec. 2007.
Miller, Billie, 1 Oct. 2007.
Moore, Wayne, 13 July 2007.
Morgan, Jon, 24 July 2007.
Morrison, Kathy, 27 Sept. 2008.
Mosier, Barbara, 24 Sept. 2008.
Mosteller, Cliff, 3 Jan. 2008.
Nanney, Stuart, 17 Aug. 2007.
Nash, John, 25 Oct. 2007.
Nelson, Wanda, 27 Sept. 2008.
Nielson, Ruth, 24 Sept. 2008.
Norvell, Barbarra, 23 June 2007.
Norwood, David, 22 Feb. 2008.
Oertel, Lavonne, 27 Aug. 2007.
Ollis, Doyle, 23 Sept. 2009.
Pace, John, 11 July 2007.
Patterson, Glynis, 20 July 2007.
Pennel, Roy, 22 Feb. 2008.
Pennington, Carolyn, 10 Aug. 2007.
Peters, Dawn, 23 Sept. 2008.
Phillips, Beverly, 14 July 2007.
Pollygus, Anthony, 14 May 2007.
Pope, Margaret, 17 Aug. 2007.
Presnell, Lowell, 27 Oct. 2007.
Price, Betty, 6 Dec. 2008.
Proffitt, Bob, 29 July 2007.
Puett, Cindy, 4 Aug. 2007.
Putnam, Ed, 17 July 2007.
Reeter, Sherry, 25 Sept. 2008.
Reid, James S., 14 Sept. 2008.
Revis, Lynne, 7 Aug. 2007.
Ricks, Susan Kirby, 7 Nov. 2007.
Sand, Susan, 30 Sept. 2008.
Schurmann, Ernest, 16 July 2007.
Seagle, Don, 25 Sept. 2007.

Setzer, John L., Sr., 11 Sept. 2007.
Sheets, Ricky, 16 July 2007.
Shelton, Mike, 17 Aug. 2007.
Shepherd, Ralph, 3 Aug. 2007.
Shull, Harold, 17 July 2007.
Simpson, James F., 31 July 2007.
Smith, J.C., 17 Oct. 2007.
Snipes, William, 3 Aug. 2007.
Spicer, Julia English, 22 July 2007.
Stafford, Mike, 16 July 2007.
Starnes, Brian, 8 March 2008.
Stamey, Mike, 21 July 2007.
Stasch, Kenneth J., 5 Oct. 2007; 11 Sept. 2007.
Stephens, Trudy, 7 Aug. 2007.
Sterling, Judy, 21 July 2007.
Stonebraker, Nancy, 24 Oct. 2007.
Styles, Dan, 27 Sept. 2009.
Summerlin, Gwen, 4 Aug. 2007.
Swanson, Loretta, 23 Sept. 2008.
Tate, Timothy, 5 April 2009.
Testerman, Robert, 28 Jan. 2008.
Thompson, Gail, 3 Dec. 2007.
Thompson, Glenda, 29 Feb. 2008; 18 Feb. 2009.
Towery, Amy, 18 Feb. 2008.
Upchurch, Chris, 14 March 2009.
Wages, Anita, 9 Sept. 2008.
Wheeler, Ron, 20 Aug. 2009.
Winebarger, Keith, 27 Dec. 2007.
Wingfield, Rebecca, 11 Nov. 2007.
Winters, Randolph, 18 Nov. 2007.
Wood, Russell, 16 July 2007.
Worley, Warren, 19 July 2007.

Index

Numbers in *bold italics* indicate pages with illustrations.

Abbe, John H. 91, 193
Adairsville, Georgia 118
Alexander, Thomas 134, 172, 193, 224
Alexander, William 162, 193, 223
Alexander County, North Carolina 38, 102
Allatoona, Georgia 119, 120, 140
Alleghany County, North Carolina 22
Anderson, Burrill 173, 193
Anderson, Patton 87, 89, 93
Anglin, James 41, 49, 194
Anglin, William 27, 138, 194
Anson County, North Carolina 22
Army of Northern Virginia 44, 64, 69, 83, 97, 109, 110, 128, 145, 153, 160, 161, 164, 183, 184
Ashe County, North Carolina 14, 16, 31, 32, 47, 54, 57, 84, 104, 167, 172, 183
Asheville, North Carolina 8, 16, 85, 86, 161, 175
Atlanta, Georgia 78, 81, 84, 95, 97, 102, 104, 114, 117, *126*, 127, 129, 130, 131, *132*, 133, 134, 135, 138, 139, 142, 148, 169, 191–2
Atlanta and West Point Railroad 140
August, Jacob 106
Augusta, Georgia 98, 107, 150, 151
Austin, Thomas 86, 194,
Austin, William 27, 77, *78*, 175, 194
Autry, John 138, 174, 194
Avery, William W. 13
Avery County, North Carolina 8, 169, 173, 192
Ayers, Jacob 172, 194

Bailey, Charles 10, 194
Bailey, Isaac 52, 64, *70*, 71, 73, 75, 77, 167, 175, 179, 194
Bailey, James 173, 194
Bailey, John 14, 51, 194
Bailey, Thomas 51, 194
Bailey, William 37, 194
Bailey, Willis 134, 194
Baird, Benjamin 28, 161, 167, 168, 179, 194, 223
Baird, David F. 138, *156*, 162, 168, 179, 194
Baird, Finley 60, 194
Baker, Robert F. 26, 194
Ball, Alford 106, 194
Banks, William 174, 195
Barbour Artillery 45, 61
Barbourville, Kentucky 38, 42
Barnes, John G. 100, 102, 104, 105, 195
Bate, William 92, 93
Bean, Largent 119, 195
Bean's Station, Tennessee 39, 61
Bearden, Marcus 34–5, 85, 195
Beauregard, P. G. T. 97, 132, 150
Belton, J. Francis 39,
Benfield, Adolphus 60, 195
Bennett, Sam 181, *182*, 183, 195
Bennett Place, North Carolina 164, 166, 192
Bentonville, North Carolina, battle of 153, 154–159, 168, 188, 192
Big Creek Gap, Tennessee 43, 44, 46, 48, 49, 51, 54, 60, 61, 62, 63
Biddix, Francis 74, 195
Blackburn, John L. 123, 195
Blair, John 42, 62, 138, 139, 142, 161, 196, 223
Blalock, Samuel 8, 185, 196
Blevins, Edward 31, 53, 196
Blevins, Poindexter 31, 106, 162, 196, 224
Bolick, Jacob 83, 115, 172, 196
Boone, North Carolina 28, 47, 168, 169, 175, 178, 187

Bowman, Jacob 26, 28, 32, 50, 52–3, 175, 196
Boyden, Nathaniel 14
Bradshaw, William F. 82, 196
Bragg, Braxton 38, 41, 42, 44, 62, 64, 65, *67*, 69, 70, 72, 80, 82, 84, 85, 87, 89, 93, 97, 128, 129, 153, 154
Branchville, South Carolina 150
Brantley, William F. 162
Braswell, Thaddeus 58, 196
Breckinridge, John 81, 85, 92
Bridgeport, Alabama 142
Briggs, Suel 27, 80, 88, 162, 175, 196, 223
Bright, Alnay 138, 196
Brooks, Stephen 162, 196, 223
Brown, Asa 172, 196
Brown, George W. 119, 196
Brown, Romulus 9, 173, 196
Brown, William 50, 196
Bryan, John 102, 197
Bryant, Robert 29, 197
Bryant, Thomas 169–70, 197, 226
Buchanan, Greenberry 174, 197, 226
Buchanan, Leonard 26, 31, 197
Buchanan, Molton *64*, 197
Buchanan, Thomas 27, 197
Buckner, Simon 60, 61, 62, 64, 65, 67, 69, 70, 73, 80, 81, 84, 85, 86, 87, 102
Bumgarner, George W. 60, 197
Bumgarner, William P. 82, 124, 197, 226
Buncombe County, North Carolina 7, 13, 24, 35
Burke County, North Carolina 7, 9, 13, 35, 175
"Burke Rangers" 26
Burleson, Meredith 175, 197
Burnside, Ambrose 61, 81, 86
Burnsville, North Carolina 14, 27, 29, 35, 178, 182

Butler, Allen 94, 197, 226
Byers, William 106, 107, 197
Byrd, Carson 173, 174, 197, 226
Byrd, Cornelius 29, 198
Byrd, Moses 29, 134, 182, 198
Calaway, William 28, 198, 226
Caldwell County, North Carolina 13, 14, 16, 21, 22, 23, 28, 29, 31, 32, 37, 38, 57, 58, 82, 84, 85, 93, 98, 100, 102, 105, 106, 107, 117, 124, 136, 147, 161, 168, 174, 175, 177, 178, *181*
Calhoun, Georgia 117, 118
Callaway, James 58, 198
Camp Chase, Ohio 169
Camp Douglas, Illinois 139, 141, 187
Camp Holmes, North Carolina 84, 106
Camp Martin, North Carolina 9, 26
Camp McGinnis, Kentucky 47
Camp Morton, Indiana 111
Camp Reynolds, Tennessee 39
Camp Stokes, Tennessee 35, 38
Camp Vance, North Carolina 84
Campbell, A. P. 104
Campbell County, Tennessee 45, 50, 183, *184*, 189
Cannon, Wesley 56, 198
Carpenter, Alfred A 9, 174, 198
Carpenter, David L. 11, 198
Carpenter, Erwin 8, 10, 198
Carpenter, Jacob 5, 198
Carpenter, Jonathan 10, 198
Carter's Depot, Tennessee 38
Cassville, Georgia 118, 119
Chandler, David 31, 51, 198
Charlotte, North Carolina 98, 152, 153
Chattahoochee River 125, 126, 127, 135, 140, 142
Chattanooga, Tennessee 38, 62, 64, 65, 69, 71, 72, 76, 80, 81, 82, 96, 98, 100, 109, 124, 141, 178, 189
Chattanooga, Tennessee, battle of 86–93, 94
Cheatham, Benjamin 70, 104, *129*, 130, 131, 145, 161
Cherokee (Van Corput's) Georgia Battery 113, 114
Chickamauga, Georgia, battle of 10, 35, 57, 69–79, 81, 107, 128, 133, 185, 187–8, 189
Chickamauga and Chattanooga National Battlefield Park 1, 179, 189, *190*
Childs, John E. 74, 78, 192, 198
Church, Eli *18*, 19
Church, Jordan 187, 198, 226
Claiborne, Ellis 103, 104, 107
Clark, Henry T. 8, 10, 11, 21
Clark, John W. 174, 198

Clark, Walter 181
Clay, Andrew 84, 199
Clayton, Edwin 162, 199, 223
Clayton, Henry 101
Clayton, Robert 162, 199, 223
Cleburne, Patrick 67, 87, 104, 130, 131, 137, 145, 188
Clingman, Thomas L. 12, 13, 86
Clinton, Tennessee 60, 61, 62, 173, 183
Coffey, Bartlett 60, 199
Coffey, Drury *139*, 174, 175, 199
Coffey, Elijah 60, 113, 143, 147, 199
Coffey, Israel 28, 199
Coffey, Jesse Finley 51, 199
Coffey, John 32, 91, 199
Coffey, Thomas J. 28, *85*, 175, 199, 226
Coffey, William 58, 73, 85, 156, 158, 162, 175, 199, 223
Cole, Joseph 95, 199
Coleman, David 14
Coleman, Richard 111, 199, 225
Coleman, Thaddeus C. 161, 199, 223
Collett, Orlando 174, 199
Collett, Waighstill A. 35, 51, 85, 199
Columbia, South Carolina 79, 98, 151, 152, 176, 192
Columbia, Tennessee 144
Conley, Alfred 43, 199
Conley, Caleb 28, 58, 104, 123, 199
Conley, James 8, 162, 199, 223
Conley, Jason 28, 51, 199
Conley, Julius 125, 199
Cook, Thomas B. 172, 199
Cook, William S. *133*, 170, 199, 223
Corinth, Mississippi 146, 147
Cornell, John 119, 200
Cornett, Isaac 226
Cottrell, Calvin 115, 178, 200
Cox, Braxton 82, 119, 200
Cox, John 91, *95*, 200
Cox, Nathan 58, 200
Cox, William R. 28, 200
Craig, A. Colman *56*, 200
Craig, Alfred H. 75, 200
Craige, Johnson 139, *141*, 200
Crisp, William 151, 200
Crump, Elijah *70*, 76, 179
Cumberland Gap, Tennessee 8, 34, 38, 39, *40*, 41, 42, 43, 44, 45, 63, 64, 81, 85, 189
Curtis, Merit 43, 200

Dalton, Georgia 78, 93, 97, 99, 100, 103, 104, 105, 109, 110, 111, 113, 190
Danner, John 28, 200
Danville, Kentucky 41
Davenport, Gilson 30, 200

Davidson, Allen T. 20
Davidson County, North Carolina 84
Davis, Albert 162, 200, 223
Davis, Alfred 30
Davis, Jefferson 17, 25, 45, 59, 61, 65, 81, 82, 97, 98, 100, 105, 128, 140, 152, 164, 165, 166
Davis, William 60, 124, 161, 179, 200
Deaver, Samuel 14
DeBorde, Ezra 91, 200
Decker, Elisha 125, 200
Dellinger, Henry *8*, 200
Dellinger, James 8
Dellinger, Joseph 115, 200
Dellinger, Reuben 106, 107, 200
Denney, Samuel 28, 201
Dickson, Joseph 37, 201
Dickson, William 13
Donelson, Daniel 60
Dover, Asa 106, 201
Dugger, John 60, 65, 69, 70, 82, 101, 118, 119, 120, 121, 123, 124, 125, 126, 130, 133, 135, 201
Dula, Thomas 22, 23, 29, 32, 38, 53, 77, 80, 85, 103, 123, 136, 175, 201
Duncan, Jonathan 31, 162, 201, 223
Duncan, Phillip H. 82, 201
Dunn, J. F. 161, 201

East Tennessee and Virginia Railroad 35
Edisto River, South Carolina 150, 151
Edney, Bayles M. 14
Edwards, John W. 29, 173, 201, 227
Edwards, Lynville 29, 173, 201
Eggers, Adam 50, 201
Eggers, John 82, 201
Eighteenth Tennessee Infantry 44, 134, 151
Eighth Alabama Infantry 61
Eighth Arkansas Infantry 65
Eighth Florida Infantry 185
Eighty-fifth Illinois Infantry 101
Eighty-seventh Indiana Infantry 74
Eighty-sixth Illinois Infantry 101
Eleventh Alabama Infantry 42
Eller, Alfred 133, 20
Eller, Calvin 31, 58, 201
Eller, Jacob 60, 172, 201
Eller, Peter 124, 201
Elliott, Jasper 155, 202
Elliott, Stephen 95, 202, 227
Ellis, John 13, 16, 17
English, John M. 11, 202
English, Samuel W. 11, 26, 202
Erwin, Alpheus M. 22

Estes, Doctor 28, 37, 92, 138, 202
Estes, Henry 37
Estes, Henderson 37, 202
Estes, Langston 35, 36, 37, 45, 46, 47, 49, 51, 53, 60, 202
Etowah River, Georgia 118, 119
Ewing, Orville, Jr. 161, 202

Fagg, Henry C. 162, 202, 224
Fifth Battalion North Carolina Cavalry 18, 25, 26, 30, 35, 41, 45, 172
Fifth Indiana Battery 113
Fifth Kentucky Cavalry (US) 62
Fifth Kentucky Infantry 65, 70, 74, 76, 82
Fifty-fifth Georgia Infantry 43, 47, 61, 62, 63
Fifty-fourth Virginia Infantry 84, 85, 87, 94, 103, 104, 114, 117, 120, 124, 129, 143
Fifty-third Virginia Infantry 38
Finley, Jason 178, 202
Finley, Joseph 130
First Mississippi Light Artillery 133
First North Carolina Artillery 161
First North Carolina Cavalry 16, 28, 30, 178
First North Carolina Volunteers 17, 86, 153
First Ohio Infantry 91
Fletcher, James 30, 202
Florence, Alabama 142, 143
Folk, George N. 16
Ford, Thomas 151, 202
Forrest, Nathan B. 142, 144
Forsyth County, North Carolina 84
Forty-fifth Ohio Infantry 91
Forty-fifth Tennessee Infantry 134, 154
Forty-sixth Alabama Infantry 149
Forty-third Alabama Infantry 42, 43
Fourteenth Arkansas Infantry 65
Fourteenth Kentucky Infantry (US) 122
Fourteenth North Carolina State Troops 20
Fourth Florida Infantry 44
Fourth North Carolina State Troops 162
Fourth Virginia Infantry 120
Fowler, Sanders 130
Fox, Alexander 31, 202
Fox, Elisha 156, 202
Fox, Henry 31, 203
Fox, James 27, 47, *48*, 134, 203
Fox, Moses 134, *137*, 203

Fox, Shelton 27, 134, 203
Frankfort, Kentucky 41
Franklin, Albert J. *37*, 38, 203
Franklin, David 8, 203
Franklin, Tennessee 145, 146
Frazier, John W. 61, 62, 63, 64, 203, 227
Fugitt, Robert 95, 203
Fullwood, James 119, 203, 227

Gaddy, Samuel H. 11, 203
Gadsden, Alabama 142
Gaither, Burgess S. 21, 22
Gardner, James 29, 52, 203
Garland, Gibbs 26, 203
Garland, John C. 26, 52, 203
Garland, William 26, 203
Garner, Thomas 27
Gentry, Callaway 82, 133, 203
Gentry, William 31, 32, 52, 203
Georgia Militia 124, 130, 133, 134, 135
Gibbs, A. N. 83, 178, 203
Gibbs, Bryant 125, 203
Gibbs, Joseph 106, 107, 203
Gibbs, William 138, 203
Gibson, Odom 83, 203
Gilbert, Larkin *103*, 162, 203, 223
Gilliland, Robert 29, 204, 223
Goforth, William 84, 204, 225
Goldsboro, North Carolina 22
Goplin, George 119, 204
Gouge, Garrett 47, 49, 51, 61, 62, 78, 116, 128, 134, 139, 140, 204
Gouge, William 35, 37, 47, 48, 51, 60, 204
Gourley, John 119, 204
Gracie, Archibald, Jr. 42, 61, 62, 69, 71, 73, 74
Gragg, Empsey 56, 204
Gragg, William S. 28, 204
Graham, Daniel 57, 204
Grant, Ulysses S. 38, 87, 100, 109, 110, 166
Green, Augustus 156, 204
Green, Isaac 124, 204
Green, James M. *10*, 11, 204
Green, John C. 26, 51, 204
Green, Jonathan 37, 204
Green, Joseph 41, 74, 204
Green, Sterling P. *54*, 204, 227
Greene, Solomon 56, 204
Greensboro, North Carolina 159, 162, 164, 165, 166, 167, 168, 170, 185
Greer, Isaiah 57, 204
Greer, Jefferson 57, 204
Greer, Phillip 57, 181, 204
Greer, Thomas 57, 204
Griffin, Hamilton 161, 205
Grub, George 30, 205
Guy, Alfred 173

Haas, Emanuel 173, 205
Hall, Elijah 60, 205
Halleck, Henry 34
Hampton, Milton 53, 119, 205
Hampton, Wade 161
Hampton, William 54, 95, 205, 227
Handy, Marion 116, 205, 224
Hardee, William 65, 81, 86, 97, 98, 100, 102, 111, 113, 118, 119, 121, 124, 128, 130, 131, 135, 137, 138, 139, 154, 155, 156, 157, 161
Hardy, Washington M. 85, 86, *88*, 134
Harman, Drury 27, 32, 52, 123, 205
Harmon, Andrew 72, 205, 226
Harmon, Eli 59, *173*, 174, 205
Harmon, Ephraim *135*, 205
Harper, Ella 49, 97
Harper, George W. F. 22, 30, 32, 39, 40, 41, 42, 43, 45, 47, 48, 49, 56, 60, 62, 63, 80, 82, 83, 84, 85, 86, 93, 97, 98, 99, 100, 102, 103, 105, 106, 111, 115, 117, 140, 142, 143, 144, 145, 146, 147, 148, 150, 151, 152, 153, 156, 157, 158, 159, 160, 161, 164, *165*, 166, 167, 176, 179, 181, 185, 192, 205
Harriss, William 77, 85, 205
Harvel, Moses 82, 206
Hase, Jesse 106, 206
Havener, Alexander G. 11, 206
Hawkins, Jessie 48, 49, 63, 206
Hawks, John 95, 206
Hayes, Ransom 59
Helton, John 119, 206
Hendrick, Emanuel 22, 124, 206
Hensley, John A. 11, 35, 161, 174, 206, 223, 227
Herndon, Harrison 34, 52, 206
Herrill, Henry C. 26, 206
Heth, Henry 42, 44, 60, 80
Hicks, Carroll 41, 206
Hicks, John W. 41
Higgins, Charles 60, 206
Higgins, Curtis 172, 174, 206
Higgins, James 95, 175, 206, 227
Hill, Daniel H. 65, 67, 81, 85, 153, 154, 157, 160, 162
Hilliard, Alfred 119, 206
Hilliard, Bartlett 30, 119, 206
Hilliard's Alabama Legion 6, 41, 45
Hillsboro, North Carolina 164
Hilton, John W. 84, 95, 206, 227
Hindman, Thomas C. 67, 68, 69, 72, 81, 113, 114, 119, 122
Hobson, Benoni 123, 206
Hodge, George 61

Hodges, Gilbert 83, 135, 136, 140, 141, 143, 207, 223
Hodges, Riley **169**, 207
Hodges, William M. 30, 207
Hogler, John C. 29, 207
Hoke, Robert F. 154, 155, 159
Holcombe, Robert 27, 207, 225
Holden, William 105, 170, 172, 176
Holder, Elijah 168, 207
Hollifield, Joseph H. 29, 207
Hood, John B. 71, 72, 110, 113, 114, 118, 119, 120, 121, 124, 127, **128**, 129, 130, 132, 133, 137, 138, 139, 140, 143, 145, 146, 148, 149, 161
Hooker, Joseph 87, 122
Hopkins, George W. 47, 52, 58
Horton, James H. 30, 207
Horton, Jonathan 27, 32, 207
Horton, Lorenzo 37, 207
Horton, William 42, 105, 207
Houck, Henry A. 31
Howell, Alvin 95, 207, 227
Howell, James 139, 207, 227
Howell, Swinfield 27, 174, 207
Howell, Thomas 29, 207
Howington, William M. 28, 72, 207
Huffman, John 74, 208
Hughes, John B. 49, 208
Hughs, James 29, 208
Hunley, John 27, 82
Hunter, John W. 50, 208
Huntsville, Alabama 143
Hurley, Elisha 58, 208
Hurley, James 117, 138, 208
Hurley, Leander 31, 162, 208, 224
Hutchings, Wright 84, 106

Inglis, James 52, 85, 98, 101–2, 208
Iredell County, North Carolina 84
Isaac, Noah 63, 208, 227
Isaacs, Reuben 134, 169, 208
Isaacs, Solomon 119, 208, 227

Jacksboro, Tennessee 45, 46, 47, 61, 63
Jackson, A. E. 61
Jackson, Bill 49, 208
James, Eli 41, 162, 174, 208
Jamestown, North Carolina 164, 165
Jarrett, George Y. 82, 208
Jarrett, Levi 173, 208
Jefferson, Adkins 100, 124, 208
Jefferson, North Carolina 14
Johnson, Bartlett 72, 208
Johnson, Bushrod 62, 72, 102
Johnson, Lewis A. 22
Johnson's Depot (Johnson City), Tennessee 32, 33, 35, 38, 49, 59
Johnston, Andrew 165, 170
Johnston, Joseph E. 38, **97**, 98, 99, 100, 102, 104, 106, 107, 108, 109, 110, 111, 112, 113, 114, 117, 118, 119, 120, 121, 122, 124, 125, 127, 128, 140, 152, 154, 155, 159, 160, 161, 162, 164, 165, 166, 192
Jolly, Hile 84, 209
Jones, Jason 58, 209
Jones, Jesse 58, 60, 209
Jones, Larkin **27**, 209
Jones, Memoch 58, 209
Jones, Robert 57, 209
Jones, Samuel 59
Jonesboro, Georgia, battle of 135–9, 141, 143, 187
Justice, Henry 116, 209

Kanipe, Zephaniah 174, 209
Keener, Jesse 119, 209
Keener, John C. 28, 30, **32**, 34, 51, 61, 70, 173, 209
Keller, Joshua 74, 209
Keller, Nicholas 54, 209, 227
Keller, William 54, 60, 209
Kelly, John H. 64, 69, 70, 71, 72, 73, 74, 76, 78, 81, 82, 83
Kennesaw Mountain (Georgia), battles of 121–123, 124, 140, 191
Kennesaw Mountain National Battlefield, Georgia 191
Kenney, Simpson 104, 209
King, Jacob 31, 209
Kinston, North Carolina 22
Kirby, Edmund 34, **35**, 41, 45, 70, 72, 74, 77, 78, 79, 80, 209
Kirby, John 60, 209
Kittrell Springs, North Carolina 22
Knoxville, Tennessee 48, 55, 60, 61, 62, 63, 86, 96, 169, 173, 186
Kolb's Battery 61
Kolb's Farm, Georgia, battle of 10, 122–125, 136, 188, 191

LaFayette, Georgia 69
Lanier, David 78, 209
Lawrence, James J. **123**, 209
Leach, James 14, 105
Ledford, Henry 95, 209
Ledford, Jasper 28, 209, 227
Ledford, William 72, 209
Lee, Robert E. 22, 44, 60, 64, 97, 110, 128, 148, 152, 165, 166
Lee, Stephen D. 131, 132, 133, 135, 136, 137, 138, 140, 141, 142, 143, 144, 145, 149, 152, 159, 161, 162
Lenoir, North Carolina 98, 102, 160, 167, 168, 170, 178, **181**
Lenoir, Walter W. 13, 14, 21, 22, 23, 29, 30, 172, 192, 210
Lenoir's Station, Tennessee 63
Lexington, Kentucky 41
Lexington, North Carolina 153
Lincoln, Abraham 8, 13, 16, 20, 164
Lincoln County, North Carolina 17, 175, 176
Lindsey, George 162, 210, 223
Lingle, John 125, 210
London, Kentucky 42
Long, Hamilton 162, 210, 224
Longstreet, James 69, 71, **72**, 74, 81, 86, 87, 102, 169
Lonon, Oliver 119, 174, 210, 227
Lorance, George W. 57, 210
Loring, William M. 124
Lost Mountain, Georgia 121
Louisville, Kentucky 41, 94, 96, 113, 124, 169, 179
Lovejoy Station, Georgia 138, 139
Lovelace, Andrew 58, 100, 210
Loven, Anderson 59, 210
Loyd, George 174, 210

Mace, Jesse 131, 172, 175, 210
Macon, Georgia 78, 132, 134, 135, 138, 149, 225
Madison, Georgia 117
Madison County, North Carolina 8, 13, 14, 24, 175
Manchester, Kentucky 39
Marcus, Serug 96, 210
Marietta, Georgia 119, 121, 140, **191**
Marion, North Carolina 58, 184
Marler, James D. 28, **29**, 174, 175, 210
Marshall, Humphery 61
Martin, James B. 24
Martin, Jeremiah 74, 210
Martin, Warren 119, 210
Mason, Joseph J. 35
Mast, Finley 169, **171**, 210
Mast, John A. **152**, 210
Mast, William 28, 210,
Maury, Dabney 60
Maxwell, G. T. 61
May, Abraham 31, 211
McBee, William 74, 211
McConnico, W. L. 110
McCowan, John 44, 59
McCurry, Phineas 9, 211
McCurry, Tillman 9, 211
McCurry, Walter 9, 211
McDowell County, North Carolina 9, 16, 28, 43, 106, 174, 178, 184
"McDowell Rangers" 32
McElroy, John S. 16
McFalls, Arthur 37, 40, 56, **57**, 74, 211
McFalls, George 106, 211

Index

McGee, Jordan C. 30, 58, 161, 211
McGimsey, Theodore 75, 162, 211, 224
McGuire, George 48, 49, 124, 211
McHargue, Thomas 174, 211
McKinney, James 156, 211
McKinney, Johnson 175, 211
McKinney, Thomas 50, 211
McKissick, Robert 116, 211
McLemore's Cove, Georgia, battle of 67–68, 69, 81
McLeod, Samuel 172, 211
McVay, William 50, 211
Mecklenburg County, North Carolina 17, 124
Medaris, John 37, 161, 211, 223
Merrill, A. B. 95, 212, 228
Metcalf, Henry 138, 211
Milledgeville, Georgia 149, 150
Miller, Ephraim 30, 212
Miller, John H. 94, 95, 212, 228
Miller, Jonathan B. 32, 46, 54, 109, 120, 127, 134, 135, 141, 151, 152, 162, 167, 168, 212, 224
Miller, Lorenzo 139, 178, 212
Miller, Moses 170, 212
Miller, William 30, 52, 212
Mitchell, Michael 28, 60, 172, 212
Mitchell, Thomas 77, 212
"Mitchell Cavalry" 25
Mitchell County, North Carolina 6, 7, 9, 10, 11, 16, 26, 27, 28, 30, 32, 58, 106, 170, 172, 174, 175, 179, 185
"Mitchell Rangers" 8, 9, 10, 11, 20, 24, 25, 31, 32, 185
Mobile, Alabama 109, 110, 148
Moffitt, John 174, 212
Molly, James 96, 212
Montgomery, Alabama 141, 149
Monticello, Kentucky 47
Moore, Charles 83, 116, 212
Moore, Elijah L. *182*, 212
Moore, Hight 37, 60, 212
Moore, Jasper 37, 60, 75, 121, 212
Moore, John K. 179
Moore, Martin L. 131, 172, 212
Moore, Newton 37, 212
Moretz, William 181, 212
Morgan, Nathan 31, 213
Morris, John H. 28, 52, 213
Morrison, James D. 28, 29, 78, 213
Morristown, Tennessee 39
Morritt, John 152
Morrow, Daniel 107, 213
Morrow, John 125, 213
Morrow, Jordan 106, 107, 213
Morrow, Nathan 37, 107, 213
Moss, Benjamin 27, 52, 213

Mosteller, Daniel 29, 60, 213
Mullis, George 139, 213

Nashville, Tennessee 38, 41, 44, 94, 95, 96, 139, 141, 146, 186
Nelson, George 119, 213, 223
Nelson, William 124, 213
New Hope Church, Georgia, battle of 119–120
Newman Artillery 43
Ninth Arkansas Battalion 65
Ninth Ohio Infantry 74
Norris, Elijah 80, 91, 138, 139, 179, *180*, 213
Norris, John R. 48, 115, 213
Norwood, Joseph C. 58

Oaks, David 5
Ollis, Jacob *131*
Ollis, John 9, 51, *53*, 213
Ollis, Leonard 83, 213
Orangeburg, South Carolina 151
Osborne, Alexander 133, 213
Oxford, James 38, 121, 213
Oxford, John 38, 213

Page, Lafayette 102, 214,
Palmer, John B. 5, 6, 7, 9, 10, 11, 12, 16, 20, 24, *25*, 26, 28, 32, 34, 38, 39, 40, 41, 44, 49, 52, 53, 56, 61, 62, 70, 74, 75, 76, 80, 81, 83, 85, 86, 105, 134, 137, 176, *177*, 188, 192, 214,
Palmer, Joseph B. 134, 135, *137*, 140, 143, 145, 148, 150, 151, 152, 153, 154, 155, 156, 157, 158, 161
Palmer's Legion 25, 26
Palmetto, Georgia 140
Parker, James 115, 214
Parkes, Samuel 121, 122, 214
Parsons, William 111, 214
Patton, Robert 77, 214
Peek, John W. 29, 32, 51, 214
Pegram, John 61
Pendley, William 82, 214
Perry, Benjamin 85, 98, 161, 214
Perryville, Kentucky 41, 65
Peterson, John 94, 214
Peterson, Lawson 174, 214, 228
Peterson, Moses 182, 214, 228
Phifer, William 74, 214
Phillips, Hugh 187, 214
Phillips, Jonathan L. 47, 48, 50, 78, 80, 123, 172, 214
Phillips, Nathan 113, 214
Phillips, Payton 76, 172, 214
Phillips, Reuben 119, 214
Pierce, Joseph 111, 214
Pipes, John 95, 215
Polk, Leonidas 65, 69, 71, 72, 81, 100, 111, 113, 118, 119, 120, 121
Poteet, Samuel 74, 215
Presnell, Benjamin 156, 215

Presnell, Squire 119, 215
Presnell, Wesley 33, 101, 172, 179, 215
Preston, William, III 60, 65, 68, 69, 70, 72, 73, 74, 76, 78, 81, 84
Prestwood, Sidney 26, 215
Pritchard, Alexander 95, 215
Pritchard, Azor 26, 215
Pritchard, Rufus 95, 215
Proffitt, William W. 27, 28, 32, 34, 51, 215
Puett, Elisha 121, 215
Pyatte, Leander 169, 173, 192, 215

Rabey, John W. 105, 106, 215
Raby, George 119, 215
Raby, James 125, 215
Raleigh, North Carolina 16, 17, 22, 24, 77, 84, 100, 104, 105, 154, 159, 164, 168, 170, 171, 172, 175, 192
Ramsey, James 60
Randolph, George W. 21, 22
Randolph, Thomas 174, 215
Rankin, James E. 60, 170, 175, 215
Ray, Thomas 48, 52, 215
Reece, Aaron 116, 215
Reedy, George W. 54, 55, 216
Resaca (Georgia), battles of 111, 112–118, 140–1, 184, 188, 190
Reynolds, Alexander W. 84, 85, 87, 88, 89, 91, 92, 93, 101, 102, 107, 110, 111, 113, 114, 120, 124
Richmond, Kentucky 41
Richmond, Virginia 22, 56, 60, 62, 79, 81, 109, 127, 137, 160, 176, 183
Riddle, James 8, 174, 216
Riddle, Samuel 172, 216
Ringgold, Georgia 65, 78, 93, 94, 100
Roark, Joshua 54, 95, 96, 216
Roark, Solomon 54, 91, 216
Roark, William 54, 216
Robbins, Anderson 58, 216
Robbins, Rufus 47, 216
Robinson, Wilborn 54, 58, 216
Rock Island, Illinois 94–5, 96
Rockingham County, North Carolina 22
Rocky Face Ridge Georgia, Battle of 110–111
Rogersville, Tennessee 55
Rome, Georgia 65, 118
Rose, Wyatt 95, 216, 228
Rosecrans, William S. 65, 67, 71, 72, 76, 80, 86
Rowland, Robert 115, 183, 216
Ruff's Mill, Georgia, battle of 124–5
Rutherford County, North Carolina 106

Sales, John 162, 216, 223
Salisbury, North Carolina 22, 84, 98, 153, 165, 168, 225
Scoggins, John 60, 216
Scott County, Virginia 47
Seagle, John A. 178, 216
Second North Carolina Mounted Infantry (US) 226, 227
Selma, Alabama 141, 149, 225
Settlemire, Sydney 22, 216
Seventh Florida Infantry 87
Sheets, Linville 104, 217
Shehan, Albert 56, 58, 217
Shehan, Andrew 71, 217
Shenan, James 100, 217, 228
Shehan, Pinkney 58, 217
Shepherd, Anderson 58
Shepherd, Erwin 58
Shepherd, Grandison 50, 217
Shepherd, Thomas 27, 217, 228
Sherman, William T. 8, 87, 100, 102, 109, 110, 113, 118, 119, 121, 123, 124, 125, 132, 134, 135, 139, 140, 141, 142, 148, 151, 152, 155, 159, 164, 165, 166, 168, 192
Sherrill, Isaac 134, 217
Sherwood, Theron 74, 78, 217
Shoup, Francis 125
Silver, Edmund 174, 175, **176**, 217
Silver, Levi 47, 217, 224
Silver, Samuel 30, 32, 58, 88, **89**, 91, 136, 137, 142, 146, 149, 150, 153, 154, 174, 217
Silver, Tilman 40, 47, 217, 224
Sisemore, James 138, 217
Sisk, Marion 125, 217
Sisk, Robert 134, 178, 217
Sixteenth North Carolina State Troops 16, 183
Sixtieth North Carolina Troops 1, 44, 84, 85, 86, 87, 89, 100, 103, 104, 105, 107, 117, 121, 134, 144, 145, 149, 157, 159, 161, 162, 165, 179, 186
Sixth North Carolina Cavalry 1
Sixty-fifth Georgia Infantry 65, 70
Sixty-first North Carolina Troops 53, 77
Sixty-fourth North Carolina Troops 1, 43, 45, 47, 61, 62
Sixty-second North Carolina Troops 1, 43
Sixty-third Virginia Infantry 65, 70, 74, 76, 82, 84, 87, 103, 104, 114, 129, 149
Skyles, John W. **125**, 219
Sluder, Felix 84, **86**, 95, 218, 228
Smith, Austin 116, 218
Smith, Edmund Kirby 26, 38, **39**, 41, 42, 44, 45, 59, 60

Smith, Julius 74, 115, 218
Smith, Robert 30, 218
Smith, Solomon 30, 218
Smithfield, North Carolina 153, 154, 159, 160
Smith's Georgia Legion 45
Somerset, Kentucky 61
Sparks, Matthew 11, 218
Sprinkle, Obadiah 84, 95, 218, 228
Stafford, Joseph 103, 124, 218
Stafford, Julius 124, 218
Starnes, Valentine 124, 218
Stevenson, Alabama 142
Stevenson, Carter 38, 41, 44, 81, 111, 113, 114, 119, 122, 123, 124, 125, 129, 131, 133, 135, 137, 138, 140, 141, 144, 149, 153, 154, 155, 156, 158, 159, 160, 190
Steward, Barry 77, 123, 218
Steward, Jasper 123, 218
Stewart, Alexander 68, 69, 71, 72, 107, 113, 114, 117, 119, 129, 130, 131, 133, 139, 145, 154, 161
Stewart, Alfred 28, 32, 92, 123, 136, 137, 138, 143
Stewart, Jackson 26, 52, 170, 219
Stewart, James 11, 74, 219
Stewart, Joseph 50, 219
Stikes, Joseph 124, 219
Stoneman, George 168
Story, Walter 95, 219
Strawberry Plains, Tennessee 62
Stringfellow, Charles 40
Styles, Noah 95, 219
Swift, Wilborn 60, 219

Tate, Junius C. 26
Taylor, James 121, 122, 219
Taylor, Richard 149
Tazwell, Tennessee 39
Teague, John B. 121, 122, 219
Team, Israel **15**
Teaster, Finley 134, 219
Teaster, Ransom 59, 219
Tennessee River 143
Third Alabama Infantry 42
Third North Carolina Mounted Infantry (US) 186, 187, 226, 227, 228
Third Tennessee Infantry 134
Thirteenth Tennessee Cavalry (US) 185, 186, 226, 227, 228
Thirty-ninth North Carolina Troops 1
Thirty-second Alabama Infantry 44
Thirty-second Tennessee Infantry 44, 134
Thirty-seventh Alabama Infantry Consolidated 162, 183, 185

Thirty-seventh North Carolina Troops 1, 28, 30, 48, 172
Thomas, George 8, 86, 88, 110
Thomas, Hezekiah 28, 187, 219
Thompson, Matthew 119, 174, 219, 228
Tilman, Bryant 125
Tipton, John 29, 52, 172, 219, 228
Tipton, Thomas 73, 220
Tobey, Frederick 8, **9**, 74, 75, 162, 175, 220, 223
Todd, Joseph B. 17
Tolley, William 172-3, 220
Towery, Edward 50, 220
Townsend, Levi **130**, 220
Toxey, William 161, 220
Trigg, Robert C. 69, 71, 73, 74, 85, 120, 134
Triplett, Abner 29, 220
Trivett, Elisha 59, 220
Trivett, Joel **145**, 220
Trivett, Lewis 113, 220
Troutman, George 184, 220
Troutman, James 185
Tucker, William 91
Tunnel Hill, Georgia 78, 87, 102, 104
Tupelo, Mississippi 38, 146, 147, 148, 149, 150
Turbyfield, James 138, 220
Twenty-eighth Alabama Infantry 61
Twenty-fifth Alabama Infantry 161
Twenty-fifth North Carolina Troops 21, 186
Twenty-first Ohio Infantry 82
Twenty-first Virginia Cavalry 58
Twenty-fourth Mississippi Infantry Consolidated 162
Twenty-ninth North Carolina Troops 1, 8, 27, 29, 183
Twenty-second Alabama Infantry Consolidated 162
Twenty-sixth North Carolina Troops 1, 20, 21, 22, 28, 29, 105, 106, 124, 136, 175
Twenty-sixth Tennessee Infantry 134
Twenty-third Kentucky Infantry 91
Twenty-third New York Infantry 122

Union County, North Carolina 106
United Confederate Veterans 177, 178
United Daughters of the Confederacy 179–81
United States Navy 84, 86, 95, 187, 226, 227, 228

Vance, John 15, 220
Vance, Lewis 8, 220
Vance, Robert 85
Vance, Thomas 8, 220
Vance, William 8, *15*, 82, 220
Vance, Zebulon B. 13, 14, 20, *21*, 22, 23, 29, 53, 59, 84, 100, 105, 161, 164, 170
Vance's Legion 20–23, 29, 30, 106, 172
Vannoy, William 96, 220

Wacaster, Jacob 101, 220
Waldrope, Joseph 174, 220
Walker, David 60, 220
Walker, Jesse 95, 221
Wallace, Cornelius 175, 221
Wallis, William 58, 221, 228
Ward, Duke 59, 221
Ward, Michael 59, 106, 107, 221
Washington County, Tennessee 35
Watauga County, North Carolina 6, 7, 16, 17, 27, 28, 30, 32, 48, 56, 57, 59, 63, 106, 139, 167, 168, 169, 170, 173, 174, 175, 178, 179, 182, 183, 184
"Watauga Troopers" 30, 32

Watson, Alfred 50, 221
Weatherman, Samuel 138, 221
Weisenfeld, Moretz 30, 221
Western and Atlantic Railroad 101, 111, 113
Wheeler, Joseph 112, 113, 130
Whisenhunt, Elias 43, 221
White, James A. 174, 221
White, Robert W. 162, 221, 224
Wilcox, Francis 48, 57, 221
Wilkes County, North Carolina 84, 91, 106, 175
Williams, Hugh 72, 221
Williams, Mac 172, 221
Williamsburg, Kentucky 60, 61
Wilson, Alexander 175, 221
Wilson, Bartlett 50, 221
Wilson, Lemuel 98, 102, 222
Wilson, Levi 29, 222
Winebarger, Levi 63, 222
Wise, Jasper 74, 222
Wiseman, James H. *25*, 222
Wiseman, John 9, 78, 222
Wiseman, Josiah 94, 222
Wiseman, Martin D. 8, 9, 32, 51, 222
Wiseman, Thomas J. 11, 222
Wiseman, William H. 74, *149*, 222

Wood, Spencer 122, 222
Wood, W. 106
Wood, William 133, 222
Woodside, Benjamin 29
Woody, Green B. 37, 45, 82, *83*, 123, 174, 222
Worth, Jonathan 170, 171

"Yancey Boys" 27, 28, 32
Yancey County, North Carolina 6, 7, 13, 14, 16, 27, 29, 32, 37, 57, 58, 106, 107, 169, 173, 174, 175, 178, 182, *186*
York County, South Carolina 106
Younce, Andrew 60, 222
Younce, William H. 32, 54, 55, 56, 57, 58, 185, 222
Young, Greenbury 26
Young, Moses 175, 222
Young, Thomas 26, 27, 77, 222, 223
Youngblood, Hiram 106, 222
Younts, E. H 106

Zollicoffer, Felix 45
Zollicoffer, Tennessee 38

www.ingramcontent.com/pod-product-compliance
Ingram Content Group UK Ltd.
Pitfield, Milton Keynes, MK11 3LW, UK
UKHW050702160426
5217IPUK00038B/1953